OXFORD WORLD'S CLASSICS

THE CIVIL WAR

GAIUS JULIUS CAESAR (?100–44 BC) was born into the senatorial aristocracy which controlled the operations of the Roman empire. Always a supporter of popular measures in the politics of the city, he became consul in 59 with the support of Pompey ('the Great'), but the alliance did not last, and the two men became first political and then military rivals. A ten-year proconsular command in the Roman province of Gaul brought him immense wealth as well as control of a huge and devoted army, both of which factors in 49 BC enabled him to challenge Pompey for supremacy at Rome. The civil war which resulted left him, after Pompey's defeat at Pharsalus and death in Egypt, in sole control of Rome's affairs; the perpetual dictatorship and extraordinary honours which followed marked a shift in the structures of Roman politics which, despite his assassination on the Ides of March 44, was to prove permanent, and which played its part in the change from Republic to Principate. The accounts which he wrote of his campaigns against the peoples of Gaul, Britain, and Germany (*The Gallic War*) and against Pompey (*The Civil War*) have been valued for centuries as classics of military practice and literary excellence.

JOHN CARTER retired from a Senior Lectureship at Royal Holloway, University of London, in 1992. His other published work included a history of the young Augustus' rise to power, *The Battle of Actium* (1970), and editions of Suetonius' life of Augustus, *Divus Augustus* (1982), and of Caesar's *Civil War* (2 vols., 1991 and 1993). He also translated the Greek historian Appian's account of the Roman *Civil War* (1996) and co-operated with Ian Scott-Kilvert on Cassius Dio's *Roman History: The Reign of Augustus* (1987). John Carter died after completing this edition, in 1997.

OXFORD WORLD'S CLASSICS

*For almost 100 years Oxford World's Classics have brought
readers closer to the world's great literature. Now with over 700
titles—from the 4,000-year-old myths of Mesopotamia to the
twentieth century's greatest novels—the series makes available
lesser-known as well as celebrated writing.*

*The pocket-sized hardbacks of the early years contained
introductions by Virginia Woolf, T. S. Eliot, Graham Greene,
and other literary figures which enriched the experience of reading.
Today the series is recognized for its fine scholarship and
reliability in texts that span world literature, drama and poetry,
religion, philosophy and politics. Each edition includes perceptive
commentary and essential background information to meet the
changing needs of readers.*

OXFORD WORLD'S CLASSICS

JULIUS CAESAR

The Civil War

WITH THE ANONYMOUS

Alexandrian, African, and Spanish Wars

Translated with an Introduction and Notes by
JOHN CARTER

Oxford   New York

OXFORD UNIVERSITY PRESS

Oxford University Press, Great Clarendon Street, Oxford OX2 6DP

Oxford New York

Athens Auckland Bangkok Bogotá Buenos Aires Calcutta
Cape Town Chennai Dar es Salaam Delhi Florence Hong Kong Istanbul
Karachi Kuala Lumpur Madrid Melbourne Mexico City Mumbai
Nairobi Paris São Paulo Singapore Taipei Tokyo Toronto Warsaw

and associated companies in Berlin Ibadan

Oxford is a registered trade mark of Oxford University Press

British Library Cataloguing in Publication Data
Data available

Library of Congress Cataloging in Publication Data
Data available
ISBN 0-19-283923-3

1 3 5 7 9 10 8 6 4 2

Printed in Great Britain by
Cox & Wyman, Reading, Berkshire

CONTENTS

ACKNOWLEDGEMENTS

The translation here given of Caesar's work is a revised version of that already published by Aris and Phillips, Warminster, as part of my complete edition, with Latin text and full commentary, of Caesar's *Civil War* (Books I–II, 1991; Book III, 1993). (The translation of the remaining three works is a new one done especially for the present volume.) I am most grateful to Aris and Phillips for permission to make use of my existing work in this way. A small amount of the introductory material is also adapted from my Introduction to the first of these editions.

J. M. CARTER

21 *August 1996*

INTRODUCTION

Gaius Julius Caesar was born in 100 BC,[1] a year of great political turbulence for the Roman Republic. Between his tenth and his twenty-third years his country was torn by almost continuous war, first against its kin and oldest allies and then against itself. And his death, in his fifty-sixth year, precipitated fourteen years of armed struggle for control of the state whose traditional forms of government he had himself reduced to an empty shell. For the last fifteen years of his life he had been one of the two most powerful men in the state, that is to say one of the two most powerful men in the Mediterranean world, and for the last three and a half he had become in effect sole ruler of that Mediterranean world, his mistress a queen.[2] He is universally acknowledged (partly on his own evidence, be it said) to have been one of the best generals of all time, but one must not forget that he was also one of the finest public speakers of his day, and that his Latin style, for all its simplicity, won the admiration of so sophisticated a judge as Cicero.[3] The introduction which follows attempts to provide some background against which to set the political, military, and literary achievements of a man who was undoubtedly one of the greatest of all Romans.

[1] The year of Caesar's birth is disputed, since the ancient sources are not unanimous and by the normal rules of the Late Republic Caesar should have reached the age of 43 during his consulship in 59 BC. The best solution is to stick to Suetonius' date of 100 BC and suppose that for whatever reason (possibly the bravery which resulted in his winning the military decoration of the *corona civica* at the siege of Mytilene), he was allowed to stand for office two years early.

[2] At the time of Caesar's death, Cleopatra and her young son by Caesar were installed in a villa on the Janiculum, across the river from the city.

[3] Cicero, *Brutus*, 262: 'They [Caesar's *Commentaries*] are bare, clean-limbed and beautiful, free of every scrap of the ornamental clothing of oratory. But although Caesar intended others to have a source ready to hand if they wanted to write History, he perhaps did a favour to fools who will want to doll them up; but he certainly put sensible men off writing, because History knows nothing more agreeable than brilliant and limpid brevity.'

The Historical Context

Some Features of Rome's Constitution

Republican Rome was in theory a democracy, though like most forms of democracy an imperfect example. According to the normal practice of the ancient world, only free adult males enjoyed full citizenship and participation in the political life of the community. These citizens of Rome (a state which by 80 BC included all of peninsular Italy), or rather such of them as wished, assembled together to vote, once a year, for magistrates who changed annually (consuls, praetors, tribunes of the people, and sundry lesser figures). They also met more often, at almost any time of year and naturally in smaller numbers, to approve or disapprove of legislation that had been put forward. War was also not supposed to be declared without a positive vote of the citizen assembly, but this became something of a dead letter in the Late Republic, as governors of outlying 'provinces' (areas such as southern Gaul, Macedonia, Spain, Asia Minor, or Syria) took action on their own initiative to ensure the security of their areas. It goes without saying that the assemblies who took these important electoral and legislative decisions were dominated by those Romans who lived in or near the city, and that a very large number of citizens were virtually disenfranchised by distance from the metropolis. The detailed arrangements for voting in these assemblies, a subject too complex for discussion here, were also such as to make the assemblies in various ways still more unrepresentative of the Roman citizen body as a whole. When thuggery, bribery, and personal influence were added to preferential voting systems and unrepresentative attendance, the distortions of this seemingly democratic machinery became alarming and in the end fatal.

The two consuls, to whom the state was entrusted, had wide executive powers and commanded Rome's armies—though this function was increasingly taken over by provincial governors in Caesar's time. A consul's power was limited by the fact that he held office for only a year and was subject to the veto of his colleague, as well as to that of any of the ten tribunes of the people. The eight praetors, an office which had originated as a sort of deputy consulship and consequently still enjoyed much the same wide powers (subject again to veto and to the superior authority of a consul), now functioned ordinarily as presidents of the system of standing civil and criminal courts which had developed in the last century of the Republic's existence, but could if necessary command armies and perform all the duties of a consul. The authority which empowered consuls and praetors to give binding commands to their fellow citizens and so ensured that their legal decisions and civil and military orders were valid was termed *imperium*, a power initially conferred on them in virtue of their popular election to these offices. In the Late Republic it had become the normal practice for consuls and praetors to pass their year of office in Rome. At its conclusion they would go out as proconsuls (i.e. 'acting consuls') to the various provinces, with their *imperium* extended by senatorial decision for as long as necessary until a duly appointed successor arrived, normally after one or two years. Here they acted as the highest administrative and judicial authority, and in unruly or frontier provinces as supreme commanders with opportunity to win the much-coveted military distinction (*gloria*). Thus the men governing the provinces, and therefore commanding the armies of Rome, were men who had been previously elected by popular vote.

The 'ghost in the machine' was the senate, whose formal purpose was to serve as the consuls' advisory council. It met at least twice a month, and in the turbulent era of the Late Republic usually much more often. By this time, it numbered about six hundred life members and consisted of all who had successfully stood for the most junior of the important magistracies of the state, namely the quaestorship, to which twenty men who had to have reached the age of 30 were elected annually. Since holding a quaestorship was also a necessary qualification for proceeding to the higher public offices, the result was that the senate was composed of all serving magistrates and all ex-magistrates. Its debates and resulting recommendations (*senatusconsulta*) were thus of the greatest importance, and it was a rash and extremely rare consul who ignored the views of the senate. In practice, the views of the senate were the views of the ex-consuls (who seldom numbered more than twenty-five or so), because the presiding consul sought opinions in order of seniority and therefore debate rarely progressed beyond the circle of ex-consuls and currently serving magistrates.

Political parties in the modern sense were unknown, but temporary alliances were constantly being formed to oppose or support particular courses of action in particular circum-stances, or to oppose or support the appointment or election of particular individuals to particular posts. The most famous of these temporary alliances, that between Pompey, Caesar, and Marcus Licinius Crassus between 59 and 53 BC, has even been dignified with the somewhat misleading name of the 'First Triumvirate'; this name implies a constitutional status the alliance did not have, because it was an unofficial com-pact the only aim of which was to secure the continued dom-ination of Roman politics by the three principals. Roman politics was very largely an upper-class game conducted by the members of that class for their own short-term advant-age, and only occasionally were the interests of the ordinary citizens of Rome an important factor. The reasons for this were that contests for office were always between members of the upper class, and that legislation could only be brought before the assembly of the people by a magistrate. In neither case was there a genuine 'voice of the people', and when legis-lation was brought in with the aim of bettering the lot of the ordinary citizen (e.g. by providing subsidized sales of the staple food, corn) it rarely seems to have been actuated by any disinterested desire for social reform or any wish to distribute more evenly the massive profits of Rome's empire. One also needs to bear in mind that Roman society was held together by a network of patronage and mutual per-sonal obligation which militated against abstract 'causes' and intellectual positions, and favoured instead a perpetual bal-ancing act on the part of individuals between competing sets of obligations. For example, on the eve of the civil war, Cicero wrote: 'I fancy I see the greatest struggle . . . the greatest there has ever been. But do please consider this personal dilemma of my own. You must see that on your advice I have made friends with both the contestants . . . you persuaded me to make friends with one of them because of all he had done for me, and with the other because of his power . . . Each counts me as his supporter . . . What am I to do?' (*Letters to Atticus*, VII.1).

Such attempts at redressing social injustice or carrying out political reform as were made in the last century of the Republic were almost all initiated by holders of the anomalously powerful office of tribune of the people (*tribunus plebis*). This magistracy was instituted during the social struggles of the Early Republic to protect the ordinary citizens against the arbitrary exercise of power by the consuls. As a result the ten tribunes, who were elected by an assembly more genuinely popular in its structure and voting than the parallel body which elected consuls and praetors, enjoyed personal sacrosanctity (in practical terms, immunity from arrest or attack) and the power to veto any action or decree of another magistrate. They also acquired the right to attend, and ultimately to summon, meetings of the senate, and to propose legislation in the assembly which elected them. Such a cocktail of powers could be explosive when exploited by ambitious or unscrupulous men, as they were on several occasions in the Late Republic, and it is probably fair to say that the existence of the tribunate, with these potentially revolutionary powers, was an important factor in the breakdown of the Republic into the near ungovernability it exhibited on several occasions in its final decade of free political life between 59 and 49. A curiosity is that the tribunate was always held (with one notable exception, that of the ex-consul Fulvius Flaccus in 122) by men near the beginning of their public careers, who were on the whole likely to conform to the weight of senatorial opinion (always predominantly conservative) and make themselves useful as part of the administrative apparatus of the state, rather than play the part of firebrands. Thus the office never acquired the status it could have been given if a series of already distinguished men had

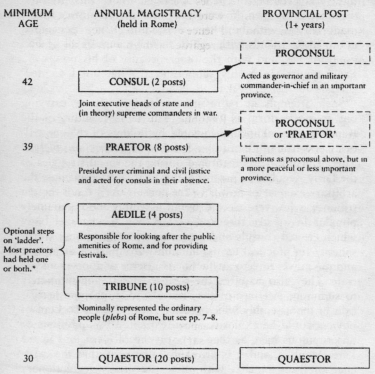

MINIMUM AGE	ANNUAL MAGISTRACY (held in Rome)	PROVINCIAL POST (1+ years)

PROCONSUL

42 — CONSUL (2 posts)

Acted as governor and military commander-in-chief in an important province.

Joint executive heads of state and (in theory) supreme commanders in war.

PROCONSUL or 'PRAETOR'

39 — PRAETOR (8 posts)

Functions as proconsul above, but in a more peaceful or less important province.

Presided over criminal and civil justice and acted for consuls in their absence.

Optional steps on 'ladder'. Most praetors had held one or both.*

AEDILE (4 posts)

Responsible for looking after the public amenities of Rome, and for providing festivals.

TRIBUNE (10 posts)

Nominally represented the ordinary people (*plebs*) of Rome, but see pp. 7–8.

30 — QUAESTOR (20 posts) — QUAESTOR

Conferred life membership of the senate after year of office was over; quaestors performed administrative duties, often financial, in Italy or acted as assistants/deputies to provincial governors.

*These two offices were typically held by men in their mid-thirties. Normally at least a 2-year interval was observed between any two offices.

FIG. 1 Roman Magistracies in the Late Republic

held it. Perhaps the reason for its always relatively low status was not that the tribunes were felt to be 'men of the people' (they manifestly were not), but that the office had no military dimension and hence offered no chance of acquiring something the Romans regarded as highly desirable, glory in war.

The Roman Aristocracy

Rome, even in the Late Republic, was a relatively undifferentiated society. The same people, who came in the main from a restricted group of élite families, functioned as leaders in war, civic heads of state, high priests of the state religion, members of the senate, judicial authorities, diplomats, cultural patrons, and chief accumulators (and therefore providers) of capital. It is true that in this period money-making activities start to be separated, in theory if not in practice, from the other more dignified pursuits of a senator, but the greatest capitalists of the Late Republic were such men as Pompey and Caesar. It could hardly be otherwise when one of a man's chief duties was the preservation and augmentation, not only of family reputation, but also of family property, and when the result of a successful political career was the holding of a provincial governorship with all its opportunities for self-enrichment. Caesar's plunder of Gaul may have enriched the treasury and swollen the revenues of the state, but it took place largely because Caesar needed to recoup a personal fortune. Roman society was always practical and materialistic, though it was not good form to be concerned with petty gain or to admit to financial motives. None the less, because service to the state was unpaid, or at least unsalaried, it was necessary for men who embarked on a public career to be rich and it is perfectly clear to the modern historian of Rome that economic considerations played an important but unadmitted part in the decisions and actions taken by leading figures on the political stage.

The Roman élite, that is to say the senatorial class and its relations and connections, was fiercely competitive, and had been since at least the fifth century BC. In this early republican society, enmeshed in annual war to preserve itself or win territory from its equally aggressive neighbours, the highest distinction a man could attain was to win the consulship (or its equivalent: constitutional niceties do not affect this discussion) and distinguish himself in peace, but above all in war, during his year of office. To triumph, that is to process in splendour from the gates of Rome to the temple of Jupiter Best and Greatest, wearing a purple robe and riding in a chariot behind a great crowd of captives and booty, was early regarded as the highest of human honours. A man could only do this if he had won a decisive victory when he himself was the chief commander in the field, and this in practice meant as consul (or later, as proconsul). Thus civic achievement, that is to say the successful holding of a series of largely administrative offices which gave one the experience and the status to be consul, was inextricably intertwined with a desire to figure as a great military commander, crush the enemies of Rome, and add to her domains. The Roman requirement that every male citizen should serve a large number of campaigns as a soldier ensured both that the future consul acquired the necessary experience of warfare, and that the state possessed a seasoned fighting force which could deliver military victories.

The competitiveness of the system of office-holding was striking. In the Late Republic, twenty quaestors (minimum age 30) were elected each year, who automatically became senators. The next compulsory step, if one wished to be able to stand for the consulship, was the praetorship (minimum age 39) but there were only eight posts. Therefore nearly all candidates would previously have stood for election to one or both of the tribunate (ten posts) or aedileship (four posts, responsible for the administration of the public facilities of the city, including the corn supply, the streets and markets, and the provision of public festivals), because in both, though in very different ways, one could be of service to ordinary members of the voting public. Then, if successful in being elected a praetor, one could think about running for the consulship (two posts, minimum age 42). Thus many a man standing as consul would have presented himself three or four times to the Roman voters in the course of the preceding twelve years, in elections where his chances of securing a post diminished steadily as he progressed up the 'ladder of office', as it is often called.

Such a system seems tolerably democratic, but in practice produced a fairly tight-knit aristocracy of office. Money was important, in two ways: first, because it provided the where-withal to woo the voters by largesse of various kinds (stopping short of outright buying of votes); and second, because there were several classes of voters, distinguished by a monetary qualification, and only members of the highest of these, the equestrian order (see Glossary), were qualified to stand for public office and become members of the senate. So those who were already at the top of the economic pile enjoyed the means to dominate the political pile as well. The Roman voting system, also, was prone to consolidate power where it already resided; for technical as well as social reasons, it was very conservative, and tended to elect men from known families. Furthermore, a man whose father had been a consul would have an advantage over a man whose father had done nothing more than achieve a quaestorship and remain an ordinary senator all his life. That is not to say that the circle of office was impenetrable to outsiders: a family might fail in the male line, or produce a black sheep that damaged its reputation, or suffer an attack of lack of ambition, while on the other hand there were always aspiring senators (and therefore aspiring consuls) from wealthy and well-connected families who might enjoy the support and patronage of men currently influential. So the charmed circle of power, influence, and wealth, though remaining small and consistent in shape and characteristics, was in reality composed of a slowly shifting selection from the wider upper class of Rome, itself likewise permeable to men of energy and ambition. Although the Roman aristocracy was small in numbers, relatively inbred, and apparently stable, it is a great mistake to see it as a fixed and unchanging group. One need only point to such figures as the Cicero brothers and Marcus Caelius (see Glossary) to see the process of renewal and replacement going on in the senatorial élite.

The clan of the Julii, to which Caesar himself belonged, was patrician, that is a clan which could claim to have been represented on the council (senate) of the last King of Rome before he was expelled at the end of the sixth century. Patricians, as the descendants of the aristocracy of regal Rome, continued under the Republic to enjoy religious and (for a long time) political privileges. Patrician status was also hereditary, unlike that of holders of the high offices and priesthoods of state. A man's father might be a consul, but that did not guarantee that he himself would even enter the senate, far less achieve a consulship. However, the Julii (represented in the early years of the Republic by the Julii Iulli) had more or less sunk from political view in the fourth and third centuries and it was not until the eve of the second century that the first known Julius Caesar restored the family's standing. A Sextus Julius Caesar then became this branch's first consul in 157, and although the Caesares achieved only subordinate magistracies in the later second century, they became very prominent in the 90s and 80s. Caesar's uncle Sextus became consul in 91, and his great-uncle (or possibly his grandfather's first cousin) Lucius consul in 90. The consular candidacy of this Lucius' brother, Gaius Julius Caesar Strabo Vopiscus, was a catalyst of civil war in 88. Caesar's aunt Julia was married to the great Gaius Marius (see Glossary), and his father, who held a praetorship in 92 and died in 85–84, might well have attained the consulship had it not been for the upheavals of the civil war between Marius and Sulla which broke out in 88. His mother Aurelia belonged to the family of the Aurelii Cottae, which had been prominent since the 120s and produced consuls in successive years in the 70s. With such an inheritance, and in such a society, a political career of some distinction for the young Gaius Julius Caesar was an almost foregone conclusion. What could not be foreseen was the scale and destructive power of his ambition.

The Origins of the Civil War

It is usual to trace this story from 60 BC. In that year, Caesar's political enemies peevishly denied him a triumph on his return from campaigning in Spain, with the result that he formed an unexpected alliance with his existing supporter Marcus Crassus, who was a distinguished and important man, and Pompey (Gnaeus Pompeius), the greatest figure of the age. The latter was then not long returned from a brilliant campaign of conquest and political reorganization in the Near East, but was finding ratification of his acts by the senate, and discharge of his obligations to his veterans, being made very difficult by some of the same men who opposed Caesar. Thus was born the so-called 'First Triumvirate', referred to above (p. x). Crassus, though not close to Pompey, had been his consular colleague in 70 and remained on sufficiently good terms with him to broker the deal between two men who had separately been antagonized but were believed to be unfriendly towards each other. Caesar stood successfully for the consulship of 59, and the deal was sealed, in the personal Roman way, by the marriage of Caesar's daughter Julia to Pompey early in that year.

As consul, Caesar was able to secure the main aims of the coalition quite rapidly, but to do so he ignored an uncooperative senate, as he was quite entitled to do. He also ignored, as he was *not* entitled to do, obstruction of his legislation on technical religious grounds by his colleague and die-hard opponent M. Bibulus. This meant that a great deal of the legislation of his consulship was theoretically invalid. However, he constructed what was simultaneously a refuge for himself and a cockpit for his military ambitions in the shape of a five-year command in Gaul, for the duration of which he was immune from prosecution for the illegal acts of his consulship.

The coalition was unpopular, but when it threatened to disintegrate in 56, partly over a proposal to repeal some of Caesar's legislation, it was not in the interests of any of the three to break ranks, and Caesar was able to persuade his partners to agree to a further consolidation of the alliance. This consolidation, worked out at Luca (modern Lucca), saw Pompey and Crassus installed by violence and obstruction as consuls for 55. They then proceeded to protect their future interests. This they did with a law (*Lex Trebonia*) by which Pompey received command of both provinces of Spain for five years, and Crassus command of Syria for the same period. They then jointly passed a law (*Lex Pompeia Licinia*) which continued Caesar in office as proconsul of Gaul by forbidding any discussion of his successor until 1 March 50. To understand the effect of this provision, one needs to know that under the system of provincial appointments in force at the time, two provinces were allocated *before* their election (usually in the late summer or early autumn) to the two consuls of the following year, who would spend that year in Rome and not proceed to these provinces until it was over. Thus under the *Lex Pompeia Licinia* Gaul could not be allocated to anyone earlier than a consul holding office in 49, who would not under normal circumstances succeed Caesar in Gaul until the beginning of 48. The effect of the law, therefore, was to allow Caesar to hold *imperium* unbroken until 48, by which time it would be legal (as he himself observed, *Civil War*, III.1) for him to become consul again (and in all probability set in train some variation on the previous scenario). His enemies were not to be allowed to get at him as a private citizen, quite apart from the fact that the longer his legislation of 59 remained unchallenged the more difficult it became to undo.

In 52, after a period of political anarchy brought on by electoral violence and murder, Pompey became sole consul. By now Crassus was dead, killed by the Parthians at Carrhae in the Syrian desert in 53, and the bond between Pompey and Caesar had been loosened by the death in childbirth of Caesar's daughter Julia in 54. Three had become two, the two had become less close, and one of the two now enjoyed a unique and constitutionally unprecedented position. To reassure Caesar of his continuing support, Pompey had the college of all ten tribunes pass a law which specifically permitted Caesar to stand for the consulship in absence. Although it apparently left it open as to which year he might invoke this privilege, it seems fairly obvious, in the light of the situation outlined above in reference to the *Lex Pompeia Licinia*, that it was intended that Caesar should stand *in absentia* in the summer of 49 for the consulship of 48. He would thus not need to lay down his *imperium* for even a short time, and so expose himself to legal action on the part of his enemies.

Pompey, however, initiated other reforms which were not so helpful to Caesar's position. One was a judicial purge, which began well with the enforced condemnation of Milo for Clodius' murder (see note on III.21), but went on, in what could be represented as a somewhat more partisan way, with the reform of the courts referred to by Caesar at *Civil War* III.1. As a result of this latter action many men were exiled or condemned who either previously or as a consequence sought Caesar's protection. More serious was a quite justified, but under the circumstances ill-timed, reform of the system of allocating and holding provincial governorships. Pompey appears to have wanted to break the close link between magisterial office in Rome and the subsequent provincial governorship, seeing it as responsible for the tendency of candidates to run up huge debts during their election campaigns, which they then conveniently recouped from the unfortunate provincials in all manner of illegitimate ways eighteen months later. To this end, he enacted a new law based on a senatorial resolution of the previous year, that five years should elapse between a magistracy and the subsequent provincial governorship. This meant that to fill the five-year gap suddenly created between those currently holding governorships (like Caesar) and their expected successors, men (like Cicero) who had been praetors or consuls but had not wished or been able to proceed to governorships thereafter were suddenly drafted to replace retiring governors. Since they were not currently holding magistracies, they were able to go out and replace their predecessors at any time.

This legislation blew a huge hole in Caesar's carefully prepared position. It was now theoretically possible for the senate to debate the question of his successor on 1 March 50, decide on the same day whom to appoint, and send that individual on his way to replace Caesar in Gaul forthwith. Even if Caesar had wished to invoke his privilege of standing *in absentia* in 51 for the consulship of 50, he still needed a dispensation from the law which forbade the holding of another consulship unless ten years had elapsed, a dispensation which in the present political climate he was unlikely to be granted. Caesar's position was still further weakened by two other laws of Pompey's. One of these prescribed that candidates for office had to announce their candidatures in person at Rome, although Pompey added a doubtfully valid rider after its passage, when in Suetonius' words 'the bronze tablet had already been inscribed', exempting Caesar from this requirement. The other extended Pompey's term as governor of Spain, and therefore commander of the strong army in that province, for another four years (five according to some sources) from 52. The effect of this was to ensure that whether Caesar became consul in 50, 49, or 48, Pompey would still enjoy *imperium* and the protection of holding a province and legions. At the same time Pompey signalled his return to the bosom of the traditionalist senatorial group whence he had come by marrying the daughter of Metellus Scipio (see Glossary). This was as clear an indication as it was possible to give that Pompey no longer saw his future in terms of a continued political alliance with Caesar.

Caesar had very nearly been outmanœuvred, but Pompey had made one mistake. He had forgotten to make his new law on the appointment of provincial governors immune to tribunician veto, as its predecessor had been. It was therefore open to Caesar to find a tribune prepared to veto any appointment to the governorship of Gaul. He did this most skilfully by paying off the large debts incurred by C. Scribonius Curio, tribune in 50 and spendthrift son of a pillar of the traditionalist group opposed to himself. Curio hid his change of allegiance and on one pretext or another blocked all attempts after the crucial date of 1 March to appoint a successor to Caesar. As the year moved to its end men sensed more and more clearly that there was likely to be an armed struggle. Pompey himself was not openly hostile to Caesar and made emollient proposals, but it was perfectly plain that his political allies were opposed to any compromise with Caesar and were itching to bring him to book for his past acts—even including genocide in Gaul. The intransigence of a handful of Caesar's bitterest opponents was illustrated in the senate on 1 December, when Curio as tribune put forward a motion that both Pompey and Caesar should give up their provinces and armies. This was passed by 370 votes to 22, but the consul C. Marcellus (cousin of his similarly named successor) dismissed the senate and (as was his constitutional right) took no steps to implement the motion.

A few days later, on the strength of a rumour that Caesar was invading Italy, Marcellus went to Pompey and placed a sword in his hands, entrusting him on his own authority with the defence of Rome and the command of troops in Italy. Meanwhile, although Caesar maintained contact with Rome and had proposed that he retain only Cisalpine Gaul and Illyricum, with two legions, until his second consulship, Pompey's own attitude was hardening. Cicero wrote on 24 December, after a long private meeting with Pompey, that not only was there no chance of peace, but Pompey did not even want it (Letters to Atticus, VII.8.4). Finally, on 7 January 49 the new consul Lentulus did what his predecessors in office had shrunk from doing, and acted. He overrode the veto of Antony and Cassius (the newly elected tribunes who had taken over from Curio the defence of Caesar's interests), had the senate declare a state of emergency, and proceeded to the long-delayed business of appointing new provincial governors, including a successor to Caesar. Caesar, who had been preparing for war (see Civil War, I.15 n.), was thus offered a pretext to start it, in defence of the safety and the constitutional rights of the tribunes—and, as he admits, of his own personal standing, his dignitas (Civil War, I.7, 9), for he preferred war to the political extinction and exile his enemies wished to inflict upon him. That Caesar could take this final step, that it appears to have been actively desired by an influential senatorial minority, and that Caesar was prepared to plan deliberately for it rather than back down, says much for the way in which the competitive ethos among the Roman aristocracy had got out of hand.

The Literary Context

Caesar's Style

It is unfortunately impossible to assess the originality of Caesar's Commentaries (i.e. the Gallic War and the Civil War) or the extent to which they may have diverged from other 'Memoirs' or 'Notes' (for such is the literal meaning of *commentarius*), because no other examples of the form survive. However, one can point to three main streams of influence on their style. One of these is the contemporary debate, known to us through Cicero's oratorical writings, concerning the appropriate style for oratory. The 'Asianists' favoured a full, rich style, employing every possible device to soothe, impress, and entertain the listener. The 'Atticists', on the other hand, believed in a spare, economical style which put a premium on clarity, simplicity, and intelligibility. Temperamentally, Caesar was drawn to the latter school. Another influence was the legacy of the Roman annalists, writers of the second and early first century BC who attempted to put together histories of Rome, or of parts of that story. They proceeded in a somewhat mechanical way, detailing year by year the various events worthy of record, from war, through civil affairs, to natural phenomena and portents. Either because they genuinely drew on terse and old-fashioned documentary sources, or because they wished to create the impression that they were so doing, they wrote in a simple unadorned way, plainly and directly, without indulging in analysis, speculation, or convolutions of thought. There thus existed a model for the 'reporting' style of history to which Caesar's *Commentarii* appear to belong. As to the third influence, it appears that the *Commentarii* were patterned on, or at any rate intended to recall, the style of the reports sent by a Roman general in the field to the consuls and senate.[4] It is reasonable to suppose that such reports would be brief and clear, and concentrate on essentials. They would also aim to convey an impression of objectivity, but not at the cost of minimizing any successes achieved by the commander (or by his subordinates, for whose actions he was of course responsible). It is further likely that these subordinates would from time to time themselves make reports to their superior of a routine and factual nature in which literary graces were neither expected nor often found.

[4] Some examples, perhaps not altogether typical in that their author is Cicero, may be found in the latter's correspondence from Cilicia, e.g. *Letters to his Friends*, XV.1, 2, and 4 (first half).

These considerations go a long way to accounting for the style of Caesar's narrative. Its most conspicuous, indeed notorious, feature is the author's habit of referring to himself in the third person ('On receipt of this news, Caesar decided . . .'). This trick at once gives the narrative a certain pseudo-objectivity and an appearance of dispassionate reporting, enabling Caesar to present, for example, simple denigration as fact.[5] (It also has an interesting counter-effect: when Caesar writes 'Caesar thought that a better plan had to be found', readers need to remind themselves that, for once, the author really *did* know what Caesar thought.) This seeming deletion of his own personality from the narrative is matched by an austere and limited vocabulary coupled with a remarkably lucid and often very simple sentence-structure. When reported in this detached and unembellished fashion, the 'facts' as presented acquire an aura of self-evident truth, against which readers need to be constantly on guard. Caesar's gift of writing limpid Latin also enables him to explain complex situations in deceptively simple words, so that once again the authenticity of the picture he presents is confirmed by the very ease with which that picture can be understood. For clarity of thought, expression, and explanation Caesar has always been deservedly praised, and not for nothing has his style served as a model for centuries. Unfortunately, what works in Latin does not work so well in English, and this translation has perforce abandoned some of the austerity, almost brutality, of Caesar's expression and sentence-structure in favour of a style that I hope is rather more palatable to readers used to modern English, with its myriad variations of expression and its inexhaustible store of metaphor.

Narrative Technique

Translation is not so unkind to those features of Caesar's works which are not intimately linked to the Latin language, such as his technique of building up a narrative, and his presentation of himself and the other characters who appear on

---

[5] e.g. at *Civil War* III.85 he says that 'by marching every day he would exhaust Pompey's army, *which was unused to hard effort*'. The words italicized are a blatant lie, as is obvious from preceding events, but the presentation lulls the reader into accepting it.

his carefully constructed stage. His narrative, like that of all good historians, depends on careful selection and moulding of material. A good example is his omission of any description at all of his desperate march from Apollonia to Gomphi after his defeat at Dyrrachium (*Civil War*, III.84 n.). He was, in effect, on the run, but it does not suit him to dwell on this because he wishes to present the upswing in his fortunes (which was to lead to the victory at Pharsalus) at starting to occur after their nadir *at Dyrrachium*, where he places both his own speech of encouragement to his demoralized army and his reflections on the hubris of the Pompeians in thinking that the war was already won. In the light of what happened at Pharsalus, the taking of Gomphi was a small matter (though important for his cause in Greece), and had he made much of the hardships of the march from Apollonia he would have needed to place correspondingly more emphasis on the capture of Gomphi, which put an end to his army's privations. Another instance of Caesar's skill is his treatment of the long siege of Pompey at Dyrrachium. Here, instead of attempting a rather shapeless day-to-day account of the type inflicted on us by the author of the *Spanish War*, he proceeds analytically. He comments on the strategic situation and describes various problems (both his and Pompey's) and their resolution, as well as a few notable incidents. He does this at sufficient length not to minimize the importance of this protracted episode, and only then, with many weeks of near-stalemate behind him, does he make the switch into narrative mode (at ch. 59) as the critical moment approaches.

Caesar also imposes coherence on the anarchic richness of events by following particular chains of consequence through to an end, and then going back in time to start another, overlapping chain. These chains are explicitly related to each other, but the temporal dislocation may be blurred or even falsified (a particularly striking instance being the last sentence of ch. 11 of Book I). An analysis of the opening of Book I yields five such chains, starting at chs. 1, 7, 11 (end), 14, and 15. This technique imposes order and clarity on a confusing and fractured series of events. Exactly how confusing the events were may be seen by reading the almost daily letters of Cicero from this period, which also (with a little other evidence) reveal the degree to which Caesar has falsified the record. Another device for creating unity, even inevitability, is the prefiguring or echoing of events, frequently through speech. The ex-centurion Crastinus goes to his death at Pharsalus after proclaiming that he is prepared to die in defence of Caesar's status (*dignitas*) and his own and his companions' freedom; yet right at the start of the *Civil War* (ch. 7) Caesar asked his troops to follow him in defence of his own *dignitas* and the rights of the tribunes of the people (long synonymous, in popular belief, with the freedom of the plebs). Making a speech (III.73) to encourage his disheartened men after their defeat at Dyrrachium, Caesar prophesies that they will eventually be able to get to grips with their enemies, because they will offer battle of their own accord—which is precisely what happened at Pharsalus later.

Perhaps the most spectacular instance of Caesar's power of imposing form on the narrative is the episode of Curio in Africa (II.23–44), where he uses the techniques of tragedy to portray a man trapped in the coils of disaster by his own temperament. We, the readers, are privy like an audience in the theatre to information of which Curio is ignorant, and we are also treated to comments about Curio's performance which hint at his fatal overconfidence. Thus we become privileged spectators as the tragedy unfolds, complete with three speeches by Curio exactly as if he were the protagonist in a stage play. And is it too far-fetched to see Caesar's treatment of his soldiers in terms of a dramatist's use of a chorus? Their valour, loyalty, and endurance keep cropping up to reinforce the message that not only is Caesar a man in control of events, who possesses superior moral quality to his opponents, but the men he commands prove it by their dedication to his cause, their selflessness (Crastinus again), and their ultimate triumph. They serve as a constant foil, not only to their commander, but also to the occasional officer of Caesar's who emerges from anonymity for a page or so, and to the assorted gang of greedy, self-seeking traitors to the Republic, and their soft army, who have the effrontery to oppose Caesar.

Caesar's characterization is in fact almost as limited as his extremely rare descriptive writing and his non-existent interest in informing us how his army actually functioned—these being details he must have taken to be unimportant or else matters of common knowledge. Out of the mass of names which fill the Glossary very few emerge as characters in any identifiable sense in the narrative, and those who do are almost all his opponents. Apart from Curio (on whom see further below), his own officers, even senior ones such as C. Fabius in Spain in Book I, D. Brutus and Trebonius at Massilia, and M. Antonius in Books I and III, remain mere ciphers, little more than mechanical links in the machinery which Caesar uses to control his army. Oddly enough, the occasional special mention of an individual or vignette of personal bravery nearly always concerns centurions, like Q. Fulginius (I.46), Scaeva (III.53), or Crastinus (III.91, 99). Is it that his higher officers were never brave, or is it that Caesar is careful of bestowing praise on fellow-senators, men too near himself in social status? Interestingly, almost the only officer who comes to life is P. Sulla, whom Caesar defends from the criticism that had he been bolder in following up a success a decisive victory could have been won (III.51). The ground of Caesar's defence is that a subordinate officer ought to act entirely in accordance with his orders and not arrogate to himself the function of his general. It would appear, then, that Caesar's view (very probably widely shared) was that since leadership resided entirely in the commander, subordinates were simply required to be efficient. In that case, their other qualities were either irrelevant, or even (if they displayed too much independence) dangerous.

The persons who do come to life, apart from his army as discussed above, are Caesar's chief opponents, particularly Q. Metellus Scipio (Pompey's new father-in-law), L. Lentulus Crus (the consul of 49), L. Domitius (Caesar's designated replacement in Gaul), T. Labienus (who deserted Caesar at the beginning of the war), and M. Bibulus (Caesar's consular, praetorian, and aedilician colleague and opponent). Bibulus, who died in uncomfortable circumstances attempting to do his duty, is more sympathetically portrayed, but the others (along with one or two other less prominent targets) attract the full force of Caesar's scorn and derision. His sketch of Scipio's behaviour as governor of Syria could serve as a satire on Roman provincial government, and his succinct analysis of the motives of Scipio, Lentulus, and Cato in the fourth chapter of Book I is damning. The worst treatment is reserved for the traitor Labienus, who cannot negotiate, murders prisoners in cold blood, and gives Pompey idiotic advice on the eve of the battle of Pharsalus. Pompey himself is exempt from personal attack of this sort, though Caesar credits him with remarks (at III.18 and 94) which show him as unwilling to compromise, and deceitful. The damage to Pompey is done obliquely by the company he keeps, precisely these persons so savagely criticized by Caesar. The cumulative effect of Caesar's portrayal is to paint Pompey's inner circle as a band of men who profess to be defending the Republic but are deeply unrepublican in their behaviour. They act illegally or in bad faith, and they place personal advantage above the interests of the state. Their numerous other failings include ineptitude, incompetence, cowardice, and poor judgement. Caesar, one may assume, was somewhat loath to attack in the same way the man who had been his political ally for eight or so years and was partly responsible for his own rise to dominance. Indirect methods would do. If these were the kind of men Pompey consorted with, what need of further denigration?

The Overall Picture, and the Purpose of the 'Civil War'

The picture that emerges is of a great man, worthy of the traditions of the Republic. Caesar is cool and omnicompetent. He stands at the head of a brave army with great powers of endurance and devotion to their commander. His reverses are due to mere chance (see III.68, 70, 72), and he is backed up by loyal and virtually anonymous subordinates. His own personality is concealed by the impersonal style of the narrative. He sometimes shares a strategic problem with us (e.g. III.78), but personal asides like his admission of fondness for Curio are extremely rare, and he does not try to communicate either emotions or states of mind in any direct way. Nor does he attempt any general assessments, for example of the state of public opinion in Italy at the outbreak of war. What he is at pains to stress are his republican credentials: he goes to war in defence of the rights of the tribunes (and, more dubiously, his own *dignitas*—but the aristocratic code gave him some justification on that point); he is keen to negotiate; he consults the senate; he offers to refer the dispute to senate and people; and he makes much of his position as consul in 48, mentioning it on several occasions. In contrast, his opponents are a self-seeking crew, as we have seen above, whose claim to be defending the Republic is belied at every turn by their behaviour. Again and again we come across a moral contrast, implicit or explicit, and this surely reveals the purpose of Caesar's writing. It is to establish the rightness of his own cause and the wrongness of his opponents', and hence to justify his own victory and his status as a true *imperator*, a successful leader of men.

However, without literary shape and a degree of restraint, this might have turned into mere invective. The restraint is present in the choice of literary style (see p. xxi above) and in the general coolness, rapidity, and matter-of-factness of the reporting. The literary shape is achieved by careful selection of material (see p. xxiv above), so that both Books I and III exhibit the pattern of an initial success (the invasion of Italy and the start of the Ilerda campaign in I, the crossing of the Adriatic up to the encirclement of Pompey at Dyrrachium in III), followed by a potentially disastrous setback (floods and famine in I, Pompey's break-out and victory in III), resolved by a decisive victory (over Afranius and Petreius in I, over Pompey in III). Exactly the same tripartite structure informs the work as a whole. This is obscured by its fragmentary state, but it is certain that Caesar either planned or more probably actually wrote an account of the disaster which was suffered by C. Antonius on the island of Curicta, off the Illyrian coast, at about the same time that Curio was defeated in Africa (III.4). The loss of this account has done great damage to a proper appreciation of the construction of the *Civil War*. We may assume that the account was fairly detailed (cf. III.67) and would therefore have possessed considerable solidity and narrative interest, perhaps even sufficient to balance that of the Curio episode. If this is so, we find in the articulation of the whole work precisely the same triple structure (success–failure–success) which can be observed giving shape, drama, and movement to the first and third books individually. The function of the story of Curio's disaster, then, is not primarily to tell us what happened in Africa in 49 BC. It is to provide a contrast, both between Caesar's previous success in Spain and Curio's failure in Africa simply as dramatic elements, and between Caesar the true *imperator* who knows how to secure victory (without bloodshed, as it happens) and Curio the false *imperator* (II.26 n.) who in spite of excellent qualities squanders his men's lives in unnecessary defeat.

We do not know why Caesar broke off his narrative in mid-course shortly after his arrival in Alexandria. (There can be no doubt that he did break off, and that little or no text has been lost, because the almost contemporary *Alexandrian War* starts where Caesar finishes.) An attractive explanation, which can be no more than a guess but has the merit of fitting the facts, is that during or shortly after the Alexandrian adventure Caesar became aware that he had become master of the Roman world and started to act in an increasingly autocratic manner. In that case, what was the point of going on proving that he was a good republican, adhering to the forms and customs handed down from earlier generations or embodied in the laws? As time went on, his own position became further and further removed from the one he had striven to represent himself as holding, at least up to the death of Pompey. His stance, perforce, had altered. Thus he simply lost the motive to go on with his now purposeless account, and unlike the *Gallic War* it was not published until after his death. An additional, though lesser, consideration may have been the very perfection in the balance, discussed above, which he had achieved so far, both within individual books and in the work as a whole, if one may judge the whole as being closed by the death of Pompey. How to go on, or indeed whether to start again, was a literary as much as a political problem, and it is hardly surprising that Caesar simply shelved the question.

The final question must be whether Caesar tells a true story, granted of course that any number of true stories can be constructed from a given complex of events. His veracity has been savagely attacked by Michel Rambaud,[6] but it is impossible to believe that at least in the *Civil War* the actual course of events did not severely inhibit falsification and invention. These events were well known to contemporaries, and Caesar's was unlikely in any case to be the only account. Propaganda that is patently untrue ceases to be effective. The other surviving sources, principally Cicero's correspondence but including also Caesar's officer Asinius Pollio, who later wrote a full-dress history of the period from 60 to 42 BC, bear out the essential correctness in factual matters of Caesar's narrative. The lie at *Civil War* I.11 is possibly the only case of importance where Caesar can be convicted of adjusting, not the interpretation of the facts, but the facts themselves. It is true that the control provided at the beginning of the work by Cicero's letters soon disappears, while Pollio himself thought that the *Commentaries* 'had been composed with too little care and with too little respect for the truth, because Caesar had given a wrong account of a number of events, either by rashly believing the exploits of others or by deliberately or through lapse of memory falsifying his own'.[7] So it is possible that there may be other falsifications of fact which we are unable to spot. None the less, it seems clear that in general Caesar prefers to influence the reader by his selection, arrangement, and presentation of the facts, rather than by altering either the facts themselves or their interrelationship.

The Continuations

Content

The present volume also contains the three works, not by Caesar himself, which continue the story of the civil wars down to the defeat of the last remaining Pompeian forces under Pompey's son Gnaeus in Spain in 45 BC. Collectively,

[6] *L'Art de la déformation historique dans les Commentaires de César* (2nd edn., Paris, 1966). [7] Suetonius, *Divus Julius*, 56.4.

they make up the so-called Corpus Caesarianum, and were probably put together by Caesar's friend L. Cornelius Balbus within a year of Caesar's death to make up, with the *Gallic* and *Civil Wars*, the collection we now have. The first, the *Alexandrian War*, is a narrative of considerable competence. It starts where Caesar breaks off and devotes something less than half its length to the rest of the Alexandrian campaign, culminating with the defeat and death of Ptolemy XIII and the installation of Cleopatra as Queen-consort to her younger brother Ptolemy XIV. The rest of the book covers, in order, the first phase of the campaign against Pharnaces, King of Pontus, which was conducted by Domitius Calvinus; then the operations of 48–47 BC on the Illyrian coast under Q. Cornificius and Vatinius; next the story of the mutiny in Spain against its governor Quintus Cassius, also in 48–47; and lastly the second phase of the campaign against Pharnaces, this time led by Caesar personally in the summer of 47 after his arrival from Egypt. Thus, like Caesar's Book II, it contains the events of several different theatres of war, and it derives its unity from the fact that they all occurred within the twelvemonth following Pharsalus.

The second, the *African War*, is a more or less seamless account of the campaign in Tunisia which started at the very end of 47 and was settled by the battle at Thapsus on 6 April of the following year. Time-frame and theatre of war are alike much more circumscribed than in either the *Alexandrian War* or the *Civil War*. The narrative, though lacking the incisiveness of Caesar's and uncertain in its emphases, remains tolerably clear. Unfortunately this is more than can be said of the third book, the *Spanish War*. This is a confused and barely literate offering which largely fails to make sense of the military operations it describes, which are those of the campaign conducted south of the Guadalquivir River over the autumn, winter, and early spring of 46–45 between Caesar and Pompey's elder son Gnaeus. The decisive battle in this case was that of Munda, fought on 17 March (Julian), to which the story of the flight and death of Gnaeus is appended.

Authorship and Point of View

The three works differ sufficiently in style, vocabulary, and linguistic usage from each other and from Caesar to make it certain that they are all by different authors. Best by far is the *Alexandrian War*, with its ability to shape a narrative, unite disparate material while preserving internal balance, and convey some overall understanding of both strategic and tactical factors. The author himself cannot have been an eyewitness of more than at best two of these theatres of war. He must therefore have been in a position where he could call upon the reports, or failing those the memory, of senior participants in the campaigns in Alexandria, Asia Minor, Illyria, and Spain. He also writes good clear Latin in a fairly close approximation to Caesar's own style. For all these reasons it has often been maintained that the author is Aulus Hirtius, who certainly wrote the Eighth Book of the *Gallic War* specifically to cover the gap between the end of the Seventh and the opening of the *Civil War*, and also claimed to have written up the events from the Alexandrian war down to the death of Caesar.[8]

It was already questioned in antiquity whether Hirtius wrote the *Alexandrian War*, and neither stylistic comparison between it and *Gallic War* VIII, nor historical argument, have been able to establish either positively that Hirtius was the author, or negatively that he cannot have been.[9] However, we must believe him when he says he put together an account of this period, and we know that he was very well placed to acquire the necessary detailed information. He served with

---

[8] *Gallic War* VIII, preface: '*Caesaris nostri commentarios rerum gestarum Galliae, non comparantibus superioribus atque insequentibus eius scriptis, contexui, novissimumque imperfectum ab rebus gestis Alexandreae confeci usque ad exitum non quidem civilis dissensionis, sed vitae Caesaris.*' ('Because of the gap which existed between his earlier and later writings, I have composed a continuation of our friend Caesar's commentaries on his campaigns in Gaul. His latter work, which was unfinished, I have completed from the operations at Alexandria right up to the end—not the end of civil strife, for the conclusion of *that* is not in sight, but the end of Caesar's life') (tr. C. Hammond).

[9] Suetonius, *Divus Julius*, 56.1; see also L. G. H. Hall, 'Hirtius and the *Bellum Alexandrinum*', *Classical Quarterly* 46/2 (1996).

Caesar in Gaul in the late 50s, probably as chief staff officer; was with him at Antioch in 47, though he did not see service either in Egypt or subsequently in Africa; held a praetorship in 46; and was consul-designate for 43 and therefore involved in the protracted winding-up of Caesar's affairs and papers after his murder. Since Hirtius entered on his consulship at a stormy moment in Roman history, and died of a wound sustained in action at Mutina in April 43, the only time he can have found free for literary composition and the concomitant research was between March and December 44. Any earlier date is excluded by the nature of his project, which cannot have come into being until after Caesar's death. It is hard to name another person better placed or better qualified, by experience and contacts, to write the continuation of the *Civil War*. None the less, the case remains unproven, and there is always the nagging question: if the *Alexandrian War* is the first part of Hirtius' continuation of Caesar, whatever happened to the rest? For one thing is absolutely certain: the Latin of the other two works which we have cannot be Hirtius' Latin. So if Hirtius *was* the author of our *Alexandrian War*, some peculiar accident has substituted the surviving *African* and *Spanish Wars* for his versions—unless he simply commissioned others to write them. In the light of this, many prefer to assume that we have none of Hirtius' work apart from *Gallic War* VIII, and that the *Alexandrian War* is the work of some unidentifiable but equally able and well-placed contemporary.

The abilities of the indisputably anonymous author of the *African War* represent a definite step down. The viewpoint is not so much that of Caesar or someone near Caesar, as of a middle-ranking officer who had access to a certain amount of strategic information, but did not always understand the full picture—or if he did, did not trouble to explain it. This man seems to have stayed with Caesar's main force throughout, as one can tell by the fairly summary treatment of other events, however important, which happen in other places— for example, the extremely effective and strategically vital campaign waged against king Juba by the mercenary captain P. Sittius. Some of the manœuvres and marches described

seem somewhat aimless, and the reader has the feeling that
there is more here than meets the eye. But although the
author may be deficient in his larger vision, he offers some
compensation with vivid details of fighting, camp life, and
training—matters which are definitely beneath Caesar's notice
unless some larger point depends on them. The description
(ch. 47) of the thunderstorm that wrecked Caesar's camp is
inserted more by way of a wonder than for any other reason, but gives us precious information about the arrangements
(or lack of them) for provisioning and sheltering soldiers in
the field. This passage is a useful corrective to the impression easily formed from a reading of Caesar that his military
operations took place in a weather-free zone. The author's
main fault, as a literary artist (a title he might not, of course,
have wished to claim), is lack of proportion and misplaced
emphasis. Good examples are the very detailed description
given to a relatively unimportant and certainly inconclusive
engagement (chs. 12–20), and the similarly detailed build-up
(chs. 58–61), with full statement of the dispositions of the
two sides, to a battle which in fact never took place. One
senses that these were episodes which were more memorable
to the author than vital in the development of the campaign.
There can be no doubt that we are reading the work of an
eyewitness of the campaign, and one who gives us a little of
the feeling of what it might have been like to have served
under Caesar instead of alongside the great man.

Of our third author, alas, it is difficult to find anything con-
structive to say. It is not his fault, one presumes, that the text
of the *Spanish War* has come down to us in a badly damaged state, so that his obscurities and awkwardnesses of expression are compounded. His Latin is distinctively different
again, embodying vocabulary and turns of syntax and expression that Caesar and Hirtius would never have employed. But
there would be no need to hold this against him if it were
not that he is also incapable of writing clearly. His most per-
nicious fault is to use 'they' indiscriminately, and without
further identification, of both parties to a situation, so that
in the more extreme cases it becomes quite impossible to be
sure which side is doing what. Here a translator simply has

to decide on a possible allocation of parts, as it were, and at least make it clear what *he* thinks is meant. The author also has almost no notion of the strategy being followed by the two generals, and is clearly much more distant from the centre of command than was the author of the *African War*. He sees almost everything from the viewpoint of the man (or cavalryman) in the field. Things happen, but their *raison d'être* and consequences tend to be a closed book to him. Trivialities displace the solid information the reader would like on strategy, or even on tactics. Many passages read like extracts from a diary, inserted because it is the next day, not because the events are of any importance. In short, selection, arrangement, and emphasis of the material are alike poor. There is some plausibility in the speculation that the author was a cavalry officer, given the much greater attention paid to cavalry operations in this work than in any of the others.[10] He was certainly of the literate classes, and can quote the old Roman poet Ennius, but he was unused to writing at this scale. Equally certainly, he was an eyewitness (as proved by, for example, the detail about the boy in the tower at the end of ch. 13), and he was also, as we have seen, someone who had no part in the larger command structure. An officer of equestrian status, or maybe some inconspicuous senator, is the most likely candidate, but to try and attach a name is hopeless.

Each of our three authors has a different viewpoint, and each moves successively further away from Caesar, although superficially the treatment is the same. The pseudo-objectivity of Caesar's own third-person narration becomes genuine now that the narrator is no longer Caesar. At the same time the insight of the author into what is going on becomes less acute, and the space given to mere military detail more generous. The author of the *Alexandrian War* has the Caesarian touch when he describes, at the opening of the book, the kinds of device each side used against each other, and the character of the street-fighting. In contrast, the author of the *African War* is concerned to tell us the shape of Caesar's

[10] R. H. Storch, 'The Author of the *de Bello Hispaniensi*: A Cavalry Officer?' *Acta Classica* (Cape Town) 20 (1977), 201–4.

counter-walls at Uzitta and to give us a day-by-day account of the progress of events. Indeed, his favourite connective is *interim*, 'meanwhile'. As a result, his narrative quite lacks the rapidity of Caesar's own, and the same goes, *a fortiori*, for the author of the *Spanish War*.

The great difference, of course, between Caesar and his continuators is that Caesar's narrative is designed to justify his actions and his success while that of his continuators has no purpose beyond the chronicling of further success. This glorificatory, at times almost hagiographic, approach (cf. *Alexandrian War*, 65; *African War*, 31) has led all three authors to ignore the dramatic possibilities of their narratives. In each of the three books Caesar came very close, in different ways, to losing his life or being defeated. Yet in none of these three accounts is there any sense of a man living dangerously. Caesar had arrived in Alexandria with two grossly under-strength legions, numbering 3,200 men in all, as he himself informs us (III.106), and rapidly annoyed the Alexandrian population and became embroiled in an unnecessary war. These facts are, on reflection, obvious, and were major determinants of the struggle, yet virtually no allusion is made to them. What even the author of the *Alexandrian War* is primarily interested in is Caesar's trajectory as a conqueror. Some attempt, granted, is made by all three men to inject a moral dimension into the contest, but somehow it lacks the bite and passion of Caesar's own aspersions on his enemies, and when he is already cast as top dog it does nothing for the drama of the narrative. Nor is there any political background, save a little in the *Alexandrian War*. So what we have is not much more than one-sided military history, written without the genius and the personal involvement of the protagonist.

Warfare in the Late Republic

Citizen Armies

It is important to realize that the armies of the Late Republic were not composed of professional soldiers, in spite of the fact that there undoubtedly were men serving in the legions who regarded warfare as their living. The citizen militia of the Early Republic, recruited annually or as required for campaigns lasting only a season, had by Caesar's time evolved some, but only some, of the way to being a professional standing army. This was because every male citizen, provided he possessed a certain minimum amount of property, had a theoretical duty to serve sixteen years (i.e. sixteen annual campaigns) in the infantry or ten years in the cavalry. As Rome became a Mediterranean power and her armies operated further and further from home for longer and longer periods, men might find themselves spending years away from Italy and home. It seems as though the period of service under these conditions dropped from its theoretical maximum to something like five to seven years' continuous service, but this was still a long enough period for many men to have difficulties in picking up their former lives. Their pay was simply subsistence, and not much more even when Caesar doubled it in Gaul, so they depended on either booty from a profitable campaign or a grant of land from a grateful state, or both, to see them back into civilian life. When Marius, at the end of the second century BC, ignored the lower property limit and recruited from men who had nothing to their name, the need for some sort of decent reward for a long period of military service became more necessary still. But the state had no mechanism for providing any reward and the problem, or the obligation, was left to the initiative of the returning army's commander, who would of course secure the lifelong political support of those he managed to help. Sulla's troops had followed him in 88 because they feared their displacement by others who would enjoy the rich pickings of a war in Asia, and they were rewarded by him with land as the price of their loyalty to him in the subsequent civil war. That event sowed the seed of what we see in the war between Pompey and Caesar, and then still more sharply in the troubles of the period after the murder of Caesar, namely the loyalty of armies, not to the state (for where or what was that?) but to whatever commander could do the best for them. Men were recruited unwillingly and

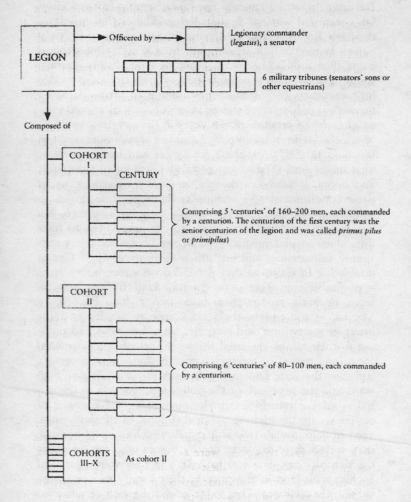

FIG. 2 Late Republican Legionary Structure

en masse in this Civil War, so the possibility of large-scale desertion and even the complete crumbling of an army was ever-present. It seems, in fact, not often to have occurred, which must be testimony to the power of the leaders to enthuse their men (or at least convince them that they had joined the winning side) and, doubtless, to the power of the formidable Roman military discipline. Against that, it is apparent that soldiers in some legions, for example Caesar's veteran Sixth and Tenth, developed during their long service a fierce *esprit de corps* and pride in their fighting abilities which made them a formidable force even when under-strength, as they were at Pharsalus and afterwards. So numbers of men were far less relevant than their fighting quality and experience, and it must have been the semi-professional veteran core of any army that kept the rest up to scratch—for they were all, on both sides, Roman citizens, supposed to be fighting in the service of their country.

Military Organization

The core of a Roman army was the heavy infantry, the legions. A legion had a nominal strength of about 6,000 fighting men, subdivided into ten cohorts of about 500, of which the first was double-strength. The cohort was the ordinary tactical unit, and a legion seldom fought as a legion, with all its cohorts together, except in set-piece battles. Within each cohort there were six centuries of about 80 men, each commanded by a centurion with further 'non-commissioned' ranks below him. The first cohort contained only five centuries, and thus there were 59 centurions in a legion. The prominence of centurions in Caesar's notices of individuals reflects the fact that they were the backbone of the army, tough, brave leaders of their men on the field of battle, and organizers and disciplinarians off it. Socially, centurions might be either ordinary soldiers who had risen from the ranks, or men of good family, possibly of equestrian status, who saw the dawning possibilities of a military career. Above the centurions came the six military tribunes of the legion, who would be equestrian—possibly sons of senators (e.g. Tuticanus Gallus, III.71) or else young men of substance performing their 'cavalry service' (officers being mounted, and the cavalry function in Rome's armies being now performed by allies such as Gauls and Germans); and above them the legionary commander (*legatus legionis*), responsible to the overall commander.

Support was provided by cavalry, officered by its own non-Roman aristocracy (like the Allobrogians Egus and Roucillus, III.59) or by a Roman *praefectus*. A legion's nominal attachment of cavalry was 300, but could vary wildly—although to operate without any cavalry at all, as Caesar did at the start of the Ilerda campaign, was to labour under a real handicap. Other auxiliaries could include archers and slingers and occasional exotics like Parthian mounted archers, but these always operated as distinct formations and were not integrated into the legionary line. Non-fighting support included camp-followers, for it appears that legionaries routinely had slaves (*Civil War*, III.6; *African War*, 47) whose main function must have been to prepare food and look after clothing, bedding, and equipment. There must also have been a system for acquiring and allocating food supplies to the men, for surely such operations as those described at *African War* 21 and 65 did not result in an uncoordinated scramble on the part of the soldiers.

Military Operation

A Roman army needed no 'lines of communication' back to any base or HQ. It was a self-sufficient organism, providing it could go on finding food and water as it went. This was why Caesar was able to march away into Thessaly after his defeat at Dyrrachium, and still face Pompey on more or less equal terms (ignoring his disadvantage in numbers). It did not matter that he was 'cut off' from Brundisium, or Larisa, or the coast of Epirus, or any other place at all. The locality of Pharsalus had no particular strategic significance—the battle simply took place when both generals, at last, desired it.

Ancient wars were decided by set-piece battles, and without such a battle clear-cut victory was very unlikely. The reason was that the victor, having pushed back (quite literally) and broken his opponents' line, was generally able to inflict great loss of life and if he acted quickly (as Caesar did at Pharsalus) also capture the enemy camp, equipment, and war-chest. But although the consequences of a set-piece battle could be so decisive, it was impossible for one to take place if one side declined to line up. The advantage, in an era of hand-propelled weapons and (on the battlefield) nothing but equine and human muscle-power, lay so much with the defence that it was enough for the side which did not want the battle to stay in camp, or else (chiefly, it seems, to avoid the charge of cowardice) deploy their battle-line where they had the advantage of a slope (*iniquo loco*). In such a case, because battle was virtually always joined at the charge, the side charging uphill had no realistic hope of dislodging the opposing line and the practical certainty of being itself broken and routed. In short, it took two to tango, and this is the explanation of the infrequency of full-scale battles. Both sides had simultaneously to see an advantage in having one.

By contrast, there was constant skirmishing, principally between the cavalry forces. The point was to harass the non-battle operations of the other side, such as foraging, construction of earthworks, gaining access to water, marching to another camp, and so forth. Sieges were another matter again, requiring specialized but well-understood techniques and counter-techniques (cf. the siege of Massilia, *Civil War*, II.1–16). Apt to be lengthy, they were sometimes begun not so much to take a place of strategic importance as to lure the opposing army into a confrontation and perhaps a decisive battle. Caesar's siege of Pompey near Dyrrachium is a good example of a siege with nothing to capture, indulged in for purely tactical reasons. Naval operations were directed almost entirely towards interrupting an enemy's line of reinforcement or supply, for example Pompey's attempt to blockade Brundisium and prevent the rest of Caesar's forces reaching him in Epirus. Otherwise they had a certain nuisance value, burning enemy dockyards for example, or raiding seaport towns, but the self-maintaining nature of a Roman army, so long as it stayed on the move, rendered it largely unaffected by naval warfare.

Caesar's Final Years and the *Civil War*

As might perhaps be expected of a work whose author abandoned it in mid-course, the fate of the *Civil War* was not straightforward. It has been suggested above (see p. xxix) that the reason for Caesar's loss of interest in his own account was the dawning realization that the picture he had been at such pains to construct, of himself as a man prepared to defend the Republic from the selfishness, abuses, and unconstitutional behaviour of the Pompeians, was rapidly becoming irrelevant. Whether this is the correct explanation or not, it is certainly true that after the Alexandrian campaign, and still more so after his defeat of Pharnaces at Zela in the summer of 47 BC, Caesar found himself unquestioned master of most of the Mediterranean. His enemies were regrouping in North Africa, and Spain, though under his control, was a somewhat uncertain area in view of its strong Pompeian connections and the recent excesses of Caesar's governor Quintus Cassius (see *Alexandrian War* 48–64). Otherwise, there was no real opposition left. Of course, the forces under Metellus Scipio and King Juba in Tunisia constituted a serious threat, as the sequel proved, and Caesar could still have been defeated and killed. However, his political position *vis-à-vis* senate and people of Rome was basically secure, yet at the same time significantly unrepublican.

The reason was that he had already been appointed dictator for a whole year once the news of the battle of Pharsalus reached Rome. However, the old republican dictatorship lasted only six months, or such lesser time as was required to perform a specific task like conducting the elections, as Caesar had done in his first dictatorship at the end of 49 BC. To hold the office for longer was inevitably to recall the only other man to have held the dictatorship in the previous century and a half, namely Sulla, who had defeated the followers of his dead enemy Marius (Caesar's uncle by marriage) in a fierce civil war which ran sporadically, and in the end bloodily, between 88 and 82 BC. Victory won, Sulla had revived the apparently obsolete office by accepting a dictatorship of indefinite duration with the right to pass laws and make binding decisions in every area of political life, as he saw fit. In virtue of these autocratic powers he had inflicted death or exile on numerous opponents, confiscated large amounts of land and property, planted numerous settlements of his ex-soldiers up and down Italy, and by constitutional reform attempted to ensure senatorial control of militarily ambitious proconsuls and populist tribunes. To the surprise of later generations, more hardened to the struggle for power, he voluntarily abdicated from his dictatorship after two years, dying soon after so that it was never clear how much influence he might have continued to exercise. But Sulla was such a potent figure that Caesar's acceptance of the same office in the aftermath, like Sulla, of a decisive battle inevitably evoked comparisons and raised the question of how far Caesar intended to go in exacting retribution from opponents and establishing personal domination of the Republic which he had claimed to be saving from the abuses of the Pompeians.

Even before this it had been clear that Caesar, when he became consul in 48 BC, was no more prepared to tolerate the obstruction and opposition which the republican constitution allowed than his opponents had been on the eve of civil war in January 49. At *Civil War* III.20–2 we can read the story of Caelius Rufus, a one-time protégé of Cicero's, who decided to employ the tactics of the 'free' or democratic republic to whip up opposition to financial measures imposed by Caesar. As is clear from the historian Dio (XLII.23), the consul Servilius passed exactly the same decree against him as had been used against Antonius and Cassius in 49, but this time Caesar's sympathies are on the side of authority and we hear nothing of unjust or arbitrary use of power. So it is scarcely surprising that from this point onwards we find Caesar's powers becoming increasingly unchallengeable and his own behaviour less and less democratically accountable. As dictator, he appointed as his deputy (called 'Master of Horse', *magister equitum*) Marcus Antonius, and Antonius with some difficulty maintained order in Italy in concert with the consuls, until Caesar himself returned to Rome in the autumn of 47 after the successful conclusion of the wars against Ptolemy in Egypt and Pharnaces in Asia Minor.

After quelling a serious mutiny among his veterans, Caesar crossed to Africa in late December with barely adequate forces to fight the Pompeians. There followed the events told in the *African War*, culminating in the defeat of Scipio and Juba at Thapsus, the subsequent deaths of these two and other Pompeian leaders, and the famous suicide of Cato at Utica. Pompey's two sons, Gnaeus and Sextus, survived and escaped to Spain, but it appeared that the civil war was effectively over. Caesar was already consul for 46, and the news of Thapsus caused him to be named dictator for a period of ten successive years, most probably 'to put the state on a working basis' (*rei publicae constituendae causa*). On his return he was voted more honours, including control over morals for three years, the right to designate magistrates for election, and the right to sit between the consuls and speak first at all meetings of the senate. However, he followed Sulla's example neither in cruelty nor in moving to reform the constitution. His policy was one of clemency to his opponents, now that the die-hard among their number were dead, and he attempted to make the necessary process of settling his discharged veterans as tolerable as he could to existing land-holders, who feared dispossession on a grand scale. But serious constitutional reform, expected and urged on him by a number of people, including Cicero, he avoided. It seems that he was content to superimpose himself on the existing framework of the state. This worked because on the one hand he now had extraordinarily wide-ranging powers with which he could control that state, while on the other the actual business of government was made possible by a personal staff which he had built up first as proconsul in Gaul, and then as commander in the field and leader of his own side in the civil war. The senate, as a decision-making body, and the traditional magistrates, as executants of those decisions, became redundant. Ever the practical man, Caesar preferred to accept his position and devote his energies to such problems as those of veteran settlement, of the swollen Roman proletariat dependent on the corn dole, of the calendar (whose celebrated reform dates to this year), and of the inadequate public spaces and buildings of Rome, to name but a few.

The four triumphs (over Gaul, Egypt, Pharnaces, and Juba
—a Roman did not triumph over other Romans) which he
celebrated between 20 September and 1 October, 46 BC, were
a magnificent and unparalleled spectacle and holiday for the
population of Rome, and should have marked the coming
of peace. Unfortunately Pompey's two sons in Spain had other
ideas, and they were so successful in detaching towns from
their newly acquired loyalty to Caesar that the dictator was
forced to set out for the province and mount the difficult
campaign described in the *Spanish War*. Not for the first time,
Caesar put his own life at risk in battle, but he survived and
the Pompeian army was finally overwhelmed at Munda on
17 March, 45 BC. Gnaeus Pompeius was tracked down and
killed, and although Sextus escaped he was forced to live as
a brigand and constituted no further threat to Caesar's control of Spain. When the news of the victory reached Rome
a month later, yet more honours were heaped upon Caesar,
including the hereditary title of *Imperator*, the right to wear
triumphal garb and the laurel wreath on all official occasions,
the consulship for ten years, and annual celebrations of the
anniversaries of his previous victories.

Caesar was not in any hurry to return to Rome and address the political problems of his own position in the state,
his relations with the Republican aristocracy, and the need
for some reform. He did not in fact reach the capital until
October, when he was tactless enough to celebrate a triumph
for the Spanish campaign in spite of the fact that his opponents had been the sons of one of Rome's greatest figures. A
sign of his increasingly cavalier attitude to established institutions was that against all precedent, and to some ridicule,
he permitted his lieutenants Q. Fabius and Q. Pedius to triumph also. On one occasion he even failed to rise to his feet
to greet the senate, who had come in a body to notify him
of a clutch of new honorific decrees. By this time more and
more honours were being conferred on him, as they continued to be until almost the end of his life, and from a number of them it seems fairly clear that he was bent on creating
(or accepting) for himself a position analogous to that of
the Hellenistic monarchs of the eastern Mediterranean world
which had been so rudely upset by the advance of Rome

from about 200 BC. These monarchs were routinely invested by their subjects with a form of divine status, and received religious offerings from them as actual or hoped-for bringers of prosperity, happiness, peace, and all the other blessings that were supposed to flow from a superhuman and of course autocratic ruler. Because the name of king had been anathema at Rome since the expulsion of the last Tarquin in the late sixth century BC, and the Romans, common people and aristocrats alike, were not disposed to treat their annual magistrates as men any different from themselves, Caesar was playing with fire. The dictatorship for life which was conferred on him in late January or early February 44 marked the abandonment of any pretence that his extraordinary powers were to meet a particular situation and would eventually be laid down.[11] This was kingship in all but name, and the Romans were well aware of it, as various episodes dating from Caesar's last months attest—for example, Caesar's fellow-consul Antonius, at the festival of the Lupercalia later in February, attempted to place a diadem (the Hellenistic equivalent of a crown) on Caesar's head, but Caesar judged the mood of the crowd to be unfavourable and insisted on passing the diadem on to Jupiter, king of the gods.

Whether Caesar actually wanted the title as well as the *de facto* position of king must remain obscure, but there can be little doubt that he was granted the other element of Hellenistic monarchy: divine status. By the time of his death it had been decreed that his house was to have a gable, an architectural feature not found on domestic frontages but characteristic of temples; his statue was to be carried among those of the gods in the solemn procession which opened the great public festivals, and have a special couch (*pulvinar*) like theirs; a statue of him with the inscription 'To the unconquerable God' was to be placed alongside that of Quirinus (the deified Romulus) in the latter's temple, and another on the Capitol among the statues of the kings; and in Dio's words (XLIV.6) 'finally they called him unambiguously Jupiter

---

[11] Caesar himself commented that Sulla's resignation of the dictatorship showed that he 'didn't know his ABC' (Suetonius, *Divus Julius*, 77).

Julius, and decreed that a temple should be consecrated to him and his Clemency'—in addition to which Antonius was elected as special priest (*flamen*) of the new god, so that Caesar was in this respect the equal of Jupiter, Mars, and Quirinus.

But Caesar had gone too far, too fast. The ingrained political attitudes and traditions of the Republic could not be changed so quickly, and history was to show that it needed another fifteen years of intermittent civil war before the old order could die and men could come into politics who had hardly known the Republic, or had had time to realize that it could not be resurrected with anything like its traditional values. Caesar's dictatorship was both a consequence and a demonstration of the inadequacy of the senatorial government which preceded it, but among his followers there were many for whom he had become no more than a tyrant, bent on maximizing his personal power. The weakness of his position was that, as we have seen, he had merely superimposed himself and his extraordinary powers on the normal machinery of the state. The result was the conspiracy to remove him, led by Marcus Brutus, who was Cato's nephew and had hoped for better things, and Gaius Cassius—both of them ex-Pompeians pardoned by Caesar, men initially willing to believe that he would somehow restore the Republic to a new working order. This is not the place to analyse or describe that conspiracy. Suffice it to say that the conspirators, though successful in murdering Caesar on the Ides of March of 44 BC, failed in their hope that the institutions of the Republic would revert to normal operation. The forces which had produced the war between Pompey and Caesar were still present. The combination of personal ambition, needy soldiery, exploitable provinces, and outdated political institutions, added to the cry of vengeance for Caesar, combined to plunge the Roman state into further years of civil war, ending only with Antonius' death in Cleopatra's arms at Alexandria in 30 BC.

These developments are more than enough to explain why Caesar himself never bothered to complete or publish the *Civil War*. But after his death the work became suddenly relevant in the arguments over the rights and wrongs of the murder: was Caesar an unscrupulous self-seeker who had trampled on the Republic, or was he a true patriot who had saved Rome from domination by a selfish clique? Antonius, as consul, had a mandate from the senate to deal with and publish as required all the papers and memoranda left by Caesar. He was also a loyal Caesarian, and so had an obvious interest in countering the claims of Brutus and Cassius by showing Caesar to be as good a Republican as they were. Hence the posthumous publication of the *Civil War*, knitted in to the end of the already published *Gallic War* by Hirtius' composition of *Gallic War* Book VIII, which must have been written in the second half of 44 BC. Thus the propagandist function which the *Civil War* was originally designed to serve paradoxically became relevant again in the battle to vindicate Caesar and save him from the charge of tyranny pressed by the murderers, the self-styled 'liberators'. It did not matter, now that Caesar was dead, that his entire behaviour, at least from 46 BC onwards, had been in blatant contradiction of the attitudes he ascribed to himself in the *Civil War*.

Of the impact of publication we know nothing, and for contemporary judgement we have only Asinius Pollio's tart remark that Caesar was insufficiently careful with the truth, being 'too ready to believe the exploits of others and either deliberately or accidentally falsifying his own'.[12] Pollio served under Caesar and himself wrote a history of the period 60–42 BC, so he was in a position to judge. We may safely assume that the *Civil War* took its place as one among a number of propagandistic pamphlets and publications which were circulated by the various protagonists in the struggles of 44–30 BC, and that it was used as an (unidentified) source, along with others, by later writers such as Livy, Plutarch, and Appian. Beyond that, it disappears from sight in antiquity. In post-Renaissance times, it has always played second fiddle to the *Gallic War*—partly no doubt because of its own incompleteness and the largely unimpressive nature of its continuations, partly because the events described appear

<hr>

[12] Suetonius, *Divus Julius*, 56.4.

in other and more balanced accounts which survive from antiquity, notably those of Plutarch, Appian, and Dio. This is unfortunate, because the story is of more central interest to Roman history than that of the conquest of Gaul, and Caesar's shaping of the events (see p. xxiii above) shows the hand of a master.

To conclude with Caesar himself, the plain fact is that despite his picture of himself as a defender of the Republican constitution and of the rights of the Roman people and their tribunes, he probably did more than any other man to bring the Republic down. First of all, he colluded with Pompey in the formation (in 60 BC) and renewal (in 56 BC) of the 'First Triumvirate' (see p. x above), an alliance which cynically exploited constitutional features to ensure long-term political dominance; it could be said that Caesar's personal enemies, by blocking his triumph, brought this on their own heads, but the signs of his extraordinary political ambition were already plain to see: he mounted spectacularly lavish shows as aedile in 65 BC, and spent quite enormous amounts of money to secure his election as Pontifex Maximus in 63 BC. Next, he was willing to start a civil war in 49 rather than allow himself to be outmanœuvred by the opposition. And finally, he used his success in that civil war to build himself a position of personal power which emphasized the weakness of the Republic and the hollowness of his own earlier claims to be acting in defence of that Republic. He himself observed towards the end of his life that 'the Republic was nothing, simply a name without form or substance'.[13] Admirers of Caesar point to the short time he was dictator, his enormous administrative energy, and the long list of projects he completed or intended, like overseas citizen and veteran settlements, overhaul of the corn dole, measures for relief of debt, the draining of the Pomptine marshes, the calendar reform, the canal through the Isthmus of Corinth, the remodelling of the centre of Rome, and so forth. But where his heir Augustus was to succeed, Caesar failed. Having seized power by military means, and quelled the disorderly

[13] Ibid. 77.

population of Rome by strong-arm tactics when necessary, he proved unable to build a political and consensual base for that power and thus make it acceptable. He was murdered on the eve of his departure for campaigns in Thrace and against the Parthians, and there is nothing to suggest that he had any long-term plans to remodel the constitution or create an organic place in it for a leader such as himself. It seems most likely that what motivated him at the end of his life was not political healing, but that dream of great eastern conquests which was associated with the semi-divine figure of Alexander the Great and was so powerful in the imagery of the late Republic. Caesar, the conqueror of Gaul, the victor of so many battlefields, preferred to follow the path he had trodden so successfully thus far: it was easier to pursue military glory than wrestle with the difficulties that surrounded him in Rome.

NOTE ON THE TEXT

The Latin text of the six works translated in the present volume has not come down to us in a very good state. All our surviving manuscripts ultimately depend on a single archetype, as is proved by transpositions and missing passages common to every one of them. This archetype, now lost, evidently contained a considerable number of errors, in addition to these transpositions and lacunae, so that the usual game of textual critics, trying to establish from the evidence at our disposal what the reading of the archetype was, is not always very helpful. As a result, there is more variation between modern editions than is often the case with classical authors. This situation led me to establish my own text of the *Civil War* for my Aris and Phillips edition (see Select Bibliography), and it is this text which I have translated here. For the other three works, I have followed the Oxford Classical Text of du Pontet so far as possible. In the *Alexandrian War* and *African War* I have occasionally diverged from du Pontet, but the reading adopted will always be found in his *apparatus criticus*. In the *Spanish War* the text has unfortunately been so badly damaged in so many places that editors often cannot make sense of the text if they stay near to the manuscript readings, and therefore have to resort to wholesale emendation or addition if they wish to present Latin which could conceivably have been written by the author. Since du Pontet belonged to the more cautious school of editing, and I have wished, in the interests of readability, to keep lacunae to a minimum, I have not infrequently diverged from his text. Where possible, I have in such cases adopted conjectures found in his *apparatus criticus*, but I have occasionally resorted to conjectures of my own, based on the general sense required, or to readings proposed by Alfred Klotz in his 1927 commentary (see Select Bibliography). I do not list these readings here, as in all these cases we are dealing with outright speculation and it will be evident to anyone using this translation in conjunction with du Pontet's text where the variations occur. An omission, or inferred omission, of one or more words in the text is indicated by . . . or < . . . >. A conjectural supplement to the text is represented by *words in italics*.

SELECT BIBLIOGRAPHY

Texts with Commentaries

For Caesar's *Civil War*, a full commentary (chiefly historical but with a newly constituted Latin text and some literary and linguistic notes) may be found in J. M. Carter, *Julius Caesar: The Civil War*, Warminster, 1991 (Books I–II) and 1993 (Book III). There is an older German commentary (without accompanying translation) by F. Kraner, F. Hofmann, and H. Meusel (12th edn., Berlin, Weidmann, 1959, being a reprint of the 11th edn. of 1906 with textual and bibliographical addenda by H. Oppermann). For the other works, there are editions by R. Schneider of the *Bellum Alexandrinum* (1888) and *Bellum Africum* (1905), both reprinted in 1962 by Weidmann, Berlin. There is also a part commentary by G. B. Townend on Caesar, *Bellum Civile* III chs. 102–112 and *Bellum Alexandrinum* 1–33, published by Bristol Classical Press, 1988, under the title *Caesar's War in Alexandria*. For the *Bellum Hispaniense* there is a German commentary by A. Klotz (1927) and an Italian edition by G. Pascucci (Florence, le Monnier, 1965) which I have not seen, but nothing in English that I am aware of.

Translations, with or without the Latin Text

There are several in English, but the best, covering exactly the same ground as the present volume, is the Penguin translation by Jane F. Gardner, *Caesar: The Civil War, together with the Alexandrian War, the African War, and the Spanish War by other hands* (1967). Of the rest, note the volumes of the Loeb Classical Library (Harvard University Press), *Civil War* by A. G. Peskett (1914) and *Alexandrian, African, and Spanish Wars* by A. G. Way (1955), which have parallel Latin and English text. In the French Budé series, which has parallel French and Latin (Collection Guillaume Budé, Les Belles Lettres, Paris), the *Guerre Civile* (ed. P. Fabre, 1936) has a particularly good Latin text.

Plain Texts

The standard editions are those of Fabre (*Civil War* only, see above, under Translations), R. du Pontet (Oxford, Clarendon Press, 1900), and A. Klotz (*Civil War* only, 3rd edn. with additions and corrections by W. Trillitzsch, Leipzig, Teubner, 1964).

Caesar as Literary Figure

F. E. Adcock's *Caesar as Man of Letters* (Cambridge, 1956) is a brief introductory essay. L. Raditsa, 'Julius Caesar and His Writings' in H. Temporini (ed.), *Aufstieg und Niedergang der römischen Welt* I. 3 (1973), 417 ff. is a useful survey, and the cultural background is well given by E. Rawson, *Intellectual Life in the Late Roman Republic* (London, Duckworth, 1985). Individual studies of aspects of Caesar's writing include J. Schlichter, 'The Development of Caesar's Narrative Style', *Classical Philology* 31 (1936), 212–24; G. O. Rowe, 'Dramatic Structures in Caesar's *Bellum Civile*', *Transactions of the American Philological Association* 98 (1967), 399–414; N. P. Miller, 'Dramatic Speech in the Roman Historians', *Greece and Rome* 23 (1975), 45–57; and H. C. Gotoff, 'Towards a Practical Criticism of Caesar's Style', *Illinois Classical Studies* 9 (1984), 1–18. More technical are P. T. Eden, 'Caesar's Style: Inheritance versus Intelligence', *Glotta* 40 (1962), 74–117, and F. Bömer's attempt to pin down the nature of *commentarii*, 'Der Commentarius', *Hermes* 81 (1953), 210–50. On the propagandistic aspect of Caesar's works, see two studies by J. H. Collins, 'On the Date and Interpretation of the *Bellum Civile*', *American Journal of Philology* 80 (1959), 113–32, and 'Caesar as Political Propagandist', in H. Temporini (ed.), *Aufstieg und Niedergang der römischen Welt* I. 1 (1972), 922–66; also K. Barwick, *Caesars Bellum Civile: Tendenz, Aufbau, Abfassungszeit* (Leipzig, 1951).

Caesar as Public Figure

The standard biography, which tends to double as a history of the period, is M. Gelzer (trans. P. Needham), *Caesar: Politician and Statesman* (Oxford, Blackwell, 1968). More ambitious and intuitive, but designed for the 'general reader' and therefore lacking documentation, is the work of Christian Meier (trans. D. McLintock), *Caesar* (London, HarperCollins, 1995), which continues an old German tradition of reverence for Caesar. Readers of German will find a useful corrective in the astringent and well-documented study by W. Will, *Caesar: Eine Bilanz* (Cologne, Kohlhammer, 1992).

The Late Republican Background

A brief introduction to the history of the peirod can be had from T. E. Wiedemann, *Cicero and the End of the Roman Republic* (London, Bristol Classical Press/Duckworth, 1994); M. H. Crawford, *The Roman Republic* (2nd edn., Fontana, 1992); and P. A. Brunt, *Social Conflicts in the Roman Republic* (London, Chatto &

Windus, 1971). Fuller accounts are those of H. H. Scullard, *From the Gracchi to Nero* (5th edn., London, Methuen, 1982), chs. 6–9, and E. S. Gruen, *The Last Generation of the Roman Republic* (Berkeley/Los Angeles/London, University of California Press, 1974). For the relationships of Pompey and Caesar see R. Seager, *Pompey: A Political Biography* (Oxford, Blackwell, 1979) and R. Syme, *The Roman Revolution* (Oxford, Clarendon, 1939), chs. 3 and 4: 'The Domination of Pompeius' and 'Caesar the Dictator'.

A more analytical view of the social, political, and economic changes of the Late Republic is given by M. Beard and M. H. Crawford, *Rome in the Late Republic: Problems and Interpretations* (London, Duckworth, 1985); G. Alföldy (trans. D. Braund and F. Pollock), *The Social History of Rome* (rev. edn. London, Routledge, 1988); and P. A. Brunt, *The Fall of the Roman Republic* (Oxford, Clarendon, 1988), ch. 1: 'The Fall of the Roman Republic'.

For an understanding of the Roman aristocracy and its values, see M. Gelzer (trans. R. Seager), *The Roman Nobility* (Oxford, Blackwell, 1975); D. C. Earl, *The Moral and Political Tradition of Rome* (London, Thames & Hudson, 1967); R. Syme, *The Roman Revolution* (Oxford, Clarendon, 1939), ch. 2: 'The Roman Oligarchy'; and W. V. Harris, *War and Imperialism in Republican Rome* (Oxford, Clarendon Press, 1979), pp. 10–40: 'The Aristocracy and War'. The political scene is well set by L. R. Taylor's very readable *Party Politics in the Age of Caesar* (Berkeley and Los Angeles, University of California Press, 1949, paperback reissue 1961) and more briefly by T. P. Wiseman (ed.), *Roman Political Life* (Exeter, Exeter University Press, 1985).

TABLE OF EVENTS

BC

100 (13 July) Birth of Gaius Julius Caesar.

88 Outbreak of civil war between Sulla and Marius.

87–85 Sulla campaigns against King Mithridates in Greece and Asia Minor.

86 7th consulship and death of Marius.

84 Caesar marries Cornelia, daughter of the Marian leader Cinna. Death of Cinna; Sulla invades Italy.

82 (1 Nov.) Defeat of Marians outside Rome (battle of the Colline Gate).

81–80 Dictatorship and 2nd consulship of Sulla. Constitutional reform designed to strengthen senatorial government.

80 Caesar does military service in Asia.

78 (early) Death of Sulla.

70 First consulship of Pompey and Crassus.

65 Caesar aedile.

63 Caesar elected *Pontifex Maximus*.

62 Caesar praetor.

61 Caesar governor of Spain.

60 Election of Caesar as consul; formation of 'First Triumvirate'.

59 Consulship of Caesar and Bibulus.

58–50 Caesar proconsul of Gaul, conquers the country.

56 (Apr.) Renewal of 'triumvirate' at Luca.

55 Second consulship of Pompey and Crassus.

53 Death of Crassus at Carrhae in Syria.

52 Pompey sole consul.

52–50 Breakdown of friendship between Pompey and Caesar.

49 (1 Jan.) Curio delivers Caesar's letter to the consuls (*Civ.* I.1).

(7 Jan.) The tribunes M. Antonius and Q. Cassius flee Rome (*Civ.* I.5).

(10 or 11 Jan.) Caesar crosses the Rubicon (*Civ.* I.8).

(17–18 Jan.) Pompey and consuls leave Rome (*Civ.* I.14).

(21 Feb.) Fall of Corfinium (*Civ.* I.23).

(17–18 Mar.) Pompey leaves Brundisium (*Civ.* I.28).

(1–3 Apr.) Caesar holds a senate in Rome (*Civ.* I.32–3).

(Apr.–Aug.) Caesar defeats Afranius and Petreius near Ilerda (2 Aug.) and Varro (Sept.?) to conquer Spain (*Civ.* I.37–55, 59–87, II.17–21).

(Apr.–Oct.) Siege of Massilia by Caesar's forces (*Civ.* I.34–6, 56–8, II.1–16, 22).

(Aug.–Sept.?) Defeat of Curio in Africa by Juba (*Civ.* II.23–44).

(Oct.?) Defeat of C. Antonius in Illyria (*Civ.* III.10).

(Dec.) Caesar in Rome, his first dictatorship (*Civ.* II.21, III.1–2).

48   Caesar consul for the second time (2), with P. Servilius (*Civ.* III.1).

(4–5 Jan.) Caesar crosses with part of his army to Illyria (*Civ.* III.6).

(Spring?) Insurrection of Caelius Rufus and Milo in Italy (*Civ.* III.20–2).

(Jan.–July) Campaign of Dyrrachium and Caesar's defeat (*c.*7 July) (*Civ.* III.7–19, 23–72).

(9 Aug.) Caesar decisively defeats Pompey at Pharsalus (*Civ.* III.73–99).

(28 Sept.) Death of Pompey, after his flight to Egypt (*Civ.* III.103–4).

(2 Oct.) Caesar arrives in Alexandria (*Civ.* III.106).

47   Caesar dictator (2) (for 1 year)

(27 Mar.) Caesar victorious in Egypt (*Alex.* 32).

(2 Aug.) Caesar defeats Pharnaces at Zela in Pontus (*Alex.* 69–77).

(Sept.) Caesar returns to Rome (*Alex.* 78).

(25–8 Dec.) Caesar crosses to Africa (Tunisia) (*Afr.* 2).

46   Caesar consul (3), dictator (3) (for 10 years)

(6 Apr.) Caesar defeats Pompeians at Thapsus (*Afr.* 79–86).

(9 Apr.) Suicide of Cato at Utica (*Afr.* 88).

(25 July) Caesar arrives back in Rome (*Afr.* 98).

(Sept.) Caesar celebrates quadruple triumph in Rome (*Span.* 1).

(Nov.) Caesar leaves Rome for Spain (*Span.* 2).

45 Caesar consul (4), dictator (4) (for life)

(17 Mar.) Caesar defeats Pompey's sons at Munda (*Span.* 26–31).

(Oct.) Caesar arrives back in Rome, and celebrates Spanish triumph.

44 Caesar consul (5)

(15 Feb.) Antony attempts to crown Caesar at the Lupercalia.

(15 Mar.) Murder of Caesar.

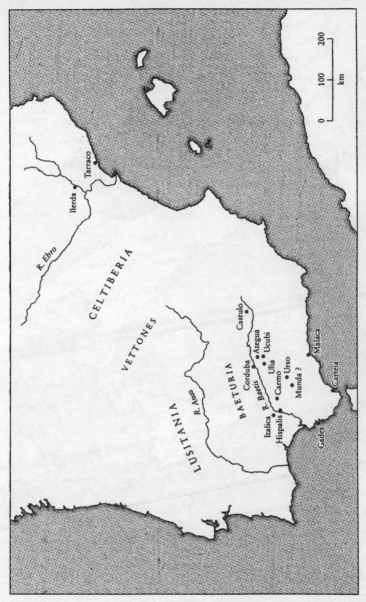

MAP 1 Spain

MAP 2 Italy, Africa, and Illyricum

MAP 3 Northern and Central Greece

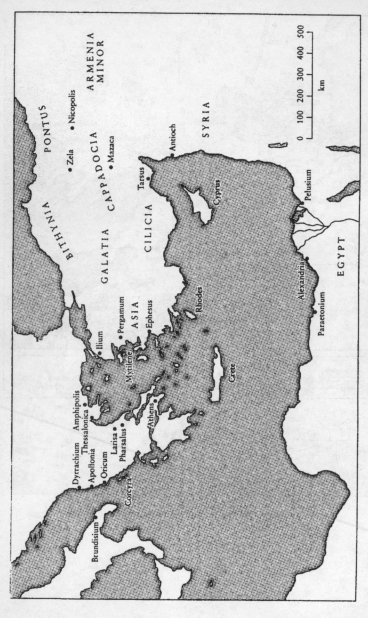

MAP 4 The Eastern Mediterranean

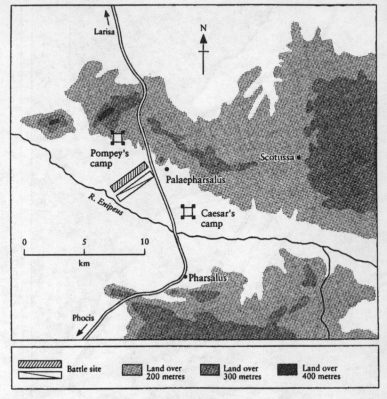

MAP 5 Pharsalus

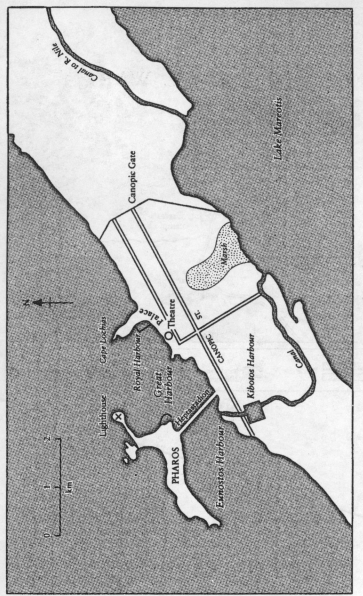

MAP 6 Alexandria

THE CIVIL WAR

Book I

The outbreak of the civil war; Caesar invades and captures Italy, Sardinia, and Sicily (1–33). Massilia refuses to admit Caesar (34–36). The campaign of Ilerda and defeat of Afranius and Petreius (37–87)

Events in Rome, early January 49. Flight of the tribunes Antonius and Q. Cassius to Caesar

(1) ... when Caesar's letter was delivered to the consuls, it was only by the most strenuous efforts that the tribunes won their agreement that the letter should be read out in the senate.* It was impossible to make them agree that a motion should be put to the senate on the basis of its contents, but they initiated a general debate on public affairs. The consul Lucius Lentulus promised the senate that he would not fail the republic, if members were willing to express their opinions boldly and forcefully; but if they kept one eye on Caesar and tried to please him, as they had done on previous occasions, he, Lentulus, would decide for himself what to do and would not obey the authority of the senate, because he too could take refuge in Caesar's favour and friendship. Scipio* spoke to the same effect, saying that Pompey's intention was to do his duty to the republic, if the senate would follow him; but if they hesitated and procrastinated they would beg in vain for his help if they wanted it later.

(2) This speech of Scipio's seemed to be launched from Pompey's very lips, since the senate was meeting in the city and Pompey was nearby.* Less impetuous views had been expressed, first for example by Marcus Marcellus, who took the line that no motion on the subject should be put to the senate until levies had been held throughout Italy and armies raised, under whose protection the senate could safely and freely make the decisions it wished; also by Marcus Calidius, who gave it as his opinion that Pompey should leave for his

provinces, so that there should be no reason for fighting; Caesar (he said) was afraid that it was to endanger him that Pompey seemed to be holding on to the two legions* that had been taken from him and keeping them near Rome; and by Marcus Rufus,* who expressed the same views as Calidius with some slight variations. These were all attacked and abused by the consul Lucius Lentulus. Calidius' motion he totally refused to put, and Marcellus took fright at the abuse and withdrew his. Thus the majority, browbeaten by the consul, frightened by an army on the doorstep, and threatened by Pompey's friends, voted unwillingly and under duress for Scipio's motion: that Caesar should dismiss his army before a certain date, and if he did not, he would be judged to be committing an act hostile to the state.* The motion was vetoed by the tribunes Marcus Antonius and Quintus Cassius, and this veto was immediately put to the senate for its consideration. Stern views were expressed; the bitterer and harsher they were, the greater their enthusiastic approval by Caesar's enemies.

(3) When the senate was dismissed towards evening, all its members were summoned by Pompey. He praised the eager and encouraged them for what lay ahead, and reproached and urged on the more hesitant. Many of the men who had served in Pompey's previous armies were re-enlisted in hope of reward or rank, and many were summoned from the two legions which Caesar had handed over. The city, and even the Comitium* itself, was full of officers, centurions, and re-enlisted men. All the friends of the consuls, and all the associates of Pompey and of the men who had long been Caesar's enemies were assembled in the senate. Their words and their numbers frightened the less resolute and emboldened the hesitant, but robbed the majority of the power of free decision. Lucius Piso, who was one of the censors,* and also Lucius Roscius, a praetor, promised to go to Caesar to inform him of these developments, and requested a period of six days to complete this business. Some also proposed that a delegation be sent to Caesar, to put the senate's wishes to him. (4) Each of these proposals was resisted, and Lentulus, Scipio, and Cato spoke against them all. Cato was driven by long-

standing enmity to Caesar and resentment at his electoral defeat.* Lentulus was motivated by the size of his debts, by the hope of an army and provinces, and by the prospect of inducements offered by kings who desired recognition; he also boasted to his intimates that he would be a second Sulla,* to whom supreme power would fall. Scipio was impelled by the same hope of a province and armies, which he thought he would share with Pompey on account of his marriage-tie with him; he was also driven on by his fear of prosecution, his love of self-display, and the flattery he received from powerful men who were particularly influential at that time in public life and the courts. Pompey himself, spurred on by Caesar's enemies and by his desire that no one should match his own status, had entirely turned his back on any friendship with Caesar and had re-established cordial relations with their joint enemies, the greater number of whom he had inflicted on Caesar at the time of their family connection;* at the same time, disturbed by the scandal of the two legions which he had deflected from their march to Asia and Syria to bolster his own power and dominance, he was keen to settle matters by fighting.

(5) For these reasons everything was done in haste and confusion. Caesar's relations were allowed no time to inform him, and the tribunes were given no opportunity to make a plea against the danger that threatened them, or even to retain their fundamental rights by veto, which Lucius Sulla had left untouched.* On the contrary, after seven days they were forced to look to their own safety, a thing which the famous revolutionary tribunes of earlier times* had not usually had to consider or fear for until eight months of the year had passed and they had a variety of actions to account for. Recourse was had to that last and final decree of the senate,* which had never before been passed except when the city was almost ablaze and the recklessness of those who were proposing laws was putting everyone's safety at risk: 'The consuls, praetors, tribunes, and those proconsuls who are in the neighbourhood of Rome are to take care that the state suffers no harm.' These words were recorded in a decree of the senate passed on 7 January. And so within the first five

days on which the senate could be convoked after the start of Lentulus' consulship (the two comitial days* excepted), decrees of the gravest and most intemperate character were passed, about Caesar's tenure of command and about persons of the highest importance, tribunes of the people. The tribunes* fled at once from Rome, and went to Caesar, who was then at Ravenna, awaiting the answer to his very modest demands to see if by some sense of natural justice the matter could be peacefully resolved.

(6) On the following days the senate met outside the city.* Pompey made the same points as he had made through Scipio, praised the senate's courage and determination, and gave details of his forces, saying he had ten legions ready; furthermore, he had discovered for a fact that the soldiers were unsympathetic to Caesar and could not possibly be persuaded to defend him or follow him. The remaining business was immediately brought before the senate: to institute recruitment in the whole of Italy, to send Faustus Sulla urgently to Mauretania, and to give money from the treasury to Pompey. There was also a proposal to make king Juba an ally and friend. Marcellus* said that for the present he would not allow this, and Philippus, a tribune, vetoed the motion about Faustus. The decisions of the senate about the other matters were duly recorded.* Provinces were allotted to men who were not holding office:* two to ex-consuls, the remainder to ex-praetors. Syria fell to Scipio, Gaul to Lucius Domitius, while Philippus and Cotta were passed over by private arrangement and their names not even put into the ballot. Praetors were sent to the other provinces. The appointees did not even wait, as had happened in previous years, for their authority to be conferred by the people, and they went out from the city in military dress after making their solemn vows. The consuls left the city <without taking the auspices>,* a thing which had never happened before, and men who were holding no elected office were attended by lictors* in the city and in the precinct of Capitoline Jupiter, contrary to all precedent. All over Italy men were conscripted, and weapons requisitioned; money was exacted from towns, and taken from shrines; and all the laws of god and man were overturned.

*Caesar invades Italy and simultaneously negotiates
for a settlement*

(7) When he learnt this news Caesar made an address to his
soldiers.* He detailed all the wrongs done him in the past
by his personal enemies, complaining that out of malice and
jealousy of his own renown they had alienated Pompey from
him and twisted his judgement, while he himself had always
supported and promoted Pompey's prestige and position. He
protested that a new precedent had been introduced into public life, whereby the tribunician veto was being censured and
suppressed by force. Sulla, who had stripped the tribunician
power of its all, had at least left the veto unimpaired; but
Pompey, who seemed to have restored what advantages had
been lost, had taken away even what they had previously possessed.* Whenever it had been decreed that the magistrates
'should take steps to ensure that the state suffered no harm'
—the words of the senate's decree which called the Roman
people to arms—this had been done when subversive laws
were proposed, when the tribunes turned to violence, when
the people seceded, when the temples and commanding positions were seized.* He also pointed out that these memorable events of earlier years had been atoned for by the fates
of Saturninus and the Gracchi;* but that at the present time
no such thing had taken place, indeed had not even been con-
templated. He exhorted them to defend against his enemies
the reputation and standing of the man under whose gen-
eralship they had for nine years played their part for Rome
with outstanding success, won a large number of battles, and
pacified the whole of Gaul and Germany. The other legions
had not yet assembled, but the soldiers of the Thirteenth,
which was there because he had summoned it at the beginning of the trouble, shouted that they were ready to defend
their general and the tribunes from harm.

(8) Having discovered the feelings of his men, he set out
with this legion for Ariminum* and there met the tribunes
who had fled to him; the rest of the legions he called out
from winter quarters and ordered to follow after him.* Young
Lucius Caesar, whose father was an officer of Caesar's, arrived

at Ariminum. When the other business which was the reason for his journey had been disposed of, he revealed that he had a mission of a personal sort from Pompey to Caesar: Pompey wished to explain himself to Caesar, to stop Caesar turning to his discredit actions which he had taken in the public interest. Pompey said that he had always regarded the advantage of the state as more important than his private obligations; Caesar too had a duty laid on him by his position to subordinate his passion and resentment to the public interest, and not to be so angry with his enemies that in the hope of harming them he harmed the state. Lucius added a little more in the same vein, along with some excuses for Pompey's behaviour. Almost the same discussion, in the same words, took place between Caesar and the praetor Roscius, who made it plain that Pompey had put these points to him.

(9) None of this appeared to have anything to do with the redress of his grievances; nevertheless, having found suitable bearers of his wishes, Caesar asked them both, as they had carried a message from Pompey to himself, not to regard it as too much trouble to take his own demands back to Pompey, bearing in mind that by making a small effort they could settle matters of serious dispute and free the whole of Italy from fear. For himself, he said, his standing had always been his first consideration, more important than his life.* He felt hurt because a favour granted by the Roman people had been insultingly wrenched from him by his enemies; he was being dragged back to Rome with six months of his governorship stolen from him, even though the Roman people had sanctioned his candidature in absence at the next elections.* This loss of office, however, he had accepted with equanimity in the public interest; yet when he sent a letter to the senate* proposing that all parties should surrender their armies, even that request had been unsuccessful. Men were being conscripted all over Italy, the two legions which had been taken from him on the pretext of a Parthian war were not being sent there, and the community was under arms. What was the purpose of all this, if not to destroy him? None the less, he was ready to descend to any depths and put up with anything for the sake of the republic.

Pompey should go to his provinces, they should both disband their armies, everyone in Italy should lay down their arms, the community should be liberated from fear, and the senate and people of Rome should be permitted free elections and complete control of the state. So that these proposals could be realized more easily and on agreed terms, and could be solemnly ratified by oath, Pompey should either come in person to meet Caesar or allow Caesar to meet him; all their differences would be resolved by discussion.

(10) Roscius accepted these instructions, and on reaching Capua, accompanied by Lucius Caesar, he found the consuls and Pompey there and reported Caesar's demands.* After considering <the matter>, their response was to send back with Roscius and Caesar a written message, which in brief was this: Caesar was to return to Gaul, withdraw from Ariminum, and disband his armies; and if he did this, Pompey would go to Spain; in the mean time, until guarantees had been given that Caesar would do what he promised, the consuls and Pompey would go on levying troops.

(11) It was unreasonable of Pompey to demand that Caesar should withdraw from Ariminum and return to his province, while he himself kept not only provinces but also legions that were not his; to want Caesar's army disbanded, but go on enlisting men himself; or to promise to go to his province but not to specify a date by which he would go, so that if he had failed to start out by the end of Caesar's consulship, he would not appear to be guilty of having broken a falsely sworn oath. Indeed, not to spare the time for a meeting, nor to promise to attend, indicated that the chances for peace were very slender. And so from Ariminum* he sent Marcus Antonius to Arretium with five cohorts; he himself stayed at Ariminum with two, and began to enlist troops there; and Pisaurum, Fanum, and Ancona he occupied with a cohort each.

(12) Meanwhile, on learning that the praetor* Thermus was holding Iguvium with five cohorts and fortifying the town, and that all the townspeople were very sympathetic to himself, he sent Curio there with the three cohorts which he had at Pisaurum and Ariminum. Thermus, hearing of

Curio's arrival and having little confidence in the loyalty of the population, withdrew his cohorts from the town, and fled. On the march his soldiers deserted him and returned home, and Curio took Iguvium with the complete approval of all.

When Caesar heard of these events, relying on the good-will of the towns he withdrew the cohorts of the Thirteenth legion from their garrison duties and set out for Auximum; Attius* had brought cohorts in to hold this town and had sent senators round to conduct a levy all over Picenum. (13) When they heard of Caesar's arrival, the members of the town council of Auximum went in a body to see Attius Varus; they told him that a decision did not rest with them; neither they, nor their fellow townsmen, could tolerate it if Gaius Caesar, *imperator*,* who had rendered great service to the state and had such great achievements to his credit, were kept outside the walls of the town; Varus should therefore think about the future and the danger he was in. Moved by what they said, Varus withdrew the garrison he had put in, and fled. A few of Caesar's leading troops caught up with him and forced him to stand his ground. When battle was then joined, Varus was deserted by his soldiers; a propor-tion of them went home, while the rest made their way to Caesar, bringing with them as a prisoner their highest-ranking centurion, Lucius Pupius, who had previously held this same post in Pompey's army. But Caesar simply praised Attius' soldiers, dismissed Pupius, and thanked the inhabit-ants of Auximum, promising that he would remember what they had done.

Caesar advances south. The siege and capture of Corfinium

(14) When news of these events reached Rome, a panic so violent and sudden occurred that although the consul Lentulus had come to open the treasury and provide funds for Pompey in accordance with a senatorial decree, he fled* from the city the moment he had opened the inner treasury.

The reason was the false report that Caesar's arrival was imminent and that his cavalry were at hand. Lentulus was followed by his colleague Marcellus and a number of the magistrates. Pompey had set out from Rome on the previous day and was making his way to the legions he had received from Caesar, which he had put into winter quarters around Apulia. Recruiting in the neighbourhood of Rome was discontinued, because everyone thought that nothing north of Capua was safe. It was at Capua that they first took heart and collected themselves, and began a levy amongst the colonists who had been settled there by the Julian Law.* The gladiators whom Caesar had in training there were brought to the town square by Lentulus, who encouraged them <with the hope> of freedom, gave them horses, and ordered them to follow him; later, because this action was universally condemned, on the advice of his friends he distributed them amongst the households of the Campanian Assembly* so that they could be kept under guard.

(15) Advancing from Auximum, Caesar overran the whole of Picenum. All the districts of the region received him most willingly and assisted his army with all kinds of supplies. Even from Cingulum, a town established by Labienus* and provided with buildings at his expense, there came a deputation promising to execute with all eagerness any orders Caesar gave. He demanded troops, and they sent them. Meanwhile the Twelfth legion caught up with him.* With the two he now had he set out for Asculum in Picenum. This town was held with ten cohorts by Lentulus Spinther, who on learning of Caesar's approach fled the town and in the attempt to bring his cohorts away with him was deserted by a large part of his force. Left with only a few men, he marched on and encountered Vibullius Rufus, who had been sent by Pompey to Picenum to stiffen resistance. After being informed by Spinther of the situation in Picenum, Vibullius accepted command of his soldiers and dismissed him.* Vibullius also assembled from the neighbouring regions what cohorts he could from the Pompeian levies, amongst them a garrison of six cohorts which he intercepted fleeing from Camerinum under Lucilius Hirrus, and by gathering these up, he put together

thirteen in all. With these he made his way by forced marches to Domitius* in Corfinium and broke the news that Caesar was close upon them with two legions. Domitius for his part had assembled twenty cohorts from Alba, from the Marsi and Paeligni, and from the neighbouring regions.

(16) Now that Firmum was in his hands,* and Lentulus had been driven out, Caesar gave orders for the soldiers who had abandoned the latter to be rounded up, and recruitment to begin; he himself paused for one day to provision, and set off for Corfinium. When he arrived, five cohorts sent forward from the town by Domitius were breaking down the bridge over the river about three miles from the town. Domitius' men engaged Caesar's advance guard there, but were quickly driven back from the bridge and withdrew into the town. Caesar brought his legions across, halted by the town, and made camp next to the wall.

(17) When he found out what had happened, Domitius sent to Pompey in Apulia* men who knew the country and had been promised a large reward, carrying a letter earnestly entreating Pompey to come and help him: Caesar, he said, could easily be trapped and cut off from food by two armies blocking the passes; and unless Pompey so acted, he himself and more than thirty cohorts and a large number of senators and Roman equestrians would be at risk. In the mean time he encouraged his men, placed artillery on the walls, and allocated each man his particular place in the defence of the town; he also called an assembly of the troops and promised them land from his own estates—twenty-four acres per head,* and *pro rata* for centurions and re-enlisted men.

(18) The news was meanwhile brought to Caesar that the population of Sulmo, a town seven miles from Corfinium, wanted to place themselves at his disposal, but were being stopped by Quintus Lucretius, a senator, and Attius the Paelignian, who were holding the town with a force of seven cohorts. He sent Marcus Antonius there with five cohorts of the Thirteenth legion. As soon as the people of Sulmo saw our standards, they opened their gates and all came out cheering, soldiers and townsfolk alike, to meet Antonius. Lucretius and Attius jumped from the wall. Attius was brought to

Antonius and asked to be sent to Caesar. Antonius returned
with the cohorts and Attius on the same day as he had set
out. Caesar incorporated these cohorts into his own army
and sent Attius away unharmed.

From the first day Caesar began to fortify his camp with
great earthworks and bring in grain from the nearby towns
and await the arrival of the rest of his forces. Within three
days the Eighth legion reached him,* and twenty-two cohorts from new recruiting in Gaul, and about three hundred cavalry from the king of Noricum. On their arrival,
he placed a second camp at the other side of the town,
with Curio in command, and on the days following began
to surround the town with a rampart and forts. When the
greater part had been finished, the messengers who had been
sent to Pompey returned with a letter. (19) After reading it,
Domitius pretended to his council of war that Pompey would
quickly come to their aid, and encouraged them not to lose
heart but to make whatever preparations would serve to
defend the town. He himself spoke secretly to a few of his
intimates and decided to make a plan of escape. The expression on his face was at odds with what he said, and he acted
in all respects with more timidity and hesitation than he had
shown previously; and since he also spent much time in private consultation with his entourage, contrary to his usual
habit, and avoided meetings and groups of people, the matter could not be hidden or the pretence maintained for very
long. Pompey had in fact written back* to say that he would
not risk putting his whole cause in extreme danger, and that
it was not by his advice or wish that Domitius had taken
up his position in the town of Corfinium; accordingly, if the
opportunity arose, Domitius was to come to him with all
his forces. That was being made impossible by the siege and
circumvallation of the town.

(20) Once Domitius' plan became known, the soldiers in
Corfinium gathered spontaneously in the early evening and
held a discussion amongst themselves through their military tribunes, centurions, and distinguished other ranks. The
points made were that they were under siege by Caesar; that
the siege-works and fortifications were almost complete; that

their commander Domitius, hoping and trusting in whom they had stood their ground, was planning to abandon them all and take to flight; and that they ought to think of their own safety. At first the Marsi started to quarrel with these views, and occupied the part of the town which seemed best fortified, and such a difference of opinion arose that they tried to begin an actual battle and fight it out with the sword; but after a little while, when intermediaries had passed between them, they found out the facts, of which they had been unaware, about Domitius' intended flight. Consequently they were unanimous in surrounding Domitius and keeping him under guard when he was brought out to face them, and they sent a deputation from their own number to Caesar to say that they were prepared to open the gates, obey his orders, and hand Lucius Domitius over alive to him.

(21) When Caesar knew this, he judged it of the greatest importance to gain possession of the town and bring the cohorts over to his camp as soon as possible, in order to prevent any change of heart brought about by bribery or improved morale or false news, because in war great events often depend on small changes. None the less, since he feared that the town might be plundered if his troops entered when darkness afforded a cover for undisciplined behaviour, he warmly praised those who had come to him, sent them back to the town, and ordered the gates and walls to be watched. He himself stationed soldiers on the siege works which he had started, not at fixed intervals as had been his practice on preceding days, but with an unbroken line of lookouts and pickets so that the whole fortification was continuously manned; he sent round military tribunes and commanders of contingents, alerting them not only to guard against organized sallies but also to watch for individuals slipping out secretly. In truth not a single man was so relaxed or apathetic as to take any rest that night. Such was the tension at this critical moment that in thought and imagination they were pulled in various directions, wondering what would happen to the Corfinians themselves, or to Domitius, or to Lentulus, or to the rest, and what fate awaited whom.

(22) Towards the end of the night Lentulus Spinther communicated from the wall with our lookouts and guards, saying

that he wished, if possible, to meet Caesar. Permission was granted and he was escorted from the town, Domitius' soldiers not leaving him until he was brought into Caesar's presence. <He asked> Caesar for his life; he begged and pleaded to be spared, reminded him of their old friendship, and rehearsed Caesar's favours to him, which were very considerable: through Caesar he had become a member of the pontifical college, had received Spain as his province after his praetorship, and had been assisted in his candidature for the consulship. But Caesar interrupted him: it was not to do harm that he had crossed the boundary of his province, but to defend himself from the insults of his enemies, to restore to their proper dignity the tribunes who had been expelled from Rome in the course of this affair, and to assert his own freedom and that of the Roman people, who were oppressed by an oligarchic clique.* Heartened by what Caesar said, Lentulus asked to be allowed to return to Corfinium, saying that his success in securing his own safety would be an encouragement to the hopes of the others, and that some were so terrified that they were being driven to consider taking their own lives. Permission granted, he departed.

(23) At dawn Caesar ordered all senators, sons of senators, military tribunes, and Roman equestrians* to be brought before him. There were five men of senatorial rank, namely Lucius Domitius, Publius Lentulus Spinther, Lucius Caecilius Rufus,* the quaestor Sextus Quintilius Varus,* and Lucius Rubrius; and in addition Domitius' son, several other young men, and a great number of Roman equestrians and members of local councils whom Domitius had called up from the towns. They were all brought forward, and after forbidding his soldiers to insult and jeer at them, Caesar spoke a few words to them, to the effect that they had shown him no gratitude for the very substantial favours he had done them, and sent them away unharmed. He returned to Domitius the six million sesterces which the latter had brought with him and deposited in the treasury, and which the four chief magistrates of Corfinium had handed over to himself; this he did in order not to seem greedier of men's money than of their lives, in spite of the fact that this was indisputably public money and had been provided by Pompey as pay for the

troops. He ordered Domitius' soldiers to take the oath of loyalty to himself, and on that day moved camp and completed a normal march;* having spent seven days in all at Corfinium, he reached Apulia by way of the territory of the Marrucini, the Frentani, and Larinum.

Pompey's forces escape from Caesar at Brundisium and cross to Epirus

(24) When he learnt what had happened at Corfinium, Pompey set out from Luceria for Canusium and thence to Brundisium. He ordered all newly recruited forces to be brought to join his, and by arming slaves and shepherds and giving them horses he created about three hundred cavalry. Lucius Manlius* fled from Alba with six cohorts, the praetor Rutilius Lupus from Tarracina with three; when these sighted Caesar's cavalry under the command of Vibius Curius, they abandoned the praetor, transferred their standards to Curius, and went over to him. Likewise on the other lines of march some cohorts fell in with Caesar's infantry, others with his cavalry. A staff officer of Pompey's, Numerius Magius from Cremona, was captured on the march and brought to Caesar, who sent him back to Pompey with the message that since up to that time there had been no chance of a meeting, and he himself was on the way to Brundisium, it would be in the interests of the republic and the common good for him to confer with Pompey; for in truth the same results were not to be expected from negotiations conducted at a distance, with terms relayed by third parties, as when all the terms could be discussed together face to face.

(25) After dispatching this message, he arrived at Brundisium with six legions,* three of them veteran, the remainder those which he had newly raised and made up to strength along the way; they did not include Domitius' cohorts, which he had sent directly from Corfinium to Sicily. He found that the consuls had left for Dyrrachium* with a large part of the army, while Pompey remained at Brundisium with twenty

cohorts. He could not discover for certain whether Pompey
had stayed there to hold Brundisium, so that he could more
easily control the whole Adriatic, including the most distant
parts of Italy and the coasts of Greece, and conduct the war
from both quarters, or whether he had stopped there because
of a shortage of ships; but as he feared that his opponent
had decided not to abandon Italy, he began to block the
entrance and impede the workings of the port of Brundisium.
This was the way he did it. Where the passage into the port
was at its narrowest, he threw out breakwaters and an earth
bank from each shore, the sea being shallow there. As the
proceeded further and the bank could not be held together
in the deeper water, he stationed double pontoons, thirty feet
long and wide, in line with the breakwater. Each of these
he kept in place with four anchors, one at each corner, so
that they would not be swung by the waves. When these
had been completed and put in place, he joined to them one
after another other pontoons of equal size, covering them with
earth and filling material so that it would not be difficult to
move rapidly on to them to defend them; at the front and
on both sides he protected them with wickerwork and pent-
houses; on every fourth pontoon he hastily raised two-storey
towers to make them more easily defensible against ship-borne
attack and fire.

(26) In answer, Pompey fitted out large cargo ships which
he had captured in the port of Brundisium. On them he
erected towers with three storeys, and having armed them
with a large number of catapults and all sorts of weapons
he drove them against Caesar's constructions so as to break
through the rafts and disturb the operations. There were
daily engagements of this kind, with both sides using slings,
arrows, and other weapons at a distance. In addition, Caesar
so directed these operations as not to consider a negotiated
peace out of the question; and although he was very surprised that Magius, whom he had sent with a message to
Pompey, had not been sent back to him,* and although his
numerous attempts to secure a peace were hindering his
assaults and his planning, he still considered that he ought
to persevere with the matter by every means possible. He

therefore sent his officer Caninius Rebilus, a friend of Scribonius Libo, to confer with the latter; he told Rebilus to encourage Libo to mediate a peace; above all he requested a meeting between himself and Pompey; he indicated that he had great confidence that, if this were granted, hostilities could be suspended on fair terms; and a great part of the praise and credit for such an outcome would be Libo's, if hostilities were brought to an end on his initiative and by his action. On leaving the meeting with Caninius, Libo went to Pompey. A little later he brought the answer back that the consuls were not there, and without them it was impossible to discuss a settlement. So Caesar concluded that the objective he had so often and fruitlessly tried to attain could not be indefinitely pursued, and that he must proceed with war.

(27) When Caesar had spent nine days in completing almost half the work, the ships which had ferried the first part of the army to Dyrrachium, and had been sent back from there by the consuls, returned to Brundisium. On the arrival of the ships Pompey, whether disturbed by Caesar's siege-works or because he had from the start indeed intended to withdraw from Italy,* began to make preparations for departure; and so that he could more easily delay Caesar's attack and stop the soldiers bursting into the town when he was in the act of leaving, he blocked the gates, built walls across the alleys and open places, and dug trenches across the streets, fixing sharpened stakes and posts in them. These he covered over level, using wickerwork and earth; as for the entrances and the two roads which led beyond the wall to the port, he made palisades across them of massive sharpened posts set in the ground. When these preparations had been made, he ordered his troops to embark in silence, and on the wall and the turrets stationed a few lightly armed men from among his veterans, <along with> archers and slingers. These he arranged to recall by an agreed signal when all the soldiers had embarked, and left light fast boats for them in a convenient spot.

(28) The townspeople of Brundisium, who resented the damage inflicted on them by the soldiery and the insulting

manner in which Pompey himself had treated them, were on Caesar's side. So when they knew about Pompey's departure, they signalled everywhere from the roofs while the Pompeians were preoccupied with mustering. Realizing through them what was happening, Caesar ordered ladders to be got ready and the soldiers to arm, so as not to lose any chance of a success. Pompey set sail* as it was getting dark. The men who had been left to guard the wall were recalled by the signal which had been agreed and ran down to the sea by paths they knew. The soldiers set the ladders in place and climbed the walls, but on being warned by the inhabitants to beware of the concealed palisade and trenches, they halted and were led by them a long way round to reach the port, where using dinghies and small boats they trapped and captured two ships carrying soldiers which had run foul of Caesar's breakwaters.

(29) Although Caesar's best hopes of putting an end to the business lay in requisitioning ships to cross the Adriatic and following Pompey before he could build up his strength with overseas reinforcements, he was still afraid of the delay and the length of time demanded by this course, because Pompey had requisitioned all the ships and removed any immediate chance of pursuit. It remained to wait for ships from the more distant regions of Gaul, Picenum, and the Straits.* That seemed to be a long and awkward business, on account of the time of year. In the mean time he was unwilling to let his absence permit a veteran army* and the two Spanish provinces (one of which was firmly attached to Pompey by his signal favours to it) to consolidate their strength, allow auxiliary troops and cavalry to be raised, and open Gaul and Italy to attack.

Capture of Sardinia and Sicily. Caesar in Rome

(30) For the moment, therefore, he abandoned the idea of pursuing Pompey, and decided to make for Spain; he ordered the chief magistrates of all the Italian towns to find ships

and see that they were sent to Brundisium. To Sardinia he sent his officer <Quintus> Valerius with one legion, to Sicily Curio as propraetor* with three; he also ordered Curio, when he had gained control of Sicily, to take his army across to Africa immediately. Marcus Cotta was holding Sardinia, Marcus Cato Sicily; <Lucius> Tubero* should, by lot, have been holding Africa. As soon as the people of Caralis heard that Valerius was being sent against them, they threw Cotta out of the town on their own initiative before Valerius had yet left Italy. Terrified because he knew that the whole province felt the same, Cotta fled from Sardinia to Africa. In Sicily Cato was busy repairing old warships and ordering the communities to provide new ones. This he did with great energy. In Lucania and Bruttium he conscripted Roman citizens through his officers, and from the communities of Sicily he demanded quotas of infantry and cavalry. These measures were almost completed when he heard of Curio's arrival, and protested at a public meeting that he had been abandoned and betrayed by Gnaeus Pompeius, who had undertaken an unnecessary war in a state of complete unreadiness and when pressed by himself and others in the senate had confirmed that everything was ready and fit for war. After making these complaints at the meeting, he fled the province.*

(31) Valerius and Curio, discovering Sardinia and Sicily deserted by their commanders, proceeded there with their armies. When Tubero reached Africa, he found Attius Varus in control of the province; the latter, having lost his cohorts at Auximum as described above,* had come to Africa immediately after making his escape; finding it without a governor* he had on his own initiative taken command, and raised two legions by conscription. He possessed the means to attempt this through his familiarity and contacts with the men and the places of the province, because a few years previously, after his praetorship, he had been its governor. When Tubero arrived at Utica with his ships, he barred him from the port and the town, and without allowing him to land his sick son forced him to weigh anchor and depart.

(32) When these matters had been dealt with, Caesar dispersed his soldiers to the nearby towns to rest from their

exertions, while he himself made his way to Rome. A meeting
of the senate was called,* and he spoke of the wrongs done
him by his enemies. He explained that he had sought no
position out of the ordinary, but had waited the legitimate
interval* for the consulate and been content with what was
open to any citizen. A law had been carried by the ten tribunes against the opposition of his enemies—and indeed Cato
had resisted bitterly and dragged out the days in lengthy
speeches in the old-fashioned way—a law which permitted
him a candidature in absence, and this in Pompey's own
consulship;* if Pompey had disapproved of it, why had he
let it be passed? And if he approved of it, why had he not
allowed Caesar to enjoy this favour from the people? He
stressed his own forbearance in requesting of his own accord
that both armies be disbanded, a move which would entail
loss of status and office by himself. He spoke of the bitterness of his enemies, who refused to do in their own case
what they demanded of a rival,* and preferred anarchy to
the surrender of command and armies. He emphasized their
injustice in taking his legions,* and their savagery and arrogance in restricting the tribunes' freedom of action; he mentioned the terms that he had put forward, the meetings that
he had proposed and been refused. In the light of these facts,
he encouraged and requested them to take responsibility for
the state and administer it jointly with himself. But, he said,
if they were frightened and ran away, he would not shirk the
task and would administer the state by himself. His view was
that delegates ought to be sent to Pompey to arrange a settlement; and he was not afraid of Pompey's recent remark in
the senate that to receive a delegation implied authority, and
to send it, fear. Such a sentiment indicated a weak and shallow spirit. He, on the other hand, wanted to win the contest
to be just and fair in the same way as he had struggled to
be superior in achievement.

(33) The senate agreed to send delegates, but none could
be found to send. The chief reason they all refused appointment was fear, because on his departure from Rome Pompey
had said in the senate that he would make no distinction between those who remained in the city and those who were

with Caesar's army. In this way three days dragged by in
arguments and excuses. Also Lucius Metellus, one of the tribunes, was put up by Caesar's enemies to disrupt this business
and to interfere with whatever else Caesar decided to do.*
After wasting several days Caesar became aware of Metellus'
purpose, and so, not wishing to lose any more time, he abandoned what he had intended to do and after leaving Rome
travelled on to Further Gaul.

The siege of Massilia commences

(34) When he reached the province,* he learnt that Vibullius
Rufus, whom he himself had captured at Corfinium a few
days previously and allowed to go free, had been sent by
Pompey <to Spain>; that Domitius likewise had set out to
gain control of Massilia* with seven light ships which he
had requisitioned from private owners at Igilium and in the
territory of Cosa and manned with slaves, freedmen, and
tenant-farmers of his own; and also that a Massiliot delegation had been sent back home ahead of him, consisting of
young nobles whom Pompey, as he left Rome, had encouraged not to let Caesar's recent favours banish from their
minds the recollection of his own earlier benefits to them.*
The people of Massilia had accepted these instructions and
closed their gates against Caesar; they had summoned to
their side the Albici, a native people who were under their
protection from of old and lived in the mountains above
Massilia; they had transported grain into the city from the
neighbouring regions and all their fortified settlements, they
had set up arms factories in the city, and they had begun to
repair the walls, gates, and fleet.

(35) Caesar summoned the Fifteen* from Massilia to his
presence. He urged them not to allow the Massiliots to bear
responsibility for starting hostilities, saying that they ought to
follow the lead of the whole of Italy, rather than humour the
wishes of a single individual.* He also drew their attention
to the other factors which he thought would help in bringing them to their senses. The delegation reported back what

he had said and on public authority made him the following reply: they understood that the <Roman> people were divided into two parties, but it was beyond their strength or their competence to decide which party was in the right. Indeed, the leaders of those parties were patrons of their own state; one had granted them public ownership of the land of the Volcae Arecomici and the Helvii, while the other, having conquered the Sallyes,* had attached this people to their state and boosted their revenues. Therefore, since the benefits the Massiliots had received were equal, their duty was to render equal goodwill to each, help neither against the other, and not receive either within the city or its harbours.

(36) While these negotiations proceeded, Domitius reached Massilia with his ships and was admitted by the city and placed in charge; he was granted supreme military command. On his orders the fleet was sent off in all directions; wherever they could they seized merchant ships and brought them back to port, those that were deficient in fastenings or in timbers and fittings being used to fit out and repair the others; any grain discovered was added to the public stock; and the other goods and provisions were kept against the eventuality of a siege. Roused by these hostile moves, Caesar brought up three legions* against Massilia; he began to deploy siege-towers and mantlets for an assault on the city, and to build warships, to the number of twelve, at Arelate. These were finished and equipped in thirty days from the felling of the timber; when they had been brought to Massilia he put Decimus Brutus in command of them and left his deputy Gaius Trebonius to take charge of the assault on the city.

Caesar establishes his position at Ilerda

(37) While he was making these preparations and dispositions, he sent his deputy Gaius Fabius ahead to Spain with the three legions* which he had stationed for the winter around Narbo and its neighbourhood, giving him orders to seize the passes through the Pyrenees which were at that time held by garrisons posted by Pompey's deputy Lucius

Afranius. He ordered the other legions,* which were in more distant winter quarters, to follow. Fabius, in obedience to his orders, made haste to eject the garrison from the pass* and headed for Afranius' army by forced marches.

(38) On the arrival of Lucius Vibullius Rufus, who as noted* had been sent to Spain by Pompey, Afranius and Petreius and Varro, Pompey's deputies* (of whom one held Nearer Spain <with three legions, the second Further Spain> from the Castulo ranges to the Anas with two legions, and the third the country from the Anas to the territory of the Vettones and Lusitania with an equal number), divided their responsibilities amongst themselves so that Petreius was to set out with all his forces from Lusitania by way of the Vettones to Afranius, while Varro guarded the whole of Further Spain with the legions he already had. When this had been decided, cavalry and auxiliary troops were demanded by Petreius from the whole of Lusitania, and by Afranius from Celtiberia, the Cantabri, and all the native tribes stretching to the Atlantic coast. When these had been collected, Petreius quickly reached Afranius by way of the Vettones, and they decided to conduct a campaign jointly at Ilerda because of the opportunities offered by the site.

(39) As indicated above, Afranius had three legions, Petreius two, and in addition there were about thirty cohorts of heavy- and light-armed native infantry from the nearer and further provinces respectively, and about five thousand cavalry from both provinces. Caesar had sent ahead to Spain six legions, no auxiliary infantry, and three thousand cavalry which he had had in all his previous campaigns, and an equal number from the parts of Gaul pacified by himself, consisting of the noblest and bravest summoned by name from all the tribal states; to this force <he proposed to add . . . > of first-rate men from the Aquitani and the mountain peoples who border the province of Gaul.* He had heard that Pompey was marching with legions through Mauretania, and would come with all speed. At the same time he borrowed money from his junior officers and centurions and distributed it to the army. By this he secured two things: by the loan, the loyalty of the centurions, and by the handout, the support of the men.

(40) Fabius began to solicit the support of the nearby peoples by writing to them and sending messengers. Over the river Segre he had two bridges built four miles apart.* By these bridges he used to send out his cavalry to graze, because he had recently used up what lay on his own side of the river. Practically the same thing, and for the same reason, was being done by the Pompeian commanders, and there were frequent cavalry engagements. When two of Fabius' legions, following their daily routine, went out in this direction to guard the grazers and had crossed the river by the nearer <bridge>, and their equipment and all the cavalry were following, suddenly the bridge was broken by a gale and flood of water, and the mass of cavalry behind were cut off. Petreius and Afranius realized what had happened from the debris and wickerwork brought down by the river, and Afranius rapidly took four legions and all his cavalry across the river by his own bridge, near his camp and the town, and went to meet Fabius' two legions. On the report of their approach Lucius Plancus, who was in command of the legions, had no alternative but to occupy higher ground and draw up his line of battle in two parts facing in different directions, so as not to be outflanked by the cavalry. In this way, although outnumbered, he withstood heavy attacks from the legions and the cavalry. Battle had been started by the cavalry when both sides sighted in the distance the standards of the two legions which had been sent round in support via the further bridge by Gaius Fabius, who suspected the likelihood of what in fact occurred, namely that the opposing generals would take advantage of the chance offered by luck to overwhelm our forces. Their arrival broke up the battle and each side withdrew its legions to camp.

(41) Two days later* Caesar reached the camp with the nine hundred cavalry he had kept to guard him. The bridge which had been broken by the storm was almost repaired, and he gave orders for it to be completed during the night. He himself, when he had seen the lie of the land, left behind all the baggage, together with six cohorts to guard the camp and the bridge, and on the next day marched all his forces, drawn up in triple column, to Ilerda. Here he halted opposite Afranius' camp, and remained there for a while

with arms at the ready, to give him the opportunity of an engagement on level ground. On being offered this opportunity, Afranius led his forces out and halted half-way down the slope below his camp. When Caesar realized that it was Afranius' decision to refuse battle, he decided to construct a camp about four hundred yards from the lowest slopes of the hill, and so that the soldiers should not be in fear of a sudden assault by the enemy while they were digging and be prevented from carrying out the work, he ordered them not to protect themselves with a rampart, which of necessity would stand out and be seen from a distance, but to make a fifteen-foot ditch on the side facing the enemy. The first and second ranks stayed under arms, as had been the case from the beginning; behind them, out of sight, the work was done by the third rank. In this way it was all completed before Afranius was able to realize that a camp was being fortified. Towards evening Caesar withdrew the legions behind this ditch and rested there the following night under arms.

(42) The next day, he kept his whole army inside the ditch and for the moment, because rampart material could only be got from some distance away, he organized a similar procedure for the work, allotting each legion a side of the camp to fortify, and ordering ditches of the same size to be dug; the rest of the legions he drew up in battle order, without their heavy equipment, facing the enemy. To spread fear and hinder the work, Afranius and Petreius brought their forces down to the lowest slopes of the hill and made harassing attacks, but Caesar did not on that account interrupt the work, trusting to the protection afforded by the three legions and the ditch. The enemy did not stay long nor advance far from the bottom of the hill, and withdrew to camp. On the third day Caesar fortified the camp with a rampart, and gave orders for the other cohorts, which he had left in the first camp, and the baggage to be brought across to him.

The battle in front of Ilerda

(43) Between the town of Ilerda and the nearest hill, where Petreius and Afranius had their camp, there was about five

hundred yards of level ground, and roughly in the middle of this was a slightly raised hillock; if he could occupy this and fortify it, Caesar was confident that he would cut off the opposition from the town, the bridge, and all the supplies which they had brought into the town. In the hope of achieving this, he led three legions out from camp, drew up his battle line in a suitable place, and ordered the élite troops of one legion to run forward and seize the hillock. When this manœuvre was observed, Afranius' cohorts which were on guard in front of his camp were quickly sent the shorter distance to seize the same spot. An engagement took place, and because Afranius' troops had reached the hillock first, our men were driven off, and when other reinforcements were sent they were compelled to turn tail and withdraw to the body of the legions.

(44) The way the opposing soldiers fought was first to make a great charge forward and boldly capture ground, not preserving much of their formation and fighting scattered and in small groups, and if they were under pressure, to think it no disgrace to retreat and give up their position, because they were accustomed <to fight> against the Lusitani and the other natives in a kind of <native> style of battle— it being common for soldiers who have served long periods in particular places to be greatly affected by the practice of those regions. This procedure at that time unsettled our men, who were unaccustomed to this style of fighting. They kept thinking that they were being outflanked on their open side* when individuals ran forward, but considered that they themselves ought to keep rank and not part company from the standards or be pushed from ground they had captured for any but the most serious of reasons. And so, when the élite formation had been disrupted, the legion which had taken up station on that wing did not maintain its position and withdrew to the nearest hill.

(45) As almost his whole line was panic-stricken, an abnormal and unexpected phenomenon, Caesar rallied his men and led the Ninth legion to lend support; he checked the enemy who were insolently and eagerly pursuing our men, and forced them to turn back again, retreat to Ilerda town

and halt beneath the wall. But the soldiers of the Ninth legion, carried away in their enthusiasm for making good the loss they had suffered, rashly followed the fugitives rather a long way, advancing to sloping ground and coming up below the hill on which the town of Ilerda stood. When they wanted to withdraw from this spot, the enemy from their higher position again exerted pressure on our men. The place was precipitous and sheer on both sides, and of such a width that three cohorts in formation filled it, so that it was impossible for reinforcements to be sent in from the flanks or for cavalry to be used to support any troops under pressure. From the town a slope with a gentle gradient stretched along for about six hundred yards. This was the way our men had to withdraw, because in their enthusiasm they had somewhat unwisely advanced that far; and it was here that the fighting took place, the ground being disadvantageous both because it was constricted and because they had halted at the very base of the hill, so that every missile hurled at them found its mark. None the less they fought with stoical bravery and did not succumb to their wounds. The enemy forces were augmented, and cohorts from their camp were constantly being sent up through the town, so that fresh troops replaced tired. Caesar was compelled to do the same and withdraw exhausted men by sending cohorts up to take their place.

(46) When the battle had gone on in this way for five hours continuously, and our men were being seriously troubled by superior numbers and had used up all their throwing weapons, they drew their swords and made an uphill attack on the enemy cohorts. They scattered a few of them and forced the rest to turn about, and having driven the cohorts up under the wall, and in some places frightened them into the town, found it easy to retreat. And although on both flanks our cavalry had taken up a position on downhill, lower-lying ground, they none the less struggled with great courage towards the crest and by riding between the two lines provided our men with a safer and more comfortable retreat. Thus the fortune of battle was varied. On our side, about seventy men fell in the first engagement, including Quintus Fulginius,

an ex-centurion of the first cohort of the Fourteenth legion, who had risen to that position from the lower ranks on account of his conspicuous courage, and the wounded numbered more than 600. On Afranius' side the dead included Titus Caecilius, a leading centurion,* and besides him four other centurions and more than 200 men.

(47) But such were the opinions put about of the day's events, that both sides thought that they had got off best: Afranius' men, because although everyone had reckoned them inferior, they had stood firm for so long in hand-to-hand fighting and withstood the attack of our men, and at the start had held the position and the hillock, which had been the cause of the battle, and had forced our men to flee when the engagement first began; our men, on the contrary, thought the same, because on disadvantageous ground and against superior numbers they had continued to fight for five hours, had made ground up the hill with their swords drawn, and had forced their opponents to flee from higher ground before driving them into the town. The other side put a fortification of mighty earthworks around the hillock for which the battle had been fought, and stationed a guard there.

Caesar in difficulties after severe flooding

(48) Within two days of these events a sudden blow fell. Such a great storm arose that it was generally agreed there had never been more extensive flooding in the area. On this occasion it in fact melted the snow from all the mountains and overflowed the banks of the river and broke down on a single day both the bridges which Gaius Fabius had constructed. This brought great problems for Caesar's army. His camp, as has been explained above,* lay between two rivers, the Segre and the Cinca, and since it was impossible to cross either for thirty miles* everyone was perforce hemmed in within this restricted space. The native communities which had come over to Caesar were unable to bring in grain, nor could the men who had gone any distance to forage, and been cut off by the rivers, make their way back, nor could

the very substantial supplies which were on their way from Italy and Gaul reach the camp. It was in any case a most difficult time of year, because there was no grain in store, nor was it quite ripe in the fields; the communities had been completely denuded, Afranius having taken almost all the grain into Ilerda before Caesar's arrival, and Caesar had consumed what remained on the preceding days; the cattle,* which could have served as a subsidiary means of support in a shortage, had been moved too far away by the neighbouring communities because of the war. The troops who set out to find grain or fodder were constantly pursued by light-armed Lusitanians and by light infantry from Nearer Spain who were familiar with the region; for them it was easy to swim across a river, because they always bring inflatable skins with them when they go on active service.

(49) By contrast, Afranius' army had plenty of supplies of all kinds. Much grain had been earmarked and gathered together previously, much was being brought from all over the province, and a large amount of fodder was to hand. Access to all this was provided without any danger by the bridge at Ilerda and the safe country across the river which Caesar was quite unable to reach.

(50) These floods lasted for several days. Caesar attempted to rebuild the bridges, but the swollen river would not allow it, and the enemy auxiliaries stationed by the bank made completion impossible; they found it easy to stop the operation both on account of the state of the river itself and the size of the flood, and because their weapons were directed from all along the banks against a single narrow spot; and it was difficult to carry out the work in a violent current and at the same time avoid the weapons that were hurled.

(51) News was brought to Afranius that a very substantial convoy which was on its way to Caesar had halted at the river. There had arrived archers from the Ruteni, and cavalry from Gaul, with a large number of wagons and much baggage in the usual Gallic style; there were about six thousand men of all sorts with their slaves and children, but there was no organization and no recognized authority among them, because each did what he thought best and they all travelled

boldly in the ill-disciplined manner of earlier times and journeys. There were <in addition> a number of well-born young men, sons of senators and of members of the equestrian order; there were delegations from native communities; there were envoys of Caesar's. All were held up by the water. To overwhelm them, Afranius set out by night with all his cavalry and three legions, and attacked them unawares by sending the cavalry on ahead. But the Gallic cavalry quickly prepared for action and joined battle. Although they were outnumbered, as long as the fighting was like against like they withstood a large body of enemy; but when the standards of the legions began to come close, they retreated with a few losses to the nearest hills. The duration of this encounter made a great deal of difference to the safety of our people, because they gained the time to withdraw to higher ground. That day saw the loss of about two hundred archers, a few horsemen, and no great quantity of servants and equipment.

(52) None the less, along with all this, the price of grain rose; this is a thing which is always triggered not only by current scarcity but also by fear of the future. By now the cost had risen to fifty <denarii> a bushel,* the soldiers had been weakened by the scarcity of grain, and their discomforts were increasing daily; and so great a change had come over the situation in a few days, and fortune had so tipped the scales, that our men were hit by a great shortage of necessities while our opponents had plenty of everything and were considered to hold the advantage. From those communities which had come over to him Caesar demanded cattle in proportion to their reduced stocks of grain; he sent the camp servants away to more distant communities; and he himself used whatever means he could to remedy the current lack of food.

(53) Afranius and Petreius and their friends wrote to their supporters in Rome describing this situation in even fuller and more glowing terms than it warranted. They invented much by way of rumour, so that the war seemed practically over. When these letters and reports reached Rome, there were great gatherings at Afranius' house and great demonstrations of joy; large numbers of people started out from Italy to join Gnaeus Pompeius,* some wanting to be the first to bring such

good news, others to avoid appearing to have waited for the outcome of the war or to be the last of all to have come.

(54) In this desperate situation, since all the roads were blocked by Afranius' infantry and cavalry, and it was impossible to complete the bridges, Caesar ordered his men to make boats of a type with which his experience of Britain* had made him familiar some years before. The keel and the main frames were made of light timber; the rest of the hull of the ship was woven from osier and covered with skins. When these were finished he carried them by night on pairs of wagons twenty-two miles from his camp,* and by transporting soldiers in these boats across the river unexpectedly seized a hill adjacent to the bank. This he swiftly fortified before the opposition could notice. To it he later sent across a legion and in two days completed a bridge that was begun from both sides. Thus he safely recovered his convoy and the men who had gone out to seek grain, and began to see an improvement in his commissariat.

(55) On the same day he put a large proportion of his cavalry across the river. They took by surprise foragers and groups of men who were scattered about without the slightest fear, and intercepted an impressive number of men and pack-animals; when light-armed infantry cohorts were sent to help they expertly divided themselves into two, some to guard their booty, the others to resist the advancing enemy and drive them off; and they cut off from the rest, surrounded, and killed one cohort which had rashly broken the line and run forward of the others. They returned to camp by the same bridge without loss and with a large amount of booty.

The first sea-battle off Massilia

(56) While these operations were taking place at Ilerda, the Massiliots, acting on the plan of Lucius Domitius, made ready seventeen warships, of which eleven had an upper deck. To these they added many smaller ships, in the hope of scaring our fleet by their numbers alone. They put on

board these ships large numbers of archers and large numbers of Albici (mentioned above) and encouraged them with rewards and promises. Domitius asked for ships of his own and manned them with the tenants and shepherds he had brought with him.* In this way, with a fully equipped fleet, they came out in great confidence towards our ships, which were commanded by Decimus Brutus. These were keeping station off the island which is opposite Massilia.*

(57) Brutus was greatly outnumbered in ships; but Caesar had seconded from all his legions to this fleet picked men who had volunteered for this duty—soldiers distinguished for bravery, and front-line troops,* and centurions. These had prepared iron claws and grappling irons and equipped themselves with a large quantity of heavy and light javelins and other varieties of throwing weapon. So on learning of the approach of the enemy, they took their ships out of port and engaged the Massiliots. The fight was fierce and bitter on both sides; the Albici were not much inferior in courage to our people, being tough mountaineers and practised in arms; and while these had ringing in their ears the promises of the people of Massilia whom they had only just left, Domitius' shepherds were spurred on by the hope of gaining their freedom and strove to prove their effectiveness under the eyes of their master.

(58) The Massiliots themselves, relying on the speed of their ships and the skill of their helmsmen, slipped out of our way and absorbed our attacks, and so long as they had plenty of searoom they extended their line further and attempted either to surround us or to make attacks in groups against individual ships or, if they could, to break off our oars by passing close alongside; when they were obliged to come to closer quarters, they relied on the courage of the mountaineers instead of on the skill and tricks of the helmsmen. <We> not only had less well-trained oarsmen and less skilled helmsmen, who had been hastily recruited from merchant ships and had not even had time to learn the terms for the pieces of tackle, but were handicapped by the slowness and weight of our ships, which had been constructed in a hurry from green timber and did not have the same

capacity for speed. Therefore, so long as the chance of hand-to-hand fighting was offered, our men willingly pitted single ships against two of theirs; they grappled them with the iron claws, held each of them, and fought from both sides of their own ship and climbed across on to the enemy's. They sank some of the ships, killing many of the Albici and the shepherds, they captured a few with their crews, and they drove the rest back to port. The number of Massiliot ships which came to grief that day, including the captured, was nine.

(59) This battle was reported to Caesar at Ilerda; at the same time, with the completion of the bridge, fortune swiftly changed.* The other side were terrified by the bravery of the cavalry and roamed less freely and less boldly; sometimes they went out only a short distance from the camp, so that they could quickly find shelter, and foraged in a restricted area, at others they avoided the lookouts and outposts of the cavalry by going a longer way round, or after suffering some losses or catching sight of the cavalry in the distance they dropped their loads in mid-journey and fled. In the end they had introduced longer intervals between foraging and, contrary to universal practice, adopted night-time foraging.

(60) Meanwhile the inhabitants of Osca and of Calagurris (a place under the administration of Osca) sent a delegation to Caesar and promised to obey his wishes. They were followed by the citizens of Tarraco, the Iacetani, and the Ausetani, and a few days later by the Illurgavonenses, who live along the Ebro. He requested all of them to supply him with grain. They promised to do so, collected draught animals from all parts, and brought it to his camp. In addition, a cohort of Illurgavonenses deserted to him when they heard of the decision of their people, and brought their standards across from their position. <There> rapidly <occurred> a great alteration in the situation: with the bridge finished, five important communities allied to him, the grain supply under control, and the rumours that Pompey was bringing legions to the rescue through Mauretania scotched, many of the more distant communities abandoned their loyalty to Afranius and came over to Caesar.

The Pompeian army withdraws towards the Ebro but is cut off

(61) The morale of his opponents was severely affected by these developments; and Caesar, to avoid always having to send his cavalry the long way round over the bridge, chose a suitable spot and began to dig several thirty-foot wide channels by which he could divert part of the Segre and make a ford across the river. When these were nearly finished, Afranius and Petreius became very afraid of being completely cut off from food and forage, because Caesar was far superior in cavalry. And so it was they who decided to leave the area and transfer the theatre of war to Celtiberia.* This plan had also in its favour the fact that of the two different sorts of communities which had been involved in the earlier war with Sertorius* those that had been defeated were in fear of the reputation and power of the absent Pompey; on the other hand those that had remained loyal had received great rewards and esteemed Pompey highly, while Caesar's name was relatively unknown amongst the natives. In these regions they expected to gain large numbers of cavalry and auxiliaries, and they held the view that on their own territory they would prolong the war until the winter. They adopted this plan, and gave orders for ships to be requisitioned all along the Ebro and brought to Otogesa. This was a town on the Ebro twenty miles from their camp. They ordered a bridge of boats to be made at that point on the river, transferred two legions across the Segre, and fortified a camp with a twelve-foot palisade.

(62) When he learnt of this through his scouts, Caesar had the work of diverting the river continue night and day, with enormous effort on the part of the soldiers. He had brought his situation back to the point where the cavalry, although it was difficult and barely possible, could nevertheless cross the river, and had the courage to do so. The infantry, on the other hand, could only clear the water with their shoulders and the tops of their chests, and were prevented from crossing by the swiftness of the stream as well as by

its depth. However, at almost the same time as the ford was being found in the Segre, news came that the bridge over the Ebro was nearly finished.

(63) Now indeed Caesar's opponents had all the more cause to hasten their march. Leaving two auxiliary cohorts to guard Ilerda, they crossed the Segre with all their forces and joined camp with the two legions they had sent across earlier. Caesar was left with no choice but to use his cavalry to harass and harry his opponents' column of march. This was because his own bridge entailed a long detour, so that the enemy had a far shorter march to reach the Ebro; but the cavalry he sent out forded the river, and when Petreius and Afranius had struck camp somewhat after midnight, these suddenly made their presence known to the rearguard and began to delay them and interfere with the march by swarming around them in great strength.

(64) At dawn a view could be had, from the higher ground which adjoined Caesar's camp, of the enemy rearguard under pressure from the attacks of our cavalry; sometimes the tail of the column was <un>able to resist and they were thrown into disorder, sometimes they advanced in regular formation and our side were driven off by an attack of all the cohorts, only to follow them again when they turned round. But all over the camp the soldiers gathered in groups, sorry that the enemy had slipped from their grasp and that the war was inevitably being prolonged, and they approached the centurions and military tribunes and begged them to tell Caesar not to shrink from exposing them to toil or danger; they were prepared, and had the capability and the courage, to cross the river at the spot where the cavalry had crossed. Caesar was stirred by their words and enthusiasm, and although afraid to expose his army to such a powerfully flowing river, thought he ought to make the attempt and see what happened. He therefore gave orders for the weaker men whose strength or spirit seemed unequal to the task to be picked out from all the centuries, and these he left with one legion to guard the camp. He led the rest of the legions out without their heavy equipment, and after stationing a large number of baggage animals in the river above and below the ford, took

the army across. A few of these soldiers were swept away by the violence of the current and were rescued and given help by the cavalry; but not a single man was lost. When the army was safely across, he marshalled his forces and began to lead them in triple column. And such was the enthusiasm of the troops, that although their march was six miles longer* because of the detour, and the fording of the river had caused considerable delay, before the middle of the afternoon they caught up with men who had set out not long after midnight.

(65) When Afranius caught sight of them in the distance and looked at them with Petreius, he was alarmed by this new development. He halted on higher ground and drew up his forces in battle order. Caesar rested his army on the level, because he had no wish to commit exhausted men to battle, and when the others again attempted to move on he pursued and delayed them. Of necessity they pitched camp earlier than they had intended, for mountains were close by* and after five more miles they would be on narrow and difficult tracks. They wanted to enter these mountains to escape from Caesar's cavalry, place guards in the narrows, and so block his army's passage, while they themselves, relieved of fear and danger, took their army across the Ebro. This operation they had to attempt, and complete by any possible means; but as they were exhausted by a whole day's fighting and the effort of the march, they put it off until the next day. Caesar also made camp, on the next hill.

(66) About midnight, some men who had ventured a little too far from camp to find water were caught by the cavalry, and Caesar learnt from them that the opposing generals were moving their forces in silence out of their camp. When he discovered this, he ordered the alert to be sounded and the military cry 'Pack up' to be raised. The other side, hearing the shouts and afraid that they would be forced to fight in the dark when they were handicapped by their loads, or that they would be held up in the narrows by Caesar's cavalry, cancelled the march and kept their troops in camp. On the following day Petreius went out unobtrusively with a few horsemen to prospect the area. The same manœuvre was

carried out from Caesar's camp: Lucius Decidius Saxa was sent out with a few men to establish the lie of the land. The reports to both sides were the same, that the next five miles were level marching, and then they would be into rough and mountainous country: the one who first seized these defiles would have no trouble in blocking the enemy's path.

(67) Petreius and Afranius debated with their advisers to decide the time of their departure. Several thought they should march at night, believing it possible to reach the pass before being noticed. Others maintained that because on the previous day the signal to move had been shouted in the dark from Caesar's camp, a secret departure from their position was impossible. They pointed out that Caesar's cavalry were all round them at night, and that every route and position was held against them; also that night battles were to be avoided, because a frightened soldier involved in civil war usually obeyed the dictates of fear, not his oath. But in day-light, when all could see him, a man felt ashamed, and fur-ther ashamed beneath the gaze of the officers and centurions who stood beside him; it was by these feelings that soldiers were usually constrained and held to their duty. Therefore on any calculation they ought to break out by day; although they might sustain some losses, nevertheless their objective could be gained with the main body of the army intact. This view prevailed in the council, and they decided to start out at first light next day.

(68) When the sky was light, Caesar, after reconnoitring the surrounding country, brought his entire force out of camp and led them in a wide circuit on no very definite line of march. The reason was that the routes which led to the Ebro and Otogesa were commanded by the enemy camp in his path. He had to struggle across very deep and difficult gullies,* and rocky bluffs blocked the way in many places, so that weapons had to be passed up from hand to hand and the soldiers completed a large part of their march un-armed, helping each other along. But none of them jibbed at this labour, because they reckoned it would be the end of all their labours, if they could cut the enemy off from the Ebro and prevent him getting corn.

(69) At first Afranius' soldiers ran delightedly out of camp to enjoy the sight, pursuing our men with insults, thinking they had been forced to turn tail for lack of the necessary food and were going back to Ilerda. Their route, of course, pointed away from their destination and it seemed they were marching in the opposite direction. The generals of the other side in fact congratulated themselves on their decision to stay in camp; and their opinion was much reinforced by the sight of men who had set out on a march without baggage animals or equipment, a thing which convinced them that it would not be possible for such a force to endure a shortage of food for very long. But when they saw the column bend back little by little to the right,* and noticed that its leaders were now more than abreast of their own camp, no one was so slow or lazy as not to realize that they had to go out and engage. The cry to arms was raised, and the whole force, with a few cohorts left behind on guard, marched out and hastened directly towards the Ebro.

(70) It was a contest that depended entirely on speed to decide which of the two first gained the pass and the mountains; but the difficulty of the terrain slowed Caesar's army down, while Afranius' troops were delayed by Caesar's pursuing cavalry. For the Afranians, however, things had inescapably reached the point where, if they were the first to reach the mountains they were making for, although they would be out of danger themselves, they would be unable to rescue any of the entire army's baggage or the cohorts left in camp; these would be cut off by Caesar's army beyond any possibility of help. Caesar reached the goal first, and after emerging from the steep and rocky ground on to the level, drew up a battle-line here facing the enemy. Afranius, with his rear under pressure from the cavalry, and the enemy in sight ahead, reached a hill and halted there. From this spot he sent four cohorts of Spanish light infantry towards the highest mountain in sight, with orders to proceed at great speed and seize it; his intention was to march there with his whole force and reach Otogesa by a different route along the ridge. As these cohorts approached their objective from the side, Caesar's cavalry saw them and attacked; the light

infantry were unable to resist the assault of the cavalry for more than a moment, and they were surrounded and killed to a man in sight of both armies.

(71) Here was an opportunity for a notable success. Caesar did not fail to realize that an army terrified by suffering such a loss under their very eyes would not be able to hold out, particularly when entirely surrounded by cavalry, if there was a battle on level and open ground; and this was what was demanded of him on all sides. Senior commanders, centurions, and officers ran to him, urging him not to hesitate to join battle and pointing out that every soldier was more than ready for it, while on the other hand the Afranians had indicated their fear in several ways: by failing to go to help their own men, by not leaving the hill, by barely withstanding the attacks of the cavalry, and by huddling together with their standards all in one place, preserving neither their ranks nor the identity of their units. If, on the other hand, he was afraid of the unfavourable slope, there would still be a chance of a battle somewhere, because inevitably lack of water would force Afranius to leave his position.

(72) Caesar had conceived the hope that he would be able to bring matters to a conclusion without fighting or shedding his men's blood, because he had cut his opponents off from food. Why should he lose any of his men, even if the battle were to go his way? Why should he allow men who had served him so splendidly to be wounded? And why should he tempt fortune, especially when it was a true general's duty to secure victory as much by strategy as by the sword? He was swayed too by pity for his fellow citizens, whom he was aware had to lose their lives; he would much prefer to gain his ends by preserving them safe and sound. This plan of Caesar's met with general disapproval, the soldiers indeed openly saying amongst themselves that since such a chance of victory was being thrown away they would not fight in future even when Caesar wanted them to. He persisted in his view, and moved away a little so that his opponents should feel less threatened. Given this opportunity, Petreius and Afranius retreated back to their camp.* Caesar posted detachments in the mountains, blocking every route

to the Ebro, and fortified a camp as close as possible to the enemy's.

Fraternization between the armies stopped by Afranius and Petreius

(73) On the next day the opposing generals, troubled because they had lost all hope of getting provisions and reaching the Ebro, considered what else they could do. They had to go one way if they wanted to return to Ilerda, and another if they were to make for Tarraco.* While they were considering the matter, news arrived that the men who were fetching water were being harassed by our cavalry. After investigating, they posted numerous cavalry pickets and interspersed both legionary and auxiliary cohorts between them. They then began to construct an earthwork from the camp to the water supply so that water could be fetched in security inside the fortification without the need for pickets. Petreius and Afranius divided this work between them, and in order to see it finished proceeded a considerable distance from the camp.

(74) Gaining by their commanders' absence the chance to communicate freely, the soldiers came out in crowds, looking for and calling out the names of any acquaintances or fellow townsmen they had in <Caesar's> camp. First they all thanked everyone, because on the day before they had spared them when they were panic-stricken: it was thanks to them that they were alive. They then enquired about the great general's* good faith, whether they were right to be thinking of entrusting themselves to him, and lamented because they had not done so at the start, and because they had fought against men who were their friends and kinsmen. Emboldened by these exchanges, they asked for an assurance from the great general that he would spare the lives of Petreius and Afranius, so that they should not appear guilty of criminal behaviour towards their own side or betrayal of their own people. This agreed, they confirmed that they would immediately bring their standards over, and sent some senior centurions to

negotiate peace with Caesar. Meanwhile some soldiers brought their friends into the camp to entertain them, and others were invited out by their friends, so much so that the two camps seemed now to have become one; and a number of officers and centurions came to Caesar and put themselves at his disposal, an action imitated by some leading Spaniards whom the Pompeians had summoned and had in camp with them, effectively as hostages. These looked for acquaintances and friends to make an introduction to ask for Caesar's favour. Even Afranius' adolescent son made a request to Caesar, through the latter's senior officer Sulpicius,* to grant safety to himself and to his father. The scene was one of general rejoicing and congratulation, both on the part of men who had escaped such great danger, and on the part of men who thought they had achieved such an important result without shedding blood; Caesar was on the point of reaping a great reward, as all agreed, for his earlier leniency,* and his tactics were approved by everyone.

(75) When this was reported, Afranius broke off the work he had begun and withdrew to the camp, prepared, so it seemed, to bear with equanimity whatever had occurred. Petreius, on the other hand, remained himself. He armed his slave attendants, and with these and his praetorian cohort* of Spanish light-armed and a few native cavalry detached for special duties, whom it was his practice to have as a bodyguard, he suddenly tore towards the rampart, interrupted the soldiers' talking, drove our men from the camp, and killed any he caught. The others gathered together and, alarmed by the sudden danger, wrapped their left hands in their cloaks* and drew their swords; in this way, trusting in the proximity of their camp, they protected themselves from the light infantry and the cavalry, retreated to camp, and were defended by the cohorts which were on guard at the gates.

(76) When the episode was over, Petreius, with tears in his eyes, went around the ranks and appealed to the soldiers, begging them not to deliver either himself or their absent general Pompey to their opponents for punishment. They quickly gathered in front of the commander's tent. He demanded that they all swear not to desert or betray their army or their

leaders, nor to decide individually what they would do. He himself was the first to take this oath; he also administered it to Afranius; the junior officers and centurions followed; and the soldiers came forward a company at a time to swear the same. A proclamation was made that anyone who had a Caesarian soldier with him should bring him forward, and those brought forward were executed publicly in front of the headquarters tent; but the majority were concealed by those who had taken them in and were smuggled out at night over the rampart. Thus the terror inspired by their commanders, the savagery of the punishment, and the sanction of the new oath removed any hope of immediate surrender and changed the attitude of the men, re-establishing the previous state of war.

(77) Caesar ordered any soldiers of the other side who had entered his camp during the period of fraternization to be searched for and sent back. But some of the group of junior officers and centurions stayed with him of their own accord. These he afterwards treated with great respect, restoring to the centurions their former rank, and to the Roman equestrians their officer status.

Surrender of the Pompeian army

(78) Afranius' men were finding it difficult to obtain animal fodder, and could hardly get water. The legionaries had a certain amount of corn, because they had been ordered to carry with them from Ilerda twenty-two [?] days' rations,* but the light infantry and the auxiliaries, whose opportunities for getting food were limited and whose bodies were unused to load-bearing, had none. Consequently every day a large number of them deserted to Caesar. Such was the situation in which they were trapped. But of the two plans proposed it seemed more straightforward to return to Ilerda, because they had left a little corn there, and there they were confident that they could work out the rest of their plan. Tarraco lay further away, and they realized that over this distance the project was more exposed to hazard. This plan

was agreed, and they set out from their camp. Caesar sent his cavalry on ahead to harry and impede the rear of the column, and himself followed with the legions. In no time the rearmost were fighting with the cavalry.

(79) The fighting was of this kind. Lightly armed cohorts brought up the rear of the column, and when the ground was level several of them stood fast. If a hill had to be climbed, the lie of the land easily kept the danger at bay, because those who were in the van occupied higher ground and protected their own men as they climbed; when a depression or a down-slope was met and those in the van were unable to assist those behind them, while on the other hand the cavalry were able to hurl their weapons from above at men who were facing away from them, then things were highly dangerous. When Afranius and Petreius approached a place of this sort, they had to resort to ordering the legions to halt in battle order and drive back the cavalry with a great charge; when this had been done they all suddenly sprinted down into the depression and after crossing it in this way halted again on the higher ground. So far from receiving any assistance from their own cavalry, of which they had a considerable number, they enclosed them in the middle of the column and actually protected them because they had lost their nerve as a result of previous encounters; it was not possible for any of them to move outside the line of march without being picked off by Caesar's cavalry.

(80) When fighting goes on in this way, progress is slow and gradual, and there are frequent halts to give assistance to one's men; as then happened. After advancing four miles, and becoming more violently harassed by the cavalry, Afranius' force took possession of a high hill and there fortified a camp on one side only, facing the enemy, without unloading their baggage animals. When they saw that Caesar had pitched camp and his tents were set up and his cavalry sent away to forage, they suddenly burst out around the middle of that same day and began to march on in the hope that pursuit would be delayed because our cavalry had left camp. On seeing this, Caesar followed with his legions refreshed, leaving a few cohorts to guard the baggage; he gave

orders that <these> should follow late in the afternoon, and that the foragers should be recalled. The cavalry returned with all speed to their daily duty during the march. The fighting was so intense at the rear of the column that the enemy almost turned tail, and a number of soldiers and even some centurions were killed. Caesar's column was pressing them hard and menacing them all along its length.

(81) Then they did indeed have to stop, without the opportunity either of looking for a suitable spot for a camp or of going any further, and they made camp a long way from water and on naturally unfavourable ground. But for the same reasons as explained above Caesar made no attempt to engage them, neither did he permit tents to be erected that day, so that his men should be all the readier to give chase, whether the enemy made their break at night or in daytime. His opponents, who were aware how unsuitable their camp-site was, pushed their defences forward all night and kept exchanging one camp for another. They did the same from dawn on the following day and spent the entire day in this activity. But the further they advanced by entrenchment and pushing their camp forward, the further they were from water: by trying to cure their present predicament they were incurring others. On the first night no one left camp to fetch water; on the next day they left a guard in camp and led out their whole force to water, but no one was sent out to forage. Caesar preferred to see them racked by these sufferings and submit to the inevitable surrender than to finish the campaign by battle. However, he made an effort to surround them with a ditch and rampart, in order to impede, so far as he could, any sudden sallies on their part; these, he thought, must be their last resort. His opponents, driven to it by lack of fodder and because they wished to be less encumbered on the march, ordered all their beasts of burden to be slaughtered.

(82) Two days were consumed in these stratagems and works of entrenchment; by the third day a great part of Caesar's earthwork was finished. The opposition, to impede its completion, gave the signal and led out their legions in the middle of the afternoon, forming up in battle order below their camp. Caesar recalled his legions from fortification

work, ordered all his cavalry to gather, and drew up a battle-line; for any appearance of avoiding battle in the face of the feelings of the soldiers and the reputation he enjoyed in the eyes of all would have seriously undermined his position. But he was swayed by reasons already explained against any desire to fight, and all the more so because the restricted space could be of little help in securing a decisive victory even if his adversaries were put to flight. For there were no more than three thousand metres between the two camps, and of this space, two-thirds were occupied by the two battle formations and one-third remained empty for the soldiers to advance and attack. If battle were joined, the proximity of their camp would afford the losers an immediate refuge in their flight. For this reason he had decided to resist if the enemy attacked, but not to initiate hostilities.

(83) Afranius' battle order was a double line formed of his five legions, with the third, reserve, line made up of the auxiliary cohorts; Caesar's line was triple; but four cohorts from each of the five legions formed the first rank, backed up by three from each and then three again; archers and slingers were enclosed in the middle of the line, and the cavalry en-closed the flanks. Once these formations had been adopted, both men thought they were achieving their purpose: Caesar to avoid battle unless it were forced on him, his opponent to do likewise with the aim of impeding Caesar's fortification work. The confrontation was nevertheless prolonged and the men remained in battle order until sunset; then both sides went back to camp. On the following day* Caesar prepared to complete the fortifications he had in hand, his opponents to try a ford in the River Segre,* to discover if they could cross. On seeing this, Caesar sent some German light-armed and a part of his cavalry across the river and set up a series of guard-posts along the banks.

(84) At last, cut off from everything, their animals kept in camp for the fourth day now without grazing, and short of water, fuel, and food, Caesar's opponents asked to nego-tiate, if possible in a place away from the troops. When Caesar refused this request, but allowed them, if they wished, to negotiate in public, Afranius' son was delivered to Caesar

as a hostage. The meeting then took place in a spot chosen by Caesar. Afranius spoke in front of both armies: he said that neither they themselves nor their soldiers ought to be the objects of anger because they had wished to remain loyal to their general Gnaeus Pompeius. But they had done their duty and had suffered enough punishment: they had put up with lack of everything; and now, almost as though they were wild beasts, they were walled in, kept from water, and kept from moving, and their bodies could not stand the suffering nor their spirits the disgrace. And so they admitted they were beaten; they begged and entreated, if there were any place left for pity, that it would not be necessary for Caesar to apply the ultimate punishment.* This was the case Afranius put as humbly and unassertively as possible.

(85) To this Caesar replied that no one in the world was less well suited to make these complaints and these appeals for pity. Everyone else had done their duty: <he himself>, by his unwillingness to fight even when circumstance, place, and time had been favourable, so that the chances of peace should remain as high as possible; his own army, by saving and protecting those who were in its power when it had been wronged and its men killed; and finally, the soldiers of the other army, by taking the initiative in negotiating for peace, a course which they considered they had to adopt to secure their common safety. Thus compassion had guided the roles of all, no matter what their rank. It was the leaders themselves who had shrunk from peace. They had not respected the rules either of negotiations or of a truce, and they had brutally put to death men who were caught unawares and had been misled by the negotiations. As a consequence there had happened to them what very often happens to men who are excessively stubborn and arrogant, namely that they turn back to and seek passionately what they have just spurned. He was not now going to exploit either their abject condition, or any opportunity offered by the circumstances, in order to build up his own resources; but he wanted the armies which they had sustained against him for many years to be disbanded. There was no other reason for which six legions had been sent to Spain and a seventh raised there,

nor such large auxiliary contingents raised, nor militarily experienced commanders sent out to them. None of this had anything to do with the pacification of Spain, nor had any of it been designed for the purposes of a province which thanks to a long period of peace needed no protection,* but it had all been aimed for a long time past at himself; it was against him that new sorts of command had been invented, so that the same man could preside at the gates of Rome over the affairs of the city and also be absentee governor* for so many years of two of the most bellicose provinces; it was to counter himself that the rules for holding magistracies had been changed,* so that men were sent out to the provinces not directly after their praetorships or consulships, as had always been the case, but as approved and chosen by a narrow group; to oppose him, the excuse of age was not accepted, as witness the fact that men who had proved themselves in previous campaigns were called out of retirement to command armies; in his case alone the practice had not been maintained that had always been observed for all other victorious generals, that after gaining their successes they returned home, either with some degree of honour or certainly without disgrace, to dismiss their armies. None the less, he had borne and would continue to bear all this with patience; and he was not now going to act so as to keep for himself the army he had taken from them, easy though that might be, but to ensure that they should not have one to use against him. Accordingly, as had been proposed, they should leave their provinces and dismiss their army; if that were done, he would harm no one. This was his single and final condition for peace.

(86) It was indeed extremely welcome and agreeable to the soldiers, as could be gathered from the way they showed their reactions, that men who had expected some not unjustified penalty should win the reward of discharge without even asking for it. When argument arose about the time and place of discharge, they all began to indicate by shouting and waving from the rampart (where they had taken their places) that they should be discharged immediately, and that no guarantee, however good, could make the promise valid, if their

discharge were to be put off. After brief debate of both views, the position was reached that those who had a home or property in Spain would be discharged at once, and the others at the River Var; Caesar gave his word that they would not suffer any harm and that no one would be compelled to enlist against his will.

(87) Caesar promised to provide food from then until they reached the Var. He added that if anyone had suffered any losses in the war, he would restore whatever his soldiers might have in their possession to its owners; he compensated his soldiers on a fair cash valuation for these items. If the soldiers had any disputes amongst themselves after this, they came to Caesar of their own accord for a decision. When Petreius and Afranius were faced with a near-mutiny by their legions demanding pay, which according to their commanders was not yet due, a request was made for Caesar to settle the matter, and both sides were happy with his decision. After about a third of the army had been discharged on that day and the next, he gave orders that two of his own legions should take the lead, and the remainder follow, in such a way as to make camp not far from each other, and he placed his senior officer Quintus Fufius Calenus in charge of this operation. The march was made from Spain to the Var according to these instructions of his, and there the remainder of the army was discharged.

Book II

Siege and surrender of Massilia (1–16, 22). Defeat of Varro (17–21). Curio's disaster in Africa (23–44)

Trebonius' initial siege operations against Massilia

(1) While this was happening in Spain, Caesar's deputy Gaius Trebonius, who had been left to conduct the attack on Massilia, began to construct a siege-ramp, siege-sheds, and towers against the town in two places. One was next to the port and the ship-sheds, the other by the gate to Gaul and Spain, beside the sea that adjoins the mouth of the Rhône. Massilia, roughly speaking, is washed by the sea on three sides;* on the fourth and last side it can be approached by land. Here too, the part which constitutes the citadel is protected by its situation and by a very deep valley, and this makes any attack long and difficult. To complete these siege-works Trebonius called up a huge number of men and pack-animals from all over the province, and gave orders for timber and bundles of osier to be brought in. When these were ready he constructed a siege-ramp eighty feet high.*

(2) But so great was the store of every sort of military equipment long held in the town, and so great the mass of artillery,* that no siege-screens of woven osier could possibly resist them. Twelve-foot shafts, sheathed with metal points and fired from the largest catapults, would drive into the earth after passing through four layers of hurdles. And so galleries were constructed with foot-square beams fastened together, and in this way material for the siege-ramp was passed forward from man to man. In front, to level the ground, there went a sixty-foot 'tortoise'* similarly made from massive timbers, and draped with every device to protect it from fire and the impact of stones. But the scale of the siege-works, the height of the wall and towers, and the quantity of artillery slowed down the whole operation. Also the Albici* made frequent sallies from the town and

attempted to set fire to the siege-ramp and towers; our soldiers easily beat off these attempts, and drove those who
had made the sally back into the town, inflicting great losses
in return.

The second sea-battle off Massilia

(3) Meanwhile Pompey sent Lucius Nasidius with a fleet of
sixteen ships, amongst them a few warships, to help Lucius
Domitius and the Massiliots; he went by way of the Sicilian
straits, taking Curio,* who was being insufficiently careful,
by surprise. He landed at Messana, where resistance collapsed
as a result of a sudden panic on the part of the leading citizens and council, and he got a ship launched from the docks.
He added this to his others, and completed his voyage to
the neighbourhood of Massilia, where he secretly sent on a
boat to inform Domitius and the Massiliots of his arrival and
urge them most strongly to use the help of his reinforcements to try another battle with Brutus' fleet.

(4) The Massiliots, after their earlier reverse, had repaired
old ships which they brought out of their sheds to bring
their fleet up to its previous size. They had put much energy into putting them into a state to fight (they had plenty
of oarsmen and captains), and had increased their numbers
with fishing boats which they had decked to keep the oarsmen safe from the impact of missiles. All these they manned
with archers and equipped with artillery. When a fleet had
been got ready in this way, they embarked with no less
courage and confidence than they had before their previous
battle,* spurred on by the tears and entreaties of the older
men, the women, and the girls, who all begged them to help
the city in its hour of crisis. It is a common failing of human
nature to be more confident in strange and unprecedented
circumstances, as happened on this occasion; for Nasidius'
arrival had filled Massilia with hope and enthusiasm. When
they had a favourable wind, they came out of port and reached
Nasidius at Tauroeis,* a fortified outpost of Massilia; there
they got their ships ready and for a second time prepared

themselves mentally for battle and discussed their plans. The Massiliots took the right wing, Nasidius the left.

(5) Brutus hurried to the same spot with an increased number of ships. In addition to those which had been built at Arelate on Caesar's instructions, he had acquired six by capture from the Massiliots. These he had repaired and fully equipped during the intervening days. So exhorting his men to despise, as already beaten, opponents they had defeated when at full strength, he sailed out against them full of hope and courage. From Trebonius' camp and every piece of high ground it was easy to look over the city and see how all the young people who had remained in the town, and all those of more advanced years, together with the children and wives and men posted as guards, either stretched their hands out to heaven from the wall, or went to the temples of the immortals and threw themselves down in front of their images to implore victory from the gods. There was not a soul who did not believe that the outcome of that day's fight would determine the fortunes of all of them. The young men of good family, and the most distinguished men of any age, had been individually called up and entreated to serve, and had embarked; so that if things turned out badly, they all saw that there was nothing else left to try; but if victory should be theirs, they trusted that the city would be saved either by its own resources or with outside help.

(6) When the battle began, the Massiliots showed no lack of courage; on the contrary, remembering the exhortations they had just heard from their families and friends, they fought in a way that suggested that this was their last chance, and that those who found their lives in danger in the fight thought they were anticipating by very little what lay in store for the rest of their townspeople, on whom the fortune of war would inflict a similar fate. As our ships gradually became separated from each other, the skill of the Massiliot captains and the manœuvrability of their ships was given room, and if our side seized a chance of grappling and holding a ship alongside, the Massiliots came to its assistance from all directions. And when the ships did lie together,* the Albici were neither reluctant to fight hand-to-hand nor much

inferior in courage to our men. At the same time a great hail of missiles thrown from the smaller boats caused many injuries to our men who were unprepared, encumbered, and taken by surprise. Two triremes, spotting Decimus Brutus' ship which was recognizable by its flag, raced from opposite directions towards it. But as Brutus was on his guard against the manœuvre, his ship was quick enough to slip from between them with only a few moments in hand. The triremes, travelling fast, collided with each other so heavily that they both suffered severe damage from the impact, and one of them had her ram broken off and was in a state of collapse. Observing this, the nearest ships of Brutus' fleet attacked them in this tangle and rapidly sank them both.

(7) Nasidius' ships, however, were useless and quickly withdrew from the fighting; no sight of native land, no exhortations of families and friends forced them to risk their lives. And so none of them were lost; from the Massiliot fleet five were sunk, four captured, and one escaped with Nasidius' squadron; these latter all sailed off to Nearer Spain. As one of the other ships, which had been sent on ahead to Massilia with the news, approached the city, a great crowd poured out to find out the result, and when they knew it their grief was so great that one might have thought the city had been captured that very moment by the enemy. But all the same the Massiliots began to make their remaining preparations for defending the city.

Further siege-works, leading to first surrender and renewed resistance of the Massiliots

(8) As a result of the frequent sallies made by the enemy, the legionaries who were working on the right-hand portion of the siege-works noticed that they would have much better protection if they were to make there, under the wall, a brick tower to serve as a fort and refuge. This they first made low and small, for use in case of sudden attacks. To it they used to retreat; from it they used to offer resistance, if superior forces had overwhelmed them; and from it they

used to dash forward to drive off and chase the enemy. It was thirty feet square, but the walls were five feet thick. Later, though, learning as usual by experience, and applying their own ingenuity, they realized that it would be a great advantage if it were built up to the height of a tower.* This was done in the following way.

(9) When the tower had been built sufficiently high for the first floor to be put in, they fitted this into the walls in such a way that the ends of the beams were covered by the outermost skin of wall, so that nothing showed which the enemy's fire could lay hold of. On top of this floor, they built the brick up as far as the roof of the siege-shed and screens* allowed, and above that they laid from side to side, not far from the ends of the walls, two beams to support the deck which was going to cover the tower, and placed on these beams timbers running from front to back which they fastened together with planks. They made these timbers slightly longer, projecting a little beyond the face of the wall, so that there would be some points from which coverings could be hung in front to absorb and keep off hits while the walls were being built below this deck; they covered its planked top with a layer of bricks and clay to make it proof against attack with fire, and on top again they put padded quilts so that the bolts of the artillery could not smash through the timber, nor the stones of the catapults break up the brickwork. They made mats from anchor rope, the length of the walls of the tower and four feet wide, and tied them to hang around the tower from the projecting timbers on the three sides which faced the enemy; this was the only sort of protection, as they had proved elsewhere, through which no weapon or artillery missile could pass. When the part of the tower which had been completed was roofed and armoured against every sort of enemy projectile, they removed the siege-sheds to other duties; then taking the weight of the tower's roof, which formed a separate unit, on lifting devices placed on the first floor, they started to jack it up. When they had raised it as far as the fall of the rope mats allowed, concealed and secure inside this protection they went on constructing the brick walls, then jacked it up again to make further room

for themselves to build. When it seemed time for another floor, they put in beams as they had done at first, with their ends covered by the outer skin of bricks, and from this floor they again went on raising the top covering and the mats. In this way, safe and completely free from injury and danger, they constructed six storeys, leaving apertures for artillery in appropriate places as they built.

(10) When they were sure that from this tower they could protect any nearby siege-works, they started to construct, from two-foot square timber, a gallery sixty feet long to lead from the brick tower to the enemy wall and tower.* The gallery was like this: first two baulks of equal length were laid on the ground four feet apart, and into them were inserted uprights five feet high. These were connected by low-pitched trusses, on which were to be placed the beams to roof the gallery. There, on top, they laid two-foot-square beams and fastened them with nails and metal plates. At the edge of the roof of the gallery and the outermost beams, they fixed three-inch wide strips to hold the bricks which were to be laid on top of the gallery. The gallery was thus given a pitch to its roof and properly put together, and when the beams had been placed on the trusses it was covered with bricks and clay to make it safe from the fire being hurled from the wall. On top of the bricks hides were stretched to stop water sprayed from pipes washing them to pieces.* And the hides, for protection in turn against fire and the impact of stone, were covered with quilts.* They completed this whole work close by the tower under the shelter of screens; then when the enemy were off guard, they put rollers underneath it and suddenly moved it up to the enemy tower so as to abut it.

(11) Panic-stricken by this sudden reverse the defenders used crowbars to bring up the largest pieces of stone they could, and tipped these forward off the wall on to the gallery. The strength of the timber stood up to the impact, and everything that fell on the pitched roof of the gallery slid off. Seeing this, the defenders changed their plan. They set light to barrels full of pitch and pine-shavings and rolled these from the wall on to the gallery. The barrels spun along it and rolled

off, and when they reached the ground they were pushed away from the sides of the structure with forks and poles. Meanwhile under the gallery the soldiers were levering away the lowest stones which formed the foundations of the enemy tower. Our side protected the gallery by firing javelins and artillery bolts from the brick tower, so that the enemy were driven from their wall and towers and given no real chance of defending the wall. By now a good number of stones had been removed from under the adjacent tower, and when suddenly a part of it collapsed and the rest of it in consequence was on the point of doing so, the enemy, terrified by the thought of a sack of their city, all poured out of the gate, unarmed and with the sacred ribbons* of suppliants tied around their foreheads, stretching out their hands for mercy to the officers and army.

(12) In the face of this new development, all military activity stopped and the soldiers turned from fighting, eager to listen and discover what was happening. When the enemy reached the senior officers and army, they all threw themselves at their feet and begged them to wait for Caesar's arrival. They said that they saw their city had been taken; that the siege-works were complete, and their tower undermined; and so they were abandoning resistance. Nothing could occur to stop an immediate and total sack if, when he arrived, they did not obey his orders to the letter. They argued that if the tower had completely collapsed the soldiers could not have been prevented from bursting into the city in the hope of booty, and destroying it. This and much else of the same sort, as might be expected from highly educated men,* was delivered with great pathos and plentiful tears.

(13) Moved by all this, the officers withdrew their men from the siege operations and stopped the attack, leaving guards on the siege-works. From compassion, a species of truce was granted, and Caesar's arrival awaited. No weapon was thrown from the wall, no weapon from our side; everyone relaxed and became careless, as if the siege was over. Caesar had in fact sent the most strict instructions to Trebonius not to let the city be taken by force, in case the soldiers, incensed by the Massiliot treachery and contempt* for them, and by their prolonged labours, should kill all the

adults; they were threatening to do this, and were with difficulty restrained from bursting into the city, being much annoyed because it was apparently Trebonius' fault that they were not masters of the town.

(14) The enemy, on the other hand, deceitfully looked for the right moment for an act of treacherous cunning.* After an interval of a few days our men were relaxed and unconcerned, and one midday, when some soldiers had gone off duty and some were resting from their daily tasks at the siege-works themselves, and all their weapons and armour were laid aside and wrapped up, the enemy suddenly burst out of the gates and in a strong and favourable wind set fire to the siege-works. The wind spread the flames to such effect that a ramp, siege-sheds, the 'tortoise', a tower, and artillery caught fire simultaneously and were all destroyed before anyone realized how it had happened. Our men responded to this sudden blow of fortune by seizing what weapons they could, and others rushed from camp. They attacked the enemy but were prevented from pursuing them as they withdrew by arrows and bolts fired from the wall. The enemy retreated beneath the wall where they had a free hand to burn the gallery and the brick tower. In this way the labour of many months was destroyed in a moment by the treachery of the enemy and the force of the gale. The Massiliots attempted exactly the same thing on the next day. With the same gale blowing, they sallied out and fought with greater confidence at the other tower and siege-ramp and set fire to them at many points. But just as earlier our men had completely relaxed their previous concentration, so now they had learnt their lesson from the events of the day before and had thoroughly prepared their defence. As a result they killed many of the enemy and drove the others back unsuccessful to the town.

(15) Trebonius began to take his losses in hand and make them good, with greatly increased determination on the part of his soldiers. They saw that their immense efforts and preparations had come to nothing, and were bitter that a mockery had been made of their courage by the criminal violation of the truce; and so, because no material was available anywhere to build a ramp, since all the trees far and wide throughout the territory of Massilia had been cut down

and brought in, they began to make a ramp of a new and unprecedented sort by laying two brick walls six feet thick and bridging these walls with a timber roof; this ramp was of about the same breadth as the previous solid ramp. When either the distance between the walls or the weakness of the timber seemed to demand it, uprights were placed in between and cross beams laid on them to support the structure, and the roofed parts were covered with wicker hurdles and coated with clay. In the space beneath this roof the men, protected to left and right by the walls and in front by the advanced siege-shed, quite safely brought forward whatever was required for the construction. Progress was swift; by the ingenuity and courage of the soldiers the lost fruits of their long-drawn-out labours were soon regained. Doorways were left in the walls at suitable spots to allow sallies.

(16) When the enemy saw that the damage, which they had hoped could not be repaired for a long time and without considerable delay, had been made good by a few days' toil and exertion in such a way that there was no opportunity for deception or sallies, and no means at all remained of injuring either the soldiers with weapons or the siege-works with fire; when, by the same token, they became aware that the whole city could be encircled on the landward side by a wall and towers, so that they would have no chance of standing firm at their own defences because their fortifications seemed to have been virtually enclosed in building by our army, and were within range of weapons thrown by hand; and when they realized that owing to the shortness of the range* their own artillery, on which they rested their hopes, had become useless, and that once the fighting was conducted on equal terms from wall and towers they could not match our men in strength and courage, they requested the same conditions again for surrender.

Varro surrenders to Caesar in Further Spain

(17) When Marcus Varro* in Further Spain initially learnt what had happened in Italy he had little confidence in the

Pompeian cause and spoke of Caesar in the most friendly terms: he said his position was predetermined by the command he held on Pompey's behalf and that he was bound by loyalty; however, he also enjoyed no less a degree of friendship with Caesar, and he was perfectly well aware what the duties were of a deputy holding a position of trust, what forces were available to him, and how the whole province felt towards Caesar. Such was the tone of all his conversations, and he made no move towards either side. But later he learnt that Caesar was held up at Massilia, that Petreius' forces had joined Afranius' army, and that large auxiliary contingents had gathered while as many more were hoped for and expected; he also realized that the whole of Nearer Spain was unanimous for Pompey, and when the news reached him of the difficulties that had later occurred over the food supplies at Ilerda, a crisis much exaggerated to him by Afranius, he too began to dance to Fortune's tune.

(18) He conducted a levy throughout the province, brought his two legions up to strength, and added about thirty auxiliary cohorts to them. He requisitioned a large quantity of grain to send to Massilia and also to Afranius and Petreius. He instructed the people of Gades to build ten warships and had several more built at Hispalis. He brought all the money and treasures from the shrine of Hercules into Gades, and sent six cohorts from the province to guard that town; in charge of it he placed Gaius Gallonius, a Roman equestrian who was an associate of Domitius and had been sent there by Domitius to see to a legacy; and he collected all privately and publicly owned weapons in Gallonius' house. He himself spoke against Caesar at public gatherings. From his official platform he more than once announced that Caesar had suffered a reverse and that large numbers of his men had deserted to Afranius, alleging that he had discovered these facts from reliable reports and reliable authorities. By these means he frightened the Roman citizens of the province and forced them to promise to contribute to the public account 18 million sesterces and 20,000 pounds of silver, and 120,000 bushels of wheat. He imposed harsher burdens on those communities he suspected of favouring Caesar, and sent for trial

ordinary citizens who might have spoken, whether privately or publicly, against the interests of the state;* the property of these people was confiscated. He began making the entire province swear an oath of loyalty to himself and Pompey. On learning of the course of events in Nearer Spain, he prepared to fight. His plan was to take himself to Gades with the two legions, and keep his ships and all his food supplies there, because he had realized that the entire province supported Caesar. On an island,* with food and ships to hand, he did not consider it difficult to drag out the campaign.

Caesar had many urgent matters which were calling him back to Rome, but had decided to leave no trace of war in the two Spanish provinces, because he knew that Pompey had done many favours and exercised extensive patronage in the Nearer one. (19) He therefore sent two legions to Further Spain with Quintus Cassius, tribune of the people,* while he himself went ahead with six hundred cavalry by forced marches, sending on an edict announcing the day on which he wished the magistrates and leading citizens of every community to be ready to meet him in Corduba. After this edict had been published all over the province there was not a community that did not send members of its council to Corduba at the right time, not a single Roman citizen of any standing who did not gather on the day. At the same time the association of Roman citizens* at Corduba closed the gates against Varro on its own initiative and stationed guards and lookouts on the towers and wall; they also detained two cohorts of the sort called 'settler',* which arrived there by chance, to protect the town. At about the same time the people of Carmo, by far the best fortified township of the whole province, spontaneously ejected a garrison of three cohorts which had been put into the citadel by Varro, and shut the gates against them.

(20) Because of this Varro hurried all the more to make for Gades with his legions as soon as possible, so strong and so favourable to Caesar were the feelings of the province found to be. When he had gone a little further a letter from Gades informed him that as soon as the news of Caesar's edict became known, the leading citizens of Gades had

agreed with the officers of the cohorts of the garrison there to expel Gallonius from the town and hold the city and island for Caesar. After adopting this plan they had invited Gallonius to leave Gades voluntarily while he could safely do so; if he refused, they would act as they thought best. Thus frightened, Gallonius had quitted the town. When this news became known, one of the two legions, called the local one,* pulled up its standards, marched out of Varro's camp under his very eyes, and withdrew to Hispalis where the men stayed in the town square and colonnades without harming anyone. The local association of Roman citizens approved of this behaviour so much that they vied with one another to offer the soldiers the hospitality of their homes. These events caused Varro to panic, and after turning back on his line of march he sent ahead to Italica to announce his arrival, when he was informed by his staff that the gates had been shut against him. Then finally, with every destination barred, he sent a message to Caesar that he was ready to hand over the legion to anyone he might name. Caesar sent him Sextus Caesar and ordered the handover to be made to him. When this had been done, Varro came to Caesar at Corduba; he gave his word for the correctness of the accounts he presented of the public finances, handed over the money which was with him, and made a statement of what ships and food supplies he had anywhere.

(21) Caesar called a public meeting in Corduba and expressed his thanks to all in their various categories: to the Romans because they had made an effort to keep the town in their own control, to the Spaniards because they had expelled the garrisons, to the people of Gades because they had sabotaged the efforts of their opponents and had asserted their own freedom, to the officers and centurions who had come to Gades to garrison it because they had courageously supported the plans of the townspeople. He remitted the contributions which the Romans had promised Varro they would pay to the treasury, and restored the property of those he had discovered to have suffered this penalty for speaking too freely. To some he granted rewards, both public and private, and to the others held out the hope of benefits to come, and

after staying two days in Corduba set out for Gades; there
he ordered the money and treasures which had been transferred to a private house to be taken back to the temple.
He put Quintus Cassius in charge of the province and gave
him the four legions.* He himself reached Tarraco in a few
days with the ships which Varro, and the people of Gades
on Varro's orders, had built. There delegations from almost
the entire Nearer province were waiting for him. He followed
the same pattern of distributing honours, both private and
public, to various communities, and after leaving Tarraco
travelled by land to Narbo and thence to Massilia.* There
he heard that a law had been passed about the appointment
of a dictator* and that he had been named dictator by the
praetor Marcus Lepidus.

Final surrender of Massilia to Caesar

(22) The Massiliots, exhausted by all their sufferings, their
food running critically low, twice defeated at sea, unsuccessful in numerous sallies, ravaged by disease on account of the
long blockade and change of diet (they were all living off
old millet and rotting barley, which they had contributed
long ago to the public provision against such an event), their
tower ruined, long stretches of their walls seriously weakened,
and without hope of assistance from provinces or armies
which they had learnt had come under Caesar's control,
decided to surrender in good faith. However, a few days
previously Domitius, when he became aware of the wishes
of the Massiliots, had made ready three ships. He put two
of these under the command of his personal friends, embarked on the third himself, and took advantage of some wild
weather to set out. The ships which on Brutus' orders were
keeping their usual daily watch off the port spotted him,
hoisted anchor, and set off in pursuit. Of the three, Domitius'
own vessel made a great effort and continued its escape, and
with the help of the storm disappeared from sight, but the
other two were frightened by the encounter with our ships
and went back to port. The Massiliots, as instructed, brought
their weapons and artillery out of the town, took their ships

out of the port and the ship-sheds, and handed over the money in their treasury. When this had been done, Caesar spared them, more in accordance with the fame and antiquity of their state than with what they deserved of himself. He left two legions there as a garrison and sent the others to Italy, while he himself set off for Rome.

Expedition of Curio to Africa, and his defeat near Utica by King Juba

(23) Concurrently with these events* Gaius Curio set out from Sicily for Africa, and since from the start he had a poor opinion of the forces of Publius Attius Varus, he took across only two legions out of the four he had been given by Caesar, and five hundred cavalry. After a voyage of two days and three nights he landed at a place called Anquillaria. This place is twenty-two miles from Clupea, possesses an anchorage that is quite convenient in summer, and is enclosed by two headlands. Young Lucius Caesar* had been waiting for him off Clupea with ten warships (these being ships which had been hauled out at Utica after the war with the pirates* and been repaired for this war on Attius Varus' orders), but he had taken fright at the size of Curio's fleet and abandoned the open sea; he had driven his decked trireme ashore on the nearest beach, left it there, and fled by land to Hadrumetum, a town which was held by Gaius Considius Longus with a garrison of one legion. On Caesar's flight, the rest of his squadron withdrew to Hadrumetum. The quaestor Marcius Rufus gave chase with twelve ships which Curio had brought out from Sicily to guard the transport vessels, and when he noticed the ship left on the shore he towed it off, and himself rejoined Curio with his squadron.

(24) Curio sent Marcius ahead to Utica with the ships, while he himself made for the same place with his army, reaching the River Bagradas after two days' march. There he left his deputy Gaius Caninius Rebilus in command of the legions, and went ahead himself with the cavalry to reconnoitre Scipio's Camp,* because the site was considered perfect for a

camp. It is a level ridge jutting into the sea, steep and difficult on both sides, but with a slightly more gentle slope on the side towards Utica. As the crow flies, it is rather more than a mile from Utica, but there is a spring in the way, to which the sea comes up from a fair distance; the ground is boggy over a wide area, and anyone who wants to avoid it has a six-mile detour to reach the town.

(25) After inspecting the place Curio observed Varus' camp which lay alongside the town wall at the gate named after Baal; it was quite well protected by the nature of its site, having on one side the town of Utica itself, on the other the theatre (which is outside the town), which with its massive supporting walls gave a difficult, constricted, approach to the camp. At the same time he noticed that the roads were packed with people carrying or driving great quantities of the sorts of things which are brought into town from the countryside when fear of war suddenly strikes. He sent his cavalry off in that direction to pillage and have something to call booty; and simultaneously Varus dispatched from the town, to help these people, six hundred Numidian horse and four hundred infantry, whom King Juba had sent as aid to Utica a few days previously. The king had been influenced by ties of friendship with Pompey which he had inherited from his father, and by enmity with Curio,* who as tribune had proposed a law which made Juba's kingdom the property of the Roman people. The cavalry charged each other; but the Numidians were unable to stand up to the first shock of our attack and after losing a hundred and twenty dead the rest retreated to their camp beside the town.

Meanwhile the warships arrived and Curio ordered a proclamation to be made to the merchant vessels, of which about two hundred were at anchor at Utica, that he would regard as hostile those who did not forthwith bring their ships over to Scipio's Camp. When this proclamation had been made, they all immediately weighed anchor, left Utica, and came over as ordered. This manœuvre gained the army supplies of every kind.

(26) After these exploits, Curio went back to the camp at the Bagradas and was hailed as 'Victorious General'* by the

whole army, and on the following day led his army to Utica and encamped near the city. While the camp was still being fortified the cavalry outposts brought news that large reinforcements of infantry and cavalry sent by the king were on their way to Utica; at the same time a great cloud of dust was seen and in a moment the head of the column appeared. Curio, who was disturbed by the unexpectedness of this, sent his cavalry forward to absorb the first assault and delay the attackers, while he himself quickly took the legions off the fortification work and drew them up in battle order. The cavalry engaged, and before the legions could fully deploy and take up their positions had put to flight all the king's reinforcements (who were encumbered with baggage and thrown into confusion because they had been travelling confidently and in no sort of order), and killed a large number of infantry; the enemy cavalry escaped practically unhurt because they rapidly fled along the shore to the town.

(27) The following night two Marsic centurions with twenty-two of their men deserted from Curio's camp to Attius Varus. Whether they communicated their true opinion to him, or whether they told Varus what he wished to hear (for we are both ready to believe the things we want to believe, and also hope other people feel what we feel ourselves), at any rate they definitely asserted that Curio did not have the support of any of his army and that it was vitally important for Varus to show himself to the army and offer them the opportunity of negotiation. Under the influence of these views Varus led his legions out of camp early the next day. Curio did the same, and they both drew up their forces separated by a single small valley.

(28) Present in Varus' army was Sextus Quintilius Varus, who had been at Corfinium, as mentioned above.* On being released by Caesar he had come to Africa, while Curio had brought across the legions which Caesar had earlier taken into his army at Corfinium in a state in which they retained, with the alteration of a few centurions, their original structure of ranks and companies. Seizing this chance of making an appeal, Quintilius began to go round Curio's ranks and beg the soldiers not to put aside the memory of their first

oath,* which they had sworn before Domitius and himself as quaestor, nor to bear arms against men who had shared the same fortunes and endured the same hardships in the siege, nor to fight for those by whom they had been insultingly labelled deserters. To this he added a few words to raise the hope of a cash payment which they could expect out of his generosity if they chose to follow himself and Attius. After he had finished speaking, there was no reaction from Curio's army, and so both withdrew their forces.

(29) But in Curio's camp they all began to be very frightened, and their fear grew rapidly as they talked amongst themselves. Each one of them gave his imagination play and added something of his own fright to what he had heard from someone else. When this had spread from its original author to a larger group, and they had passed it from one to another, there seemed to be wide authority for it. *Civil war ... the sort of men ... freely doing what they liked and seeking what they wanted ... these legions which had very recently been on the opposing side ... for Caesar's favour to them had also altered ... the practice by which they were being offered ... their towns also connected with the different sides ... nor had they come from the Marsi and Paeligni as men who on the night before in their tents ... and some fellow soldiers ... more serious matters ... talk amongst the soldiers ... what was uncertain was interpreted for the worse ...* Some details too were invented by those who wished to seem better informed.

(30) For these reasons Curio called a council and began to consider his general strategy. Opinions were expressed in favour of making every possible effort and attacking Varus' camp, because <when> soldiers were contemplating moves of this sort, idleness was the most harmful thing of all; they said that it was better, in the end, to try the fortune of war by being brave in battle than to be deserted and thwarted by their own men and suffer the ultimate punishment. Some thought that they should retreat to Scipio's Camp during the latter part of the night, to give the men a longer interval to come to their senses; at the same time, should any more serious setback occur, the large number of ships there would allow them to withdraw to Sicily with greater ease and safety.

(31) Curio disapproved of both plans, saying that what the one lacked in spirit the other possessed to excess: one side were planning a highly discreditable withdrawal, the other thought they ought to fight even when the ground was unfavourable. 'What confidence can we have', he said, 'that it is possible to storm a camp whose defences, both natural and man-made, are so strong? And where is the advantage, if we suffer great losses and have to abandon our attack on the camp? You forget that it is success that earns generals the goodwill of their armies, and failure their loathing. Does a move of camp mean anything other than ignominious retreat, lack of any hope, and disaffection among the troops? Good soldiers should not suspect they are distrusted, nor bad soldiers know they are feared, because the fear we feel provokes greater insubordination among the latter and erodes the loyalty of the former. But if', he said, 'we were now quite certain of what is being said about the disaffection in the army (and I think this is either quite untrue or at the least much exaggerated) would it not be better for it to be suppressed, and not admitted, than reinforced by our own actions? Surely it is true that the defects of an army, like the wounds on a body, should be concealed so as not to encourage the enemy? Furthermore, the advocates of this course add that we should set out in the middle of the night, in order, I suppose, that any who try criminal behaviour may have more freedom. For actions of that sort are held in check either by fear or by a sense of shame, and darkness is particularly hostile to both. Consequently I am neither so brave as to think we ought to make a hopeless assault on the camp, nor so timid as to give up hope; I think we should first try every alternative, and I am now confident that my judgement and yours will largely agree.'

(32) After dismissing his council, Curio called the soldiers together for an address. He reminded them of the use Caesar had made of their support at Corfinium, so that thanks to their services and their example he had made a large part of Italy his. 'Because all the towns then imitated you and your action, not without reason did Caesar judge you most favourably, and our enemies judge you most harshly. Pompey, without suffering a reverse on the field of battle, was pushed aside by

the verdict you had already passed, and left Italy; while Caesar committed to your trust both myself, whom he held very dear,* and the provinces of Sicily and Africa, without which he cannot keep Rome and Italy safe.* But there are men here who advise you to abandon us. What more can they desire than to cheat us and at the same time make you guilty of an awful crime? In their fury, what worse fate can they imagine for you than that you should betray those who believe they owe everything to you, and come into the power of those who think you have ruined them? Or perhaps you have not heard of Caesar's exploits in Spain? Two armies defeated; two generals overcome; two provinces gained; and this done in forty days from the time when Caesar set eyes on his opponents. Or do you think that men who could offer no resistance when they were fresh can resist now they are finished? Are you who followed Caesar when his victory still hung in the balance really going to follow the loser now that the result of the war is settled and you ought to reap the reward of your services? They say they have been deserted and betrayed by you, and make mention of your previous oath. But did you desert Domitius, or did Domitius desert you?* Did he not reject you when you were prepared to hold out to the bitter end? Did he not seek safety in flight without telling you? When he had betrayed you, were you not saved by Caesar's kindness? As for the oath, how could he have held you to it, when after throwing away his insignia of office and laying down his command he passed into another's power as a private citizen and a prisoner himself? We have arrived at a new sort of obligation, when you pay no attention to the oath you are under now, but respect the one which has been annulled by your leader's surrender and loss of legal rights.* But what logic! You approve of Caesar, but are now turning on me. I am not going to make any premature claims on your gratitude for services which are as yet less substantial than I would like, or you hope; all the same, soldiers have always sought the rewards of their labours in the result of a war, and not even you can be in doubt as to what that will be. I need not, surely, be silent about my conscientiousness,* or my good fortune so far?

Perhaps you regret that I brought this army across safe and sound without the loss of a single ship? Or that on arriving I scattered the enemy fleet at the first attack? Or that I won a cavalry victory twice in two days? Or that I got two hundred loaded vessels from the enemy's harbour and anchorage and put him in the position of being unable to receive supplies, whether by land or sea? Are you going to turn your backs on such good fortune and such leaders, and be attracted by the disgrace of Corfinium, the flight from Italy, and the surrender of the two Spains—and there you have a foretaste of the outcome of the war in Africa! For my part, it was my wish to be called a footsoldier on Caesar's side, but you have saluted me as a victorious general. If you regret this, I give you back your gift; but you must restore to me my good name, to avoid appearing to have given me an honour in order to insult me.'

(33) The soldiers were moved by this speech and frequently interrupted Curio while he was still speaking, so that they appeared to be very hurt by the suspicion of their disloyalty; but as he left the gathering they all encouraged him to be of good heart, and not to hesitate to join battle on the spot and put their loyalty and courage to the test. This caused a general change in attitudes and opinions, and Curio decided, with the agreement of his advisers, to proceed with a battle as soon as the opportunity offered; and next day he led them out and formed them up in battle order in the same position as they had occupied a few days before. Nor for his part did Attius Varus hesitate to bring his forces out for battle, so as not to miss any opportunity, if the chance arose, either of appealing to the soldiers or of fighting on favourable ground.

(34) Between the two lines there was, as described above, a depression, not particularly deep but with sides that were difficult and strenuous to climb. Both commanders were waiting to see if the opposing forces would try to cross it, so that battle could be joined where the ground was more favourable to themselves; at the same time, on the left wing, all Attius' cavalry together with a number of interspersed light-armed were observed going down into the depression. To meet them Curio sent his cavalry and two cohorts of Marrucini. The

enemy horse failed to withstand their first attack and fled at full gallop to their own lines; and thus abandoned, the light-armed troops who had run forward along with them were surrounded and killed by our men. Varus' whole army was watching and saw the flight and death of their men. Then Rebilus, one of Caesar's officers, whom Curio had brought with him from Sicily because he knew he was an extremely experienced soldier, said 'You see the enemy are terrified, Curio; why hesitate to seize your opportunity?' Curio said just one thing to his soldiers, that they should remember what they had promised him the day before, then ordered them to follow him and ran forward at their head. In fact the edge of the depression was so difficult that the leading soldiers could not easily climb up out of it unless they were helped by their comrades; but the morale of Attius' troops had been so undermined by the panic and flight and slaughter of their men that they had no thoughts of resistance and believed that they were all surrounded by cavalry already. And so before a weapon could be hurled or our troops could come any nearer, Varus' whole formation turned round and retreated to camp.

(35) In this rout, Fabius, a Paelignian from the lowest ranks of Curio's army who was leading the pursuit of the retreating forces, kept shouting out Varus' name and asking for him, so that he appeared to be one of his soldiers who wanted to speak to him and tell him something. Varus, hearing his name constantly called, looked at him and stopped and asked who he was and what he wanted. Then Fabius lunged at Varus' unprotected shoulder with his sword and almost killed him, but Varus escaped the danger by raising his shield to block the thrust, and Fabius was surrounded and killed by the nearest soldiers. The gates of the camp were choked and the way blocked by the chaotic mass of fugitives; more died there without a wound on them than were killed in the rout and fighting, and they were nearly driven from the camp as well, some in fact heading directly for the town without stopping. But at the time Curio's men *were prevented* from entering not only by the natural position and fortifications of the camp, *but* also by the fact

that they had come out for a battle and lacked the equipment needed to attack a camp. And so Curio led his army back to camp, having killed about six hundred of his opponents and wounded a thousand, without losing a man except Fabius; when he had gone, all the wounded, and many more who pretended to be so, were frightened enough to leave their camp and go into the town. When Varus saw this and sensed the fear in his army, he left a trumpeter and a few tents for appearances' sake in his camp, and during the third watch of the night silently took his army back into the town.

(36) The next day Curio began to lay siege to Utica and surround it with a palisaded earthwork. In the town were the populace, whom long peace had left unaccustomed to war; the citizens of Utica, who were very well disposed to Caesar on account of certain favours he had done them; the association of Romans,* which was composed of people of various sorts;—and great fear, produced by the recent battles. And so they all now talked openly of surrender, and approached Attius to persuade him not to ruin them all by his obstinacy. While the matter was under discussion, messengers arrived who had been sent ahead by King Juba to say that he was at hand with a large force and to encourage them to guard and defend the city. This news restored their shattered morale.

(37) The same news reached Curio, but for a while he did not believe it, so great was his confidence in what he was doing. Already, too, reports and letters about Caesar's successes in Spain were being passed about. Encouraged by all these factors, he thought that the king would take no action against him. But when he discovered on good authority that the king's forces were less than twenty-five miles from Utica, he left his fortifications and withdrew to Scipio's Camp. Here he began to bring in grain, fortify a camp, and collect timber, and sent at once to Sicily for the two legions and the rest of his cavalry. The camp was an ideal base for a campaign, with its natural position, its man-made defences, the sea close by, and plenty of water and salt, of which a huge quantity was already there, collected from the nearby salt-pans. There could be no shortage of timber, as the trees were numerous,

nor of grain, as the fields were full of it. And so with the agreement of all his staff Curio prepared to wait for the rest of his forces and prolong the campaign.

(38) When things had been thus organized, and his plans were agreed, he was told by some deserters from the town that Juba had been called back by a border invasion and some trouble to do with the inhabitants of Leptis and had stayed behind in his kingdom,* while Saburra, his general, had been sent on with a modest force and was approaching Utica. Rashly believing this source of information, he changed his plan and decided to proceed by giving battle. In thinking that this was the correct course, he was much affected by his youth, his nobility of spirit, his previous successes, and his self-confidence. Under the influence of these factors, he sent off all his cavalry as night fell to the enemy camp at the River Bagradas, where Saburra, about whom he had previously heard, was in command; but the king with all his forces was following behind and had stopped six miles away. The cavalry completed their journey while it was still dark and attacked the enemy off guard and unawares. The Numidians had camped indiscriminately, in no sort of formation, as seems to be the habit of foreign peoples, and when the cavalry swept in on them as they lay fast asleep in scattered groups a large number were killed and many fled in panic. After this the cavalry returned to Curio, bringing him the prisoners.

(39) Curio had left camp before dawn with all his forces, leaving five cohorts behind on guard. After six miles he met the cavalry and learnt what they had done; he asked the prisoners who was in command of the camp at the Bagradas, and they replied 'Saburra'. In his eagerness to reach his objective, he omitted to enquire about the rest of the facts, and turning his gaze to the detachments nearest to him said 'You see, men, that the prisoners' story agrees with the deserters? That the king is not present,* and that a weak force was sent which could not stand up to a few cavalry? Hurry on then to booty and to glory, so that we can now start to think about rewarding you and showing you our gratitude.' The achievement of the cavalry was in fact great, particularly when their small numbers were compared with the great

mass of Numidians. But it was exaggerated in their account of it, since men are always willing to speak up in their own praise. In addition, many items of loot were held up to view, and captured men and horses were produced, so that any time lost seemed only to be putting off the moment of victory. Thus Curio's hopes were supported by the enthusiasm of his men. He ordered the cavalry to follow and speeded up his march so that he could fall on the enemy when they were at their most panic-stricken as a result of the rout. But the cavalry, exhausted by travelling all night, were unable to keep up and stopped one after another. Not even this fact moderated Curio's optimism.

(40) On being informed by Saburra of the night battle, Juba sent forward to him two thousand Spanish and Gallic cavalry, whom it was his practice to have with him as a body-guard, and also the most reliable part of his infantry; he himself followed behind more slowly with the rest of his army and sixty elephants. Because he suspected from his cavalry patrols that Curio himself was in the vicinity, Saburra drew up his cavalry and infantry in formation and told them to give way gradually, pretending to be afraid, and retreat; he himself would give the signal to engage when it was necessary, and would give them such orders as he saw were demanded by the circumstances. Curio's previous optimism was reinforced by his view of the present situation, and thinking that the enemy were turning tail he led his troops down from higher ground on to the level.

(41) When he had gone some distance from this position, he halted his exhausted army, which had now marched sixteen miles. Saburra gave the signal to his men, formed them into battle order, and began to go round the ranks and encourage them; but he used his infantry only in the rear, for appearances' sake, and put the cavalry into the front line. Curio did not shirk his task, and encouraged his men to regard bravery as their only hope. And neither the infantry, though tired out, nor the cavalry, though few and exhausted by their efforts, lacked enthusiasm or courage for the fight; but the latter numbered only two hundred because the remainder had stopped along the way. Wherever they attacked, they forced the enemy to give ground, but they could neither

pursue fugitives any distance nor spur their animals to additional speed. But the enemy cavalry started to go round to the rear of our line and pick off men whom they took from behind. Whenever cohorts ran forward from the line, the Numidians were fresh enough to escape the attack by a quick retreat, and then when our men were re-forming into their ranks they surrounded them and prevented them rejoining the line. Thus it appeared safe neither to stay in the same place and keep formation, nor to run forward and risk the outcome. The enemy forces were continually augmented by reinforcements sent up by the king; tiredness sapped the strength of our troops, and at the same time those who had been wounded could neither drop out of the line nor be carried to any safe spot, because the whole line was held fast inside the circle of the enemy cavalry. These men, despairing of escape, behaved as men do in the last moments of their lives, either bewailing their own deaths or commending their parents to anyone whom good fortune might be able to save from this danger. Fear and grief were everywhere.

(42) When Curio realized that in the general panic neither his exhortations nor his pleas were being heard, he considered the situation to be so desperate that the only hope was for them all to take up a position on the adjoining high ground, and he ordered the standards to proceed in that direction. But Saburra had already sent some cavalry and seized this too. Then our men indeed despaired utterly. Some took to their heels and were cut down by the cavalry, others collapsed even though they were unwounded. Gnaeus Domitius, Curio's cavalry commander who was guarding him with a few troopers, advised him to save himself by flight and make all speed back to the camp, and promised that he would stay with him. But Curio swore that after losing the army which Caesar had given him on trust he would never let Caesar see him again, and so died fighting. Of the cavalry a handful extricated themselves from the battle; but those who, as mentioned above, had halted at the rear to rest their horses, saw from afar the total rout of the army and got themselves safely back to camp. The infantry were killed to a man.

(43) When he learnt the news Marcius Rufus, the quaestor who had been left in the camp, encouraged his men not to lose heart. They begged and pleaded with him to take them back to Sicily in the ships. Promising to do so, he instructed the captains of the ships to see that all their small boats were at the beach in the early evening. But they were all so terrified that some said Juba's forces were near, others that Varus was on them with his legions and they could already see the cloud of dust as they came (none of which had in fact happened), and yet others suspected that the enemy fleet would swiftly descend on them. And so in the general panic it was every man for himself. Those aboard the warships hurried to set sail. Their flight provoked the captains of the merchantmen, and not many ship's boats gathered for their appointed task. But on the packed beaches the struggle to settle who from this large number of men should embark was so fierce that some of the boats sank from weight of numbers and the rest were reluctant to approach because they feared the same fate.

(44) For these reasons it came about that only a few soldiers and fathers of families, being those who could make a claim on the good will or pity of others, or could swim to the ships, were taken on board and reached Sicily safely. The troops who were left sent some centurions at night to Varus as their representatives and surrendered to him. On the following day Juba, when he saw the cohorts of these soldiers in front of the town, declared that they were his spoil and gave orders for the greater part of them to be put to death; he picked out a few prisoners and sent them back to his kingdom, while Varus complained that his word of honour had been violated by the king, but did not dare to resist. Juba himself rode into the city with several senators in train,* amongst them Servius Sulpicius and Licinius Damasippus, decided what he wanted to do with Utica and gave his orders, and a few days later withdrew with his entire army to his own kingdom.

Book III

Caesar crosses to Epirus to face Pompey (1–19).
Troubles in Italy (20–22). Caesar receives
reinforcements, checks Scipio (23–38). He blockades
Pompey outside Dyrrachium but is defeated (39–72).
The campaign of Pharsalus (73–99). Naval
operations (100–101). Flight and death of Pompey
(102–104). Start of the Alexandrian War (105–112)

*Caesar in Italy. Summary of forces available to
Caesar and Pompey*

(1) In his capacity as dictator* Caesar held the elections, at
which <Gaius> Julius and Publius Servilius were elected consuls; for this was the year when he was legally permitted to
become consul.* When this business was finished, he decided
to appoint assessors, since credit had become difficult* all
over Italy and debts were not being paid; these assessors
were to make valuations of landed and other property at the
prices ruling for individual items before the war, and such
property was to be handed over to creditors. Caesar thought
this would be the most appropriate measure, both to remove
or reduce the fear of a general cancellation of debts, and to
protect the value of debtors' assets. Also, by means of legislation brought before the people by praetors and tribunes*
he restored their property in full to some people who had
been condemned under Pompey's law on electoral corruption.* This had taken place at a time when Pompey had
legionary forces in the city and trials were being completed
each in a single day, with one set of jurors to hear the case
and a different set to give the verdict.* At the outbreak of
the civil war the victims had offered their services to Caesar
if he wished to avail himself of them, something which he
valued in exactly the same way as if he had taken up the
offer, since they had put themselves at his disposal. He acted
like this because he had decided that such persons ought to

receive restitution by decision of the Roman people before being seen as restored by his own favour, so that he would not seem to be either churlish in repaying a kindness or arrogant in pre-empting the right of the people to confer a favour.

(2) He spent eleven days* on this business and on completing all the elections and the celebration of the Latin Festival before abdicating from the dictatorship and travelling from Rome to Brundisium. He had given orders for twelve legions and all his cavalry to assemble there. But he found only as many ships as would permit the tightly packed transport of twenty thousand legionaries and five hundred cavalry, and this was the one resource Caesar lacked to finish the war rapidly. Also his military units themselves were under strength at embarkation, because there had been so many campaigns that many of the Gauls* had deserted, the long march from Spain had reduced numbers greatly, and the oppressive autumn in Apulia and around Brundisium, coming after the healthiness of Gaul and Spain, had spread sickness throughout the whole army.

(3) Pompey, who undisturbed by any enemy had gained the space of a year free from war to gather forces, had assembled a great fleet from Asia, the Cycladic islands, Corcyra, Athens, Pontus, Bithynia, Syria, Cilicia, Phoenicia, and Egypt, and had arranged for another great fleet to be built in various places. He had also extracted from Asia, from Syria, from all the kings, dynasts, and tetrarchs, and from the free communities of Achaea the large amount of money which he demanded, and had forced the tax companies of the provinces which he himself held* to pay him a vast sum.

(4) He had assembled nine legions of Roman citizens: five which he had brought over from Italy; a veteran one from Cilicia, which was formed from two and called 'twin' by him; one from Crete and Macedonia, composed of individual veterans who had been discharged by previous commanders and settled in these provinces; and two from Asia, raised by the consul Lentulus. In addition he had distributed amongst the legions, by way of reinforcement, a large number of men from Thessaly, Boeotia, Achaea, and Epirus; with these he had mixed the soldiers who had been serving with Antonius.* Apart from these he was expecting two legions from Syria

with Scipio. He had archers from Crete, Sparta, Pontus, Syria, and the rest of the states to the number of 3,000, two 600-strong cohorts of slingers, and 7,000 cavalry. Of the latter, Deiotarus* had brought 600 Gauls, and Ariobarzanes* 500 from Cappadocia; Cotys* had supplied the same number from Thrace and had sent his son Sadalas; from Macedonia there were 200 under Rhascypolis,* excellent men; from Alexandria Pompey's son had brought with his fleet 500 Gauls and Germans of the 'Gabinians', the troops Aulus Gabinius had left there as a garrison with King Ptolemy;* he himself had conscripted 800 from his slaves and his <body> of shepherds; 300 had been given by Tarcondarius Castor and Domnilaus from Galatia, of whom the one had come in person, the other had sent his son; 200, most of them mounted archers, had been sent from Syria by Antiochus of Commagene,* whom Pompey rewarded generously. To these he had added Dardani and Bessi who were partly mercenaries and partly ordered or cajoled into service, likewise Macedonians, Thessalians, and men belonging to other tribes and states, and so had reached the number mentioned above.

(5) He had gathered a very large quantity of grain from Thessaly, Asia, Egypt, Crete, Cyrene, and the other regions. He had decided to put his army into winter quarters at Dyrrachium, Apollonia, and all the seaboard towns, to prevent Caesar from crossing the Adriatic, and for that reason had disposed his fleet all along the coast. The ships from Egypt were commanded by Pompey's son, those from Asia by Decimus Laelius and Gaius Triarius, those from Syria by Gaius Cassius, those from Rhodes by Gaius Marcellus* assisted by Gaius Coponius, and the Liburnian and Achaean fleet by Scribonius Libo and Marcus Octavius. But Marcus Bibulus, who was put in charge of the whole naval operation and organized everything, was their overall commander.

Caesar crosses the Adriatic, takes Oricum and Apollonia

(6) When Caesar arrived at Brundisium, he addressed the soldiers, saying that as they had almost reached the end of

their labours and dangers, they should be happy to leave their slaves and personal belongings in Italy and embark without baggage, to allow a greater number of troops to be carried, and place all their hopes in victory and in his generosity. They all shouted for him to give what orders he liked and they would gladly carry them out. On 4 January he set sail with seven legions, as stated above, and on the next day made his landfall at the Ceraunian range. Amongst the rocky cliffs and other hazards he found a sheltered anchorage, and mistrusting all the harbours, because he believed them to be held by his opponents, disembarked his soldiers at a place called Palaeste without the loss of a single ship.

(7) At Oricum there were stationed Lucretius Vespillo and Minucius Rufus with eighteen of the Asian ships which had been placed under their command on Decimus Laelius' orders, and at Corcyra there was Marcus Bibulus with 110 ships. The former, however, were unsure of themselves and did not dare to come out of port, although Caesar had brought as an escort a total of no more than twelve warships and only four of these had an upper deck; and Bibulus, with his ships unready for sea and his rowers dispersed, was late in coming to meet him, because Caesar was sighted off the mainland before any report of his arrival could reach the area.

(8) Caesar disembarked his men and sent his ships back the same night to Brundisium, so that the rest of the legions and cavalry could be brought over. This task was given to his senior officer Fufius Calenus, with the object of speeding up the ferrying across of the legions. But the ships put out from land rather late, failed to make use of the night breeze, and met with disaster on their way back, because Bibulus, who had heard at Corcyra about Caesar's arrival and hoped to succeed in meeting some of the ships while they were loaded, met them empty. He fell in with about thirty and vented on them the anger and resentment produced by his own carelessness. He burnt them all and put the crews and captains to death in the same blaze, in the hope of deterring the rest by the enormity of the punishment. After doing this he had his squadrons seize the anchorages and the whole coastline from the port of Sason to that of Oricum. He stationed guard-ships with considerable care, and himself spent

nights on board ship in the most severe winter weather, shirking no task and no labour, and waiting for no reinforcement, if only he could sight Caesar . . .

(Some sentences are here missing from the text)

(9) After Libo's departure from Illyricum, Marcus Octavius reached Salonae with the ships he had with him. There, he stirred up the Dalmatians and the other natives and detached Issa from its loyalty to Caesar. At Salonae, he could make no impression on the association of Roman citizens,* whether by promises or threats, and started to attack the town (which is <*not adequately*> protected either by natural or artificial defences). But the Roman citizens quickly defended themselves by constructing wooden towers, and since their resistance was weak because of their lack of numbers, and they were enfeebled by the many wounds they suffered, as a last resort they set free all the adult slaves, and cut off the hair of all the women to make artillery.* When he became aware of their decision, Octavius surrounded the town with five camps and began a simultaneous siege and assault. They were prepared to endure every kind of hardship, but were particularly short of grain supplies. On this last they sent a delegation to Caesar asking for help, but put up with their other difficulties in whatever way they could. After a long time, when the protracted siege had made Octavius' men rather careless, the besieged took advantage of the midday lull. When their enemies went off duty, they stationed women and children on the walls so as not to make any break with their daily routine, formed themselves into a body with those they had so recently freed, and burst into Octavius' nearest camp. They took this and swept on to the next, then to the third and fourth and so to the remaining camp, driving their opponents out from all of them with great loss of life, and forcing the rest, along with Octavius himself, to flee to the ships. This marked the end of the attack on the town. Winter was now approaching, and Octavius, despairing of taking it after such losses, withdrew to Pompey at Dyrrachium.*

(10) We have explained that Lucius Vibullius Rufus, an officer of Pompey's, was twice released by Caesar after falling

into his hands, once at Corfinium and a second time in Spain. On account of the favours he had done him, Caesar thought him a suitable person to send with proposals to Pompey, and he knew that Vibullius carried weight with Pompey. The essence of the proposals was that both of them ought to put an end to their obstinate behaviour, abandon armed struggle, and not risk their luck any further. It was enough that great losses had been incurred on both sides, which could be read as a lesson and a warning to be afraid of further misfortunes: Pompey had been driven out of Italy and lost Sicily and Sardinia, the two Spanish provinces, and 130 cohorts of Roman citizens in Italy and Spain, while Caesar had suffered the death of Curio and disaster to his African army, and the surrender of Antonius and his troops at Curicta. Accordingly they should have mercy on themselves and their country, <because> thanks to their reverses they were in their own persons an adequate proof of how great the power of fortune was in war. This was the one time to negotiate peace, while they were each confident and appeared to be equally matched; but if fortune tilted even slightly towards one of them, the one who thought he had the advantage would have no interest in a negotiated peace, and the one who believed that he was about to take the whole would not be content with a fair share. Because they had previously been unable to agree peace terms, these ought to be requested from senate and people at Rome; this was in the common interest, and was a course of action which they ought to approve. If each of them were immediately to swear an oath in a public assembly that he would dismiss his army within the next three days, then when they had laid aside their arms and the support in which they now placed their hopes, they would both have to be content with the verdict of people and senate. To make this proposal more acceptable to Pompey < . . . . . >.*

(11) After receiving these instructions, Vibullius considered it no less necessary that Pompey should be informed of Caesar's sudden arrival, so that he could decide what to do about that before negotiations began on the proposals Vibullius brought. Vibullius therefore broke his journey

neither by night nor by day, and changed his animals at every town in the interests of greater speed, as he hurried to Pompey to tell him that Caesar was present. Pompey was at that time in Candavia, on his way from Macedonia to winter quarters in Apollonia and Dyrrachium. Much disturbed by the new turn of events, he began to make for Apollonia by forced marches, to stop Caesar seizing the coastal towns. However, the latter, after landing his men, set off the same day for Oricum. On his arrival, Lucius Torquatus, whom Pompey had put in charge of the town with a garrison of Parthini, shut the gates and attempted to defend it, but when he ordered the Greeks to arm themselves and man the walls, they said they would not fight against the legitimate authority of the Roman people.* In addition the townspeople* were trying of their own accord to admit Caesar. Torquatus therefore despaired of any help, opened the gates, and surrendered himself and the town to Caesar, who spared him unharmed.

(12) After taking Oricum, Caesar immediately set out for Apollonia. When Lucius Staberius, who was in command there, heard the news of his approach, he began to take water up to the citadel and put it in a state of defence and require hostages from the Apollonians. But they refused to give them, or close their gates against a consul, or take a decision that went against the judgement of all Italy and the Roman people. On realizing their sympathies, Staberius fled secretly from Apollonia, and they sent a delegation to Caesar and let him into the town. They were followed by the people of Byllis and Amantia and by the rest of the nearby communities and the whole of Epirus, who sent deputations to Caesar and promised to obey his orders.

(13) Pompey, on the other hand, when he learnt what had happened at Oricum and Apollonia, feared for Dyrrachium and marched day and night to reach it. At the same time Caesar was said to be approaching; and such panic struck Pompey's army, because in his haste day and night had become one and he had not broken his march, that almost all the men who came from Epirus and the adjacent areas deserted the colours, a number threw their arms away, and the march resembled a rout. But after he had halted near

Dyrrachium and given orders for a camp to be laid out, and the army was still terror-stricken, Labienus came forward and took an oath* that he would not desert Pompey and would share with him whatever fate had been allotted him by fortune. The other senior officers took the same oath, followed by the military tribunes and centurions, and the whole army swore in the same terms. Now that his march on Dyrrachium had been forestalled, Caesar stopped hurrying and encamped by the River Apsus on the borders of the territory of Apollonia, so that the communities that deserved well of him should be safely protected, and decided to wait there for the arrival of the rest of his legions from Italy, and spend the winter under canvas.* Pompey did the same, established his camp on the other side of the Apsus, and brought all his troops and auxiliaries there.

Caesar suffers naval blockade; abortive negotiations for peace

(14) Following Caesar's instructions,* Calenus embarked as many legions and cavalry at Brundisium as was possible with the number of ships he had, and put to sea. When he was a little way out from port, he received a letter from Caesar telling him that the harbours and the entire coastline were held by enemy fleets. As a result of this information he put back into port and recalled all his ships. One of them, which carried on and refused to obey his authority because it had no soldiers on board and was being managed privately, made landfall at Oricum and was attacked and taken by Bibulus, who exacted retribution from all, slave and free, down to mere boys, and put them to death to the last man. Thus the preservation of the army hung on a matter of minutes and a remarkable chance.

(15) Bibulus, as mentioned above,* was with his fleet off Oricum, and just as he prevented Caesar from having access to the sea and the harbours, was himself prevented from landing anywhere in that area. Caesar had stationed guard-posts

and controlled all the coast, and there was no possibility of taking fuel or water on board or of tying up to shore. Things were extremely difficult, and Bibulus' men laboured under severe shortages of essentials, so much so that they were forced to bring fuel and water, just like the rest of their provisions, in merchant ships from Corcyra; and there was even an occasion during a period of bad weather when they were forced to collect the night dew off the leather awnings with which the ships were covered. However, they endured these difficulties patiently and in good spirits, and thought they ought not to leave the coast unguarded or move away from the harbours. In the difficult situation I have described,* after Libo had joined up with Bibulus they both parleyed from their ships with Caesar's senior officers Marcus Acilius and Staius Murcus, of whom one was in command of the town defences, the other of the guard-posts on shore: their message was that they wanted to speak to Caesar on matters of the highest importance, if they could have access to him. To this they added a few words to reinforce the impression that their business was to discuss a settlement. Meanwhile they asked for a truce, and succeeded in obtaining it from Acilius and Murcus. For the proposal seemed important, they knew Caesar passionately desired it, and it was thought that something had come of Vibullius' mission.

(16) Caesar had at that point set out with one legion to win over the more distant communities and improve his supplies of grain, which were short, and he was at the town of Buthrotum <opposite> Corcyra. On being informed by letter from Acilius and Murcus of the requests made by Libo and Bibulus, he left the legion and himself returned to Oricum. When he arrived, the other side were summoned to a conference. Libo appeared and made excuses for Bibulus, because the latter was in a state of deep anger and in addition had private grounds for enmity towards Caesar, arising from their aedileship and praetorship;* his reason for not attending the conference was that his anger might interfere with business of the greatest promise and advantage. Libo said that Pompey, both now and previously, had always

wanted to reach an agreement and bring an end to armed conflict. He and Bibulus themselves possessed no competence in the matter, because by resolution of council* they had allowed Pompey control of the war and of all other matters, but if they could find out Caesar's demands, they would send them to Pompey, and he would take further action through themselves and on their advice. Meanwhile, the truce should stay in force, until Pompey could return an answer, and neither side should harm the other. To this he added a few words about the matters at issue and about his troops and auxiliaries.

(17) On these topics Caesar thought no reply necessary at the time, nor do we consider there is sufficient reason now to set one down in the record. Caesar asked to be allowed to send a delegation to Pompey under a safe-conduct, and that the other side should themselves accept responsibility for that, or else that they should receive the delegates and take them to him. As for the truce, he said that the balance of the war was so arranged that they were using their fleet to interfere with his ships and support, while he stopped them obtaining water or coming in to land. If they wanted some relaxation on this score, they could themselves relax their naval blockade; but if they maintained theirs, he would keep his. He said it was still possible, none the less, to negotiate for an agreement even granted that the blockades were not lifted, and the one was not an obstacle to the other. Libo, however, would neither receive delegates from Caesar nor guarantee their safety, but wanted to refer the whole business to Pompey; the truce was the one point he insisted on and pressed for most vigorously. When Caesar realized that Libo had embarked on the whole scheme to escape from his present danger and solve his shortage of supplies, and was not putting forward any prospect or terms of peace, he went back to considering other plans for the war.

(18) Bibulus was prevented from landing for many days, and fell seriously ill as a result of the cold and his exertions. Lacking medical attention, and unwilling to abandon the task he had undertaken, he was unable to withstand the force

of the disease. After his death, no one inherited the overall command, but each admiral operated his own fleet as he thought best.

When the disturbance caused by Caesar's sudden arrival had subsided, Vibullius chose his moment, summoned Libo and Lucius Lucceius and Theophanes,* men with whom Pompey habitually discussed matters of the highest importance, and began to discuss Caesar's proposals. As he was speaking Pompey interrupted him and forbade him to say any more: 'What use', he said, 'are life or citizen rights to me, if I am seen to enjoy them by Caesar's favour? That view will be impossible to change, if ever people think I have been brought back . . . to Italy, which I left . . .' Caesar discovered this after the end of the war* from those who had been present at the conversation. However, he still tried by other means to negotiate a peace.

(19) Between the two camps of Pompey and Caesar there was only the single stream of the River Apsus; the soldiers frequently talked to each other, and by agreement between the participants no missiles were thrown while they were so engaged. Caesar sent Publius Vatinius, one of his senior officers, to the very edge of the river to discuss the questions thought to be most important for peace, and to ask over and over again at the top of his voice whether Romans were allowed to send delegates to Romans (a thing that had been permitted even to fugitives from the mountain uplands of the Pyrenees and to pirates),* especially when their business was to stop a civil war. He spoke at length, in a pleading fashion, as was right in a matter of life and death for himself and them all, and was heard in silence by both groups of soldiers. A reply came from the other side promising that Aulus Varro would attend a conference the next day and examine with Vatinius how delegates could come in safety and present their demands; and a time was settled for this. When the hour came the next day, a great crowd converged from both sides, expectation was high, and everyone seemed to desire peace. From out of this crowd, Titus Labienus came forward and without raising his voice began to speak about a peace, and argue with Vatinius. In the middle of this dis-

cussion they were interrupted by missiles suddenly thrown from all directions; Labienus, protected by his soldiers' shields, escaped them, but several people were wounded, amongst them Cornelius Balbus, Marcus Plotius, Lucius Tiburtius, and some centurions and ordinary soldiers. Then Labienus said: 'Well then, stop talking about peace; there can be no peace for us unless we get Caesar's head.'

Insurrection of Caelius Rufus and Milo in Italy

(20) During this period Marcus Caelius Rufus, one of the praetors, took up the cause of the debtors; at the beginning of his magistracy he set up his dais next to the official seat* of Gaius Trebonius, the urban praetor, and promised that he would take up the cases of any who appealed against valuations and payments arrived at by assessors under the system set up by Caesar* when he was in Rome. But it so happened, thanks to the fairness of the decree and the decency of Trebonius, who thought that under these circumstances the law ought to be applied with kindness and moderation, that nobody could be found to initiate an appeal. Perhaps one does not need to possess an unusual character in order to make excuses for poverty, to complain of private or public disaster, and to allege the difficulties of selling at auction; but to expect to keep assets untouched, while admitting debts, what sort of character and what sort of effrontery does that require? As a result no one was found who was prepared to make such a demand, and Caelius was shown up as being too hard on the very people whose interests were at stake. And to avoid appearing to have wasted his time backing a discreditable cause, he went on from where he had started, and promulgated a law to permit the repayment of a loan free of interest <on its fifth(?) anniversary>.*

(21) In face of opposition from the consul Servilius and the rest of the magistrates, Caelius achieved less than he had expected and set about winning popular support by withdrawing the first law and promulgating two others, one giving a year's remission of rent to tenants, the other cancelling

debts; he also made an attack with a mob on Gaius Trebonius and forced him off his dais, injuring several people. Servilius as consul referred the episode to the senate, which passed a motion suspending Caelius from public duties.* On the strength of this decree the consul barred him from the senate and dragged him off the Rostra* as he was attempting to address a public meeting. Mortified by the disgrace, he made a public pretence of going to Caesar; in private he sent messengers to Milo, who after Clodius' murder* had been found guilty of that crime, and summoned him to Italy, because Milo still owned the remnants of a troop of gladiators from the great public shows he had put on. He allied himself with Milo and sent him ahead to the country around Thurii to win over the shepherds.* He himself reached Casilinum, but when weapons and military standards of his were seized at Capua, and simultaneously at Naples the gladiators were seen making ready for the defection of the town, his schemes were revealed. He was shut out of Capua, and because he was fearful of the danger posed by the association of Roman citizens who had armed themselves and considered they should treat him as an enemy, abandoned that plan and went by a different route.

(22) Milo, meanwhile, circulated letters around the towns saying that he was acting as he was by Pompey's orders and on Pompey's authority, the instructions having been conveyed to him by Vibullius, and he tried to gain the support of those he thought were in difficulties with debt. Having no success with them, he broke open some slave quarters and began to attack Compsa in the territory of the Hirpini. When a praetor, Quintus Pedius, <came> with a legion <to give assistance>, Milo was hit by a stone thrown from the wall, and died. Caelius, making his way (as he maintained) to Caesar, reached Thurii, where after making approaches to some inhabitants of that community and promising money to Caesar's Gallic and Spanish cavalry who had been sent there to protect the town, he was killed by the latter. Thus the beginnings of a great upheaval, which caused much anxiety in Italy on account of the preoccupations of the magistrates and <the problems> of the times,* came to a speedy and simple end.

Antonius breaks Libo's blockade of Brundisium

(23) Libo set out from Oricum* with a fleet of fifty ships under his command, and on arriving at Brundisium seized the island which lies off the town's port, because he thought it was better to blockade the single place where our forces had to come out, than the entire shoreline and harbours. His sudden arrival let him attack and burn some merchant ships, capture one laden with grain, and create panic on our side. He landed legionaries and archers at night, forced a garrison of cavalry to decamp, and made such good use of the possibilities of the position that he wrote to Pompey to say that, if he wished, Pompey could give orders for his other ships to be hauled out and repaired: with his fleet he himself would stop reinforcements reaching Caesar.

(24) At that time Antonius was at Brundisium; trusting in the courage of his troops, he covered about sixty ship's boats with wickerwork and screens, put picked men in them, and stationed them separately by the shore in various places; he also ordered two triremes, which he had had built at Brundisium for rowing practice, to appear at the harbour entrance. When Libo saw them come out somewhat recklessly, he despatched four quadriremes towards them in the hope of being able to intercept them. When these got near our ships, our veterans turned round and made for harbour, while the others in their enthusiasm followed too incautiously. Then suddenly, when the signal was given, Antonius' boats headed from every direction for the enemy, and with their very first attack captured one of the quadriremes with its rowers and marines and forced the others to flee ignominiously. Apart from this loss, the enemy were prevented from obtaining water because Antonius had stationed cavalry along the shore. Libo gave in to necessity and disgrace, left Brundisium, and stopped blockading us.

Reinforcements reach Caesar by sea

(25) Many months had now elapsed and winter was far advanced,* and still the ships and legions from Brundisium had

not reached Caesar. He supposed that some opportunities to cross had been missed, because the steady winds which he thought necessary for the operation had often blown. And the more time went by, the more attentive the fleet commanders became to the blockade and the greater their confidence of stopping the reinforcement. They were also admonished by frequent letters from Pompey, to the effect that since they had begun by failing to stop Caesar's arrival, they must obstruct the rest of his army; and with every day they expected the winds to be lighter and the weather more difficult for crossing. Disturbed by these considerations, Caesar wrote in fairly stern terms to his officers in Brundisium that when the wind went into the right quarter, they should not let slip any opportunity to sail, so long as they could manage to hold a course right to the Apollonian coast* and drive the ships ashore there. This area was mostly clear of blockading ships, because they did not dare to commit themselves too far from harbour.

(26) Led by Marcus Antonius and Fufius Calenus, Caesar's force was bold and courageous. The ordinary soldiers themselves gave strong support and balked at no danger to save Caesar. When they got a south wind, they set sail and on the next day were carried past Apollonia. They were sighted from the mainland, and Coponius, who was in command of the Rhodian fleet at Dyrrachium, brought his ships out from harbour. When he was just closing on our fleet, with the wind dropping, the same south wind came up again and helped us.* Not that he was thereby put off, because he hoped that by determined effort his sailors could overcome even the force of the storm, and he followed the ships, regardless, when they were swept past Dyrrachium by the gale. Although our side benefited from this stroke of fortune, they none the less feared an attack by Coponius' fleet if the wind were to drop, and when they reached a port three miles beyond Lissus, by the name of Nymphaeum—a port sheltered from the southwest but open to the south—they put their ships in there, thinking the weather a less serious danger than Coponius' fleet. The moment they entered harbour, with amazing luck the south wind which had blown for two days swung to the south-west.

(27) And now a sudden change of fortune could be observed. Those who had a moment ago been in fear for their lives found shelter in the safest of ports; while those who had put our ships in danger were forced to fear danger themselves. So when the conditions changed, the gale not only protected our side, but inflicted such damage on the Rhodian ships that every single one of the sixteen vessels with an upper deck was smashed and lost, and out of the great number of rowers and marines some were dashed against the rocks and killed, and some were picked up by our men; all the survivors were spared and sent home by Caesar.

(28) Two of our ships, which had been less swift in completing their passage, were overtaken by night, and as they had no knowledge of the whereabouts of the rest, anchored off Lissus. Otacilius Crassus, who was in command at Lissus, sent a collection of ship's boats and smaller vessels against them and made preparations to take them by boarding; at the same time he offered terms of surrender and promised that captives would go unharmed. One of these two ships had taken on board 220 men from a legion of recruits, the other slightly fewer than 200 from a veteran legion. And here one may recognize how great a defence men possess in resolution of spirit. For the recruits, terrified by the number of boats and exhausted by seasickness, accepted on oath that the enemy would do them no harm and surrendered to Otacilius; and they were all paraded in front of him and brutally put to death* before his very eyes, contrary to the obligation of the oath. But the soldiers from the veteran legion, who had been severely shaken in exactly the same way by the discomforts of the storm and the slopping of the bilges, far from thinking it was right to forget their previous standards of courage, spun out the first part of the night in discussing terms and feigning surrender, and then forced their captain to beach the ship. They found a suitable spot to see out the remainder of the night, and when dawn came and Otacilius sent against them about 400 cavalry who were guarding that part of the coast, and behind them some armed men from the garrison, they fought them off, killed a number of their opponents, and withdrew unharmed to join our forces.*

(29) After this exploit the association of Roman citizens at Lissus, a town which Caesar had earlier assigned to them and provided with fortifications, received Antonius and gave him every assistance, while Otacilius, in fear for his life, fled the town and made his way to Pompey. When Antonius had landed all his forces, which totalled three legions of veterans, one of recruits, and 800 cavalry, he sent most of the ships back to Italy to bring over the remaining infantry and cavalry,* but left the 'pontoons' (a type of Gallic vessel) at Lissus. He wished to ensure that if Pompey thought that Italy was empty of troops and went across there with his army—an opinion widely held by the ordinary public—Caesar would have some means of pursuing him. He also sent an urgent message to inform Caesar where he had landed and what forces he had brought across.

(30) Caesar and Pompey discovered what had happened at almost the same time. They had themselves seen the ships passing Apollonia and Dyrrachium, but for a day or two did not know where they had come in to land. When they found out, they adopted different plans: Caesar intended to join up with Antonius as soon as possible, Pompey to place himself in the path of the arriving force in an attempt to ambush and attack it unawares. The two of them led their armies from their permanent camps on the Apsus on the same day, Pompey secretly by night, Caesar openly by day. But Caesar had a longer march, with a more roundabout route upstream to ford the river; Pompey, because his route was clear and he had no river to cross, made towards Antonius with forced marches and when he knew that the latter was approaching found a suitable position, stationed his forces there, kept them all in camp, and banned the lighting of fires so that there should be less evidence of his arrival. This was at once reported by the Greeks* to Antonius, who sent a message to Caesar and remained in camp for a single day; on the next, Caesar reached him. When Pompey heard of his arrival, to avoid being surrounded by two armies he abandoned his position, and marched with all his forces towards Asparagium,* in the territory of Dyrrachium, where he encamped in a suitable spot.

Scipio's behaviour as proconsul of Syria

(31) At this time Scipio had suffered some reverses around the Amanus ranges and styled himself 'Victorious General'.* After this he had demanded large amounts of money from the city-states and local rulers, likewise exacted from the tax contractors of his province the payment owed for a two-year period and made them advance as a loan the sum due for the following year, and required the whole province to supply cavalry. When these forces had been raised, he turned his back on the Parthian enemy on his borders,* who not long previously had killed our general Marcus Crassus and put Marcus Bibulus* under siege, and took his legions and his cavalry away from Syria. Although the province was deeply anxious and afraid of a war with Parthia, and although not a few of the soldiers said that they would go to war if they were led against an enemy, but would not take up arms against a fellow Roman and a consul, Scipio put the legions into winter quarters in Pergamum and the wealthiest cities, distributed huge bonuses, and to secure the loyalty of the soldiers handed the communities over to them to plunder.

(32) Meanwhile the contributions which had been ordered were being exacted with great harshness throughout the province. In addition, many new categories were thought up to satisfy Scipio's greed. A poll tax* was levied on every individual, slave and free; imposts were levied on columns and doors, and demands were made for grain, recruits, weapons, rowers, artillery, and transport; if a name could be found for something, that was deemed enough to raise a tax on it. Officials were appointed to take charge not only of each city but of almost every village and little outpost, and those of them who acted with the utmost severity and cruelty were called excellent men and excellent patriots. The province was full of lictors and official attendants, and packed with officers and collectors, who in addition to demanding the money officially payable acted to line their own pockets: to have a good excuse to cover their disgraceful behaviour, they would say that because they had been driven from their homes and their country they were short of all the necessities of life. On

top of this came very high rates of interest, the usual result of war when every kind of wealth is requisitioned; in this context, they called a postponement of the settlement date a gift. And so in these two years the debt of the province was increased* many times over. Nor were Roman citizens living in the province any less liable because they were Romans: specified sums were required from individual associations and individual communities, under the pretext that these were loans exacted under the terms of a senatorial decree; and from the tax contractors, inasmuch as they had accumulated capital, the sum due for the next year was taken and reckoned as a loan.

(33) In addition, Scipio was in the process of giving orders for the wealth that had been deposited there since ancient times to be taken from the shrine of Diana at Ephesus.* He appointed a day for the business and came to the temple accompanied by a number of senators* whom he had summoned, when a letter from Pompey was delivered to him with the news that Caesar had crossed the sea with his legions: Scipio was to hurry to him with his army and postpone everything else. On receipt of the letter he dismissed the men he had summoned and began to make preparations for a march to Macedonia. A few days later he set out, and so the treasures of Ephesus were saved.

Caesar's generals check Scipio in Macedonia and Thessaly

(34) After Caesar had joined up with Antonius' army, he withdrew from Oricum the legion he had stationed there to guard the coast, and thought he ought to probe the provinces and advance somewhat further; and when delegates came to him from Thessaly and Aetolia, who promised that if he provided protection the communities of those peoples would do his bidding, he sent Lucius Cassius Longinus to Thessaly with a legion of recruits (the Twenty-seventh), and 200 cavalry, and likewise Gaius Calvisius Sabinus to Aetolia with five cohorts and a few cavalry; and he particularly urged the

delegates to supply him with grain, because their regions were nearby. He ordered Gnaeus Domitius Calvinus, with two legions (the Eleventh and Twelfth), and 500 cavalry, to set out for Macedonia; and from the area of this province known as 'free',* the leading man of the region, Menedemus, came as an envoy to profess the greatest good will on the part of all his adherents.

(35) Of these commanders, Calvisius was welcomed enthusiastically by all the Aetolians as soon as he arrived, and after the enemy garrisons at Calydon and Naupactus* had been ejected gained control of the whole of Aetolia. Cassius reached Thessaly with his legion. Here there were two factions and in consequence he met with a mixed reception: Hegesaretos, a person of long-established influence, supported the Pompeian cause; Petraeus, a young man of the highest birth, helped Caesar energetically from his own resources and those of his connections.

(36) At the same time Domitius entered Macedonia; and as numerous delegations from the communities began to meet him, there came the news, accompanied by much rumour and general speculation, that Scipio and his legions were near; for when some new development occurs, in most cases rumour outruns fact. Scipio did not stop anywhere in Macedonia, but aimed with great determination for Domitius and when he was only twenty miles from him suddenly turned aside towards Cassius Longinus in Thessaly. This he did so quickly that the news of his arrival came at the same time as the news that he was on the way; also, to ensure faster marches he left Marcus Favonius with eight cohorts at the River Haliacmon,* which divides Macedonia from Thessaly, to guard the legions' baggage and equipment, and told him to establish a fort there. At the same time Cotys' cavalry,* which was usually stationed on the borders of Thessaly, moved very rapidly in the direction of Cassius' camp. Cassius was thoroughly frightened, and having learnt of Scipio's arrival and sighted cavalry which he believed to be Scipio's, turned towards the mountains which ring Thessaly* and from this area began to march in the direction of Ambracia. As Scipio hurried to follow, a letter from Marcus Favonius caught up

with him, saying that Domitius with his legions was near and that he could not keep guard where he had been positioned without Scipio's assistance. On receipt of this letter, Scipio changed his plan and his direction of march: he stopped pursuing Cassius, and hurried to help Favonius. And so, marching day and night, he arrived in the nick of time, and his first outriders were seen at the very moment when the dust of Domitius' army was sighted. Thus Domitius' energy saved Cassius, and Scipio's speed Favonius.

(37) For two days Scipio stayed in his fixed camp by the river, the Haliacmon, which ran between him and Domitius. On the third day he forded the river at dawn with his army, pitched camp, and early on the following day drew up his battle-line in front of his camp. Then Domitius too thought he ought not to hesitate to deploy his legions and fight it out. But although there were about <three(?)> miles of level ground between the two camps, Domitius brought his line close up under Scipio's camp, while the latter refused to move from his rampart and palisade. However, although Domitius' soldiers could hardly be restrained, in the end there was no engagement, mostly because there was a stream with difficult banks next to Scipio's camp which impeded our troops' advance. When Scipio became aware of their enthusiasm and readiness to fight, he suspected that on the next day he would either be forced to fight against his will or incur much disgrace by keeping his forces in camp, and having come with high hopes, and gone too far, the result he achieved was discreditable: without even making the signal for breaking camp, he crossed the river by night, returned to his starting-point, and pitched camp there on a natural height near the river. A few days later, he laid a cavalry ambush at night, at a spot where on nearly all the preceding days our men had habitually grazed their animals, and when Quintus Varus, Domitius' cavalry commander, appeared according to his normal routine, the enemy suddenly emerged from their ambush. But our men resisted their charge bravely, quickly returned to their own formations, and all together actually made an attack on the enemy. After

killing about eighty of them and putting the rest to flight, they returned to camp with the loss of two men.

(38) As a result of this exploit, Domitius hoped that Scipio could be drawn into battle and pretended that he was being forced to move camp by a shortage of grain supplies. After giving the military signal to strike camp, he travelled three miles and stationed his whole army and all his cavalry in a suitably concealed spot. Scipio, who was ready to follow, sent on the greater part of his cavalry to search out and gain information about Domitius' route. When they had gone ahead and the leading squadrons had entered the ambush, their suspicions were aroused by the noise of horses and they began to withdraw, and those who were following them, seeing their rapid retreat, came to a halt. When the ambush was revealed, our troops, so as not to wait in vain for the rest, caught and cut off two of their squadrons, <of whom only a handful managed to flee back to their own side,> amongst whom was Marcus Opimius, a cavalry commander. All the other men from these squadrons were either killed or brought as prisoners to Domitius.

Caesar cuts Pompey off from Dyrrachium and starts to invest his army

(39) When Caesar, as mentioned above,* withdrew his garrisons from the coast, he left three cohorts at Oricum to guard the town, and placed under their protection the warships he had brought across from Italy. <Marcus Acilius> Caninianus was the senior officer in charge of the town and this task. He moved our ships into the inner harbour behind the town* and made them fast to the shore, and sank a merchant ship to block the way into the port, with another fastened to it; over this he built a tower facing the actual entrance of the port, manned it with soldiers, and made them responsible for keeping it safe against any sudden danger.

(40) Hearing of this, Gnaeus Pompeius the younger, who was in command of the Egyptian fleet, sailed to Oricum and

dragged away the sunken ship using a winch, a large number of cables, and a great deal of effort. With several of his own ships, on which he had constructed towers to the same level, he attacked the other ship which had been positioned by Acilius to guard the harbour; he fought from a higher position, he constantly replaced tired men with fresh, and he attacked the town walls in the other sectors, both from the land with scaling-ladders and from shipboard, in order to disperse his opponents' manpower; the result was that by his efforts and his barrage of missiles he got the better of our men, ejected the defenders, who were all picked up by small boats and made their escape, and took the ship. At the same time, on the other side of the town, he occupied the natural mole which makes it almost an island and dragged four biremes across to the inner harbour by putting them on rollers and using levers. By attacking the warships, which were tied up to shore and unmanned, from both directions like this he succeeded in towing away four of them and setting fire to the rest. After this, he moved Decimus Laelius from the command of the Asian fleet and left him to stop supplies from Byllis and Amantia being taken into the town. He himself sailed towards Lissus, where he attacked and burnt all thirty merchant ships which had been left in the port by Marcus Antonius; he tried to storm Lissus, which was defended by the Roman citizens of the local association and by troops sent by Caesar to defend it, but after staying for three days and losing a few men in the attack departed without attaining his objective.

(41) After Caesar had found out that Pompey was near Asparagium,* he set out in that direction with his army. On the way he took a town belonging to the Parthini, in which Pompey had a garrison, and reached Pompey on the third day. He pitched camp close to him, and on the following day brought all his forces out, drew up his line of battle, and offered Pompey the chance of a decisive engagement, but when he realized that the latter was going to stay put, he led his army back to camp and decided that he had to adopt a different plan. So on the next day he set out for Dyrrachium with his whole force by a difficult, narrow, and

very roundabout route, in the hope that he could either compel Pompey to make for Dyrrachium or cut him off from it, because his opponent had gathered there all his supplies and material for the whole conduct of the war. Pompey, not knowing Caesar's plan, and seeing him set out in a different direction, at first thought that he had been forced to withdraw by a shortage of food; but on receipt of later intelligence from scouts, he struck camp the next day, expecting that his shorter route would allow him to confront Caesar. Caesar, who suspected that this would be the case, encouraged his soldiers to endure hardship without complaining, and after breaking his march for a small part of the night reached Dyrrachium early in the morning, to see Pompey's advance guard in the distance, and pitched camp there.

(42) Cut off from Dyrrachium and unable to do as he had intended, Pompey fell back on the plan of fortifying a camp on a height called Petra,* which had a passable anchorage for ships and sheltered them from some winds. He gave orders for a part of his war fleet to gather there, and for grain and supplies to be brought from Asia and all the areas which he controlled. Caesar thought that the war was going to be further prolonged, and despaired of receiving provisions from Italy, because the whole coast was being guarded so diligently by the Pompeians, and his own fleets, which he had built in the winter in Sicily, Gaul, and Italy, were slow in coming. He therefore sent Quintus Tillius and Lucius Canuleius as senior officers to Epirus to arrange grain supplies, and because these regions were some distance away he set up granaries in particular spots and informed the surrounding communities of the deliveries of grain they were to make. He also gave orders for whatever grain there was at Lissus, amongst the Parthini, and in all the little outposts to be sought out and collected. This was an extremely small quantity, both because of the nature of the land, since the country is rough and mountainous and they mostly consume imported corn, and also because Pompey had foreseen this and in the preceding days had plundered the Parthini, looted and dug out* their homes, and used his cavalry to carry in to Petra the grain he had gathered.

(43) Once he had discovered these facts, Caesar based his plan on the nature of the terrain. Around Pompey's camp there was a large number of steep, rough hills. These he first seized, garrisoned, and strengthened with forts. Then, by making an earthwork from fort to fort as the lie of the land dictated in each case, he began to wall Pompey in. His objectives were these: because he was short of provisions, and because Pompey's strength lay in the number of his cavalry, to make it less dangerous for himself to bring in corn and supplies for his army from any direction; at the same time to cut off Pompey from grazing and render his cavalry operationally ineffective; and thirdly to undermine the authority which his opponent seemed to enjoy, especially with foreign nations, when the whole world came to hear that he was under siege from Caesar and did not dare fight him on the field of battle.

(44) Pompey had no wish to leave the coast and Dyrrachium, because he had placed all his war equipment, missiles, weapons, and artillery there, and was supplying his army with grain by sea; but neither was he able to stop Caesar's earthworks unless he were willing to engage in battle—a thing which he had decided not to do at that time. It remained for him to adopt his final military expedient: be the first to seize as many hills as possible, hold with garrisons as wide an area as possible, and stretch Caesar's forces as far as he possibly could; and that happened. He succeeded in setting up twenty-four forts embracing a circuit of fifteen miles, and in this space was able to get grazing; there were also many cultivated crops in the area, on which for the time being the pack-animals could feed. And just as our men had continuous fortifications leading from each fort to the next, so that the Pompeians could not break through anywhere and attack them from the rear, in the same way the Pompeians were building continuous fortifications on the inner side, so that our men could not enter at any point and get round behind them. But the enemy were having the better of it with the earthworks, because they not only possessed more men* but also, being on the interior, had a shorter circuit. Although Pompey had decided not to stop Caesar by an engagement with his full forces, none the less, whenever Caesar had to

occupy a particular spot, he used to send archers and slingers, of whom he had a large number, to take up their positions. As a result many of our men were getting wounded, the arrows had spread terror, and almost all the soldiers had made tunics or coverings out of felt, quilts, or hides to protect themselves from the missiles.

(45) Both sides expended great efforts in seizing strongpoints: Caesar, to hem Pompey in as much as he could, Pompey, to occupy as many hills as possible with as extended a circuit as possible; and for that reason there were frequent clashes. One of these occurred when Caesar's Ninth legion had occupied a particular strongpoint and begun to fortify it, while Pompey occupied a hill near to and opposite this and started to prevent our men from working; and since it had an almost level approach on one side he interfered with the fortifications first by stationing archers and slingers all round and then by sending forward a great crowd of light-armed troops and bringing up artillery; and it was not an easy task for our men to defend their position and at the same time fortify it. When Caesar saw his men being wounded from every direction, he ordered them to withdraw and leave the place. The way back was by a downward slope. Our opponents then pressed on all the more eagerly and would not allow our men to retreat, because they thought it was fear that was making them abandon their position. It is said that at that moment Pompey boasted in front of his associates that he was prepared to be considered an incompetent general if Caesar's legions managed to withdraw without severe loss from the point to which they had rashly advanced.

(46) Apprehensive about his men's retreat, Caesar gave orders for wicker bundles to be brought up and mounted facing the enemy at the very end of the hill, and for a trench of moderate width to be dug behind them by the soldiers so concealed; the ground was also to be obstructed as much as possible in every direction. He stationed slingers in suitable positions to cover our men as they retreated. When all this was done, he ordered the legion to withdraw. At this the Pompeians began to put pressure on our men and attack them more insolently and boldly, and knocked over the bundles that had been put up in front of the fortification,

so that they could cross the trenches. When Caesar saw this, he was afraid that it would seem that his soldiers had not been withdrawn, but driven away, and that a worse reverse would be sustained. So from about midway* he gave a message of encouragement to his men through Antonius, who was commanding the legion, and ordered the trumpet to sound the signal for an attack on the enemy. Suddenly united by resolve, the soldiers of the Ninth legion hurled their throwing-spears, charged up the slope from their lower position, and drove the Pompeians headlong and compelled them to turn tail, their retreat being greatly impeded by the overthrown bundles and poles in their path and the beginnings of the trenches. In contrast, our men were satisfied to retreat without suffering a defeat. After killing several opponents and losing in all five of their own number, they withdrew very calmly, and when they had seized some other hills a little further on finished their fortification works.

The nature of the warfare at Dyrrachium. Temporary stalemate

(47) This type of warfare was new and unprecedented, on account of the large number of forts, the great distances involved, the extent of the fortifications, and the whole nature of the siege. There were other reasons also. For whenever people have attempted to besiege others, they have attacked a weak and shaken enemy and held down men who have been defeated in battle or thrown into disarray by some misfortune, while they themselves have had numerical superiority in cavalry and infantry; and usually the reason for the siege has been to cut the enemy off from food. But in this case Caesar was holding down sound, intact forces with an inferior number of troops, while his opponents had plentiful supplies of everything; every day a large number of ships came in from every direction to bring supplies, and no wind could blow that was not favourable for some. He himself, though, was in extreme difficulties, because the grain available from a very wide area had been consumed. None the

less the soldiers bore this with remarkable patience. They remembered that in Spain the previous year* they had endured similar privations and by uncomplaining effort had brought a vital campaign to an end; they recalled that by enduring near-famine at Alesia, and much worse at Avaricum,* they had ended up as conquerors of mighty peoples. Neither when they were given barley, nor when they were given pulses did they refuse them; but meat, of which there was plenty in Epirus, they particularly appreciated.

(48) There is also a kind of root, which was found by the men stationed on the fortifications, and is called 'chara'.* When mixed with milk this was a great relief to their hunger, and there was plenty of it. Our men made loaves out of it, and when in verbal exchanges with the Pompeians they were taunted with being hungry, they threw these in handfuls at them to undermine their hopes.

(49) The crops were now beginning to ripen and hope herself sustained them in their privations, because they were sure they would soon have plenty; and the soldiers were often heard to say on watch and in conversation that they would rather live off bark from the trees than let Pompey slip out of their hands. They also learnt with satisfaction from deserters that their opponents' horses were being allowed to live, but that the remainder, the draught animals, had been killed; and that the men were in poor health not only because of the restricted space, the foul odour from the number of dead bodies, and the daily toil to which they were unused, but also on account of an extremely serious shortage of water. Caesar had either diverted or obstructed with great dykes every river and every stream which ran towards the sea, and where the ground was steep and rough he had blocked the narrow parts of the valleys with stakes driven into the ground around which earth was heaped to hold back the water. His opponents were thus of necessity forced to choose places that were low-lying and marshy and dig wells, and this work was additional to their daily tasks; but these sources of water were a fair distance from some of the outposts and used to dry up easily in periods of hot weather. Caesar's army on the other hand <not only> enjoyed

excellent health and an abundance of water, but also had plenty of supplies of every kind except grain; for them the passing of time offered more assistance every day, and they saw their hopes growing greater as the crops ripened.

(50) In this new sort of war, new methods of fighting were invented by both sides. When the Pompeians noticed from the fires that at night our cohorts kept watch near the fortifications, they approached in silence, discharged their arrows all together into the mass of men, and hastily retired to their own lines. Learning by experience, our men found the following answers to such attacks, namely to make their fires in one place . . .*

(A chapter or more is here missing from the text)

(51) . . . In the mean while, Publius Sulla, whom Caesar had put in command of the camp when he left, brought two legions to help the cohort; and his arrival easily repulsed the Pompeians. They failed to stand firm against our men, either when they appeared or when they attacked, and after the front rank had been dislodged the others turned round and abandoned their positions. Sulla, however, recalled our men from the pursuit to stop them carrying it too far. Now many people think that if he had been willing to pursue the enemy more vigorously, the war could have been ended that very day. But his decision ought not to be criticized. A senior officer's role is one thing, a general's another: the former ought to act entirely in accordance with his orders, the latter ought to take decisions flexibly with an eye on the overall picture. Sulla had been left at the camp by Caesar, and once he had saved the men of his own side he was content with this and had no wish to fight a full battle, an action which might bring the risk of seeming to play the part of general himself. The situation put the Pompeians in great difficulty with their retreat. They had left a position on lower ground and had come to a halt at the top of the slope; if they re-treated downhill, they were afraid of our men pursuing them from above; furthermore, there was little time left before sunset, because in the hope of bringing the operation to a successful conclusion they had prolonged the struggle until

almost nightfall. Thus forced to improvise a plan, Pompey seized a small isolated hill which was far enough away from our fort to be out of range of an artillery missile. He settled down in this position, fortified it, and gathered all his forces there.

(52) In addition there was fighting at the same time in two other places, Pompey having made simultaneous attacks on a number of forts in order to stretch our manpower and ensure that help would not be available from the adjoining forts. In one of these places Volcacius Tullus with three cohorts withstood the attack of a legion and forced it to give ground, in the other some Germans went forward from the fortifications and after killing several of the enemy retired unharmed to their own lines.

(53) So six engagements took place on a single day, three at Dyrrachium and three at the lines of fortification,* and when the tally was made of all of these we found that about two thousand of the Pompeians had fallen, including a fair number of re-enlisted men and centurions (one of their number being a Valerius Flaccus, son of that Lucius who had been governor of Asia*); six military standards were also captured. Of our own men, no more than twenty were lost in all the engagements. But in the fort there was not one man who was unwounded, and four centurions from a single cohort lost eyes. When they wanted to provide proof of their efforts and the extent of their danger, they counted out for Caesar about thirty thousand arrows which had been fired at the fort, and when he was brought the shield of the centurion Scaeva a hundred and twenty holes were found in it. Caesar gave Scaeva 200,000 sesterces for his services to himself and to the state, and declared that he was promoting him from centurion in the eighth cohort to leading centurion of the legion (for it was agreed that it was largely due to him that the fort had been saved), and he afterwards rewarded the cohort generously with double pay, grain, clothing, and rations, and with military decorations.*

(54) At night, Pompey added large-scale fortifications, and on the following days constructed towers; then he raised his earthworks to a height of fifteen feet and shielded that side of his camp with protective screens. Five days later he

took advantage of another somewhat overcast night, blocked all the gates of the camp, put ... in the way to impede the enemy, and at the start of the third watch silently led his army out and retired to his old fortifications.

(55) Every day after that Caesar led his army forward in battle order on to level ground, to give Pompey the opportunity of a decisive battle, and as a result brought his legions up almost under Pompey's camp. His front line was only just far enough away from the ramparts to be out of range of artillery missiles. Pompey, on the other hand, to preserve his public reputation, drew his army up in front of his camp, but in such a way that his third line was in contact with the ramparts, and indeed the whole army could be protected by missiles thrown down from there.

Fufius Calenus' activities in Central Greece

(56) Now that he had won Aetolia, Acarnania, and the Amphilochians, as explained, through Cassius Longinus and Calvisius Sabinus, Caesar thought he ought to try Achaea* and make a little further progress. He therefore sent Quintus <Fufius> Calenus in that direction and added to his force Sabinus, Cassius, and their cohorts. When he heard of their approach, Rutilius Lupus, who had been sent by Pompey to administer Achaea, began to build defensive works across the Isthmus to keep Fufius out of Achaea; the latter took control of Delphi and of Thebes and Orchomenus by the wish of those communities, took some cities by force, and sent delegations round the other states in an attempt to win them over to Caesar's side. Such was the general nature of Fufius' activity.

Further abortive peace negotiations.
Pompey's cavalry starve

(57) While these operations were taking place in Achaea and at Dyrrachium, and when it was established that Scipio had

reached Macedonia, Caesar, not forgetting his original policy,* sent Aulus Clodius to him; this man was a friend of both himself and Scipio, and Caesar had been in the habit of regarding him as one of his circle after Scipio had initially recommended and passed him on. Caesar gave him a letter and a message for Scipio, of which this was the gist: he himself had tried everything to obtain peace, but considered that it was the fault of the people he had wanted to be its agents that nothing had been done, because they had been afraid of delivering his message to Pompey at an inopportune time.* But Scipio had enough authority not only to explain without demur the course of action he favoured, but also to exert a great deal of pressure and bring a man who was going astray back to the right path; furthermore he commanded an army in his own right,* so that in addition to moral authority he also possessed the power to coerce. If he were to do this, to him alone everyone would give the credit for bringing calm to Italy, peace to the provinces, and salvation to the empire. Clodius gave him this message, and was apparently listened to willingly for a day or two; but subsequently, when Favonius had rebuked Scipio (as we found out when the war was over), he was not given audience and went back to Caesar without achieving his purpose.

(58) So that Caesar could more easily contain the Pompeian cavalry at Dyrrachium* and stop them going out to graze, he built large earthworks by the two approaches, which we have explained were narrow, and sited forts at these spots. When Pompey realized that no advantage was being gained by his cavalry, after a few days he brought them back again by ship inside his fortifications. There was an extreme shortage of fodder, so much so that his men kept the horses alive by stripping leaves off the trees and mashing the soft roots of reeds; for they had eaten the crops which had been planted inside the fortifications. They were forced to bring in fodder a great distance by sea from Corcyra and Acarnania, and as the supply of it was reduced, to supplement it with barley, and keep the cavalry going by these expedients. But when not only the barley, and the fodder from all sources, and the plants they reaped, but even the leaves from the trees ran

out, and the horses had become weak with emaciation, Pompey thought he must make some attempt to break out.

Pompey breaks out and defeats Caesar

(59) On Caesar's side, among the cavalry, there were two brothers from the Allobroges,* Roucillus and Egus, sons of Adbucillus, who had over many years held the headship of his people. They were men of outstanding courage, of whose splendid and valiant assistance Caesar had made use in all his campaigns in Gaul. For these reasons Caesar had given them the highest offices at home and seen that they were appointed to their senate outside the ordinary procedures; he had given them land in Gaul captured from his enemies, and great rewards in the form of money, and transformed them from paupers into rich men. Thanks to their courage they were not only honoured by Caesar, but also popular with the rest of the army; however, relying on their friendship with Caesar and carried away by a foolish and uncivilized arrogance they were treating their own people with contempt, cheating the horsemen over pay, and diverting all the booty back home. Disturbed by this, their men came in a body to Caesar and complained openly about the injustices inflicted by the pair, and added to their other grievances the charge that they had made false returns of the number of cavalrymen in order to appropriate their pay.

(60) Not considering this the time to punish them, and making considerable allowances for their courage, Caesar adjourned the whole business; privately, he reprimanded them for treating their cavalry as a source of profit, and advised them to expect everything of his friendship and to base their hopes for the future on his past kindnesses. None the less, this affair brought them into universal dislike and contempt, a state of affairs which they realized not only from the taunts of others, but also from their own judgement and consciences. Impelled by the disgrace, and perhaps thinking that they were not being allowed to go free, but were being held over to be dealt with at another time, they decided to leave us

and try new fortunes and new friendships. They shared their plan with a few of their dependants to whom they dared entrust such a crime, and first tried to kill the cavalry commander Gaius Volusenus (as was afterwards discovered at the end of the war), so that they would not appear to have deserted to Pompey without bringing him some gift; but when that seemed too difficult and no opportunity of carrying it out arose, they borrowed as much money as they could, as if they wanted to satisfy their men and pay back what they had misappropriated, bought a large number of horses, and deserted to Pompey with their accomplices.

(61) Because they were well-born and lavishly equipped and had come with a great retinue and many draught animals, and were considered men of courage and had been honoured by Caesar, and because this was a new and abnormal event, Pompey took them round and displayed them to all his troops. Before that time no one, whether he was a footsoldier or a cavalryman, had abandoned Caesar for Pompey, while desertions from Pompey to Caesar took place almost every day; but commonly the latter were the soldiers conscripted in Epirus and Aetolia and from all the regions controlled by Caesar, who came over *en masse*. But these two knew everything; they knew if there was something unfinished on the fortifications, or if something was thought by the military experts to be lacking, and they had observed the times things happened, and distances between sites, and the varying watchfulness of the guards according to the character and enthusiasm of the man in charge in each case. All this information they presented to Pompey.

(62) Pompey had previously decided, as has been mentioned, on an attempt to break out, and so, having learnt all this, he ordered his troops to make wicker coverings for their helmets and gather together filling material. When preparations were complete, after dark he put a great number of light-armed troops and archers and all the material on board small boats and merchant ships and at about midnight took sixty cohorts drawn from his main camp and his outposts towards that part of the fortifications which adjoined the sea and was furthest away from Caesar's main camp.* He despatched to

the same place the ships which (as we have explained) were loaded with material and light-armed troops, and also the warships which he had at Dyrrachium, and gave each their orders. Caesar had the quaestor Lentulus Marcellinus posted at these fortifications with the Ninth legion; as Marcellinus was not in good health, he had sent Flavius Postumus to assist him.

(63) At that spot, facing the enemy, there was a ditch fifteen feet wide and a bank and palisade ten feet high; the earth bank of this fortification was of the same breadth, and after an interval of 150 feet there was another palisade facing the opposite direction with a slightly lower earthwork. The reason was Caesar's fear during the preceding days, that our men would be outflanked from the sea, and he had constructed a double fortification there so that if there were to be fighting on both sides there would be some possibility of resistance. But the scale of the earthworks and the non-stop daily labour, because he had extended the circuit of his fortifications seventeen miles, had not allowed time for them to be finished. And so he had not yet completed the transverse bank and palisade facing the sea which was to join up these lines of fortification. This fact was known to Pompey, having been reported by the Allobrogan deserters, and caused a great setback for our men. When our cohorts had taken up their night stations by the sea, at first light the Pompeians suddenly approached, and at the same time the soldiers who had been transported round in ships launched their missiles at the outer palisade. The ditches began to be filled in with material, the legionaries brought up ladders and with artillery and missiles of various kinds struck fear into the defenders of the inner line of fortification, and a great mass of archers was deployed on both fronts. Furthermore the wicker coverings which the Pompeians had attached to their helmets gave them considerable protection from the impact of stones, which were the only missiles available to us. And so, when our men were under every sort of pressure and were barely holding their own, the defect in the fortifications (explained above) was noticed and men were put ashore from ships between the two palisades, where the work was not finished.

These took our men in rear, cleared them from both lines of fortification, and forced them to flee.

(64) On the news of this emergency, Marcellinus sent . . . cohorts from the camp to help our struggling forces. When they came in sight of the fugitives they were unable to steady them by their arrival, nor did they stand up themselves to the enemy attack. Thus whatever reinforcement was provided, it was undermined by the fugitives' fear and contributed to the panic and danger, the retreat being hampered by the mass of men. In this engagement the legionary standard-bearer was seriously wounded. As his strength ebbed, he caught sight of our cavalry and said: 'This eagle, when I was alive, I defended assiduously for many years, and now as I die I give it back to Caesar with the same trust. Do not, I beg you, allow to occur what has never before happened to Caesar's army and suffer a military disgrace,* but take this safe to him.' By this chance the eagle was saved when all the centurions of the first cohort* had been killed except the second most senior.

(65) By now the Pompeians, inflicting heavy casualties on our men, were approaching Marcellinus' camp and making the remaining cohorts extremely apprehensive, and Marcus Antonius, who held the nearest of the fortified positions, had received the news and was seen coming down with twelve cohorts from higher ground. His arrival checked the Pompeians and encouraged our men to recover from their panic. Not much later, after a smoke signal had been made from fort to fort, as had previously been the practice, Caesar arrived on the spot with a number of cohorts which he had taken from the garrisons of the forts. When he learnt the extent of the reverse and saw that Pompey had made his way outside the fortifications, so that he could freely graze his animals along the coast without losing access by ship, Caesar changed his tactics, as he had failed to achieve his aim, and gave orders to fortify a camp next to Pompey.

(66) When this had been done, it was observed by Caesar's scouts that some cohorts, amounting apparently to a legion, were behind a wood and being taken to an old camp. This was the arrangement of the camp. When on the preceding

days Caesar's Ninth legion had blocked Pompey's forces and was completing the earthworks to encircle them, as we have explained, it had encamped at this spot. The camp adjoined a wood and was no more than 300 yards from the sea. Later Caesar for a number of reasons changed his plans and moved his camp a little further away. A few days afterwards Pompey had taken possession of this same site,* and because he intended to accommodate a greater number of legions there, had added a more extensive fortification, leaving the inner ramparts in being. Thus the smaller camp was contained within the larger and functioned as a fort and strongpoint. Pompey had also built a fortification about 400 yards long from the left-hand corner of the camp across to a stream, so that his men could get water more easily and without danger. But he too, changing his plans for reasons which it is unnecessary to detail, had left the place. Thus although the camp had remained empty for several days, its entire defensive system was still intact.

(67) Caesar's lookouts reported* that legionary standards had been taken into this camp. They confirmed that the same thing had been seen from some of the higher forts. The place was about 500 yards from Pompey's new camp. Hoping to be able to crush this legion, and wanting to mitigate the day's defeat, Caesar left two cohorts busy on earthworks, to give the impression that fortification was in progress; his remaining cohorts numbered thirty-three, amongst them the Ninth legion (reduced in numbers and with many of its centurions missing), and these he took by a roundabout way in double line* as unobtrusively as possible towards Pompey's legion and the smaller camp. His initial thoughts proved right, because he arrived before Pompey could observe him, and although the fortifications of the camp were substantial, none the less he quickly attacked on the left wing, where he himself was, and dislodged the Pompeians from the rampart. A 'hedgehog'* had been put in to block the gates. Here there was a struggle for a little while, while our men were trying to break in and the opposition were defending the camp; the resistance in this area was led by Titus Pullienus, by whose agency, as we have explained, Gaius Antonius' army had been

betrayed.* But nevertheless our troops' courage brought them victory; they cut out the 'hedgehog' and burst first into the bigger camp and then also into the fort which was incorporated in it, because that was where the beaten legion had withdrawn; and there they killed some of the enemy who were fighting back.

(68) But luck, a force universally powerful but particularly so in war, brings about great changes by slight adjustments of her balance; as then occurred. The cohorts of Caesar's right wing were ignorant of the ground and in their search for a gate thought the fortification, which as we explained above led from the camp to a stream, was the fortification of the camp, and followed it. But when they realized that it connected with the stream, they broke it down, as there were no defenders, and all our cavalry followed these cohorts.

(69) In the mean time Pompey, having received news of this event after a rather long delay, withdrew his five legions from their work of fortification and led them to the relief of his men; his cavalry was approaching ours at the same time as his battle formation was sighted by those of our troops who had seized the camp, and the whole situation was suddenly altered. The Pompeian legion, heartened by the hope of swift relief, tried to resist from the rear gate of the camp and actually took the offensive against our men. Caesar's cavalry, because they were making their way up through the ramparts by a narrow path, were afraid they might not be able to retreat and began the flight. The right wing, which was separated from the left, noticed the terror of the cavalry, and began to withdraw at the point where they had destroyed the fortifications, to avoid being overwhelmed inside them. Not a few of them, to escape the narrow opening, jumped down into the ditches of the fortifications, where the first men in were crushed and the rest used their bodies to provide a way out to safety for themselves. On the left wing, when the soldiers saw from the rampart that Pompey had arrived and their own men were in flight, they became afraid of being cut off in a confined space, as they had the enemy both outside and inside them. They attempted to save themselves by a retreat in the direction from which they had

come, and there was such confusion, panic, and flight all around that although Caesar seized the standards of his fleeing men and ordered them to halt, some *<abandoned their horses and ran off together in the same direction>*, others in their fear even threw away the standards, and not a single man halted.

(70) In this disastrous situation, the factors which contributed to prevent the destruction of the entire army were that Pompey was afraid of an ambush, I think* because events had turned out contrary to his expectations after he had seen his own men fleeing from the camp shortly beforehand, and so did not dare for some time to approach the fortifications; and that his cavalry were slowed down in their pursuit by the narrow gaps which were in any case already occupied by Caesar's infantry. And so a trivial matter tipped the balance strongly in each direction: the fortifications which had been extended from the camp to the stream interfered with the victory which Caesar had all but won after storming the Pompeian camp, and the same thing saved our men by slowing down their pursuers.

(71) In these two battles fought on a single day Caesar lost 960 legionary soldiers and the military tribunes *<Titus>* Tuticanus Gallus, who was a senator's son, Gaius Felginas from Placentia, Aulus Granius from Puteoli, and Marcus Sacrativir from Capua, who were all four prominent Roman equestrians, and 32 centurions (but a large proportion of these perished in the ditches and on the fortifications and the banks of the stream, quite unwounded but overwhelmed by the panic-stricken flight of their fellows), and 32 military standards* were lost. The battle earned Pompey a salutation as 'Victorious General'.* He accepted the title and allowed himself to be so greeted afterwards, but never adopted the practice of putting it at the head of his letters, nor wreathed his rods of office with laurel. Labienus, on the other hand, succeeded in getting Pompey to order the prisoners to be handed over to him, and apparently in order to make a show and create more confidence in himself, deserter that he was, when they had all been brought forward he addressed them as 'fellow soldiers', asked them in the most insulting fashion

whether veteran soldiers usually ran away, and publicly put
them to death.

(72) These events gave the Pompeians such confidence
and courage that they did not reflect on the nature of the
struggle, but considered that they had already secured victory. They did not recognize as causes either the small numbers of our men, or the difficult terrain and restricted passage
arising from the previous occupation of the camp, and the
fear of attack from inside and outside the fortifications, or
the fact that the army had been cut in two and neither section could help the other. Apart from this, they failed to
consider that the fighting had taken place neither when line
had fiercely charged line, nor in pitched battle, and that our
men had inflicted more harm on themselves because of their
numbers combined with the lack of room than they had suffered at the hands of the enemy. And finally they failed to
remind themselves of the everyday accidents of war, how
factors which are frequently trifling—mistaken suspicion, or
sudden alarm, or religious scruple—have caused great dis-
asters, or how often an army has come to grief through the
shortcomings of a commander or the fault of a tribune; but
just as if they had triumphed by their own courage, and no
change of fortune could occur, they made that day's victory
famous, by letter and by word of mouth, to the whole world.

Caesar withdraws to Thessaly and encamps near Pharsalus. Pompey's army comes up with him

(73) As his previous plans had been thwarted, Caesar thought
he ought to change his entire plan of campaign. He therefore withdrew from all his fortified positions simultaneously,
and abandoned the siege. Gathering the army together, he
addressed his men and encouraged them not to be down-
hearted at what had happened or to be demoralized by
these events and allow one defeat, and that not serious, to
outweigh many victories. They should be grateful for their
luck because they had taken Italy without loss of any kind,
had imposed peace on the two Spains with their extremely

warlike population led by highly experienced and practised generals,* and had brought under their own control the nearby provinces* and their supplies of grain; finally they ought to remember the happy chance by which they had all been brought safe across from Italy, through hostile fleets, when not only the harbours but even the beaches had been packed with the enemy. If not everything was going well, luck needed to be helped along by their own efforts. The blame for such loss as they had incurred ought to be attributed to anything or anyone except themselves. They had offered level ground for a battle, they had taken possession of an enemy camp, they had driven their opponents out and got the better of them in combat. But whether it was their own disarray, or some mistake, or indeed luck which had intervened to rob them of a victory which had seemed to be already in their hands, they must all strive to redeem by their courage the defeat they had suffered. If they did this, <the result would be> that their loss would turn to profit, as had happened at Gergovia,* and their opponents, men who had previously been afraid to fight, would offer battle of their own accord.

(74) After delivering this address he formally reprimanded some standard-bearers and demoted them. The whole army, in fact, was so hurt by defeat and so eager to restore their reputation that nobody waited for orders from an officer or a centurion and each of them, by way of punishment, voluntarily undertook even harder labour; at the same time they all longed to fight, while even some of the higher ranks, not without reason, thought the right policy was to stay there and seek a result by battle. Caesar disagreed; he had little confidence in his demoralized troops and thought they needed time to regain their courage, and he was very concerned about his food supplies now that he had moved away from the fortifications.

(75) And so without any delay, apart from that required to attend to the sick and wounded, he silently sent ahead to Apollonia* at the beginning of the night all the baggage and equipment from his camp, forbidding anyone to rest before the march was finished. One legion was sent to escort the

train. When this operation was complete, he made two legions stay in the camp but brought the remainder out before dawn by a number of gates and sent them the same way. Shortly afterwards, to observe military routine but also ensure that his departure should be discovered as late as possible, he ordered the signal for breaking camp to be given, then immediately emerged and swiftly disappeared out of sight of the camp in pursuit of the rear of his column. When he realized Caesar's plan, Pompey had no hesitation in following, and bearing the same consideration in mind, that is the possibility of catching troops demoralized and hindered by baggage* on their march, he led his army out of camp and sent his cavalry ahead to slow down Caesar's rearguard; but he was unable to catch up with the latter, because Caesar had had a long start and was marching without equipment. But when they reached the River Genusus, the banks of which were difficult, the cavalry caught up with the rearmost troops and delayed them in fighting. Against them Caesar sent his own horse, reinforced by four hundred light-armed frontline troops, and they were so successful that as a result of the cavalry engagement that took place they drove all the enemy off, killing a number of them, and themselves withdrew without loss to rejoin the column of march.

(76) After completing the normal march which he intended for that day, and getting his army across the River Genusus, Caesar halted for the night in his old camp facing Asparagium.* He kept all his infantry inside the fortifications, and ordered his cavalry, which had been sent out as if to forage, to come rapidly back again into camp by the rear gate. Likewise Pompey halted in his old camp at Asparagium when his day's march was done. Some of his soldiers, who were free from entrenchment work because the fortifications were intact, went rather far afield in search of firewood and fodder, while others, because the decision to march had been sudden and they had left most of their baggage and possessions behind, were tempted by the nearness of their previous camp to deposit their arms in their tents and abandon the defences. They were thus prevented from following, as Caesar had foreseen would be the case, when at about midday he

gave the signal to leave camp, led his army out, and by repeating the day's march proceeded eight miles further; this Pompey was unable to do because of the absence of his soldiers.

(77) On the following day Caesar, in the same way, sent his baggage and equipment on ahead and himself left camp before dawn, so that if circumstances compelled him to fight, he could respond to the emergency with his army ready for battle. He did the same on subsequent days. By these means he was successful in avoiding any loss or defeat although the rivers were very deep and the way very obstructed.* For Pompey, after suffering the first day's delay and undertaking the effort of the following days without result, although he pressed on with forced marches and very much wanted to catch up with the men ahead, called off the chase on the fourth day and decided that he ought to adopt a different plan.

(78) Caesar had to go to Apollonia to leave the wounded, pay his troops, rally his allies, and put garrisons in the towns. But he gave only as much time to these matters as a man in haste was forced to; he was anxious about Domitius,* fearful that Pompey might succeed in reaching him first, and hurried with all speed and energy in his direction. His whole strategy depended on the following considerations: if Pompey made for the same area, he would be drawn away from the sea and separated from the supplies of grain and provisions he had collected at Dyrrachium, and be forced to fight Caesar on equal terms; if he crossed to Italy, Caesar could join forces with Domitius and go to the help of Italy by way of Illyricum;* and if he attempted to attack Apollonia and Oricum and keep Caesar out of the whole coastal area, by blockading Scipio Caesar would force him to come to the aid of his own forces. Caesar therefore sent messengers ahead to Domitius with written instructions about what he wanted done; then he garrisoned Apollonia with four cohorts, Lissus with one, and Oricum with three, and after leaving the wounded, began to make his way through Epirus and Athamania.* Pompey too, guessing what Caesar's plan would be, was of the view that he ought to hurry to Scipio; if Caesar were to march

there, he could support Scipio; but if Caesar were unwilling to leave the coast and Oricum, because he was expecting legions and cavalry from Italy, he could himself attack Domitius with his entire force.

(79) For these reasons each of them made all speed, intending on the one hand to help his own side <and on the other> not to let slip the chance of defeating the enemy. But while Caesar had been diverted from the direct route by his visit to Apollonia, Pompey had an easy journey to Macedonia through Candavia. On top of this came another, unforeseen, setback: <although> Domitius had been encamped alongside Scipio for a number of days, he had moved away from him to find supplies of food, and had taken his force to Heraclia, which is on the borders of Candavia, so that fortune herself seemed to be putting him in Pompey's path. These facts were unknown to Caesar at this stage. At the same time Pompey had sent letters to all the provinces and communities about the battle at Dyrrachium, and a wildly exaggerated rumour had spread, that Caesar had been routed and was fleeing with the loss of nearly all his men. This news had not only made the journey dangerous, but was even turning some places against him. And so it happened that although messengers were sent off by several routes from Caesar to Domitius and from Domitius to Caesar, they completely failed to reach their destination. But some Allobroges, companions of Roucillus and Egus, who as we explained above* had deserted to Pompey, caught sight as they rode along of Domitius' scouts, and whether from old acquaintance, because they had fought together in Gaul, or from elation over their great achievement, recounted the whole story of what had happened, and told them that Caesar had left and that Pompey was about to appear. The scouts brought the news to Domitius, who with a start of barely four hours avoided danger, thanks to the enemy, and met Caesar as he arrived in the neighbourhood of Aeginium, a town which faces Thessaly and closes it off.

(80) His forces now united, Caesar went on to Gomphi, which is the first town in Thessaly as you come from Epirus; the people had of their own accord sent a delegation to Caesar

a few months beforehand to invite him to make use of all the help they could give, and they had asked him for soldiers to protect them. But he was preceded there by the rumour we have mentioned above about the battle at Dyrrachium, which it had grossly exaggerated. So Androsthenes, the chief magistrate of Thessaly, preferring to associate himself with Pompey in victory than to be Caesar's ally in adversity, gathered the whole rural population, slave and free, inside the town, barred the gates, and sent messengers to Scipio and Pompey to come to his rescue, saying that he was confident of the town's defences, if help came quickly, but they could not withstand a lengthy assault. Scipio, hearing that the armies had left Dyrrachium, had brought his legions to Larisa; Pompey, however, was not yet near to Thessaly. Caesar fortified a camp, then gave orders for ladders and mantlets to be constructed, and fascines to be prepared, for an immediate attack. When these were ready, he fired the soldiers' enthusiasm by pointing out how advantageous it would be to alleviate their desperate shortage of everything* by capturing a rich and well-provisioned town, and at the same time terrify the remaining communities by its example, and have this happen quickly, before help could arrive. And so, thanks to the remarkable efforts of his soldiers, on the same day as he arrived, he attacked in the middle of the afternoon, and took by assault before sunset, a town with imposingly high walls, handed it over to his soldiers to plunder, and immediately moved camp away from the town and arrived at Metropolis, so that he reached it before any message or rumour of the storming of Gomphi.

(81) The people of Metropolis were at first of the same way of thinking, being influenced by the same rumours. They shut their gates and manned the walls, but later, when they heard of the fate of Gomphi from prisoners whom Caesar had had brought forward to the foot of the wall, they opened their gates. Caesar was most careful to see that they suffered no harm, and apart from Larisa, which was occupied by substantial forces of Scipio's, there was no state in Thessaly which on comparing what had happened to Gomphi with the good fortune of Metropolis did not submit to Caesar

and obey his orders. He took up a position in farmland convenient <for securing supplies of corn>, now nearly ripe, and decided to wait for Pompey there and make this the centre of his whole campaign.*

(82) A few days later Pompey reached Thessaly. Addressing the whole army, he expressed his gratitude to his own men and encouraged Scipio's soldiers, now that victory was theirs, to share in the booty and the rewards. He brought all the legions into a single camp and shared the honours with Scipio, ordering a second commander's tent to be pitched and the bugle to be sounded in his area too. Now that Pompey's forces were enlarged and two great armies united, the opinion previously held by them all was confirmed and their hopes of victory were increased. So much so, indeed, that any intervening time appeared simply to delay their return to Italy, and whenever Pompey acted a little slowly or cautiously, they used to say that although the business needed no more than a day, he took pleasure in exercising command and liked to count among his slaves men who had been consuls and praetors. Some were already openly competing among themselves for rewards and priesthoods, and allocating consulships for years ahead, while others were asking for the houses and property that belonged to the men in Caesar's camp; they also had a great dispute in council about whether Lucilius Hirrus, who had been sent by Pompey on a mission to Parthia, should be permitted to be a candidate *in absentia* at the next praetorian elections—his friends begging Pompey to stand by the promise he had made when Hirrus was leaving, so as not to give the impression that the latter had been deceived through Pompey's exercise of authority, the others jibbing at special treatment for one man when the effort and the risk were the same for all.

(83) By now Domitius,* Scipio, and Lentulus Spinther in their daily quarrelling over Caesar's priesthood* had sunk to open and serious insult: Lentulus made much of the honour due to his seniority, Domitius boasted of his position and popularity in Rome, and Scipio relied on his relationship to Pompey. Acutius Rufus even demanded that Lucius Afranius be brought before Pompey on a charge of betraying

his army, on the grounds that he had <been negligent> in conducting the <war> in Spain. Lucius Domitius even said in council that after the end of the war he favoured giving three voting tablets to those members of the senatorial order who had taken part in the war on their side, and that they should give their verdict on each person who had stayed in Rome or had been with Pompey's various forces but failed to lend support in the field: one tablet would be for those they thought should be entirely exonerated, one for those on whom they would pass a capital sentence, and one for those whom they would fine. In short, all of them were concerned with either office, or monetary reward, or pursuit of their private enemies, and thought not about how they could achieve victory, but how they ought to use it.

Caesar secures victory at Pharsalus

(84) Now that he had secured supplies of grain and his soldiers had recovered their strength, and a sufficient interval had elapsed since the battles at Dyrrachium* for him to consider that he could reliably judge the troops' morale, Caesar decided to test Pompey's intention, or willingness, to fight. So he brought his army out of camp and formed it up for battle, at first on his home ground and at a good distance from Pompey's camp, but as the days went by in such a way as to progress forward from his own camp and draw up his line close under the hills where the Pompeians were. This action made his army daily more confident of itself. He adhered, however, to his previous practice, as explained, with the cavalry: since he was greatly inferior in numbers, he ordered young lightly equipped men from his front-line troops, armed with weapons chosen with an eye to rapid movement, to fight among the cavalry, so that by daily practice they became experienced in this sort of fighting also. By these means it came about that even on the more open sort of ground his thousand cavalry, as they were trained, would dare to stand up to the charge of seven thousand Pompeians without being much terrified of their numbers. To prove

it, during this very period he carried out a successful cavalry engagement, and killed among others one of the two Allobroges who, as we noted above, had deserted to Pompey.

(85) Pompey, whose camp was on a hill, was in the habit of drawing up his battle-line at the very bottom of the slope, always, it seemed, waiting to see whether Caesar would accept the disadvantage of the ground. Caesar, believing that there was no means of tempting Pompey to battle, judged that his best plan of campaign was to shift his camp away and always be on the march. His idea was that by moving from camp to camp and coming to more places he would find provisioning easier; at the same time he might get some chance of a battle while *en route*, and by marching every day he would exhaust Pompey's army, which was unused to hard effort. In consequence of this decision, the signal for departure had already been given and the tents struck when it was observed that Pompey's line had shortly beforehand advanced further from his defences than was his daily custom, so that it appeared possible to fight without one side having the advantage of the slope. Then Caesar, although his column of march was already at the gates, said to his companions: 'We must delay the march for the moment and put our minds to a battle, as we have always wanted. We are mentally prepared to fight; we shall not easily get the chance again.' And hurriedly he led his forces out in battle order.

(86) Pompey too, as was later discovered, had decided to settle matters by a battle, on the urging of all his advisers. He had even said in council within the preceding few days that Caesar's army would be routed before the battle-lines met. When there was general astonishment at this, he said: 'I know I am promising something almost incredible; but here is the logic of my plan, so that you can go out to battle in better heart. I have convinced our cavalry of this, and they have confirmed that they will do it, namely attack Caesar's right wing on its open flank* when the armies are nearly upon each other; they will outflank his line, take it in rear, throw his army into confusion, and rout it before a single weapon of ours is hurled at the enemy. In this way we shall finish off the war without any danger to our legions and

virtually without bloodshed. This is really not difficult, as we are so strong in cavalry.'* At the same time he instructed them to be mentally ready for the next day and, since the opportunity of fighting now existed, as they had often repeatedly asked, not to disappoint the hopes held both by themselves and by the rest.

(87) Labienus spoke next, and because he had a low opinion of Caesar's forces enthusiastically praised Pompey's plan: 'Do not think, Pompey,' he said, 'that this is the army which conquered Gaul and Germany. I took part in all the battles* and my view is not put forward without consideration or based on facts beyond my knowledge. A very small fraction of that army remains; a large proportion has died (something which was bound to occur given the number of battles), many fell victim to disease in the autumn in Italy, many have gone home, and many were left behind on embarkation. Or have you not heard that cohorts were put together in Brundisium from men who had stayed behind because they were sick? These forces you see have been reconstituted from the levies of recent years in Cisalpine Gaul, and a good number of them are Transpadane settlers.'* With these words, he swore not to return to camp unless victory was theirs, and urged the rest to do the same. Pompey praised him for this, and took an oath in the same terms; and not one of the rest hesitated to do likewise. After these proceedings in council were over, they separated with high hopes and much cheerfulness; and they imagined they had already secured victory, because they thought it impossible in a matter of such importance and from a general of such experience* to receive assurances that were groundless.

(88) On drawing close to Pompey's camp, Caesar saw that his line of battle was arranged as follows. On the left wing were the two legions handed over by Caesar at the beginning of the quarrel in accordance with a decree of the senate; one of these was called the First, the other the Third.* This was where Pompey placed himself. The centre of the line was taken by Scipio with the legions from Syria. The Cilician legion was positioned on the right wing together with the Spanish cohorts which Afranius, as we said,* had brought

with him. These were the units which Pompey thought were his most reliable. He had inserted the rest of the cohorts between his centre and his wings, bringing the total to 110. This made 45,000 men,* plus about two thousand re-enlisted veterans, men of his personal entourage from his previous armies who had gathered to join him; these he had distributed over all parts of the line. The remaining seven cohorts he had stationed to guard his camp and the neighbouring forts. A river with difficult banks* protected his right wing; he had therefore put his whole body of cavalry and all his archers and slingers on his left wing.

(89) Following his previous practice, Caesar had put the Tenth legion on the right wing; on the left he had put the Ninth, although it had been terribly weakened in the battles at Dyrrachium, and placed the Eighth next to it in such a way as to make virtually a single legion out of the two, and had instructed each to protect the other. He had 80 cohorts formed up in the line, 22,000 men in all,* and had left seven cohorts to guard the camp. In command of the left wing he had put Antonius, of the right wing Publius Sulla, and of the centre Gnaeus Domitius. He himself took up a position opposite Pompey. At the same time, because he had noticed the dispositions we have explained, and was afraid that his right wing might be outflanked by the mass of cavalry, he quickly withdrew individual cohorts from his third line and made a fourth from them, which he formed up opposite the cavalry; he made it clear to them what he wanted, and impressed on them that victory that day depended on the courage of these cohorts. At the same time he gave instructions to the third line that they were not to engage without orders from him; when he wanted them to, he would give a signal by flag.

(90) In delivering his exhortation (following military custom) to the army to fight, and declaring his undying commitment to its interests, Caesar recalled above all that he was able to use his soldiers as witnesses to the enthusiasm with which he had sought peace, the initiatives he had taken through Vatinius in discussions and through Aulus Clodius with Scipio, and the ways in which he had struggled with Libo at Oricum* to arrange the despatch of an embassy. Nor

had he ever wanted to waste soldiers' blood, or deprive the state of one or other army. At the conclusion of this address, as the soldiers clamoured and burned with eagerness to fight, he gave the signal on the trumpet.

(91) In Caesar's army there was a re-enlisted veteran, Crastinus, who in the previous year had served under him as senior centurion in the Tenth legion and was a man of extraordinary courage. When the signal was given, he said: 'Follow me, you men who were in my company, and give your general the aid you have promised. This is the only battle left; once it is over, he will regain his position and we our freedom.' And looking at Caesar he said: 'I shall do things today, general, that you will thank me for, whether I live or die.' After uttering these words, he was the first man to run forward from the right wing, followed by about 120 picked volunteers.

(92) Between the two lines enough space was left for the two armies to make their charge at each other. But Pompey had previously instructed his men to absorb Caesar's attack without moving from their positions, and to allow Caesar's line to become distorted; this he was said to have done on the advice of Gaius Triarius, so that the first vigorous charge of Caesar's troops should be blunted and their line stretched, while they themselves, with their formation intact, could attack men in disorder; and he hoped that the throwing-spears would fall with less effect on his troops if they stood their ground than if they threw their own weapons and advanced, and also that Caesar's men, because they had run twice the distance, would be out of breath and overcome by exhaustion. At least in our view, Pompey was wrong to do this, because there is in all of us some naturally inborn excitement and ardour of soul, which is fired by the desire to fight. This quality generals ought not to repress, but encourage; and not without reason did it become the custom a very long time ago for trumpet calls to be sounded on all sides and for everyone to raise a shout; people thought that by these means the enemy were terrified and their own side urged on.

(93) But when the signal was given and our soldiers ran forward with their spears ready to throw, they saw that the

Pompeians were not running to meet them; being experienced and practised from previous battles, they spontaneously checked their charge and halted approximately half-way, to avoid being in a state of exhaustion when they came to close quarters; then after a short pause they renewed their charge, threw their spears, and quickly drew their swords, as had been ordered by Caesar. Not that the Pompeians were not up to the task. They withstood the hail of spears, took the shock of the legions, kept their formation, and after throwing their spears resorted to their swords. At the same time the cavalry on Pompey's left wing all charged, as they had been instructed, and his entire mass of archers streamed forward. Unable to withstand their attack, our cavalry were driven from their positions and retreated a little, and Pompey's cavalry pressed on all the more eagerly and began to operate in individual squadrons and go round behind our line on its open side.* When Caesar observed this, he gave the signal to the fourth line which he had formed by detachment from the total number of his cohorts. They rapidly ran forward and with colours flying made an attack of such force on Pompey's cavalry that none of them stood their ground; they all turned round and not merely retreated, but immediately proceeded to gallop on in flight towards some very high hills.* When they had gone, all the archers and slingers, left unarmed and defenceless, were killed. Without pausing in their advance our cohorts outflanked the left wing of the Pompeians, who were still resisting in the set-piece fighting, and attacked them from behind.

(94) At the same time Caesar gave orders to his third line, which had not been in action and had up to this point stayed where it was, to charge forward. So now that fresh, unwounded men had taken the place of those who were exhausted, and furthermore others were attacking them from the rear, Pompey's men were unable to hold out and all turned and fled. Caesar was very well aware that the origins of his victory, as he himself had predicted when encouraging his troops, lay with those cohorts which had been stationed in the fourth line opposite the cavalry. It was they who had first driven off the cavalry, it was they who had slaughtered

the archers and slingers, it was they who had outflanked Pompey's line on the left* and caused the start of the rout. But when Pompey saw his cavalry beaten back and realized that the part of his force in which he placed most confidence was stricken with panic, he despaired of the others too; he left the line, rode urgently to his camp, and said in a loud voice to the centurions he had stationed at the principal gate, so that the soldiers could hear, 'Watch the camp and defend it well, if things go hard for us. I shall go round the other gates and hearten the men guarding the camp.' With these words, he went to his commander's tent, despairing of victory but still awaiting the result.

(95) On fleeing, the Pompeians had been forced inside their fortifications, but Caesar felt they should be allowed no time to recover from panic, and encouraged his soldiers to take the gift offered them by fortune and attack the camp. Although they were exhausted from the intense heat (for the battle had lasted until midday) none the less they were mentally ready for any effort and obeyed his orders. The camp was diligently defended by the cohorts which had been left there to guard it, and much more energetically by the Thracians and foreign auxiliaries. As for the soldiers who had fled from the battle, their morale undermined by fear and their bodies overpowered by weariness, the greater number of them had thrown away their weapons and their military standards and were thinking more of further flight than of defending the camp. Not that those who had made a stand at the fortifications were able to withstand the rain of missiles for very long; overcome by their injuries, they abandoned their position and immediately sought refuge in some very high hills* which adjoined the camp, under the leadership of their centurions and military tribunes.

(96) In Pompey's camp could be viewed artificial bowers, great quantities of silver laid out, tents floored with freshly cut turf, the tents of Lucius Lentulus and some others wreathed with ivy, and much else to indicate gross luxury and confidence of victory. It was easy to deduce from their pursuit of inessential pleasures that the other side had no misgivings about the outcome of the day. Yet these were men who

accused Caesar's wretched and long-suffering army of luxury, when it had never enjoyed sufficiency in its everyday needs. When our men were already inside the fortifications, Pompey seized a horse, tore off his general's insignia, and bursting out of the rear gate of the camp immediately made for Larisa at full gallop. And he did not stop there, but after gathering up a few of his fleeing associates* travelled on in the dark without a break, accompanied by thirty horsemen, to reach the sea and embark on a grain ship, complaining only that he had been mistaken in his judgement, because he thought he had been as good as betrayed by a group of men* whom he had expected to give him victory but who had in fact set the rout in train.

(97) After gaining possession of the camp, Caesar pressed the soldiers not to become occupied in looting and miss the opportunity of completing the rest of their business. He obtained their agreement and began to ring the hill with an earthwork. Since this hill had no water, the Pompeians had no confidence in their position and they left it and all began to withdraw along the adjoining ridge towards Larisa. When he saw this, Caesar split his forces: some of his legions he ordered to remain in Pompey's camp, some he sent back to his own camp, and four he took with him. By marching a less difficult route he began to converge on the Pompeians, and after six miles he drew up his battle-line. On observing this, the Pompeians halted on a hill, at whose foot ran a river. Caesar urged on his soldiers, and although they were exhausted from the unbroken exertions of a whole day, and night was starting to fall, he none the less cut off the hill from the river by a fortification, to stop the Pompeians getting water under cover of darkness. When this work was complete, the Pompeians sent a deputation and began to negotiate surrender. A few men of senatorial rank,* who had joined them, fled by night to seek safety.

(98) At dawn Caesar ordered all those who had occupied the hill to descend from the higher ground to the level and throw down their weapons. They did this without protest, and cast themselves on the ground with hands outstretched, weeping and begging him to spare them. He offered them

consolation and told them to stand up, said a few words about his leniency to them, to lessen their fear, and granted all of them their lives; he entrusted them to his soldiers, saying that none of them should suffer violence or be the recipient of demands from his men. After this scrupulous action, he gave instructions for other legions to come from camp to join him and for those he had taken with him to have their spell of rest, and reached Larisa on the same day.*

(99) In the battle his casualties amounted to no more than two hundred* soldiers, but he lost about thirty strong brave centurions. Amongst the dead was also the above-mentioned Crastinus,* who was killed, fighting heroically, by a sword-thrust full in the mouth. And what he had said as he went out to combat was proved correct, for it was Caesar's opinion that Crastinus' courage in the battle had been outstanding, and he considered himself most deeply in Crastinus' debt. In the Pompeian army, it appeared that about 15,000 had fallen, but more than 24,000 surrendered (the cohorts which were manning the forts having also surrendered, to Sulla), and in addition many of them took refuge in the neighbouring communities; and 180 military standards and nine eagles were brought back to Caesar after the battle. Lucius Domitius fled from the camp to the hills, but when he succumbed to exhaustion he was killed by the cavalry.

Naval operations in Sicily and S Italy

(100) During the same period Decimus Laelius arrived at Brundisium with his fleet and seized the island lying opposite the port in the same way as we explained earlier had been done by Libo.* Likewise Vatinius, who was in command at Brundisium, decked and equipped some small boats, enticed Laelius' ships out, and captured one quinquereme which had ventured too far and two smaller vessels in the narrow entrance of the port; he also arranged to prevent Laelius' crews from getting water by posting cavalry in different places. But Laelius had an easier time of year for sailing, and brought his men water from Corcyra and Dyrrachium in merchant

ships, and was not deterred from his plan. Nor could he be
driven away from the port and the island either by the disgrace of losing the ships or by any shortage of essential supplies, until the news came of the battle that had taken place
in Thessaly.

(101) At about the same time Cassius* arrived in Sicily with
a fleet of Syrian, Phoenician, and Cilician ships. Caesar's fleet
being divided—Publius Sulpicius, a praetor, commanding one
half <at> Vibo, and Marcus Pomponius the other half at
Messana—Cassius descended with his ships on Messana before Pomponius could hear of his arrival. He caught him in
a state of confusion, without guards set or definite dispositions, and in a strong following wind let cargo vessels filled
with resinous pine, pitch, tow, and other inflammable material drift down on to Pomponius' fleet, and burnt all 35 of
his ships, including 20 with an upper deck. Such fear was
created by this exploit that although there was a legion gar-
risoning Messana the town was scarcely being defended, and
if the news of Caesar's victory had not been brought at that
very moment by relays of horsemen, it was the general opinion that the result would have been its loss. But the news
arrived in the nick of time and the defence was successful,
and Cassius departed for Vibo to attack Sulpicius' fleet. Affected by the same panic, our ships, <numbering about 40>,
had been moored up to land, and Cassius, using the same
tactic as before and getting a favourable breeze, let go cargo
vessels previously made ready for firing, and five of our
ships were burnt as the flames caught hold from either end
of the line. When the fire began to spread further because of
the strength of the wind, the soldiers from the group of sick
who had been left behind from the old legions to guard the
ships could not endure the disgrace, but of their own accord
boarded the ships, cast them off from their moorings, and
attacked Cassius' fleet. They captured two quinqueremes,*
Cassius being on board one of them, but he was taken off
in a small boat and made his escape; in addition two triremes*
were captured. Not long afterwards the result of the battle
in Thessaly became known, so that even the Pompeians, who
had previously thought it was invented by Caesar's officers

and friends, came to believe it; and on learning the facts Cassius departed from the area with his fleet.

Flight and death of Pompey

(102) Caesar thought he ought to abandon everything else and pursue Pompey wherever he might have taken refuge after his escape, to prevent him from again* being able to gather other forces and renew the war. He therefore covered as much ground as he could with his cavalry every day, and ordered one legion to follow him by shorter stages. An edict had been proclaimed at Amphipolis in Pompey's name, that everyone of military age in the province, whether Greeks or Roman citizens, should assemble for enlistment. But it was impossible to decide whether Pompey had made the proclamation as a bluff, to hide for as long as possible his plan of fleeing further afield, or whether, if no one attacked him, he would attempt to hold Macedonia with fresh levies. Pompey himself stopped for one night, which he spent at anchor, summoning his contacts from Amphipolis and raising money from them for essential expenses, and when he heard of Caesar's arrival made his departure, arriving at Mytilene a few days later. He was kept there by a storm for two days and then went on, after collecting some fast light ships, to Cilicia and thence to Cyprus. There he discovered that the citizen body of Antioch and the Romans who were in business there had agreed they should arm to keep him out, and that messages had been sent to those who were reported to have fled to the shelter of neighbouring communities not to come to Antioch; they were told that if they did, they would be placing their lives at risk. The same thing had happened at Rhodes to Lucius Lentulus, the consul of the previous year, and Publius Lentulus the ex-consul, and some others; after their escape from the battle, they were following Pompey and had come to the island, but they had not been admitted to the town or port, and when a message was sent telling them to go away, they sailed off reluctantly. And already a rumour about Caesar's arrival was going round the cities.

(103) When he learnt these facts, Pompey abandoned his plan of going to Syria. He confiscated money from the tax companies, borrowed from certain private individuals, and put a great quantity of cash for military purposes aboard his ships. He armed two thousand men, partly chosen from the slaves of the tax companies,* and partly forcibly recruited from the business community, by taking from each establishment whoever was thought suitable by its master for the task, and proceeded to Pelusium. As it happened, King Ptolemy, who was only a boy, was there at the head of a large force, at war with his sister Cleopatra,* whom he had ejected from the kingdom a few months beforehand through the agency of his relatives and friends; and Cleopatra's camp was no great distance from his. Pompey sent him a request that for the sake of his ties of friendship and hospitality* with the king's father he be given refuge at Alexandria and protected in his misfortune by the king's power. But when their duty as emissaries had been performed, those who took the message began to talk rather too freely with the king's soldiers and urge them to support Pompey and not treat his present condition with contempt. Among this group were a considerable number of soldiers who, after serving with Pompey, had been transferred from his army to the command of Gabinius, and he had taken them across to Alexandria and left them behind with Ptolemy, the boy's father, at the conclusion of the campaign.

(104) Because of the king's age his friends* were acting as regents, and when they found this out they were induced to make a friendly reply in public to Pompey's emissaries and tell him to come to the king. They did this either because, as they afterwards alleged, they were afraid that Pompey, having made approaches to the royal army, would take possession of Alexandria and Egypt, or because they despised his present state (friends very often turning into enemies in times of disaster). They themselves formed a secret plan and sent Achillas, one of the king's officers and a man of remarkable nerve, together with Lucius Septimius, a military tribune, to kill Pompey. On being greeted in a friendly manner by these men, and encouraged by some acquaintance

with Septimius, because this man had served as a centurion under him in the war against the pirates, Pompey boarded their little boat with a few friends, and was killed there by Achillas and Septimius. Lucius Lentulus was also seized by the king and put to death in custody.

Caesar pursues Pompey to Egypt, and becomes involved in the dynastic war between Cleopatra and Ptolemy XIII

(105) When Caesar reached the province of Asia, he discovered that Titus Ampius had attempted to remove treasure from the shrine of Diana at Ephesus and for that reason had summoned all senators from everywhere in the province to act as witnesses to the sum taken, but on being interrupted by Caesar had fled. Thus on two occasions Caesar had saved the treasure of Ephesus . . . Likewise it was agreed, after checking and counting the days, that on the day of Caesar's success in battle the image of Victory, which stood in the sanctuary of Minerva* at Elis in front of the goddess herself, and had previously faced her statue, had turned towards the double doors and threshold of the sanctuary. And on the same day, at Antioch in Syria, such a loud shout of an army and sound of trumpets had twice been heard that the citizens armed themselves and rushed to their posts on the walls; exactly the same thing occurred at Ptolemais. And at Pergamum drums sounded in the secret hidden parts of the sanctuary, which the Greeks call <adyta, and where none but the priests may go>. Also at Tralles, in the precinct of Victory, where they had dedicated a statue of Caesar, a palm-tree* was pointed out as having come up at that time, within the building, between the joints of the paving-stones.

(106) Caesar stayed a few days in the province of Asia, but when he heard that Pompey had been seen in Cyprus he guessed that he was making his way to Egypt because of his connections with the kingdom and the other possibilities of the place. He therefore pressed on to Alexandria with one legion which he had ordered to follow him from

Thessaly, another which he had summoned from his lieu-tenant Quintus Fufius in Achaea, 800 cavalry, and ten war-ships from Rhodes along with a few from Asia. These legions contained 3,200 men;* the rest of the men, incapacitated by battle injuries and by the difficulty and length of the marches, had been unable to join in the pursuit. But Caesar had trusted in the reputation his achievements had earned him and had not hesitated to set out with weak support, in the belief that he would be equally safe anywhere. At Alex-andria, he learnt of Pompey's death, and there as soon as he disembarked he heard the shout raised by the soldiers the king had left to garrison the town, and saw them running to meet him, because the consul's rods* were being carried in front of him. The body of the population all declared that this constituted treason against the king. This disorder was brought under control, but for a period of days the crowd continued to assemble and provoke frequent disturbances, and a number of soldiers were killed in the streets of the city.

(107) In the light of this situation he ordered other le-gions, which he had formed from Pompey's soldiers, to be brought from Asia. He himself had no alternative to stay-ing, because of the Etesian winds,* which blow absolutely dir-ectly against anyone sailing out of Alexandria. Meanwhile, thinking that the dispute between the rulers was a matter of concern to the Roman people and to himself, because he was consul, and that it had an even greater claim on his atten-tion because it was in his previous consulship* that an alli-ance had been made by law and by decree of the senate with Ptolemy (the father), he made it known that it was his de-cision that King Ptolemy and his sister Cleopatra should disband their armies and conduct their argument by judicial process before himself rather than by armed struggle between themselves.

(108) Because of the boy's age, his guardian, a eunuch called Pothinus, was in charge of the kingdom. First he began to complain and to express indignation to his intimates that the king had been summoned to a legal hearing. Next he obtained from among the king's friends some helpers for his designs, and secretly called the army back to Alexandria

from Pelusium and put the same Achillas we mentioned before in command of all the forces. He then both wrote and sent verbal messages to explain his wishes to Achillas, who was roused by his own promises and egged on by those of the king.

By the elder Ptolemy's will his heirs were named as the elder of his two sons and the one of his daughters who had precedence of age.* In the same will Ptolemy, swearing by all the gods and by the treaties which he had made at Rome, called upon the Roman people to ensure that his wishes were put into effect. One copy of the will had been brought to Rome by his representatives, to be deposited in the treasury (this could not be done because of pressure of public affairs, so it was deposited with Pompey), while the other identical copy, which had been left and witnessed at Alexandria, was now produced.

(109) While these matters were being disputed before Caesar, he himself being particularly anxious to play the part of friend and arbitrator to both parties and settle the quarrel between the rulers, news suddenly came that the king's army and all its cavalry were on their way to Alexandria.* Caesar's forces were much too small for him to place any confidence in them if he had to fight outside the city. The only course open to him was to remain in his position in the town and find out Achillas' intentions. None the less he ordered all his men to stay under arms, and pressed the king to send as ambassadors to Achillas those members of his entourage whom he considered to possess the most authority, and make plain what would be acceptable to him.* The king sent Dioscorides and Serapion, who had both been at Rome as ambassadors and had possessed great influence with his father Ptolemy. They reached Achillas, but when they came into his presence, he ordered them to be seized and put to death before he could listen to them or find out why they had come; one of them was wounded but was rescued by his friends and carried away as dead, while the other was killed.* After this, Caesar took care to keep the king in his power, because he considered that the royal name had great authority with his people. He was also careful to make it

apparent that the war had been started not by design of the king, but privately, by a small faction of buccaneers.

(110) Achillas was accompanied by forces of a sort not to be despised, either in quantity and type of troops or in military experience. He had 20,000 men under arms. These consisted of Gabinius' soldiers, who had by now become habituated to the ill-disciplined ways of Alexandrian life and had unlearnt the good name and orderly conduct of Romans and had taken wives* by whom most of them had children. In addition to these there were men gathered from among the pirates and brigands of Syria, the Cilician province, and adjoining regions. Also many exiles and men condemned to loss of citizen rights had collected here. All runaway slaves of ours had a guaranteed refuge and a guaranteed way of life at Alexandria, provided they enrolled and became soldiers; and if any of them was arrested by his master, he was snatched away by agreement among the soldiers, who protected their companions against violence as though they were themselves in danger, because they were tarred with the same brush. By a long-established custom of the Alexandrian army, these men habitually demanded that friends of the king be put to death, plundered the property of the rich, laid siege to the king's residence to win higher pay, and removed some and appointed others to the throne. There were in addition two thousand cavalry. All these men had done long service in the numerous wars at Alexandria, had put the elder Ptolemy back on the throne, had killed two sons of Bibulus,* and had participated in campaigns against the Egyptians.* This was the source of their military experience.

(111) Confident in these forces and contemptuous of the small numbers of Caesar's men, Achillas occupied Alexandria except for the part of the town which Caesar held* with his soldiers. With his first assault he attempted to break into Caesar's quarters, but Caesar had his cohorts spread about the streets and withstood the assault. At the same time there was fighting by the harbour, and that brought by far the most serious struggle. Fighting was taking place between forces positioned at intervals over a considerable number of streets, and simultaneously the enemy were trying with a large body

of men to gain control of the warships: fifty of these had been sent to help Pompey and had returned after the battle in Thessaly, all of them quadriremes and quinqueremes ready and completely fitted out for sailing; and there were twenty-two besides, eleven with upper decks, which were normally kept at Alexandria to guard the port. If the enemy got possession of them, they would have wrested the fleet from Caesar, and would have the port and the open sea entirely under their control and would stop supplies and reinforcements from reaching him. And so the battle was fought with the determination to be expected when the one side realized that it would give them a quick victory, the other that their lives depended on it. But Caesar carried the day; he burnt all these ships, together with the remainder which were in the dockyards,* because he was unable to defend such a wide area with his small force, and hastily landed soldiers on Pharus.

(112) The Pharus* is a tower of great height and of amazing architectural construction, standing on the island from which it takes its name. This island lies off Alexandria and creates its harbour; but from the higher ground a causeway nine hundred paces long* has been pushed out into the water so that there is a connection to the town by a narrow track and a bridge. There are native dwellings on the island, forming a settlement the size of a town; and if ships go a little off course there, through carelessness or bad weather, the people are in the habit of behaving like pirates and plundering them. Moreover, on account of the narrow channel, it is impossible for a ship to gain entrance to the harbour against the wishes of those who hold Pharus. This was Caesar's immediate fear, and while the enemy were occupied with the fighting he landed soldiers, seized the lighthouse,* and stationed a garrison there. By these means he secured the safe delivery to him by ship of food and reinforcements (for he sent a summons to all the nearby provinces to provide the latter). In the other parts of the town the fighting ended with honours even and neither force was driven back (this was due to the confined space); and after the loss of a few men on each side, Caesar took control of the most essential

positions and under cover of night made fortifications in front
of them (in that stretch of the town there was a small section of the palace, where he himself had been accommodated
at the beginning, and also, attached to the living quarters, a
theatre which served as a citadel and had access to the harbour and the royal dockyards*). He enlarged these fortifications on the following days, in order to have a barrier which
would function like a city wall, and to avoid being forced
to fight against his will. Meanwhile, King Ptolemy's younger
daughter,* hoping to take unencumbered possession of the
throne, went over from the palace to Achillas and began to
direct the war in co-operation with him. But very soon they
fell out over the leadership, and this brought an increase in
bribes to the soldiers as they both threw away large sums
in trying to win their support. While this was happening on
the enemy side, Pothinus was sending messages to Achillas
and encouraging him not to slacken his efforts or lose heart;
but his go-betweens were betrayed and arrested, and he was
put to death by Caesar.

THE ALEXANDRIAN WAR

The Alexandrian War (1–33). Domitius Calvinus'
unsuccessful attack on Pharnaces (34–41). Caesarian
victory on the Illyrian coast (42–47). Revolt against
Caesar's governor Q. Cassius in Spain (48–64).
Caesar defeats Pharnaces at Zela (65–78)

*Operations at Alexandria, by land and sea,
culminating in the defeat of King Ptolemy
on the Nile*

(1) Now that war had broken out at Alexandria, Caesar
summoned his entire fleet from Rhodes and from Syria and
Cilicia, sent to Crete for archers, and for cavalry to Malchus,
the Nabataean king, and ordered artillery* to be gathered
from all sources, wheat to be supplied, and auxiliary forces
to be provided. Meanwhile additional fortifications were constantly being added to his defences, and all apparently vulnerable parts of the town were attacked from the shelter
of movable galleries and screens;* from the buildings, too,
battering-rams were directed through apertures in the walls
to pound the neighbouring buildings, and his defences were
pushed forward to incorporate any ground gained by collapse
or capture. This was done because Alexandria is virtually
proof against fire, since the buildings have no floor-beams
or timber, and are constructed of arched masonry and con-
crete and roofed with rubble or paving-stone. Caesar was
particularly anxious to advance his defence-works and siege-
huts* and isolate from the rest of Alexandria the district
where the marsh* that cuts into the city from the south
makes it particularly narrow. His considerations were, first,
that although his fighting effort would be split against the
two parts of the city, it could be directed by a single command operating to a single plan, and second, that if his men
were under pressure on one side of the town help and reinforcements could be brought across from the other; but above

all, his aim was to enjoy plenty of water and forage, because he was short of the one and entirely lacked the other, and the lagoon was able to provide both in generous measure.

(2) Nor were the Alexandrians at all idle or hesitant in their operations. They had sent officers and recruiting sergeants to levy troops from all the regions which belong to the territory of the kingdom of Egypt, they had brought a large amount of weapons and artillery into the town, and they had assembled an enormous number of men. With no less energy, huge workshops for making weapons had been set up in the city. They had also armed the adult slaves, for whom the richer owners provided daily rations and pay. This great mass of men was posted in various places to guard the fortifications of the separated parts, while they kept their seasoned cohorts in the most frequented places in the city, without fixed duties, so that wherever fighting might break out fresh forces could offer resistance and bring help. They had blocked all the streets and alleys with a triple wall— built of cut stone and at least 40 feet high—and had fortified any parts of the city that were lower with lofty ten-storey towers. In addition they had constructed other towers, with the same number of storeys, which were mobile; they put wheels under these, attached ropes and draught animals, and moved them along the straight avenues* in the desired direction.

(3) The city, being extremely fertile and well supplied, provided the wherewithal for everything. Its population, who are clever and very quick-witted people, put into effect whatever they saw us do with such skill that it seemed our troops had imitated their work. They thought up many stratagems of their own and harassed our fortifications at the same time as they defended their own. Furthermore, their leaders argued in meetings and public speeches that the Roman people had gradually become used to occupying their kingdom. A few years previously, Aulus Gabinius had been in Egypt with an army; Pompey had betaken himself there after his flight; Caesar had arrived with a military force, and Pompey's death had been of no use in preventing Caesar from remaining with them. If they failed to expel him, their kingdom would

become a province, and they must act swiftly, because thanks to the time of year he was cut off by gales* and could not receive reinforcements from overseas.

(4) Meanwhile, because a difference had arisen between Achillas, who commanded the seasoned troops, and Arsinoe, the younger daughter of King Ptolemy, as explained above, they were plotting against each other; each wanted to obtain the supreme command for themselves, but Arsinoe moved first through the eunuch Ganymedes, her guardian, and killed Achillas. Once he was dead she gained complete control without any associate or regent, and the army was entrusted to Ganymedes. On taking up his post he increased the bonuses to the soldiery,* and gave like attention to the rest of his duties.

(5) Almost the whole of Alexandria has galleries beneath it and conduits extending to the Nile by which water is brought to private houses. After a while this water gradually becomes clear and settles, and is habitually used by house-owners and their households because what is brought by the Nile* is so muddy and turbid that it causes all kinds of disease; but the mass of ordinary folk have to be content with the latter, because there is not a single spring in the city. However, the watercourse was in the portion of the town which was under Alexandrian control. This circumstance gave Ganymedes the idea that it was possible to deprive our forces of water, because in order to protect their fortifications our men were distributed over various quarters of the city and used water taken from the conduits and wells of private houses.

(6) This plan was approved, and he embarked on a huge and difficult task. He drove tunnels to intercept the conduits, and after isolating all the areas of the city which he himself controlled, strove to raise an enormous quantity of water from the sea, using water wheels; and this he endlessly poured into Caesar's area from the higher levels. Consequently slightly saltier water than usual was drawn from the nearest houses, causing people great puzzlement as to how this had happened. They were not even sure they were right, since those who lived at a lower level said they were drawing water of

the same quality and flavour as usual, and everyone was making comparisons and tasting the water to decide how much the samples differed from each other. But within a short space of time the nearer supply was quite undrinkable, and the lower was already found to be less pure and more salty.

(7) As a result, all doubt was removed and a great surge of fear made everyone feel they were in serious danger; some accused Caesar of being slow to give the order to embark, while others were much more deeply afraid, because the short distance between themselves and the Alexandrians made it impossible to conceal their preparations for withdrawal, and with the enemy hanging on their heels and pursuing them no retreat to the ships would be feasible. Moreover, in Caesar's part of the city there was a very large number of townspeople, whom he had not turned out of their homes because in public they pretended to be loyal to us and seemed to have deserted their own side: on the other hand, if I had to defend the Alexandrians against the charges of deceitfulness and opportunism, I could speak for a long time to no purpose; indeed, the moment you recognize their race* you also recognize their character, and no one can doubt that this is a people made for treachery.

(8) Caesar consoled his men and sought to allay their fear by argument. He asserted that it was possible to find fresh water by sinking wells, because every coast naturally possessed veins of fresh water. But even if the coast of Egypt differed in nature from all others, none the less, because they had unchallenged control of the sea, and the enemy had no fleet, they themselves could not be stopped from fetching daily supplies of water by ship, either from the direction of Paraetonium to their left or the island* to their right; these sailings, being in different directions, could never be simultaneously prevented by contrary winds. But any plan to withdraw was ruled out, not simply for men who put their honour above everything else, but even for men who thought of nothing but saving their lives. It was a great effort to withstand the enemy attacks when they were facing them from their defences; and if they abandoned these, they could not match the enemy in numbers or in position. Furthermore,

embarkation on the ships would be a slow and difficult business, especially from small boats, while the Alexandrians on the contrary possessed great speed of movement and intimate knowledge of the ground and the buildings. They were bold, particularly in victory; they would dash forward and seize the higher ground and buildings, and in this way prevent our forces from retreating or reaching the ships. His men therefore had to forget that notion and realize that they must employ every means to win.

(9) After addressing his men in this way and firing them all to action, he gave the centurions orders to halt other work and devote their attention to sinking wells, without taking any break during the night. The job was begun, and with every man roused to throw himself into the work a copious supply of fresh water was discovered in a single night. Thus an effort of no great duration provided an answer to the elaborate machinery and enormous exertions of the Alexandrians. Two days later the Thirty-seventh Legion, which was composed of surrendered Pompeian soldiers* and had been embarked by Domitius Calvinus along with supplies of wheat, arms, missiles, and catapults, made landfall on the shore of Africa a little beyond Alexandria. Because the east wind had been blowing continuously for many days this fleet was prevented from making port, but there are excellent places all along that coast for lying to anchor. They were detained there for a long time and were suffering from a shortage of water, so they sent a fast vessel* to inform Caesar.

(10) In order to decide for himself what had best be done, Caesar embarked and ordered his whole fleet to follow him without taking any soldiers on board,* because he was going to be away a little too long and was reluctant to denude the defences. When they reached the place, which is called Chersonensus, and they had landed rowers to get water, some of these went too far from the ships in search of booty and were cut off and captured by enemy cavalry. From them the enemy found out that Caesar had come in person with the fleet and that he had no soldiers on board. On discovering this they believed that fortune had offered them a splendid opportunity to score a success. They therefore put fighting men aboard

all the ships they had ready to sail and met Caesar as he was returning with his fleet. He was reluctant to fight that day, for two reasons, because he had no soldiers on his ships and because the engagement was taking place in the late afternoon and he thought darkness would bring greater assurance to his opponents, who were confident in their knowledge of the area; he would also be without the help obtained by encouraging his men, because any encouragement which could pick out neither courage nor cowardice would be inadequate. For these reasons Caesar put in towards land with what ships he could in a place where he thought the enemy would not move in on him.

(11) One of the Rhodian ships on Caesar's right wing was well separated from the rest. On seeing her, the enemy did not hold back, and four decked ships and several open ones made for her very aggressively. Caesar was forced to help her, to avoid suffering a disgraceful indignity in full view of the enemy, although he considered that if anything serious happened to her she well deserved it. Battle was joined with great commitment from the Rhodians; and although they were outstanding in every engagement in both technique and courage, at this moment above all they did not shirk the whole burden, to prevent their compatriots appearing responsible for any loss that occurred. A very favourable result was thus obtained. One enemy quadrireme* was captured, another sunk, and two stripped of all their marines; in addition, on the other ships a very large number of the fighting men were killed. And if nightfall had not put an end to the battle, Caesar would have captured the whole enemy fleet. Since the enemy were thoroughly frightened by this disaster, and the contrary wind had fallen light, Caesar towed the merchant ships back to Alexandria behind his victorious warships.

(12) The Alexandrians saw that they had now been worsted, not by the courage of the fighting men, but by the skill of the ships' crews, and they were so demoralized by this defeat that they hardly had any confidence that they could defend themselves from the buildings, which had given them strength

on earlier occasions.* They made barriers out of all available material, because they were afraid that our fleet would even attack the land. Also, after Ganymedes had declared in council that he would replace the ships that had been lost and add to their numbers, they began confidently and optimistically to repair their old ships and devote more care, time, and effort to this project. And although they had lost more than 110 warships* in the harbour and dockyards, they had none the less not abandoned thoughts of reconstituting a fleet. This was because they observed that neither reinforcements nor supplies could reach Caesar if they themselves enjoyed naval superiority; besides, the people of the city and coastal region, being seafarers and trained from childhood by daily practice, longed to have recourse to their own natural advantage and were aware how expert they were in small boats. So they turned with all their energies to making a fleet ready.

(13) There were guard-ships stationed at all the mouths of the Nile to collect the customs duties, and in secret docks within the palace old ships which had not been sailed for many years: they repaired the latter and recalled the former to Alexandria. There were no oars: so they took the roofs off colonnades, gymnasia, and public buildings, and the rafters became oars; their natural cleverness provided some things, their plentiful resources others. Finally, it was no long voyage they were preparing; they were slaves to the necessity of the present, and saw that the conflict must take place in the harbour itself. And so within a few days, contrary to what everyone thought possible, they completed twenty-two quadriremes and five quinqueremes.* To these they added a fair number of smaller undecked ships, and risking the consequences of what each could do under oars in the harbour, put on board the appropriate soldiers and prepared themselves with everything for the conflict. Caesar had nine Rhodian ships—for although ten had been sent him one had deserted *en route* along the Egyptian coast—along with eight Pontic, five Cilician,* and twelve from Asia. Ten of these ships were quinqueremes and quadriremes, but the rest were

smaller and many not decked. None the less he had faith in the courage of his soldiers, and after taking stock of the enemy forces prepared himself for battle.

(14) Now that the point had been reached where each side was confident of itself, Caesar took his fleet round Pharos* and halted his ships facing the enemy. He stationed the Rhodian ships on the right and the Pontic on the left, leaving between them a space of 400 yards, which appeared sufficient to deploy his fleet. Behind this line he distributed the rest of his ships in support. He decided which ship should follow and help which, and issued his orders accordingly. Without hesitation the Alexandrians brought out their fleet and drew it up: they placed the twenty-two in front and the rest in support in a second line. In addition, they brought out a great quantity of smaller craft and boats along with incendiary missiles and fire, to see if their very number and the clamour and the flames could inspire some degree of terror in our side. Between the two fleets lay narrow shallows, which extend in the direction of Africa—for as they say, half of Alexandria belongs to Africa*—and they waited for quite some time to see which of them would begin to pass these, because the side which had entered the gap would enjoy less freedom of movement, both in deploying its fleet and in withdrawing if something should go wrong.

(15) The commander of the Rhodian ships was Euphranor, a man who for his great spirit and courage ought to be compared with us Romans and not with Greeks. He had been chosen admiral by the Rhodians on account of his celebrated expertise and greatness of spirit. When he noticed Caesar hanging back, he said: 'Caesar, I fancy you are afraid that if you enter these shallows with your leading ships you will be forced to fight before you can deploy the rest of your fleet. Give the job to us: we shall sustain the struggle—and not betray your judgement—until the rest can follow. For these people to preen themselves any longer under our very noses disgraces and pains us greatly.' Caesar encouraged him, heaped praises on him, and gave the signal to engage. Four Rhodian ships advanced past the shallows and were surrounded and attacked by the Alexandrians, but withstood

the attack and skilfully and cleverly made room between themselves. Indeed their proficiency was such that although they were outnumbered not one of them lay broadside to the enemy, or had her oars broken off, and they kept meeting approaching ships head-on.* Meanwhile the rest followed. Then skill was perforce abandoned because of the restricted space, and the whole struggle turned on bravery. And there was not a soul in Alexandria, whether Roman or townsman, except for* those whose attention was engrossed in fortification work or fighting, who did not make for the highest buildings and take their place to see the show from any vantage point, and with prayers and vows demand victory for their own side from the immortal gods.

(16) The terms of battle were far from equal. Our side, if routed, would have no escape, whether by sea or land, once they were defeated, and if victorious possessed no certainty about the future. The enemy, on the other hand, would control everything if they triumphed at sea, but if they were worsted they could hazard their remaining fortunes. It seemed hard and at the same time pitiable that a handful of men should fight the decisive battle for their national existence and the lives of all, and if any of them failed in commitment or courage, the remainder, who had no opportunity of fighting on their own behalf, would also have to fend for themselves. Caesar had frequently put these points to his men on the preceding days, so that they should make all the greater an effort because they realized that the lives of all were in their hands. Each man followed and made the same appeal to his messmates, friends, and acquaintances not to betray the opinion held of them by himself and by everyone whose judgement had led to them being chosen to go out to battle. In consequence, the fight was carried on with such spirit that their skill and ingenuity afforded no protection to the sailors and seafarers, nor was their mass of ships any advantage in spite of their superiority of numbers, nor could the men who were picked for their courage from such a crowd match the courage of our side. In this battle we captured one quinquereme and a bireme with marines and rowers, and sank three quinqueremes, without suffering any

harm ourselves. The rest of their ships beat a short retreat towards the town, and our opponents, fighting from the moles and overhanging buildings, protected them from attack and prevented our ships coming any closer.

(17) To avoid the possibility of this happening more often to him, Caesar judged that he must make every effort to bring the island* and the causeway leading to the island under his own control. He was confident that as his fortifications in the town were for the most part complete, he could make assaults on both the island and the city at the same time. Having decided on this plan, he put ten cohorts, some picked light-armed troops, and those of his Gallic cavalry he thought suitable on board boats and small vessels. He also launched an attack with decked ships on the other side of the island, in order to stretch the defences, and offered large rewards to whoever first took it. At first the islanders were equal to our attack, fighting from the roofs of the houses* and at the same time defending the shore with armed men. This was difficult for our side to approach because of its rockiness, and the enemy moved quickly and skilfully with small boats and five warships to protect the restricted channels. But as soon as landing-places had been identified and the shallows attempted, a few of our men established a firm foothold on the beach. Others followed them, and they kept up steady pressure on the men who had taken up their position on the level shore. Then all the Pharians turned tail, and once they were routed, the enemy abandoned any defence of the harbour, beached their ships at the settlement on Pharos, and jumped out to defend the buildings.

(18) Even so they were unable to hold that line of defence for very long, although the houses, to compare less with great, were not dissimilar in kind to those of Alexandria, with their continuous line of high towers* serving as a wall, and our men had come unprepared with ladders or fascines or anything else for an assault. But terror robs men of the power to make rational decisions and physically weakens them, which is what happened on this occasion. The same people who believed that they were our equals on level ground that gave them no advantage, became panic-stricken

by the flight of their men and the loss of a few of them. They did not have the courage to stand firm thirty feet above us on the houses, and jumped into the sea from the causeway and swam the intervening 800 yards to the town. Many of these were none the less caught and killed, but the number of prisoners totalled 6,000 altogether.

(19) After giving his soldiers permission to keep their booty, Caesar ordered the houses to be sacked, fortified a strongpoint beside the bridge nearer to Pharos, and stationed a garrison there. The Pharians had abandoned this bridge when they fled, leaving the Alexandrians guarding the narrower one nearer to the town.* But Caesar attacked this in a similar manner on the following day, because he thought that if he gained control of both of them all naval sorties and sudden raids would be stopped. By catapult and arrow fire from his ships he was successful in forcing the garrison holding the place out of it and back to the town, and landed the equivalent of three cohorts—the restricted space not al lowing any more to stay—while the remainder of his forces were stationed on the ships. After this, he gave orders for a palisaded barrier to be constructed facing the enemy in front of the bridge, and for the arch which supported the bridge and allowed ships an exit to be blocked with a filling of boulders. When the latter operation had been completed, so that not a single small boat could get out, and the former had been started, all the Alexandrian forces burst out of the town and took up a position in a rather broader place opposite the fortifications. At the same time they laid alongside the causeway the ships which they used to send out through the bridges to attend to fires on cargo vessels. We fought from the bridge and from the causeway, they from the open area which faced the bridge and from their ships against the causeway.

(20) While Caesar was busy with these operations and urging his soldiers on, a large number of rowers and marines poured on to the causeway from our warships, some of them keen to watch, others actually eager to fight. At first they kept the enemy ships away from the causeway with stones and slingshot and seemed to be having a good deal of success

with their considerable firepower. But once a few of the Alexandrians had found the courage to land further out, on their unprotected side,* they began to retreat haphazardly to the ships in the same way as they had come ashore, without standards, formation, or thought. Encouraged by their flight, more Alexandrians landed and pursued our disordered troops still more vigorously. At the same time, the men who had remained on board our warships hurried to pull up the ladders and push the ships off from land in case the enemy captured them. The soldiers of our three cohorts which were in position on the bridge and the first part of the causeway were disturbed by all this, and when they heard the uproar behind them, saw their side in flight, and received a hail of weapons in their faces, they were afraid that they were being surrounded from the rear and cut off from any retreat by the departure of the ships, and so they abandoned the fortification they had begun on the bridge and ran towards the ships at a great pace. Some of them reached the nearest ships and were drowned as these sank under the weight of so many men, others were killed by the Alexandrians as they resisted, in doubt as to what to do; some were luckier, reached ships lying ready at anchor, and came away unscathed; and a few, by holding their shields above their heads and making a great effort, managed to swim to the nearest vessels.

(21) As long as he could rally his men and keep them at the fortifications and the bridge, Caesar was in the same danger, but when he saw they were all retreating he withdrew to his own vessel. A crowd of men followed him, swarming on board and not allowing any opportunity to work the ship or push off from shore. Guessing what was going to happen, he jumped overboard and swam to the ships which had stopped somewhat further away. From here he sent boats to help his men in difficulties, and saved some, while his own ship did indeed sink under the number of soldiers, and was lost along with them. About 400 legionaries and a slightly greater number of marines and rowers perished in this battle. The Alexandrians then strengthened the fort in that spot with substantial defences and plenty of artillery, and when they had removed the boulders from the sea made free use of it subsequently for the passage of shipping.

(22) So far from being put off by this reverse, our troops were angered and roused and had substantial success in storming the enemy defences. In the daily encounters, whenever the occasion offered, when the Alexandrians ran forward and made sorties, <our men were passionately keen to take the chance of fighting>;* nor could Caesar's circulated exhortations match the efforts of the legions in working on their fortifications or their eagerness to fight, so that they needed to be deterred and held back from the riskiest engagements, rather than encouraged to fight.

(23) When the Alexandrians saw that the Romans drew strength from success and were stimulated by failure, and since they knew no third condition of war under which they could be any safer, we can conjecture that it was either the advice of the king's friends who were inside Caesar's defences, or else their own initiative approved by the king through secret messengers, which led them to send a delegation to Caesar to ask him to release the king* and allow him to go over to his own people. They said that the whole population were dispirited and tired of the girl, the throne she held in trust, and the brutal tyranny of Ganymedes. They were ready to obey the king's orders, and if his authority were behind a surrender to Caesar and acceptance of his friendship, no fears for their own safety would prevent the general mass of people from surrendering.

(24) Although Caesar was very well aware that the Alexandrians were a deceitful people, always keeping one aim in view and pretending to another, none the less he thought it advantageous to treat their request graciously because he believed that if they were in any way genuine in what they were asking, the king would remain loyal when sent away; but if, as was more likely given their nature, they wanted to have the king as their leader in conducting the war, it would be more glorious and honourable for him to be waging war against a king than against a gang of refugees and runaway slaves. So he urged the king to think of his ancestral kingdom; to take pity on his glorious homeland, which had been disfigured by the disgrace of fire and ruin; to begin by bringing his people back to their senses, and then save them; and to trust the Roman people and himself, Caesar,

whose faith in him was firm enough to send him to join enemies who were under arms. He clasped the king's right hand in his and started to dismiss the lad, who was now of age. But the king, highly trained as his mind was in deceit, in order not to betray the standards of his people, began to weep and beg Caesar not to send him away, for his throne itself was no sweeter to him than the sight of Caesar. When the lad had mastered his tears, Caesar, who was moved himself, declared that if he felt like that he would very soon be back with him, and sent him to his own people. Then the king, like a racehorse given his head, started to wage war against Caesar with such energy that the tears he had shed when talking to Caesar were obviously tears of joy. A large number of Caesar's officers, companions, and centurions were delighted that this had happened and that Caesar's over-kindness had been mocked by the lad's trickery—as if his action had been prompted solely by kindness and not by the most careful consideration.

(25) When the Alexandrians realized that in spite of acquiring a leader they had become no more secure, nor the Romans any less energetic, and when their soldiers laughed at the king's youth and weakness, they were much hurt. Seeing they were no better off, and since rumours were about, which had not yet come to Caesar's ears, that strong reinforcements were on their way to him by the land route from Syria and Cilicia, they decided to intercept the supplies which were being brought in by sea to our forces. They therefore kept light vessels on station in suitable spots near Canopus and ambushed our ships and supplies. On being informed of this, Caesar gave orders for his entire fleet to be made ready and equipped, and put Tiberius Nero in command of it. The Rhodian ships sailed as part of that fleet, and on board them was Euphranor, without whom no naval battle either occurred in the first place or failed to end in success. But fortune, who all too often saves for a harsher fate those to whom she has been particularly generous, did not attend Euphranor in the same guise as before. When they had reached Canopus, and the fleets on either side had been drawn up and battle joined, Euphranor, as was his habit, was the first to engage.

He rammed and sank an enemy quadrireme, then as he pursued the next for some distance the other ships followed too slowly and he was surrounded by the Alexandrians. No one went to help him, whether because they thought that in view of his courage and good fortune he was well enough able to defend himself, or because they feared for themselves. Thus the single man who was successful in the battle perished alone, along with his victorious quadrireme.

(26) Mithridates the Pergamene, who came of a family illustrious in those parts and was expert in military matters, as well as possessing great courage, loyalty, and standing as a friend of Caesar, had been sent to Syria and Cilicia at the start of the Alexandrian war to assemble reinforcements. At about this time he arrived at Pelusium by the land route which connects Egypt with Syria, accompanied by a large force which he had quickly raised through the enthusiastic support of the city-states and his own diligence. Achillas had put a strong garrison into the town because of the strategic importance of the place—the whole of Egypt being, so to speak, closed by a bolt at Pharos against approach by sea, and by another at Pelusium against approach by land. Mithridates suddenly surrounded it with large numbers of troops, and although the numerous garrison defended it tenaciously, the size of his force, which kept sending forward fresh men to replace the wounded and exhausted, and his unremitting perseverance in attack, allowed him to win control of it and install his own garrison on the day he launched his assault. After this success he hurried on towards Alexandria, and thanks to the authority which almost invariably attends a victor, he had pacified and won over to Caesar's side all the regions through which he marched.

(27) Among the most celebrated of these regions is that which lies not very far from Alexandria and is called the Delta. It takes its name from the shape of that letter because a part of the River Nile splits into two branches and gradually leaves space between them, with the widest distance at the coast as it joins the sea. When the king heard that Mithridates was approaching this area and knew that he had to cross the river, he sent a large force to oppose him

in the belief that Mithridates could be either overcome and wiped out or at any rate halted. He wanted to defeat him, but thought it would be just as satisfactory if he could halt him and cut him off from Caesar. The first body of troops which was able to cross the river and attack Mithridates joined battle hurriedly, to prevent those who were following behind from sharing in their victory. Mithridates very prudently took the shock of their attack from a palisaded camp, Roman fashion, but when he saw them coming unwarily and insolently up under the defences, he burst out from every point and killed a large number of them. If the rest had not been protected by their knowledge of the locality, and some had not retreated in the ships they had used to cross the river, they would have been completely destroyed. But when they had taken a little time to recover from their fright, they united with the men following them and again started to attack Mithridates.

(28) Mithridates sent a messenger to tell Caesar the result of the engagement, and the king learnt of the same events from his own men. In this way the king set out to crush Mithridates at almost the same time as Caesar set out to rescue him. The king used the quicker method of sailing by the Nile,* on which he had a large fleet ready. Caesar was unwilling to take the same route, in case there should be a naval battle on the river, but went round by the part of the sea which is said to be on the African side, as we have explained above.* None the less he met the king's forces before the king could attack Mithridates, and welcomed the latter as victor at the head of an intact army.

The king and his forces had taken up a position which was naturally fortified* because it was itself on an eminence above the plain, which lay below it on every side. It was protected on three sides by defences of various sorts: one side adjoined the River Nile, another ran along a rise so steep as to serve as an element of the camp, and the third was bounded by a marsh. (29) Between this camp and Caesar's line of march lay a narrow watercourse* with very high banks, which flowed into the Nile but was about seven miles distant from the king's camp. When the king had discovered that Caesar was coming that way, he sent his entire force of cavalry and some picked light-armed troops to this water-course, to stop Caesar crossing it and to begin a battle on unequal terms from the banks: for brave men had no way forward and cowards no risks to run. Our soldiers and cavalrymen burned with resentment at this, in that they were struggling for so long and gaining no advantage over the Alexandrians. Therefore some of the German cavalry, who had scattered to look for a ford, swam across the watercourse where its banks were lower at the same time as the legionaries, who had cut down trees big enough to reach from bank to bank, threw them across, packed on to them whatever filling material they could quickly find, and made their crossing. The enemy were so terrified of their attack that they hoped to save themselves by flight—but in vain, since few of those who took to their heels found their way back to the king and almost all the remainder were killed.

(30) Following this spectacular success Caesar thought that his sudden arrival would strike panic into the Alexandrians, and pressed on straight from his victory to the king's camp. When he realized that the camp was fortified with great ramparts and defended by its natural position, and when he saw a solid mass of armed men stationed on the rampart, he did not want his soldiers, tired by the march and the battle, to approach and attack the camp. He therefore made camp at no great distance from the enemy. The king had fortified a strongpoint in the nearby village, not far from his own camp, and joined it with extensions to his main defences so as to hold the village. Caesar now attacked and took this strongpoint with all his forces, not because he thought this would be a difficult task to achieve with a smaller number of men, but in order to make an immediate attack on the king's camp while the Alexandrians were demoralized by his success. And so the soldiers, coming up under the defences with the momentum of their chase of the Alexandrians as they fled from the strongpoint to their camp, began to engage vigorously at long range. We had an opening for attack on two sides: one, as I have indicated, was unobstructed, and on the other there was a gap of moderate

size between the camp and the River Nile. A very large body of élite Alexandrian troops guarded the side which offered the easiest access, while the defenders on the side next to the Nile were very successful in beating off and wounding our men, who were hit by missiles from different directions, some from in front, from the ramparts of the camp, and some from behind, from the river, where a considerable number of ships carrying slingers and archers were attacking them.

(31) Caesar saw that his soldiers could not fight any harder, or make much progress because of the difficulties posed by the position. He also noticed that the very highest spot of the camp had been abandoned by the Alexandrians, because it possessed natural protection and its defenders, out of desire partly to watch and partly to join in, had run down to where the fighting was taking place. He therefore ordered some cohorts to go round to that spot and attack the very top, placing them under the command of Carfulenus, a man outstanding for his great spirit and military expertise. When they reached the place, there were few at the defences while our men on the contrary fought very hard. Then the Alexandrians, made fearful by the noise of combat from different sides, started to scatter in terror to all parts of the camp. Their discomfiture so encouraged our men that they won ground at almost the same moment from every direction, but first at the summit of the camp, from which point they ran down and killed a great number of the enemy within the camp. In their flight from this threat, most of the Alexandrians jumped down from the rampart in heaps on the side adjoining the river, and after the first men had been catastrophically overwhelmed there in the ditch the rest had an easier escape.* It is generally agreed that the king himself got away from the camp and was taken on board ship, but died when the ship sank under the numbers of men who swam out to the nearest vessels.

(32) Confident in a great victory after the extremely rapid and successful end to this operation, Caesar hurried to Alexandria with his cavalry by the nearest land route and entered as victor through the area of the city which was held by

the enemy garrison. His judgement did not betray him, in that the enemy, after hearing of the battle, had no further thoughts of resistance, and on arrival he reaped a reward worthy of his courage and great spirit: the entire population of the town threw down their weapons, left their defences, assumed the garb in which suppliants commonly crave pardon from their masters, and after bringing out all the sacred objects with whose religious awe they used to appeal to their displeased or angry monarchs, went to meet Caesar as he approached, and surrendered to him. After accepting the surrender, Caesar consoled them and proceeded through the enemy lines into his own part of the town, to the great rejoicing of his men, who were delighted that not only the war itself and the fighting, but also an arrival like this, had turned out so fortunately.

(33) Now that he was in control of Egypt and Alexandria, Caesar established on the throne the monarchs whom Ptolemy had appointed in his will and bound the Roman people by oath to see were not altered. Since the elder of the two boys, who had been king, was no more, Caesar gave the throne to the younger boy and to Cleopatra,* the elder of the two daughters, who had remained loyal to him and stayed within his lines. He decided to remove from the kingdom the younger girl, Arsinoe, in whose name as I have said Ganymedes had ruled intemperately for some time, so that no fresh disturbance should again be stirred up by revolutionaries before the passage of time had consolidated the power of the rulers. Caesar took his veteran Sixth legion away with him but left the others to bolster the power of monarchs who were unable to enjoy either popular affection, since they had not wavered in their loyalty to Caesar, or long-established authority, since they had been placed on their thrones only a few days previously. He considered that it was in keeping with the dignity of our power, and at the same time in the public interest, that the monarchs should be safeguarded by a garrison of our troops, if they remained loyal, while if they proved ungrateful, they could be coerced by this same garrison. Everything was thus settled and all arrangements made, and Caesar set off for Syria.*

Domitius Calvinus attacks King Pharnaces at Nicopolis and is defeated

(34) While these events were taking place in Egypt, King Deiotarus came to Domitius Calvinus, to whom Caesar had entrusted the administration of Asia and the neighbouring provinces, to plead with him not to allow either Lesser Armenia, his own kingdom, or Cappadocia, the kingdom of Ariobarzanes, to be occupied and plundered by Pharnaces. He said that if they were not rid of this nuisance, they would be unable to comply with orders from Caesar or pay him the promised money. Domitius not only thought the money necessary to meet military expenses, but decided it was also discreditable to himself and an insult to the Roman people and to Caesar in his hour of victory, that the kingdoms of men who were allies and friends were being appropriated by the king of an external power.* He therefore sent an urgent message to Pharnaces to tell him to withdraw from Armenia and Cappadocia and not seize the occasion of a civil war to undermine the rights and majesty of the Roman people. He also thought that this declaration would have greater force if he moved his army nearer to those areas; so he went to join his legions, and taking one of the three (the Thirty-sixth) with him, he sent the other two to Egypt in response to Caesar's letter calling for their mobilization, although one of them did not take part in the Alexandrian war, because it was sent overland by way of Syria. To the Thirty-sixth Gnaeus Domitius added the two legions trained and equipped in Roman fashion which Deiotarus had maintained for several years; he also took 100 cavalry,* and the same number from Ariobarzanes. He sent Publius Sestius to the quaestor Gaius Plaetorius, to fetch the legion which had been put together from an emergency levy of troops in Pontus, and Quintus Patisius to Cilicia, to summon auxiliaries. All these forces rapidly gathered in Comana in response to Domitius' orders.

(35) Meanwhile an embassy from Pharnaces brought his reply: he had withdrawn from Cappadocia but annexed Lesser Armenia, to which he had a legal claim on his father's account. At worst, the case of this kingdom should be left as

it was for decision by Caesar, because he was prepared to accept whatever Caesar decided. Gnaeus Domitius saw that Pharnaces had withdrawn from Cappadocia not from choice but from necessity, both because it was easier for him to defend Armenia, which lay up against his own kingdom, than Cappadocia, which was further away, and because he had been expecting Domitius to bring all three legions against him. After hearing that two of them had been sent to Caesar, he had hung on more boldly in Armenia, but Domitius began to insist that he withdrew from that kingdom as well. Domitius said that his claim to Cappadocia was no different from his claim to Armenia and that he had no right to ask that the matter should be left as it was until Caesar arrived, because 'as it was' meant a state of affairs that was as it had been.* After returning this answer, Domitius set out for Armenia with the forces I have described above and began to make his way along the higher ground, for there is a lofty forested range which extends from Comana in Pontus and connects it with Lesser Armenia, which divides Armenia from Cappadocia. He saw that this route had definite advantages: there could be no sudden enemy attack against higher ground, and Cappadocia, lying below these ranges, would provide him with plentiful supplies.

(36) In the mean time Pharnaces sent several embassies to Domitius to negotiate peace and bring him regal gifts. Domitius steadfastly rejected everything and replied to the ambassadors that nothing was more important to him than to restore the dignity of the Roman people and recover the kingdoms of their allies. By constant forced marches he arrived at the town of Nicopolis, which is in Lesser Armenia on a site that is itself level but has high mountains blocking it in on two sides at a fair distance from the town, and made camp some seven miles away. From this camp he had to traverse a narrow, difficult place. Pharnaces therefore laid an ambush with some picked infantry and almost all his cavalry; he also ordered a great quantity of sheep and cattle to be dispersed within the pass, and people from both town and country to move openly about. His object was that if Domitius came amicably through the pass he would see men

and cattle there in the fields, as though they were expecting friends, and not suspect an ambush, but if he came like an enemy into hostile territory, his soldiers would scatter to seize their plunder and be slaughtered when they were dispersed.

(37) While Pharnaces was making these arrangements, he still did not stop sending ambassadors to Domitius asking for peace and friendship, since he thought that this in itself would make it easier to deceive him. On the contrary, the hope of peace gave Domitius a reason for staying on in the same camp. Thus Pharnaces, having lost the immediate opportunity, recalled his troops to camp because he was afraid that the ambush would be discovered. On the following day Domitius moved nearer to Nicopolis and made camp opposite the town. As our men were constructing the rampart, Pharnaces drew his forces up for battle according to his well-established practice: in front there was a single line of men, stiffened on each wing by three lines of reinforcements, while in the centre the reinforcements were arranged in the same way, with single lines placed in the gaps to right and left.* Domitius posted part of his forces in front of the rampart and completed the work he had begun on his camp.

(38) On the next night Pharnaces intercepted messengers bringing Domitius a letter about the situation at Alexandria, and learnt that Caesar was in great danger and that Domitius was being insistently asked to send Caesar reinforcements as soon as possible and himself move closer to Alexandria by way of Syria. On discovering this, Pharnaces thought that it would amount to a victory if he could drag things out, since he reckoned that Domitius would swiftly have to withdraw. Therefore from the town, at the point where he saw that our troops had the easiest approach and the most level ground for fighting, he dug two straight ditches, not very far apart and four feet deep, to the spot beyond which he had decided not to extend his line. He always drew up his battle-line between these ditches, although he stationed all his cavalry on the flanks beyond the ditch, because they far outnumbered ours and would otherwise have been useless.

(39) Then Domitius, who was disturbed more by Caesar's danger than his own, and thought that he would not be able

to retreat in safety if he went back to accepting conditions he had already rejected, or if he withdrew for no reason, led his army out to battle from his camp nearby. He put the Thirty-sixth legion on the right wing, the one from Pontus on the left, and Deiotarus' in the centre (to whom, however, he left only a very narrow sector of the line), with the remaining cohorts in reserve. Such being the order of battle on each side, they proceeded to engage.

(40) The signal was given at about the same moment on both sides, and they charged together. The fight was hard and varied in result: the Thirty-sixth legion made so successful an attack on the king's cavalry outside the ditch that they came up under the walls of the town, crossed the ditch, and took the enemy from behind. But the Pontic legion on the other wing, having briefly turned away from the enemy and given ground, still tried to go round and across the ditch to attack the opposition on their unprotected side, and was struck down and overwhelmed in the act of crossing the ditch. As for Deiotarus' legions, they barely withstood the attack. Thus the victorious royal forces on the king's right wing and in the centre converged on the Thirty-sixth legion. This stoutly resisted the winners' attack, and although surrounded by large enemy forces fought with great resolution all round the circle and retreated to the foot of the mountains, a point to which Pharnaces was unwilling to continue his pursuit because of the steepness of the terrain. Thus after the Pontic legion had been almost totally lost and a substantial proportion of Deiotarus' men killed, the Thirty-sixth legion made its way to higher ground without losing more than 250 men. Several distinguished and illustrious Romans belonging to the equestrian order* fell in the battle. After this reverse, Domitius gathered together the remains of his scattered army and retreated by a safe route through Cappadocia to Asia.

(41) Elated by his success, and expecting to hear what he wanted to hear about Caesar, Pharnaces moved to invade Pontus with his full army. There he behaved as a victorious king, and a king of extreme cruelty. With the object of making his father's fortune* his own, but with a happier result,

he attacked and took many towns, plundered the property
of Roman and Pontic citizens, inflicted punishments more
harrowing than death* on those who possessed any distinction of beauty or youth, and in the absence of defenders
took possession of Pontus, boasting that he had taken back
his father's kingdom.

Gabinius fails to secure the Illyrian coast; after his death Vatinius defeats the Pompeian admiral Octavius

(42) At about the same time a reverse was sustained in
Illyricum, a province which in the preceding months had
been held not merely without disgrace but even with credit.
Quintus Cornificius, Caesar's quaestor, had been sent there
in the summer* as governor with two legions, and although
the province had poor resources for maintaining armies and
had been worn down and devastated by war on its borders*
and by internal quarrels, his caution and care nevertheless
enabled him to recover and defend it, because he took great
pains not to make any risky advance. He stormed a large
number of fortified settlements built on heights, the commanding positions of which induced their inhabitants to
make raids and conduct hostilities, and he gave his soldiers
the booty, which although exiguous was still welcome, especially as it had been acquired by valour, given that the state
of the province was so pitiful; and when Octavius* in the
rout after the battle of Pharsalus made his way with a large
fleet into the gulf,* Cornificius used a few ships belonging
to the people of Iader, whose sense of duty to the state had
always been exceptional, to seize Octavius' scattered ships,
with the result that by combining the ships of his allies with
the ones he had captured he even had a fleet to fight with.
In a very different part of the world, Caesar was pursuing
Gnaeus Pompeius after his victory, but when he heard that
a number of his opponents had collected the remnants of their
routed forces and betaken themselves to Illyricum because
of its proximity to Macedonia, he sent a letter to Gabinius*

with orders to set out for Illyricum with the legions of new recruits which had recently been raised. There he was to join forces with Quintus Cornificius and beat off any threat to the province; and if the province could be kept secure without a large force, he was to take the legions on to Macedonia, because Caesar believed that that entire region would restart the war so long as Pompey was alive.

(43) When Gabinius reached Illyricum it was winter and a difficult time of year. He may have thought the province better supplied than it was; he may have set much store by the luck that had given Caesar his victory; or he may have relied on his own courage and military skill, with which he had often run risks in war and secured great successes by his daring leadership. But he received no support from the resources of the province, which was on the one hand stripped bare and on the other disloyal, and it was imposs- ible for supplies to be brought in by way of the sea, which was stormy and closed to shipping. He was constrained by great shortages and conducted his campaign not as he wished, but as necessity dictated. Thus when lack of food compelled him to storm fortified settlements or towns in the most se- vere weather, he suffered frequent setbacks and was held in such contempt by the natives that when he retreated to Salona, a town on the coast where there were Roman inhabitants of the greatest bravery and loyalty, he was forced to fight a set battle. In this battle he lost more than 2,000 men, thirty-eight centurions, and four military tribunes,* and withdrew with the remainder of his forces into Salona where he laboured under extreme shortages of every kind and died of disease within a few months. His lack of success when alive and the suddenness of his death gave Octavius high hopes of taking possession of the province; but luck, which has the most powerful effect on wars, and Cornificius' care, and Vatinius' courage did not allow Octavius to enjoy his favourable cir- cumstances for very long.

(44) Vatinius, who was at Brundisium and knew what had happened in Illyricum, was sent a stream of letters by Cornificius asking him to bring assistance to the province. He also heard that Marcus Octavius had made alliances with

the natives and was bringing places garrisoned by our troops under attack, some by his fleet under his own command, others by land forces of native origin. Although Vatinius was so seriously ill that his body barely had the strength to obey his mind, his courage none the less overcame the difficulties created both by the winter and by the suddenness of his preparations. Since he himself had only a few warships in port, he wrote to Calenus in Achaea with a request to send him a fleet. But as this took longer than was demanded by the threat to our troops, who were unable to hold out against Octavius' assault, he fitted rams to his light ships, of which he had a fair number, though they were of a size quite inadequate for battle. To these he added his warships. He then increased the strength of his naval force by embarking veteran soldiers, of whom he had a large number from every legion, left behind among the sick when the army had been ferried across to Greece,* and set out for Illyricum. A number of communities on the coast had either defected or surrendered to Octavius; some of these he recovered, some, if they would not change their minds, he bypassed, and he avoided any kind of delay or commitment which would prevent him coming up with Octavius himself as soon as possible. Octavius was attacking Epidaurus, where we had a garrison, from land and sea, but Vatinius' arrival compelled him to abandon his assault, and our garrison was relieved.

(45) When Octavius discovered that Vatinius had a fleet that was composed for the most part of small light ships, he decided to rely on his own fleet and stopped at the island of Tauris. Vatinius was sailing that way in pursuit of him not because he knew that Octavius had made a halt there but because he had decided to chase him further. When he drew nearer to Tauris, with his ships well scattered because the weather was rough and he had no suspicion of the enemy presence, he suddenly sighted a ship coming to meet him with her yard-arms half-lowered and fighting men on board. Immediately he saw her, he gave orders to furl the sails, lower the yards, and arm the soldiers, and by hoisting the ensign which was the signal for battle indicated to the ships immediately astern of him that they should do the same.

(46) When Vatinius realized that for this fortuitous encounter he was at a disadvantage in both number and size of ships, he preferred to trust to luck. He therefore made the first attack with his own quinquereme on Octavius' own quadrireme. The latter rowed very fast and with great determination at him, and the ships struck each other so hard with their rams that Octavius' ship had hers ripped off and was held entangled by her timbers. Battle was fiercely joined elsewhere, but the clash was at its most intense around the commanders, because as they all tried to help their own man an intense hand-to-hand fight developed in a restricted patch of water. The more the ships grappled each other and gave the opportunity for coming to grips with opponents, the more Vatinius' men had the upper hand. With astonishing bravery, they had no hesitation in jumping from their own ships on to those of their opponents, and once the terms of engagement were equal their far superior courage brought them success. Octavius' own quadrireme foundered, and many besides were captured, or sank after being holed by ramming; some of Octavius' marines were butchered, others thrown into the sea. Octavius himself took to a small boat, and when more men sought refuge on it and it sank, in spite of a wound he swam to a galley of his.* He was taken on board, and when darkness began to put a stop to the battle he fled under sail in the storm, followed by a number of his ships which chance had saved from this dangerous situation.

(47) As for Vatinius, when success had been achieved, he sounded the signal to withdraw and came victoriously and with all his forces intact into the very port from which Octavius' fleet had gone out to fight. In the battle he had captured one 'five', two triremes, eight 'twos',* and a number of Octavius' rowers. The following day he spent there while he repaired these captured ships and his own. The day after, he pressed on to the island of Issa, where he believed Octavius had taken shelter after his flight. On this island was the most notable of the towns of these parts, which was very supportive of Octavius, but when Vatinius arrived the inhabitants threw themselves on his mercy and he discovered that Octavius himself with a few small ships and a

following wind had set course for Greece with the intention of going on from there to Sicily and then to Africa. Thus in a short time Vatinius had won a spectacular success, recovered the province and restored it to Cornificius, completely cleared the gulf of the enemy fleet, and made a victorious return to Brundisium without sustaining any losses to his fleet or troops.

The civilian plot and subsequent army mutiny against Q. Cassius in Spain

(48) During the period when Caesar besieged Pompey at Dyrrachium, won the battle at Palaepharsalus,* and was in great danger, rumoured to be even greater, in the fighting at Alexandria, Quintus Cassius Longinus had been left in Spain as governor of the Further province.* Whether it was his own natural disposition that was responsible, or the hatred he had developed against the province after being wounded there as quaestor* in an ambush, his feelings of dislike had become greatly exacerbated; perhaps this was because he was well aware that these feelings were reciprocated by the province, or perhaps it was because he could detect from numerous tell-tale signs the hatred felt by people who were not good at hiding their feelings, and he longed to compensate for being disliked in the province by becoming popular with his army. Accordingly, as soon as he had concentrated the army in one place he promised his men a hundred sesterces each, and not long afterwards, having attacked and taken the town of Medobrega in Lusitania, along with Mount Herminius where the inhabitants of Medobrega had taken refuge, he was saluted there as 'Victorious General'* and presented his soldiers with their hundred sesterces. In addition, he made large rewards to many individuals, and these, although they gave him an impressive temporary popularity with the army, gradually and imperceptibly undermined strict military discipline.

(49) Cassius dispersed his legions to winter quarters and went back to Corduba to hear court cases. He decided to pay off debts of his which had caused great hardship to the

province; and as is the way with largesse, the fine pretext of generosity entailed finding more funds for the donor. Sums of money were demanded from the rich, sums which Longinus not merely permitted, but required, in the form of personal payments to himself;* men of modest means were lumped in with the rich because of private quarrels; and there was no source of profit, whether grand and open or petty and sordid, which went untapped by the governor's household or his legal hearings. There was no one capable of standing any loss at all who was not bailed to come to court or found himself included in the list of accused. Thus besides financial losses and damage to family fortunes, people were worried about the risks to their persons.

(50) The result was that since Longinus in his capacity as governor was acting exactly as he had when quaestor, the provincials again started to lay a similar plot to kill him. Their loathing of him was strengthened by some of his entourage, who in spite of being partners in his robbery, none the less hated the man in whose name they were doing wrong and credited to themselves what they had seized, but held it against Cassius when loss or obstruction occurred. He also recruited a new, Fifth, legion,* increasing his unpopularity both by the levy itself and by the cost of the additional legion. His cavalry numbers were made up to 3,000 and equipped at enormous expense, and the province had no respite.

(51) Meanwhile, instructions came from Caesar that Cassius was to take his army across to Africa and march through Mauretania to Numidian territory, because Juba had sent a great deal of help to Pompey and intended to send still more. After he had received these instructions, he was beside himself with delight at being offered such a wonderful chance of laying his hands on new provinces and a highly fertile kingdom. He therefore departed himself for Lusitania to assemble his legions and mobilize auxiliaries, while the responsibility for making ready supplies of food and commissioning a hundred ships, and for allocating and demanding contributions of money, was delegated to specific individuals so that there should be no delay of any kind when he returned. He came back sooner than anyone anticipated; for Cassius could work

hard and do without sleep, particularly when he had his heart set on something.

(52) He mustered his army in a single place, made camp outside Corduba, and in an address to his soldiers explained what actions he had to take, on Caesar's orders. He promised that he would give them one hundred sesterces each when he had crossed to Mauretania, and that the Fifth legion would stay in Spain. After this speech he went back into Corduba, and on that very day, in the afternoon, as he was going into the basilica,* one Minucius Silo, who was a hanger-on of Lucius Racilius, pretended to be a soldier and handed him a petition as though he was asking something of him. He then took his place, as if he was wanting an answer, behind Racilius, who was walking beside Cassius. Racilius quickly made room for him, and after slipping between them Minucius grabbed Cassius with his left hand while he was facing away from him, and stabbed him twice with a dagger. Yells arose and all the conspirators attacked. Munatius Flaccus thrust his sword through the nearest lictor, and after killing him wounded Quintus Cassius,* one of the governor's deputies. At this point Titus Vasius and Lucius Mercello showed similar boldness in aiding their townsman Flaccus—all being from Italica. Lucius Licinius Squillus flew at Longinus himself and inflicted some minor wounds on him as he lay there.

(53) There was a rush to defend Cassius, because it was his habit always to have with him some armed Berones and a number of re-enlisted veterans. They stopped the rest who were moving in behind to do the killing, amongst them Calpurnius Salvianus and Manilius Tusculus. Minucius fled, but after being overpowered among the boulders which lay across his path was taken before Cassius when the latter had been brought home. Racilius slipped into a house very close by which belonged to one of his relations, until he could find out for certain whether Cassius had been finished off. Lucius Laterensis had no doubts on this score, ran happily into the camp, and wished joy to the soldiers of the Second and the locally raised legions, whom he knew loathed Cassius. The mob hoisted him on to the dais and saluted him as governor; for no one who had either been born in the province,

like the men of the local legion, or had become a provincial by long residence there, a group which included the Second legion, failed to share the feelings of the whole province in detesting Cassius. On the other hand the Thirtieth and Twenty-first legions, which had been recruited in Italy a few months previously, had been assigned to Cassius by Caesar, and the Fifth legion had only just been raised in the province.

(54) Meanwhile the news was brought to Laterensis that Cassius was alive, and on receipt of it, more annoyed than alarmed, he quickly reassumed his previous demeanour and went to see Cassius. When the Thirtieth legion heard what had happened, it marched into Corduba to help its general. The Twenty-first did the same, and the Fifth followed. Two legions now remained in camp, and the men of the Second, afraid that they would be left by themselves and their sentiments inferred from that, followed the example of the previous legions. The local legion refused to change its mind and was not deflected from its course by any fear.

(55) Cassius ordered the arrest of those who were named as privy to the plan to kill him and sent the legions back to camp, retaining five cohorts from the Thirtieth. On the evidence of Minucius he established that Lucius Racilius, Lucius Laterensis, and Annius Scapula, a provincial of the highest standing and influence who was as much one of his intimates as Laterensis and Racilius, were all involved in the same plot, and he soon gratified his bitterness by giving orders for their execution. He handed Minucius over to his ex-slaves* to torture, likewise Calpurnius Salvianus, who talked and gave the names of additional conspirators—genuinely, some think, but as others complain, under duress. L. Mercello . . . Squillus* was similarly tortured and produced the names of more men, whom Cassius ordered to be put to death with the exception of those who bought themselves off: certainly he openly agreed a fee of six million sesterces with Calpurnius and five million with Quintus Sestius.* And if these men who were chiefly guilty were fined, the fact that the danger to his life and the pain caused by his wounds were paid for in cash still meant that in Cassius cruelty and greed were fighting a close contest.

(56) Some days later he received a letter from Caesar, from which he learnt that Pompey had been defeated in battle and had fled with the loss of his troops. At the news he felt both resentful and glad: the tidings of the victory gave him joy, but the ending of the war put an end to the licence which the times had allowed him. Thus he was uncertain which he preferred, freedom from fear or the power to be able to do anything he pleased. When his wounds had healed, he summoned all those who had him down as a debtor in their accounts, and ordered them to show him as a creditor for those amounts; he also demanded more generous sums from those to whom he thought he had been over-lenient. He also began a levy of Romans qualified for cavalry service; they were called up from all the colonies and associations of Roman citizens,* terrified by the prospect of service overseas, and invited to buy immunity from the military oath. This produced a great deal of revenue, but brought him into even greater odium. Once this business was concluded, he performed a ceremony of purification* for the whole army and sent the legions which he intended to take to Africa, along with the auxiliaries, to make the crossing. He himself went to Hispalis to inspect the fleet he was preparing, and stayed there a while because he had published an edict all over the province requiring anyone from whom he had demanded money and who had failed to pay it, to appear before him. This summons caused severe and general disquiet.

(57) Meanwhile Lucius Titius, who was at that time a military tribune with the local legion, brought news that this legion had parted from the Thirtieth, which like itself was under the command of the governor's deputy Quintus Cassius, when they were encamped outside the town of Ilipa. There had been a mutiny, some centurions who had refused to allow the men to break camp had been killed, and they had marched towards the Second legion, which was being taken by another route to the crossing. On receipt of this information Cassius set out at night with five cohorts of the Twenty-first legion and reached Naeva* early in the morning. He waited there that day, to see what was happening, and hurried on to Carmo. Here, after the Thirtieth and Twenty-

first legions, and four cohorts of the Fifth legion, and all his cavalry, had assembled, he heard that four cohorts had been overpowered by the men of the local legion near Obucula and with them had reached the Second legion, where they had all united and chosen Titus Thorius of Italica as their commander. Cassius quickly called a council of war and sent his quaestor Marcus Marcellus to Corduba to keep the town under control, and his deputy Quintus Cassius to Hispalis. In a day or two news came that the association of Roman citizens at Corduba had rejected his authority and that Marcellus, whether voluntarily or not (and reports varied), was taking the side of the Cordubans. Also the two cohorts of the Fifth legion which were on garrison duty in Corduba were following suit. Furious at these developments, Cassius struck camp and arrived at Segovia on the River Singilis on the following day. There he addressed the troops to test their attitude, and discovered that they were totally loyal to him, not for his own sake but for that of the absent Caesar, and would not seek to be excused any danger provided that they could be the means of winning the province back for Caesar.

(58) Meanwhile Thorius brought the veteran legions to Corduba. He did not wish it to appear that the trouble sprang from his own and the soldiers' mutinous natures, and he also wanted to counter Quintus Cassius, whom he thought enjoyed a stronger position by virtue of Caesar's name, with an equally powerful and prestigious figure. He therefore repeatedly and publicly claimed that he desired to win the province back for Pompey. And perhaps he even did this out of hatred of Caesar and love of Pompey, whose name was very potent with the legions which had been Marcus Varro's.* But whatever his intentions, about which there was general speculation, this was certainly what he maintained in public; as for the soldiers, they were so keen to declare it that they had Pompey's name written on their shields. A full gathering of the Roman citizens' association, not simply the men but also their wives and young sons, came to meet the legions and beg them not to fall like enemies on Corduba and sack it: they said they shared the universal feeling against Cassius, but pleaded not to have to act against Caesar.

(59) Moved by the tearful entreaties of such a crowd, and seeing that they had no need of the memory or name of Pompey to hunt Cassius down, that Longinus was detested equally by every supporter of Caesar and by every supporter of Pompey, and that they could induce neither the association nor Marcus Marcellus to oppose the Caesarian cause, the troops removed Pompey's name from their shields. Having adopted as their commander Marcellus, who declared that he would defend Caesar's cause, they saluted him as governor, allied themselves with the association, and encamped at Corduba. Two days later Cassius made camp within sight of the town on high ground about four miles away, to the south of the River Baetis, and wrote to King Bogud of Mauretania and to Marcus Lepidus, the proconsul of Nearer Spain, to come as quickly as possible to help him and the province, for Caesar's sake. He himself, in enemy fashion, ravaged the land and set fire to the houses of the Cordubans.

(60) The disgrace and humiliation brought by this action on the legions which had chosen Marcellus as their commander made them crowd around him and beg him to lead them out to battle and give them the chance of fighting before the splendid and cherished possessions of the inhabitants of Corduba vanished so degradingly before their very eyes in plunder, fire, and slaughter. Although Marcellus thought that to fight was the most wretched thing of all, because the losses of both the winners and the losers would affect the same man, Caesar, and he would not be in control, he crossed the Baetis with his legions and drew up his line of battle. When he saw that Cassius opposite had formed up his line in front of his camp on higher ground, Marcellus advanced the excuse that his opponent had not come down to level ground, and persuaded his soldiers to withdraw to their camp. He therefore began to lead his forces back, but Cassius attacked with his cavalry, the arm in which he was strong and knew that Marcellus was weak, and as the legionaries retreated killed a number of the rearguard on the banks of the river. This loss made Marcellus aware of his mistake in crossing the river and of the difficulty of this operation. So he transferred his camp across the Baetis, and both commanders

kept leading their men out to battle; however, battle was never joined because of the problems of the terrain.

(61) Marcellus was much stronger in infantry, because he had veteran legions with considerable experience of battle. Cassius put his faith in the loyalty of his legions rather than their fighting qualities. So when the camps were lying beside each other and Marcellus had captured and fortified an outlying position which allowed him to deprive Cassius' men of access to water, Longinus became afraid of being virtually besieged in territory that was neither under his control nor friendly to him. Silently, he left his camp by night and marched rapidly to Ulia, a town which he believed was loyal to him. There he constructed a camp so close against its walls that not only its natural position—Ulia is situated high on a hill—but also the very defences of the town made him safe from attack from any direction. Marcellus pursued him and encamped opposite him as close to Ulia as he could. When he realized the nature of the ground, he had no choice but to adopt the course of action he most desired: neither to give battle—from which, if the chance had offered, he would have been unable to restrain his eager troops—nor to permit Cassius any freedom of movement, in case more towns and their territories suffered as the Cordubans had. He placed strongpoints in suitable spots and by constructing a continuous earthwork all round the town enclosed Ulia and Cassius within his fortifications. Before these works were complete, Longinus sent all his cavalry out, because he believed they would be very useful to him if they could stop Marcellus getting forage and provisions, but would be a great handicap if they consumed vital supplies of food when trapped by siege and useless.

(62) A few days later King Bogud, having received Cassius' letter, arrived with troops and added a number of Spanish auxiliary cohorts to the legion he had brought with him. For as usually happens in civil wars, at that time some of the townships took Cassius' side, while a majority favoured Marcellus. Bogud and his force approached Marcellus' outer fortifications. Both sides fought fiercely, and they clashed repeatedly as fortune gave victory now to one side and now

to the other; Marcellus, however, was never driven from his siege-works.

(63) Meanwhile Lepidus reached Ulia from the Nearer province with thirty-five legionary cohorts and a large number of cavalry and other auxiliaries. His intention was to settle the differences between Cassius and Marcellus without prejudice. As Lepidus arrived, Marcellus unhesitatingly came forward and accepted his authority. Cassius, in contrast, stayed behind his defences, whether because he considered that he ought to be accorded more rights than Marcellus, or because he feared that his opponent's deference had already affected Lepidus' attitude. Lepidus encamped at Ulia, and acted in complete harmony with Marcellus. He forbade any fighting and invited Cassius to come out, giving him his own personal guarantee of complete safety. Cassius hesitated for a long time, wondering what to do and how far he could trust Lepidus, but could see no satisfactory outcome if he decided to stick to his present course. He therefore asked for the fortifications to be dismantled and an unobstructed exit granted him. Not merely had a truce been made, but peaceful conditions had almost been established, with the earthworks being levelled and the guards withdrawn from the defences, when the king's auxiliaries, to the surprise of all—if, that is, 'all' can include Cassius, since it was uncertain whether he was in the know—attacked and overwhelmed a number of soldiers there. And if Lepidus' angry provision of assistance had not swiftly broken up this fighting, more serious losses would have been suffered.

(64) After a way had been cleared for Cassius, Marcellus and Lepidus amalgamated their forces and set out with their troops for Corduba at the same moment as Cassius set out for Carmo. This was about the time when Trebonius came as proconsul to govern the province. When Cassius heard of his arrival, he placed the cavalry and the legions he had with him in various winter quarters, rapidly gathered together all his personal property, and made for Malaca. There he took ship, at the wrong time of year for sailing. He himself stated that he did not want to put himself in the hands of Lepidus, Trebonius, and Marcellus; the friends of the latter asserted

that he did not want to make a less than dignified journey through a province the greater part of which had rejected his authority; and everyone else thought that he did not want any others to lay their hands on the cash he had accumulated from countless robberies. He enjoyed good weather, considering it was winter, and put into the River Hiberus to avoid a night passage. He went on from there in a somewhat stronger wind, in the belief that his voyage would be no more dangerous, and ran up against a heavy sea at the entrance to the river. Since the strength of the current prevented him turning back, and he could not hold a straight course ahead in such a sea, his ship sank, right at the mouth of the river, and he was drowned.

Caesar proceeds to Pontus and defeats Pharnaces at Zela

(65) When Caesar reached Syria* from Egypt, he learnt from people who had arrived from Rome, and realized from letters written from the city, that many matters there were being handled badly and incompetently and that no aspect of public life was running tolerably smoothly. Tribunician agitation was giving rise to damaging riots,* while ambition and favouritism on the part of military tribunes and legionary commanders were responsible for much that broke military custom and practice and contributed to the collapse of strict discipline.* He saw that all this demanded his presence, but none the less thought it preferable to leave the provinces and regions, to which he had come, organized in such a way that they were free of internal strife, subject to the rule of Roman law, and rid of the fear of foreign enemies. He hoped to manage this quickly in Syria, Cilicia, and Asia, because these provinces were unaffected by war, but in Bithynia and Pontus he could see that there was a heavier task awaiting him. Reports were reaching him that Pharnaces had not left Pontus, nor did he think he would, because the king was mightily conceited by the battle he had won against Domitius Calvinus.

Caesar stayed briefly in almost all the more important communities, distributing rewards both individually and communally to those who deserved them, and hearing and deciding old disputes. He also took under his protection the kings, despots, and dynasts bordering on Syria, who all converged on him; he made them agree to watch and defend the province, and sent them away firm friends* to himself and the people of Rome.

(66) After spending a few days in the province, he put Sextus Caesar, a relation and friend of his, in charge of Syria and its legions, and went on himself to Cilicia with the fleet he had come with. He summoned all the communities of that province to Tarsus, the strongest and most celebrated town of virtually the whole of Cilicia. Once he had made all the administrative and constitutional arrangements there for the province and its neighbouring communities, his eagerness for war allowed him to stay no longer. After a series of forced marches through Cappadocia and a break of two days at Mazaca, he reached Comana, which is the oldest and most sacred sanctuary of Bellona in Cappadocia.* It commands such religious respect that among those folk the priest of the goddess is by common consent held to be second only to the king in majesty, authority, and power. This priesthood was awarded by Caesar to Lycomedes, a Bithynian of high nobility, who was descended from the royal family of Cappadocia. His right to it was not in doubt, but he was seeking its return after a long intermission due to the misfortunes of his ancestors and a change of descent.* To Ariarathes, the brother of Ariobarzanes, he granted authority over . . . to be under his sovereignty and power,* since both men deserved well of Rome and he did not want Ariarathes either to be tempted by his position as successor to the kingdom, or as heir to intimidate Ariobarzanes. He then started to complete, equally fast, his interrupted march.

(67) Deiotarus was at that time the tetrarch of almost the whole of Galatia, a position which the other tetrarchs maintained was permitted neither by law nor by custom, but he had without doubt been given the title of King of Lesser Armenia by the senate. When Caesar approached Pontus

and the borders of Galatia, Deiotarus laid aside his regal insignia and put on not simply ordinary clothes, but the garb
of a man summoned for prosecution,* and came to Caesar
to pray for pardon. He explained that he lived in a part of
the world where there had been no Caesarian forces and that
orders backed by armies had forced him to join Pompey's
camp; his duty, he said, was not to sit in judgement on
the quarrels of the Roman people, but to obey the present
holders of authority.

(68) In response Caesar called to mind the many services
he had rendered Deiotarus in official decrees passed when
he was consul.* He showed that no defence could possibly
acquit the king of folly, because a man of his common sense
and attentiveness was able to know who controlled Rome
and Italy, which side the senate and people of Rome and
the state itself supported, and finally who had succeeded to
Lentulus and Marcellus as consul.* None the less, he would
overlook what Deiotarus had done in the light of his own
past favours,* the long-established relations of friendship and
hospitality between them, Deiotarus' status and age, and the
entreaties of a crowd of the king's friends and acquaintances
who had gathered to intercede for him. He said that he would
give a decision later on the quarrel between the tetrarchs, and
gave the king back his regal costume. He also ordered him
to bring with him on campaign the legion which he had
formed from his own people and had trained and armed in
Roman fashion, as well as his entire force of cavalry.

(69) When Caesar reached Pontus he gathered all his forces
together in one spot. They were modest in numbers and in
experience of war, with the exception of the veteran Sixth
legion, which he had brought with him from Alexandria;
but this had gone through such toil and danger and been so
reduced in size, in part by the difficulties of marches and voy-
ages, and in part by the frequency of campaigning, that it
contained less than a thousand men. The other three legions
were Deiotarus' one and the two involved in the battle we
described between Gnaeus Domitius and Pharnaces. An embassy from Pharnaces now approached Caesar and asked
him, above all, not to act in hostile fashion on his arrival,

because Pharnaces would do whatever he was ordered. And they laid particular emphasis on the fact that Pharnaces had refused to give Pompey any help against Caesar, whereas Deiotarus, who had given help, had made his peace with him.

(70) Caesar replied that he would treat Pharnaces with absolute fairness, provided that he carried out his promises. He cautioned the embassy, gently as was his habit, not to hide behind Deiotarus or make too much of the service they had done himself by not sending help to Pompey, because nothing was dearer to his heart than pardoning suppliants, but neither could he condone public injury done to Roman provinces by those who had professed to be dutiful towards him. Moreover the dutifulness they mentioned had been more profitable to Pharnaces, who had taken care not to be on the losing side, than to himself, to whom the immortal gods had granted victory. He would therefore take no action against Pharnaces for the very serious harm he had inflicted on Romans who had been in business in Pontus, since he could not make full restitution: it was not possible to restore life to the dead or virility to the castrated—the punishment worse than death to which some Romans had been subjected. However, Pharnaces must immediately move out of Pontus, send the staff of the tax contractors back, and restore to the allies of Rome and to Roman citizens anything else that was in his possession. If he did this, he could then send Caesar the gifts and presents which successful commanders-in-chief commonly receive from their friends (the reason for this being that Pharnaces had sent him a golden crown). After making this answer, he sent the embassy back.

(71) Pharnaces obligingly promised everything. But he hoped that Caesar, in his haste and eagerness to press on, would also believe his promises more readily than the facts warranted, in order to leave sooner and with greater credit to deal with more essential matters—for everyone knew that there were a host of reasons calling Caesar back to Rome. He therefore began to spin things out, request a later date for his departure, insist on making agreements, and in short practise obstruction. Realizing Pharnaces' cunning, Caesar had no choice but to do what at other times was his natural

habit, and come to grips with the enemy more quickly than anyone expected.

(72) Zela is a town in Pontus, which for a place situated on flat ground is fairly well fortified in itself, because a natural mound resembling an artificial tumulus supports the wall and gives it greater height all round. The town is encircled by high hills separated by valleys. The highest of these hills, which is extremely famous in those parts on account of Mithridates' victory over Triarius* and the losses inflicted on our army, is almost joined to the town by high-level paths, and is no more than three miles from Zela. Pharnaces occupied this spot with all his forces after repairing the defences of the old camp which had brought his father good luck.

(73) Caesar, who had made camp five miles from the enemy, realized that the valleys whose width protected the royal camp would similarly protect his own, provided that the enemy had not previously seized those sites which were much nearer the king's camp. He therefore ordered material for a rampart to be collected and brought inside his defences. This was rapidly done, and then, in the fourth watch* of the following night, he left the baggage behind in camp and with all his legions ready for battle made a dawn seizure of the very place where Mithridates had won his victory over Triarius. He ordered slaves to fetch from the camp all the material that had been collected, to prevent any soldier leaving the work of fortification—it being a distance of no more than a mile across the valley which separated the enemy camp from where Caesar was starting his earthworks.

(74) As it grew light, Pharnaces suddenly noticed what was happening and formed his whole force up in front of his camp. Because such steep ground lay between the two positions, Caesar assumed that this deployment had been made in accordance with a common enough military practice, in order either to keep more of his men on guard and slow down their work of fortification, or to demonstrate Pharnaces' confidence and avoid giving the impression that he was sheltering behind his ramparts rather than using the sword to defend his position. Caesar was therefore happy to do no more than station his front line in front of his

ditch and bank while the rest of his army continued working. Pharnaces may have been swayed by the lucky associations of the place, or encouraged by omens and superstitious beliefs, to which we afterwards heard he had bowed; or he may have been influenced by discovering how few men of ours were under arms, when in the light of our usual way of fortifying a camp he had originally thought that the great crowd of slaves who were carrying material were soldiers; or he may have had faith in his own veteran army (which his officers boasted had fought and won twenty-two pitched battles), while at the same time despising ours, which he knew he had beaten when it was under Domitius' command. Anyway, he took the decision to fight, and began to descend the steep valley. For a while Caesar laughed at his empty bravado and the way he packed his troops into a place to which no enemy in his right mind would advance. But in the mean time Pharnaces, with his men in battle order, was making an unbroken continuation of his progress down into the precipitous valley by beginning to climb the slope of the hillside facing him.

(75) Disturbed by this incredible temerity, or self-confidence, and caught unprepared and unsuspecting, Caesar all at once called his troops away from their labours on the fortifications, told them to arm, put the legions across Pharnaces' path, and drew up his line of battle. The sudden excitement of this made our men very frightened. The king's four-horse chariots fitted with sickles threw Caesar's ranks into confusion when the ranks were still out of position, but were none the less quickly overwhelmed by a huge storm of weapons. Hard on their heels came the enemy battle-line, and shouts filled the air as the fight began; the natural strength of the position was a great advantage, but greater was the blessing of the immortal gods, who have a hand in all the accidents of war, and particularly those where rational action is impossible.

(76) The origin of our victory lay in the bitter and intense hand-to-hand battle joined on the right wing, where the veteran Sixth legion was stationed. Here the enemy were thrust down the slope, while on the left and in the centre, the whole

of the king's forces were being decisively defeated—much more slowly, but with the same help from the gods. The ease with which they had approached uphill was matched by the speed with which they found themselves in difficulties with the slope once they were dislodged. And so they lost many of their men, some slain, some crushed by their falling companions. Those who were able to escape at the cost of throwing away their weapons crossed the valley, but without arms could do nothing from higher ground. Our men, on the other hand, were fired by their victory and did not hesitate to climb the slope facing them and attack the enemy fortifications. Since the defence consisted of the cohorts left behind by Pharnaces to guard the camp, it was soon taken. His whole army having now been either killed or taken prisoner, Pharnaces fled with a handful of cavalry; and if the attack on his camp had not allowed him an improved chance of escape,* he would have been captured alive and brought to Caesar.

(77) Caesar was quite overjoyed at such a victory, although he had been victorious in so many battles. He had brought a major war to an astonishingly rapid end, and recollection of his sudden danger made his easy victory under difficult circumstances all the sweeter. Pontus now recaptured, he allowed his soldiers to keep all the booty plundered from the king, and himself took the road the next day accompanied by cavalry equipped for action. He ordered the Sixth legion back to Italy to receive their rewards and honours, sent Deiotarus' auxiliaries home, and left two legions with Caelius Vinicianus in Pontus.

(78) So he made his way through Galatia and Bithynia to Asia, hearing and settling disputes in all those provinces, and granting rights to tetrarchs, kings, and communities He installed Mithridates the Pergamene, whose swift and successful action in Egypt we have described earlier,* as king of the Bosporan kingdom which had been ruled by Pharnaces; this man was of royal stock* and had also been given a royal upbringing, because Mithridates, king of the whole of Asia, had taken him from Pergamum as a small boy, on account of the nobility of his birth, and kept him on military service

with himself for many years. Caesar thus protected the provinces of the Roman people against hostile foreign kings by interposing an extremely friendly ruler. He also assigned to Mithridates, by right of family succession and national custom, the tetrarchy of Galatia which had been seized and appropriated a few years previously by Deiotarus. But he stayed no longer anywhere than the pressure of the disturbances in Rome allowed, and after this remarkably swift and successful settlement of affairs arrived in Italy sooner than anyone expected.*

THE AFRICAN WAR

After crossing to Africa, Caesar is tied down at Ruspina (1–33). He moves camp and goes on the offensive at Uzitta, but can make no impression on the Pompeians (34–64). Leaving Uzitta, inconclusive manœuvres by both sides lead finally to Caesar's victory at Thapsus (65–86). Collapse of resistance in Africa (87–98)

Caesar crosses to Africa and after a drawn battle establishes a defensive position near Ruspina

(1) By marching the regular daily distances, but not taking any days' rest, Caesar reached Lilybaeum on 17 December* and immediately made it clear that he wanted to embark in spite of the fact that he had no more than a single legion of recruits and barely 150 cavalry. He pitched his tent right by the shore, so that the waves almost broke on it. He did so in order to stop anyone hoping that anything would delay him, and to ensure that everyone was ready whatever the day and the hour. As it happened, the weather at the time was not suitable for sailing; but he none the less kept the crews and his soldiers aboard the ships and let slip no opportunity of setting out, especially as news came from the inhabitants of the province of Africa that his opponents' forces comprised countless cavalry, four legions belonging to the king,* a large quantity of light-armed troops, ten legions of Scipio's, 120 elephants, and several squadrons of ships. But he was undismayed and placed his trust in hope and courage. Meanwhile, as each day passed, his fleet of warships grew, numbers of merchant ships converged at the same point, and four legions of recruits* gathered, along with the veteran Fifth legion and nearly 2,000 cavalry.

(2) When six legions and 2,000 cavalry had been assembled, the former were embarked on the warships in the

order in which they had arrived, and the latter on the merchant ships. Caesar ordered the greater part of the ships, thus loaded, to go on ahead and make for the island of Aponiana, < ... > miles distant from Lilybaeum, but he himself stayed on <at Lilybaeum>. He sold the property of a few persons for the benefit of the treasury, and then, after giving general instructions to Allienus, the governor of Sicily, and making him responsible for the rapid embarkation of the remaining forces, boarded his ship on 25 December and immediately followed the others. In this way, travelling on a fast vessel before a steady wind, he sighted Africa three days later, in company with a small number of warships, because the merchantmen which made up the rest of his fleet were (except for a few) scattered by the wind and once off course made for various places. Caesar sailed his squadron past Clupea, then Neapolis, and also passed by a number of forts and towns not far from the sea.

(3) Caesar reached Hadrumetum, where there was an enemy garrison under the command of Gaius Considius, and when Gnaeus Piso appeared at the head of about 3,000 Moors, <making for> Hadrumetum with his cavalry along the shore from Clupea, he delayed for a little while off the harbour to give his remaining ships a chance to join him. He then landed his troops, who at that point numbered 3,000 infantry and 150 cavalry, and after pitching camp in front of the town stayed there without harming anyone or allowing his men to go out and plunder. Meanwhile the inhabitants of the town packed the walls with armed men and massed in front of the gates to defend themselves, their strength equivalent to two legions. Caesar rode round the town and when he had seen the lie of the land returned to camp. Some regarded it as culpable lack of foresight that he had failed to instruct the captains of the ships and his subordinate officers which of the surrounding places they should make for, and that he had not adhered to his previous custom of giving them sealed orders so that they could read these and all make for a particular point at the right time. But Caesar had not been guilty of the slightest omission: for he suspected that he could not rely on a single African port

where his squadrons might come in being free of an enemy garrison, and was waiting for Chance to offer him some opportunity of making a landing.

(4) Meanwhile one of Caesar's senior officers, Lucius Plancus, asked him for permission to negotiate with Considius to see if he could somehow be brought to his senses. The permission granted, he wrote a letter and gave it to a prisoner to take to Considius in the town. As soon as the prisoner arrived and began, as instructed, to proffer the letter to Considius, the latter, before taking it, said 'Who is that from?' 'From Commander-in-Chief Caesar' replied the prisoner. 'Scipio', said Considius, 'is the sole commander-in-chief appointed by the Roman people at the moment.' He then ordered the prisoner to be put to death in front of him immediately, and gave the letter, still sealed and unread, to a reliable man to take to Scipio.

(5) A day and a night passed at the town without any reply being received from Considius. Caesar's other forces had not come to his aid, he was short of cavalry, he did not have enough troops (who were in any case recruits) to mount an assault on the town, and he had no wish for his army to suffer casualties directly after its arrival. The fortifications of the town were excellent and the ascent to attack them difficult, and news had come that large reinforcements of cavalry were on their way to help the inhabitants. Caesar accordingly dismissed any plan of staying to attack the town, for fear that while he was busy with the assault he would be surrounded from the rear by the enemy cavalry and find himself in trouble.

(6) He therefore wanted to move camp, when suddenly there burst out from the town a mass of men who were fortuitously assisted at the same moment by some cavalry sent by Juba to collect their pay. They occupied the camp which Caesar had left as he began his march, and started to harass the rear of his column. The legionaries halted immediately this was observed, and his cavalry, in spite of their lack of numbers, none the less very courageously charged this enormous body of men. The result was incredible: fewer than thirty* Gallic horsemen dislodged 2,000 Moorish cavalry

and made them flee to the town. Once they had been beaten off and driven back inside their fortifications, Caesar pressed on with his planned march. Since they repeatedly did this, now making harassing attacks, now being beaten back again into the town by Caesar's cavalry, Caesar placed at the rear of his column a few of the veteran cohorts which he had with him and some of the cavalry, and began to march slowly on with the remainder. In this way, the further away from the town he proceeded, the slower the Numidians* were to attack. Meanwhile, as he marched on, representatives came from towns and fortified outposts, promising him supplies of food and readiness to obey his orders.

(7) From there he moved on and reached the town of Leptis,* which is an independent community not subject to Roman taxation. A delegation came out to meet him and said they would willingly obey his orders. So he put centurions and detachments of guards at the town gates to stop any soldier entering the town or harming any of its inhabitants, and made camp along the shore not far from the town. By chance some of his merchant ships and warships reached the same spot; the rest, as was reported to him, were unsure of where to go and seemed to be heading in the direction of Utica. Because his ships had lost their way he did not, for the moment, leave the coast and make inland; he also kept his entire cavalry force on shipboard, in order I presume not to devastate cultivated land, and gave orders for water to be taken out to the ships. The crews meanwhile, who had come ashore to fetch water, were suddenly and unexpectedly attacked by the Moorish cavalry, and many were wounded and some killed by their javelins. (The Moors hide in ambush with their horses in the folds of the ground and suddenly emerge, and avoid the close combat associated with open ground.)

(8) During this time Caesar sent messengers to Sardinia and the other nearby provinces with letters containing instructions to arrange for the immediate despatch of reinforcements, supplies, and grain. He also unloaded some of his warships and sent Rabirius Postumus to Sicily to gather a second instalment of supplies. Meanwhile, he ordered < . . . > to set

out with ten warships to find the rest of the merchant ships which had gone off course, and at the same time keep the sea safe from the enemy. Similarly he instructed Gaius Sallustius Crispus, a praetor, to proceed with some of the ships in the direction of the enemy-held island of Cercina, because of a report that there was a large quantity of grain there. He gave each of these men his orders and instructions in such a way that they could be carried out without leaving any room either for excuses or for hesitation and delay. In the mean time he found out from deserters and local inhabitants the conditions agreed to by Scipio and his supporters in the war against himself, namely the upkeep of the king's cavalry by Scipio from the resources of the province of Africa, and pitied them for being so insane as to prefer to pay tax to a king rather than enjoy their fortunes in safety beside their fellow citizens in their own country.

(9) Caesar moved camp on 3 January, leaving a garrison of six cohorts* at Leptis under Saserna. He himself returned to Ruspina, whence he had come the previous day, and deposited the army's baggage there. Then, with his force ready for combat, he set out around the rural estates to collect grain, and gave orders to the townsfolk that all their carts and draught animals should follow. Consequently he found a large amount of grain, and returned to Ruspina. I suppose he returned there to avoid leaving the towns on the coast vacant behind him, and to provide well-garrisoned havens for the fleet.

(10) He therefore left Publius Saserna, who was the brother of the man he had left in neighbouring Leptis, with one legion in Ruspina, and ordered as much wood as possible to be brought into the town. He himself marched out of the town to the port two miles away with seven cohorts which were from veteran legions and had served on shipboard with Vatinius and Sulpicius,* and there, as evening approached, embarked this force. No one in the army knew what was happening; they all wanted to know their commander's intentions, and were racked by fear and despondency. They realized that they had been landed in Africa as part of a small force, a force moreover which was made up of recruits and

had not been landed in its entirety, to face large forces and the innumerable cavalry of a treacherous people; and they could see no comfort for the present, nor any help to be had from the advice of their companions, if it had not been for the expression, the vigour, and the amazing cheerfulness of their commander himself, who constantly exhibited a lofty and undaunted spirit. This was soothing, and they all hoped that everything would run their way under his expertise and direction.

(11) Caesar spent one night on board and was attempting to set sail as the sky grew light, when suddenly the part of the fleet about which he was worried turned up there after its wanderings. As soon as he realized this, he ordered everyone to disembark rapidly and wait on shore for the rest of his soldiers to arrive. And so, when the ships had been hastily brought into port and the infantry and cavalry disembarked, he went back again to Ruspina, and after making camp there set off in person to collect grain accompanied by thirty cohorts ready for action. This revealed his plan, that he had wanted to go with his fleet, without alerting the enemy, to help the merchant ships which had lost their way, lest his own ships should accidentally and unsuspectingly come upon the enemy fleet. He had also not wished the troops he had left behind on garrison duties to know this, in case they were overcome by fright at their own small numbers and the large numbers of the enemy.

(12) Meanwhile, when Caesar had already travelled about three miles from camp, scouts and cavalry outriders reported to him that they had seen enemy forces not far away; and as the report arrived, a huge cloud of dust did indeed begin to come into view. In response to this Caesar quickly gave orders for all his cavalry, of which he had no great quantity at the time, and his archers, whose numbers were small, to be summoned from camp, and for the standards to follow him slowly in battle order, while he himself took the lead with a few soldiers. When the enemy could be seen in the distance, he told his troops to put on their helmets and prepare for battle on the plain. His forces totalled thirty cohorts, plus 400 cavalry and 150 archers.

(13) In the mean time, the enemy, under the command of Labienus and the two Pacidei, formed a line of battle of remarkable length thick not with foot-soldiers but with cavalry, between whom they had stationed light-armed Numidian infantry and archers on foot, and they had so packed them together that at a distance Caesar's men thought they were all infantry; they had also strengthened their right and left wings with large bodies of cavalry. Meanwhile Caesar drew up a single line of battle, as best he could in view of his shortage of numbers; he placed his archers in front of the line, and his cavalry opposite the right and left wings with instructions to be careful not to be outflanked by the mass of enemy cavalry: for he was under the impression that his battle-line was about to fight a force of infantry.

(14) Both sides waited. Caesar made no move, and saw that with his small numbers he had to fight with brain rather than brawn against the large enemy force. Suddenly the opposing cavalry began to lengthen their line, move outwards, and take in the hill slopes, stretching Caesar's cavalry and at the same time preparing to outflank them. The Caesarian horse found difficulty in standing up to their numbers. Meanwhile when the battle-lines in the centre tried to engage, the light-armed Numidian infantry, accompanied by the cavalry, suddenly ran forward from the close-packed squadrons and hurled their javelins in amongst the legionaries. When Caesar's men moved forward to attack them, their cavalry made off but the infantry continued to resist until the cavalry could make another charge and support them.

(15) Caesar saw that in this new sort of fighting his men lost formation as they ran forward. His infantry, as they pursued the cavalry some distance from their own standards, exposed their flanks and were wounded by the javelins of the nearest Numidians, while the enemy cavalry easily avoided the legionary throwing-spears as they wheeled away at speed. He therefore had an order passed round the ranks that no infantryman should advance more than four feet in front of the standards. In the mean time, Labienus' cavalry, relying on their numerical superiority, did not hesitate to outflank Caesar's small body of horse; exhausted by the weight

of enemy numbers, Caesar's few cavalrymen, their animals severely wounded, gradually gave ground while the enemy brought more and more pressure to bear. So in a few minutes the whole legionary body was surrounded by the enemy cavalry, Caesar's forces were penned inside a ring, and they were all forced to fight within a limited space.

(16) Labienus rode about bareheaded in the front line, encouraging his own men and sometimes calling like this to Caesar's legionaries: 'You there, recruit: aren't you a fierce little chap? And the rest of you, are you bewitched by his words too? He's certainly put you in terrible danger. I'm sorry for you.' A soldier answered: 'I'm no recruit, Labienus. I'm a veteran of the Tenth legion.'* To which Labienus replied: 'I don't see the standards of the Tenth.' Then the soldier said: 'It's time for you to understand the kind of man I am'; and casting his helmet aside so that he could be recognized, he instantly took aim like that at Labienus and hurled his throwing-spear with great force. He severely wounded the commander's horse full in the chest, and said: 'Now understand, Labienus, that it is a soldier of the Tenth attacking you.' Nevertheless, they were all terror-stricken, particularly the recruits, who kept looking around for Caesar and doing no more than avoid the enemy missiles.

(17) Caesar meanwhile, realizing the enemy plan, gave orders for his line to stretch out sideways as far as possible with alternate cohorts facing opposite ways, one behind and one in front of the standards. In this way he split the enemy ring in half with his right and left wings. He then used his cavalry, in conjunction with the infantry, to attack one part after it had been isolated from the other; he put them to flight with a hail of weapons, but went no great distance after them, because he was afraid of an ambush, and came back to join his force. The other section of his cavalry and infantry did the same. After this exploit, having driven the enemy well back and inflicted serious casualties on them, he began to withdraw in the same formation to his defensive lines.

(18) Meanwhile Marcus Petreius and Gnaeus Piso with a picked force of . . . Numidian cavalry and a fair number of

infantry of the same race came straight from the march to the aid of their fellows. The enemy overcame their panic, recovered their courage and began to attack the legionary troops, who were retreating with their cavalry faced about, and to interfere with their withdrawal inside their camp. When Caesar saw this he ordered the standards to turn round and battle to recommence on open ground. The enemy employed the same tactics as before, without any return to combat at close quarters; Caesar's cavalry had mounts which were suffering from recent seasickness, thirst, tiredness, low numbers, and wounds and were too slow to pursue the enemy or maintain a sustained gallop; and there was little of the day remaining. He therefore placed his cohorts around the cavalry and urged them to deliver a single thrust and not let up until they had driven the enemy back beyond the furthest hills and taken control of them. Accordingly he gave the signal when the enemy had begun to throw their weapons perfunctorily and carelessly, and suddenly launched his cohorts of foot and squadrons of horse at them. In an instant they drove the enemy effortlessly from the field, pushed them back beyond the high ground, and won the position. After remaining there for a little while, they retired at a gentle pace in the same formation to their own defences. In the face of this reverse, the enemy then finally likewise withdrew to their camp.

(19) Meanwhile, after the engagement was over and battle had been broken off, men of all classes deserted the enemy, and in addition a number of their cavalry and infantry were captured. These revealed the enemy plan, that they had come intending to try new and unusual battle tactics, and overwhelm the inexperienced legionaries, few in number as they were and alarmed by what had happened to Curio,* by surrounding them with cavalry. Labienus was reported to have made an address in which he said that he would provide Caesar's opponents with so many reinforcements that at the moment of victory Caesar's men would actually become exhausted by the work of slaughter and would be defeated and overcome by their countrymen. Labienus' reasons for his confidence were, first, that he had heard that

the veteran legions at Rome were mutinous and unwilling to cross to Africa, and second, that he had kept his men for three years in Africa and made them loyal to himself by force of habit; he also had very large auxiliary forces of Numidian cavalry and light infantry. In addition he had given arms to the German and Gallic cavalry he had brought with him from Buthrotum after the Pompeian rout at Pharsalus, and to others whom he had conscripted in Africa from ex-slaves, slaves, and men of mixed birth, and taught how to ride a horse with reins. Furthermore, he had the support of the king's auxiliary forces, 120 elephants, and countless cavalry, and finally legions composed of more than 12,000 men of all sorts.* Fired by his hopes of them and by his own boldness, he had led into battle 1,600 Gallic and German cavalry, 8,000 Numidian cavalry not using reins, an auxiliary force of 1,600 of Petreius' cavalry, four times that number of heavy and light infantry, and a large quantity of archers, slingers, and mounted archers. These were the forces with which the battle was fought, on 4 January, six days after Caesar's arrival in Africa, from late morning until sunset, on completely level and unencumbered ground. In this battle Petreius was seriously wounded and retired from the fight.

(20) In the mean time Caesar improved the fortifications of his camp, stiffened his garrisons with more troops, and built two ditch-and-bank ramparts down to the sea, one from the town of Ruspina and the other from his camp, so that passage to and fro would be safer and reinforcements could come to his aid without danger. He also brought weapons and artillery from his ships to the camp, armed some of his crews, Gauls, Rhodians, and marines, and brought them ashore to his camp so that he could if possible intersperse light-armed troops among his cavalry, positioning them like his opponents. He gathered into camp from all the ships a substantial number of Ituraean, Syrian, and miscellaneous archers, and packed his army with them, because he heard that Scipio would be arriving two days after the battle and consolidating his forces, reported to number eight legions and 3,000 cavalry, with those of Labienus and Petreius. He set up smithies, had quantities of arrows and throwing-

weapons manufactured, cast slingshot, and prepared sharpened stakes. He sent messengers to Sicily with instructions to gather fascines and material for making battering-rams, of which there was a shortage in Africa, and to have iron and lead sent to him as well. He also realized that he could not lay his hands on any grain in Africa, unless it was imported, because the levy conducted by his opponents, which had made soldiers out of the farmers who paid tax in grain, had prevented the harvest the previous year. Furthermore, he was aware that his opponents had denuded the whole region of grain by transporting it from all over the province of Africa into a few well-fortified towns, and that apart from these few towns which they were able to protect with their garrisons the others were ruined and deserted, their inhabitants forced to move into the protected areas and their agricultural land abandoned and laid waste.

(21) In these straits, Caesar had gone round and coaxed a certain amount of grain out of private individuals and after gathering it inside his strongpoints was using it sparingly. Meanwhile he personally inspected the fortifications every day and kept half his cohorts on watch alternately, because of the enemy numbers. Labienus ordered his wounded, of whom there were a great number, to be bandaged up and taken in wagons to Hadrumetum. In the meantime Caesar's merchant ships, lost, sailing fruitlessly about, and uncertain of the places he held or of the whereabouts of his camp, were being attacked one by one by groups of their opponents' small craft, and set on fire and captured. When he heard this, Caesar spread his fleet out around the islands and harbours so that supplies could more safely reach him.

The Pompeian commanders move on to the offensive

(22) Meanwhile Marcus Cato, who was in charge at Utica, never ceased to speak reproachfully and at length to the younger Gnaeus Pompeius. 'Your father', he said, 'when he was your age and saw the state oppressed by criminally wicked fellow Romans, and decent men punished by death or exile and so without a country or rights as a citizen, was

inspired by glory and nobility of soul; as a young man holding no public office, he gathered together the remains of his
father's army and restored to freedom an Italy and a city of
Rome whose spirit and very existence were on the brink of
extinction. He also recovered by arms, and with amazing
speed, Sicily, Africa, Numidia, and Mauretania. By these
actions he won for himself that brilliant reputation known
to all the world, and celebrated a triumph when still only a
young man and not yet a senator.* And he made this entry
into public life without remarkable achievements on the part
of his father, without the help of some outstanding reputation won by his elders, and without exercising any great patronage or enjoying such a famous name. You, on the other
hand, possess fame and reputation through your father, and
are well enough endowed on your own account with nobility of soul and conscientiousness; will you not exert your-
self, and go to those who saw your father as their patron,
to demand that they give assistance to you, to our country,
and to every right-thinking man?'

(23) Roused by these words from a figure of such authority, the young man set out from Utica with a fleet of
thirty vessels of various sorts, including a few warships. He
invaded Mauretania and the kingdom of Bogud, and with a
lightly equipped army of slaves and free men to the number
of 2,000, some armed and some unarmed, began to advance
on the town of Ascurum, where there was a garrison installed
by the king. On his arrival the townspeople allowed him
to come closer and closer until he was almost at their very
gates and wall. Then they suddenly burst out and chased
his defeated and terrified men in disorder down to the ships
and the sea. Having suffered such a serious reverse, young
Pompeius left the place and set course towards the Balearic
Islands without coming ashore again.*

(24) Meanwhile Scipio left a strong garrison at Utica and
set out with the forces we have described above,* first making camp at Hadrumetum, where he stayed for a few days,
and then marching by night to join up with the forces of
Labienus and Petreius. They constructed a single camp and
took up a position three miles distant from Caesar. Their
cavalry meanwhile patrolled around Caesar's defences and

captured any men who had gone outside the rampart in search of fodder or water; they thus penned all their opponents within their fortifications. In consequence Caesar's forces were desperately short of food, as supplies had not yet arrived from Sicily and Sardinia and it was unsafe at that time of year for flects to sail as they liked. Furthermore, they controlled no more than six miles of African land in any direction, and the shortage of grazing was a severe problem. To meet this emergency the veterans among the infantry and cavalry, who had seen through to a finish many a campaign by sea and land, and had often been racked by dangers and shortages of this kind, prolonged the lives of their starving beasts by giving them seaweed which they collected from the beach and washed out in fresh water.

(25) So long as this state of affairs lasted, King Juba, having become aware of Caesar's difficulties and the small size of his forces, thought he ought not to allow him any room to recover and build up his resources; he therefore gathered a large force of infantry and cavalry, left his kingdom, and hastened to march in support of his allies. Meanwhile Publius Sittius and King Bocchus had united their forces and when they heard that Juba had gone moved them towards his kingdom and attacked its richest town, Cirta. Within a few days it fell to storm, along with two Gaetulian towns. Sittius offered his opponents terms, namely that they should quit their town and hand it over empty to him, but they rejected these and were later all captured and put to death by him. Advancing further, he continued to harass the towns and the countryside. When Juba received intelligence of this, although he had nearly reached Scipio and his commanders, he took the view that it was better to go and look after his own kingdom and interests than to be driven out of that kingdom while he was on his way to help others and risk being a loser on both counts. He therefore retreated again, and was so concerned for himself and his fortunes that he even withdrew his auxiliaries from Scipio, leaving the latter with only thirty elephants, and went to relieve his own territory and towns.

(26) Meanwhile, as there was some doubt about whether he had arrived in the province and nobody believed that it

was he, and not some deputy commander, who had come with the troops, Caesar wrote letters to all the communities of the province to let them know of his arrival. Meanwhile various persons of importance who had fled from their towns turned up in Caesar's camp, and began to detail the cruelty and harshness of his opponents. Caesar was so moved by their tears and complaints that although he had previously decided to stay in a permanent camp and leave it to the beginning of summer to summon all his troops and supporting forces and campaign actively against his opponents, he began <to . . . >. He hastily sent a letter by light reconnaissance vessel to Allienus and Rabirius Postumus in Sicily, giving instructions that the army was to be ferried over to him as quickly as possible, without delaying at all or making winter gales an excuse. He pointed out that the province of Africa was collapsing and being thrown into chaos by his enemies, whose criminal and treacherous behaviour meant that apart from the soil itself there would be nothing left of Africa, not even a roof to take shelter under, unless his allies lent assistance. Caesar himself was so impatient and in such a state of anticipation that the day after he had sent the letter he said that the messenger to Sicily and the fleet and army were being slow, and his eyes and thoughts were directed and concentrated on the sea. And no wonder: he saw farmhouses in flames, cultivated land laid waste, cattle stolen and slaughtered, towns and small fortified settlements destroyed and deserted, prominent men put to death or held in chains, and their children carried off into slavery in the guise of hostages. In spite of their misery and their pleas for protection, it was impossible for him to help them because his forces were too few. His soldiers in the mean time never ceased their fortification work, making defences for the camp, erecting towers and forts, and building moles out into the sea.

(27) Meanwhile Scipio began to train his elephants in the following way. He drew up two battle-lines, one of slingers to act as enemy and bombard them from in front with very small stones; then came the row of elephants, and behind them his own battle-line, so that when stones began to be hurled by the 'enemy' and the elephants turned in terror

on their own side, another barrage of stones was thrown from this line to make them face the enemy again. This they did eventually and with reluctance, because elephants are primitive creatures and can scarcely be rendered tractable by many years' training and long habituation; none the less, they are employed in battle, where they are equally dangerous to both sides.

(28) While the leaders on either side were busy with all this at Ruspina, the ex-praetor Gaius Vergilius, who was in command at the coastal town of Thapsus, noticed that single ships with Caesar's troops on board were sailing by aimlessly, uncertain of the places their side held or where their camp was. He seized his opportunity, manned a light warship he had there with soldiers and archers, put some ships' open boats with it, and began to pursue individual Caesarian ships. He attacked several, but although he was driven away and forced to make off in flight, he still persisted with his dangerous operations. He happened to come upon a ship which had on board two Titii from Spain, young military tribunes of the Fifth legion whose father had been enrolled by Caesar in the senate, and with them Titius Salienus, a centurion of the same legion. The latter had obstructed Marcus Messalla,* one of Caesar's senior officers, at Messana, using highly mutinous language to him, and had also been responsible for detaining and impounding money and trappings intended for Caesar's triumph. Conscious of his wrongdoing, he persuaded the young men to offer no resistance and to surrender to Vergilius. They were accordingly taken by Vergilius to Scipio, placed under guard, and put to death two days later. It is said that when they were being led to execution, the elder Titius begged the centurions to kill him before they killed his brother, and the request being cheerfully granted, that was how they died.

Scipio attempts to make Caesar give battle

(29) Meanwhile the squadrons of horse, which were habitually posted in front of the ditch and rampart, were constantly

engaged in minor actions against each other; sometimes the Germans and Gauls in Labienus' force would actually make a truce with Caesar's cavalry, and the two sides would talk to each other. In the mean time Labienus attempted with part of his cavalry to attack Leptis, where Saserna was in command with six cohorts, and break forcibly into the town. The defenders were easily able to defend it without risk, thanks to its excellent fortifications and large quantities of artillery. But Labienus' cavalry persisted in making frequent attacks, and a squadron happened to be packed in front of the gates when a carefully aimed 'scorpion'* was fired, hit their commander, and skewered him to his horse. The others fled in terror back to their camp, and the upshot was that they became scared of making any further attempt on the town.

(30) Scipio meanwhile used to draw up his battle-line almost every day not far from his camp, at a distance of about a quarter of a mile, and after the greater part of the day had passed withdraw again to camp. He did this on many occasions, but no one came out from Caesar's camp or approached his troops. So, despising the endurance of Caesar and his army, he led out his entire force, stationed his thirty elephants, equipped with turrets, across the front of his line, and extended his mass of cavalry and infantry as far as possible. He advanced with all these at once and halted on open ground not very far from Caesar's camp.

(31) When he saw this, Caesar ordered all the soldiers who had gone outside the defences in order to gather fodder or firewood, or look for earth and rubble and other material they needed to strengthen the fortifications, to make their way back inside one by one in a controlled manner, without noise or panic, and take their places on the rampart. To the cavalry who had been posted out in front, he gave instructions to stay where they had recently stationed themselves until they were within range of the enemy weapons; but if the enemy came any nearer, to withdraw as honourably as possible into the camp. The remaining cavalry he told to be ready, armed and prepared, in their allotted places. He was so remarkably skilled in the art of warfare that he

did not himself survey the scene from the rampart and give the orders for what he wanted done where all could hear them, but sat in his commanders' tent and issued his instructions through scouts and messengers. For he was conscious that although his enemies relied on large forces, he had none the less often put them to flight, routed them, and filled them with fear, and had spared their lives and pardoned their offences; in the light of this, their own bad consciences and their lack of enterprise would never allow them to be confident enough of victory to risk an attack on his camp. In addition, the impressiveness of his own reputation greatly reduced the belligerence of their army. Another point was that the excellent defences of his camp, the height of the rampart and ditches, and the cunningly concealed spikes outside the rampart stopped opponents from approaching even if there were no defenders: but he had plenty of 'scorpions' and catapults and other weapons usually deployed in defence. He had taken these measures in view of the small numbers and inexperience of his present force, and it was not because he was alarmed and disturbed by the strength of the enemy that he gave the latter grounds to think that he was submissive and fearful. And the reason that he refused to lead his troops out to battle was not that he did not believe they would win, although they were inexperienced and outnumbered, but he considered that it mattered what kind of victory it would be: for he reckoned it would be a stain on his character if after achieving so many successes, defeating such great armies, and winning so many splendid victories, he was generally thought to have wrung a blood-soaked victory from the remnant of his opponents' forces when these had only been scraped together after a rout.* He had accordingly made up his mind to put up with their boastful self-glorification until some of his veteran legions appeared as part of his second convoy.

(32) Scipio meanwhile, as I have previously said, waited for a short time in his position to give the impression that he had no respect for Caesar, and then gradually withdrew his forces into camp. He then addressed the troops, and after

speaking of the fear and hopelessness felt by Caesar's army*
urged on his men and promised that he would very soon give
them a victory of their own. Caesar ordered his soldiers back
to their toil, and in the interests of his fortifications never
allowed his recruits a break from their exhausting labour.
Meanwhile Numidians and Gaetulians melted away daily from
Scipio's camp; some made their way to the king's territory,
while a continuous stream of others deserted to Caesar's
camp because they and their fathers or grandfathers had enjoyed favours from Gaius Marius, whom they were told was
a relation of Caesar's.* Caesar picked the more distinguished
of their number, gave them letters for their fellow citizens,
and dismissed them after urging them to band together to
defend themselves and their friends and refuse to obey his
opponents and personal enemies.

(33) While this was going on at Ruspina, a deputation
came to Caesar from Acylla, which was an independent town
free of Roman taxation. They promised that they were ready
and willing to carry out any orders of his; but they begged
for one thing, that he would give them a garrison to allow
them to do so with less risk to themselves; they said that
in the interests of their common survival they would themselves provide this garrison with grain and whatever else they
needed. Caesar willingly granted the request, provided a garrison, and ordered Gaius Messius, a former aedile, to set out
for Acylla. On hearing this, Considius Longus, who was in
command at Hadrumetum with two legions and 700 cavalry, took swift action, leaving part of his force there and
making a rapid march with eight cohorts towards Acylla.
Messius travelled more quickly and reached Acylla first, accompanied by his cohorts. When Considius in the mean time
arrived at the city with his troops and saw that there was
a garrison of Caesar's there, he did not dare to expose his
men to danger, and having achieved nothing commensurate
with the size of his force withdrew again to Hadrumetum.
Finally, after Labienus had brought him some cavalry, he returned to Acylla a few days later, encamped there, and began
a siege of the town.

Caesar receives reinforcements, moves camp, and wins a cavalry engagement

(34) During this period Gaius Sallustius Crispus, whom we said had been despatched by Caesar a few days previously, reached Cercina.* On his arrival the former quaestor Gaius Decimius, who was in charge of the stores there with a large garrison of his own slaves, boarded a small vessel and took to flight. Meanwhile Sallustius was welcomed as praetor by the inhabitants of the island, and when he discovered a large quantity of grain loaded it aboard merchant ships, of which there were a good number there, and sent it to Caesar in camp. Meanwhile the proconsul Allienus embarked the Thirteenth and Fourteenth legions on merchant ships at Lilybaeum, along with 800 Gaulish cavalry and 1,000 slingers and archers, and sent a second convoy to Caesar in Africa. These ships picked up a favourable breeze and reached harbour safely three days later at Ruspina, where Caesar had established his camp. In this way Caesar's spirits were doubly lifted by his delight at the arrival at one and the same moment of both grain and reinforcements. At last he could forget his concern for his men, now cheered and no longer short of food; and after telling the infantry and cavalry who had disembarked to rest and recover from their fatigue and seasickness, he dismissed them and sent them to various outposts and positions on the defences.

(35) Scipio and his associates were surprised at this and began to ask questions: they suspected that Gaius Caesar, whose habit had been to take the military initiative and attack aggressively, had not changed his ways without some very good reason. They became nervous of his passivity and by promises of large rewards induced two Gaetulians, whom they thought were particularly well disposed to their cause, to pretend to be deserters and go to Caesar's camp as spies. Immediately they were brought to Caesar, they asked if they might be permitted to speak freely without risk to themselves. Permission granted, they said: 'Time without number, general, many of us Gaetuli, who are beholden to Gaius

Marius, and virtually all the Romans in the Fourth and Sixth legions have wanted to escape to you and the places defended by you; but we were always prevented from doing this safely by the Numidian cavalry who were on watch. Now that we have been given the chance, we have come with enthusiasm. Scipio has sent us as spies to see whether any ditches or traps for elephants have been constructed in front of the camp or the gates through the rampart, and at the same time to learn your plans to counter these same animals and your assessment of the battle, and to report back.' Caesar praised them and gave them money, and they were taken to join the other deserters. The truth of what they said was soon confirmed, for on the following day a number of men from the legions which had been named by the Gaetulians deserted from Scipio to Caesar.

(36) While this was happening at Ruspina, Marcus Cato, who was in command at Utica, endlessly conscripted ex-slaves, Africans, or even slaves, in fact any one at all so long as they were old enough to fight; these he sent to Scipio's camp and turned over to him. Meanwhile a delegation from the town of Thysdra, into which 20 tonnes* of wheat had been brought by the growers and Italian dealers, came to Caesar, told him how much grain there was in the town, and pleaded with him to put a garrison in for the better protection of both the grain and their own supplies. For the moment Caesar thanked them and said that he would send a garrison shortly, and after stiffening their resolve told them to return home. Meanwhile Publius Sittius, who had invaded Numidia with his troops,* stormed and captured a mountain fort within defensive works where grain and other military supplies had been gathered by Juba in aid of his war effort.

(37) Having augmented his forces with the two veteran legions and the cavalry and light-armed troops from the second convoy, Caesar at once ordered the empty ships to set sail for Lilybaeum to bring over the rest of his army. As for himself, about the time of the first watch on 25 January he told all his scouts and attendants to stand by. And so without anyone knowing or suspecting what was going to

happen he gave orders in the third watch that all the legions were to leave camp and follow him towards the town of Ruspina, where he had a garrison and which had been the first place to declare for him. From there he went down a slight slope and led the legions beside the sea along the left-hand side of the plain. This plain, extraordinarily flat and extending for twelve miles, is enclosed by a low ridge running in from the sea which makes it resemble a theatre. On this ridge are a few high hills, where separate towers and lookout posts had been built long previously, and on the last of these there was an outpost and detachment of Scipio's men.

(38) Caesar then climbed up to the ridge described and began to make his way along hill by hill, examining the towers and forts and taking less than half an hour to do so. When he was not very far from the final hill and tower, nearest to the enemy camp, where as I have said there was an outpost and detachment of Numidians, he stopped for a short while to survey the lie of the land. Then he posted a shield of cavalry and set the legionaries to work, ordering them to dig and fortify an outwork extending along the middle of the ridge from the point he had reached to his starting-point. When Scipio and Labienus observed this, they brought all their cavalry out of camp, drew them up for battle, and advanced about a mile from their defences; they also drew up their infantry in a second line less than 600 yards away from their camp.

(39) Caesar urged his troops to continue with their labours and was not disquieted by the enemy forces. But when he saw that there was now no more than a mile and a half between the enemy line of battle and his own fortifications, and realized that the enemy were coming nearer in order to interfere with his men and force them to stop working, and that he must take the legions off the fortifications, he ordered a squadron of Spaniards to gallop to the nearest hill, expel its detachment of guards, and seize it. He also ordered a few light-armed troops to follow to help them. These forces were quickly despatched and attacked the Numidians. They captured some alive, wounded a number of the cavalrymen as they fled, and succeeded in gaining possession of the

position. On noticing this, Labienus, in order to bring them help more quickly, detached almost the whole of his right wing from their place in his line of cavalry and hastened to go to their support as they fled. When Caesar observed that Labienus had already gone some way from his troops, he launched the left wing of his cavalry forward to cut the enemy off.

(40) On the plain where this engagement was taking place there was a very large farmhouse with four turrets, which obstructed Labienus' vision and prevented him noticing that he was being cut off by Caesar's cavalry. He saw nothing of his opponent's squadrons until he realized his own men were being cut down from behind. As a result, the Numidian cavalry immediately panicked and made off in flight straight back to the camp. The Gauls and Germans, who resisted, were attacked from higher ground and from the rear and after putting up a brave fight were all killed. Scipio's legions were drawn up in front of the camp, and when they saw this they succumbed to blind panic and began to flee back into their camp through every gate. Now that Scipio and his troops had been dislodged from the plain and the hills and driven back inside their camp, Caesar had the signal sounded for retreat and pulled all his cavalry back within his fortifications. When the field had been cleared he noticed the remarkable bodies of the Gauls and Germans. Some of these had come from Gaul in response to Scipio's summons, some had been induced to go over to him by money or promises, and not a few, who had been captured but spared after Curio's defeat,* had wished to repay this favour by displaying equivalent loyalty; and their bodies, of wonderful size and appearance, lay slaughtered and strewn all over the battlefield.

(41) On the following day, after this success, Caesar took the infantry away from all his guard-posts and drew up his entire force in the plain. But Scipio, whose men had suffered a defeat with deaths and severe injuries, now began to keep inside his own fortifications. With his line ready for battle, Caesar followed the lower slopes of the ridge and slowly drew nearer to Scipio's fortifications. His legions were already

less than a mile from the town of Uzitta, which Scipio held, when Scipio, fearing that he might lose the town, which his army used to rely on for water and other things it needed, led all his forces out. He adopted his usual quadruple formation, with his first line consisting of a row of cavalry squadrons interspersed with elephants carrying turrets, and proceeded to the town's defence. When Caesar saw this, he assumed that Scipio was coming to meet him with the firm intention of giving battle, and halted in front of the town in the position I have just described. Scipio, however, used the town to protect the centre of his line, and stationed his right and left wings, where the elephants were, in full view of his opponents.

(42) Caesar waited until it was nearly sunset, but saw that Scipio made no advance towards him from the position in which he had stopped, and realized that if his opponent was forced to it his preference was to defend himself where he was rather than dare to stand and fight at close quarters in the open. He rejected any plan of moving against the town that day, since he was aware that there was a large garrison of Numidians there and the enemy had used the town to protect the centre of his line; he realized that it would be a difficult task to attack it and simultaneously fight a set battle uphill on the right and left wings, especially as the troops were tired and hungry from standing all day without food. He therefore led his troops back into camp and on the following day began to extend his fortifications nearer to his opponents' line of battle.

Scipio's cruelty to captured Caesarian soldiers

(43) Meanwhile Considius with eight cohorts and some Numidian and Gaetulian mercenaries was besieging Acylla, where Gaius Messius was in command with three cohorts.* He made protracted and valiant efforts, including several attempts to bring massive siege devices up to the walls, but they were set on fire by the people in the town and he made no progress. Suddenly he received news of the cavalry battle.

Worried, he burnt the considerable quantity of grain he had in his camp, deliberately spoilt the wine, oil, and other customary items of food, and abandoned his siege of Acylla. He marched through Juba's kingdom,* handed over some of his forces to Scipio, and retired to Hadrumetum.

(44) Meanwhile, a single ship, aboard which were Quintus Cominius* and Lucius Ticida, a member of the equestrian order, had become separated from the second convoy sent from Sicily by Allienus. This ship was driven by the wind to Thapsus, captured by Vergilius with his boats and small vessels, and brought to shore. Likewise another ship from the same convoy, a trireme, lost its way and was blown in by the storm to Aegimurus where it was captured by the fleet commanded by Varus and Marcus Octavius. Aboard this ship were some veterans along with one centurion and some recruits, whom Varus rescued and arranged to have sent without disgrace to Scipio. When they reached him and halted in front of his tribunal, he said: 'I am sure that it is not by your own wish that you indulge in this wicked persecution of your fellow Romans and every right-thinking man. You have been forced to do so by the pressure and authority exerted by that criminal commander-in-chief of yours. Fortune has delivered you into our power, but if you join every right-thinking man in doing your duty and defending the republic, that will certainly secure you life and money. So declare your opinion.'

(45) After he had delivered this speech, Scipio, being of the view that the men before him would definitely thank him for his kindness, gave them permission to say some words. One of them, a centurion of the Fourteenth legion, said: 'I thank you, Scipio—for I do not address you as commander-in-chief—for your great kindness in promising to spare my life and exact no punishment although I am a prisoner-of-war; and I might indeed accept that kindness, if it did not entail a crime of the highest order. Am I to stand in arms and oppose my commander-in-chief Caesar, under whom I have held this rank and for whose honour and victory I have fought for <*thirteen?*> years?* I am not going to do that, and I urge you most sincerely to desist from your project. For you

now have the chance to discover, if you were not sufficiently aware of it before, whose troops you are up against. From your men, pick the cohort you think the most resolute and line it up against me; I, on the other hand, will choose no more than ten of those fellow soldiers of mine whom you now hold in your power. Then our courage will make you understand what expectations you ought to have of your forces.'

(46) After the centurion had spoken with this ready courage and proved Scipio's opinion wrong, the latter, shaken and inflamed by anger and pique, nodded to the centurions of his guard and had the centurion put to death at his feet. The remaining veterans he ordered to be separated from the recruits. 'Take them away,' he said, 'stained as they are by a dreadful crime, and fattened on the blood of Romans.' So they were taken outside the rampart and tortured to death. As for the recruits, he ordered them to be dispersed among his legions, while Cominius and Ticida were refused all audience with him. Caesar was so disturbed by this episode that he took steps to dismiss from his army with ignominy, for dereliction of duty, those whom he had instructed to maintain a guard of warships at sea off Thapsus to protect his merchantmen and warships. He also had an edict published condemning them in the gravest of terms.

(47) At about that time Caesar's army had an extraordinary experience. The Pleiades had set,* and one night around midnight a huge rain-storm suddenly came up with hail the size of pebbles. The discomfort caused was made worse because Caesar was not keeping his men in winter quarters as he had done previously, but was strengthening the defences of his camp as he proceeded forward for the third or fourth day in his approach to the enemy, and the soldiers were too busy with their labours to keep a lookout. In addition, the transport of his army from Sicily was such that he would allow no equipment or slaves* or anything a soldier generally uses, apart from his person and his arms, to be put on board ship. But in Africa the men had not only not acquired or organized anything for themselves, but also the high price of corn meant that they had used up what they had

previously obtained. Weakened by these circumstances, a tiny handful were sleeping under proper canvas* while the rest lived in little shelters improvised from clothing, reeds, and plaited twigs. The shelters were overpowered by the weight of the sudden downpour and the hail which followed, and washed away and broken apart by the force of the water; the stormy night put out the fires; and with everything that served to keep them alive ruined, the soldiers wandered aimlessly about the camp holding their shields above their heads. That same night the tips of some throwing-spears of the Fifth legion burst into flames of their own accord.

Juba joins Scipio. Inconclusive skirmishing around Uzitta. More legions reach Caesar

(48) Juba, meanwhile, who had been informed about Scipio's cavalry battle, received a letter from him in which Scipio called on him to leave his general Saburra in command of part of his army against Sittius and come in person to assist him, his intention being that Juba's appearance alongside himself should lend some prestige to his own army and strike terror into Caesar's. Juba therefore left his own territory and set out to join Scipio with three legions, 800 cavalry with reins,* a mass of light-armed infantry and Numidian cavalry without reins, and thirty elephants. On arrival, he took up a position not very far from Scipio in a separate royal camp with the forces I have detailed. (There had previously been a great feeling of dread in Caesar's camp, and his army was much more apprehensive about the royal forces before Juba's arrival; but once they compared camp with camp, they ceased to have any respect for his forces and shrugged off all their fear. Thus by making his appearance Juba had forfeited all the prestige he had possessed in his absence.) After this, it took no great intelligence to see that the king's arrival had given Scipio new courage and confidence, because on the next day he brought out his own and the king's entire strength, including the sixty elephants.

He formed them up as impressively as possible, advanced slightly further from his defences, and waited there, but not for very long, before retreating back to camp.

(49) When Caesar saw that almost all the reinforcements expected by Scipio had gathered, and that battle would be joined without delay, he began to advance with his forces along the top of the ridge. He made a great effort to extend arms forward from his earthworks, fortify outposts, and by dint of seizing the heights nearer to Scipio forestall any move by his opponents, relying on their numbers, to occupy the next hill before he did and so deny him the ability to proceed any further. Labienus had planned to seize the same hill, and as he was nearer to it reached it first.

(50) There was a valley which Caesar had to cross before he could reach the hill he wanted to capture. This valley was fairly wide and precipitous, and had been eroded in many places into cave-like formations. Beyond it lay an old olive-grove thick with trees. Here Labienus had seen that Caesar, if he wanted to occupy the position, had first to cross the valley and go through the olive-grove. His familiarity with the ground allowed him to conceal himself in ambush with some of his cavalry and light-armed infantry, and he had also placed cavalry out of sight on the other side of the hill, so that when he himself attacked and took the legionaries by surprise, the cavalry could appear from behind the hill; Caesar and his army would thus be thrown into confusion by the double attack, find it impossible either to fall back or to go forward, and be surrounded and cut to pieces. Caesar, who had sent his cavalry on ahead, reached the spot quite unaware of the ambush; but the troops who were in hiding, whether because they forgot Labienus' orders or were frightened of being overwhelmed at the bottom of the steep valley by the cavalry, emerged in ones and twos from the rocks and made for the top of the hill. Caesar's cavalry pursued them, killing some and taking others alive; they then pressed eagerly forward up the slope, and swiftly occupied the hill after ejecting Labienus' garrison. Labienus managed to save himself by taking to flight with some of his cavalry.

(51) Following this success on the part of the cavalry, Caesar allocated the labour among the legions and fortified a camp on the hill he had taken. Then he started to push two extensions of his defensive works from his main camp across the middle of the plain in the direction of Uzitta, which lay on level ground between his camp and Scipio's and was held by Scipio, aligning these extensions so that they converged on the right and left corners of the town. The purpose of building these earthworks was to keep his flanks protected by his own defences once he had moved his troops nearer the town and begun to attack it, so that his men would not be surrounded by a mass of cavalry and forced to abandon the attack. He also wished to make it easier for conversation with opponents to occur and to allow anyone wishing to desert (which they had often done previously, but at great risk) to do so without difficulty or danger. He further wanted to find out, when he had come to closer quarters with the enemy, whether they intended to fight. An additional reason was that this ground lay in a depression and some wells could be sunk there—for his present sources of water were scanty and distant. During the construction by the legionaries of the earthworks I have just described, some of their number were stationed in battle formation in front of the work, close to the enemy, while the foreign cavalry and light-armed infantry fought constant small hand-to-hand engagements.

(52) Towards evening, when Caesar was already bringing his troops away from this work and back into camp, Juba, Scipio, and Labienus, at the head of all their cavalry and light-armed, made an attack of great vigour on the legionaries. Caesar's cavalry briefly gave way, overwhelmed by the sudden power of the united enemy numbers. But the result was not what their opponents expected, because in order to help the cavalry Caesar brought his infantry back in the middle of their march home. Heartened by the arrival of the legions, the cavalry turned their horses round and launched an attack on the Numidians, who had become scattered in their eagerness to give chase. They inflicted severe casualties and drove the Numidians right back to the king's camp,

killing many of them. If the battle had not been prolonged beyond nightfall and the dust raised by the wind had not seriously reduced visibility, both Juba and Labienus would have been captured and fallen into Caesar's hands, and the cavalry together with the light-armed troops would have been slaughtered to a man. Meanwhile, unbelievably, soldiers from Scipio's Fourth and Sixth legions were slipping away, some to Caesar's camp, some to any region they could reach; and a number of the cavalry who had once served under Curio,* having likewise lost confidence in Scipio and his forces, took themselves off to the same destinations.

(53) While the commanders on either side were busy with these manœuvres at Uzitta, two legions, the Tenth and Ninth, which had sailed from Sicily aboard merchant ships, sighted Caesar's ships which were in position off Thapsus. Fearing that they were inadvertently meeting some enemy fleet waiting there to ambush them, they ran for the open sea and finally, after a long and stormy passage, reached Caesar many days later suffering badly from hunger and thirst.

(54) Caesar remembered the previous ill-discipline of the soldiery in Italy and the looting carried out by particular individuals. So when these legions had disembarked he took as a pretext the trifling matter that Gaius Avienus, a military tribune of the Tenth legion, had occupied an entire ship in the convoy with his slaves and draught animals and not brought a single soldier from Sicily, and on the following day summoned before his dais the tribunes and centurions from all the legions and said: 'Above all, it would have been my wish that individuals, sooner or later, had put an end to their wilful and excessively selfish behaviour and taken the measure of my leniency, self-control, and patience. But since they have not drawn the line anywhere themselves, I shall follow military custom and set an example to ensure that others do not act in the same way. Gaius Avienus, you have looted towns and encouraged soldiers of the Roman people to mutiny against the state. You have also done a disservice to me and the state by embarking your own slaves and draught animals in place of soldiers, so that thanks to you the state is short of soldiers at a time of crisis. For these

reasons you are dismissed with ignominy from my army and I order you to leave Africa today and go as far away as possible. Likewise I dismiss you, Aulus Fonteius, because you have been a mutinous officer and a worthless citizen. Titus Salienus, Marcus Tiro, and Gaius Clusinas, you attained the rank of centurions in my army by favour and not by your qualities as men; but since you have so conducted yourselves as to be neither brave in war nor good and useful persons in peace, and you have been more concerned to foster mutiny and incite soldiers against your commander-in-chief than to behave in a restrained and decent fashion, I consider you unworthy to be centurions in my army and I discharge you and command you to remove yourselves as far from Africa as possible.' Accordingly he handed them over to the centurions of his guard and had them put separately on shipboard, allowing them only a single slave each.

(55) Meanwhile the Gaetulian deserters who had been despatched by Caesar, as we explained above,* reached their own people. The latter were easily induced by the authority of the deserters and the reputation of Caesar to revolt against Juba, and they all quickly armed themselves and did not hesitate to take action against the king. When Juba found out about this, torn three ways as he was by war on three fronts, he was forced to protect his kingdom against the Gaetulians by sending back to his own territory six of the cohorts which he had brought to use against Caesar.

Battle offered at Uzitta, but accepted by neither side

(56) When Caesar had completed the extensions of his earthworks and pushed them forward to the point where they were just out of javelin range of Uzitta, he constructed a fortified camp. He put the defenders of the wall in constant fear for their lives by placing catapults and 'scorpions' at close intervals along the front facing the town, and moved five legions down from his higher camp.* The more distinguished and better-known of his men took this opportunity to attract the attention of their friends and relations and talk

with them. Caesar saw the advantage of letting this occur, because the cavalry commanders and the more highly born Gaetulians in the royal cavalry were men whose fathers had once served with Marius and owed grants of farms and land to his favour, but had been placed under the sovereignty of Hiempsal after Sulla's victory.* They seized their chance, and when it was already dark enough for the lanterns to be lit about a thousand of them with their horses and servants deserted to Caesar's camp on the plain next to Uzitta.

(57) At about this time, when Scipio and his entourage had found out what had happened, and were very agitated by such a loss, they saw Marcus Aquinus in discussion with Gaius Saserna. Scipio sent a message to Aquinus to the effect that it was not proper to talk to the opposition. The messenger relayed his words, but since he none the less lingered to allow Aquinus to finish what he wanted to say, Juba also sent one of his attendants to say when Saserna was listening: 'The king forbids you to engage in discussion.' Aquinus was frightened by the message and rode away in obedience to the royal command. To think it had become normal, that a Roman, and one moreover who had been elected to public office by the Roman people and whose homeland and personal fortune were quite intact, preferred to obey a foreign king rather than either comply with Scipio's message or return safely home when fellow Romans of the same party had been killed! And Juba behaved still more arrogantly, not towards Marcus Aquinus, someone of little significance who was the first of his family to become a senator, but towards Scipio, a person so eminent by birth, status, and record of public office. For although before the king's arrival Scipio was in the habit of wearing a purple cloak, Juba is said to have put it to him that he ought not to wear the same thing as he himself wore. Thus it came about that Scipio started to wear white instead and complied with the wishes of Juba, a man of monstrous arrogance and very little energy.

(58) On the following day Scipio and Juba led their entire force out from all their camps and occupied a modest elevation not far from Caesar's camp, where they drew up their line of battle and waited. Caesar likewise brought his

troops out, quickly drew them up in front of his defences, which were on the level ground, and halted there. Doubtless he thought that his opponents, because they had the assistance of such large forces of the king's and had previously been more ready to advance, would join battle with him and come closer. He rode back and forth encouraging the legions, and after giving the signal waited for the enemy advance. He himself had good reason for not moving very far forward from his defences, because in the town of Uzitta, held by Scipio, there were armed enemy units. On his right flank, his wing was opposite the town, and he was afraid that if he advanced past it these forces would make a sally from the town, attack him on the flank, and inflict casualties. He had another reason, too, for caution: in front of Scipio's line there was a patch of heavily obstructed ground, which he thought would stop his men from themselves moving in to engage.

(59) I should not omit to explain how the two armies were deployed for battle. Scipio arranged his line as follows. In front were his own and Juba's legions, and behind them a supporting line of Numidians so thinned out and stretched towards the ends that from a distance it looked to the legionaries* as if the centre of the line was only a single man deep. He had placed the elephants, evenly spaced, on his left and right wings, and behind the elephants were stationed his light-armed troops and Numidian auxiliaries. His whole force of reined cavalry he had put on his right wing, because his left wing was hemmed in by the town of Uzitta and there was no room to deploy cavalry. In addition, he had placed a great mass of Numidians and light-armed troops level with the right-hand end of his line of heavy infantry and at least a mile from it, more against the lower slopes of the hills and at some distance from both his own and the opposing forces. His object was to allow his cavalry, when the two battle-lines had met at the beginning of the fighting, to ride a longish way round, take the enemy by surprise, and use their numbers to encircle Caesar's army and shoot their javelins into his disordered troops. Such was Scipio's battle-plan that day.

(60) As for Caesar's line, this was its order, starting from his left wing and proceeding to the right. He had the Tenth and Ninth legions on the left wing, and the Twenty-fifth, Twenty-ninth, Thirteenth, Fourteenth, Twenty-eighth, and Twenty-sixth in the centre. However, on his right wing he had stationed some of the cohorts from the second line of his veteran legions and supported them with a few cohorts from the newly recruited ones,* while he had moved his third line over towards his left wing, so that it reached only as far as the centre legion of his battle order, and had so placed it as to make his left wing three deep. His reasons for so doing were because his right wing was supported by his fortifications, and because he was anxious that his left wing should be capable of resisting the great numbers of enemy cavalry. This was where he had placed all his cavalry, but since he had little confidence in them he had sent the Fifth legion forward to protect them and had stationed light-armed troops among the horse. His archers he had disposed in various places up and down the line, particularly on the wings.

(61) Thus the armies of either side, drawn up for battle with no more than a quarter of a mile between them, remained where they were from early in the morning until late in the afternoon, a thing which had perhaps never happened before without a battle ensuing. When Caesar eventually started to withdraw his army inside his fortifications, suddenly the whole more distant force of Numidian and Gaetulian cavalry without reins moved towards the right and began to make for Caesar's camp on the hill, while Labienus' reined cavalry remained where they were and distracted the legions. Suddenly some of Caesar's horse and light-armed rashly advanced too far, without orders; they crossed the marshy ground, but not being numerous enough to withstand the weight of enemy numbers they abandoned their light-armed support and suffered serious casualties, fleeing back to their own lines with the loss of one trooper and twenty-seven light-armed, and injuries to many of their mounts. Delighted by the successful outcome of this cavalry engagement, Scipio led his forces back to camp at nightfall. But

fortune decided not to allow the combatants their proper rejoicing; for on the next day Caesar sent some of his cavalry to Leptis to fetch grain, and on the way these surprised about a hundred raiding Numidian cavalry, attacked them, and killed some and took others prisoner. In the mean time Caesar brought his legions down daily into the plain, set them to work, and pushed a ditch and rampart across the middle of the plain, constantly seeking by these means to block his opponents' freedom to sally out. Scipio likewise built counter-fortifications and hurried to prevent Caesar cutting him off from the ridge. Thus the generals on either side were busy constructing fortifications, but their daily cavalry clashes were not on that account any the less frequent.

Caesar makes a naval counter-attack

(62) Meanwhile, when Varus heard of the arrival of the Thirteenth and Fourteenth legions from Sicily, he quickly launched the fleet which he had previously hauled out for the winter at Utica, and manned it with Gaetulian rowers and marines. He then sailed from Utica with the intention of laying a trap, and reached Hadrumetum with fifty-five ships. Caesar, who knew nothing of his arrival, sent Lucius Cispius with a fleet of twenty-seven vessels towards Thapsus to take up station to guard his supply route, and likewise sent Quintus Aquila on ahead to Hadrumetum for the same purpose with thirteen warships. Cispius rapidly reached his destination, but Aquila was caught in a storm and when he was unable to round the headland found a corner safe from the gale and disappeared completely from view with his fleet. The remainder of Caesar's fleet lay in open water off Leptis, empty of defenders because the crews had landed and scattered on shore, some of them having gone as far as the town to buy provisions for themselves. When Varus learnt of this from a deserter, he seized his opportunity and put out towards midnight from the ship-basin at Hadrumetum. He arrived at Leptis early in the morning with his whole fleet, burnt the merchant ships, which were anchored in open

water rather further from the harbour, and captured unopposed two quinqueremes which had no one on board to defend them.

(63) Caesar, meanwhile, was swiftly informed of this by messenger while he was inspecting the fortification work at his camp, which was about six miles from the harbour. Dropping everything else, he gave his horse its head and quickly reached Leptis, where he urged every ship to follow him. He himself boarded a diminutive vessel and after meeting Aquila, who was terrified by the number of enemy ships, began to follow their fleet. In the mean time Varus, who was unsettled by Caesar's rapidity and daring, put his ships about and strove to escape with his whole fleet in the direction of Hadrumetum. Caesar caught up with him after four miles and recovered a quinquereme with all its marines, besides taking prisoner the enemy prize crew of 130 who were on board. He also captured the nearest enemy trireme, which had stayed behind to fight him off and was laden with rowers and marines. The remainder of the enemy ships rounded the headland and all made for the ship-basin at Hadrumetum. Caesar found it impossible to round the headland with the same breeze, spent the night anchored offshore, and reached Hadrumetum at dawn. There he set fire to the merchant ships which were outside the basin, and since his opponents had either hauled ashore all the rest or packed them into the basin, he stayed for a little while, to see whether they wanted a naval battle, and then returned to camp.

(64) Among the men taken prisoner on the ship were Publius Vestrius, an equestrian, and Publius Ligarius, who had been in Afranius' army and after having been dismissed along with the rest by Caesar in Spain* had made his way to join Pompey and then escaped from the battlefield and come to Varus in Africa. This man Caesar ordered to be executed for treacherously breaking his word. But he pardoned Publius Vestrius, because his brother had paid up when money had been demanded of him, and because he himself convinced Caesar that he had been captured by Nasidius' fleet* and saved by the favour of Varus when he was being

led to execution, but had had no opportunity afterwards to change sides.

Leaving Uzitta, Caesar and Scipio manœuvre without result against each other as they attempt to secure supplies and support

(65) In Africa, it is the practice of the inhabitants to have secret underground chambers in the countryside, and in almost every farmhouse, for concealing grain, and to stock these as a precaution above all against war or the sudden arrival of enemies. On being told of this by an informer, Caesar sent two legions accompanied by cavalry a distance of ten miles from his camp in the small hours of the night, and they returned laden with a large quantity of grain. When this came to his ears, Labienus advanced seven miles by way of the ridge of hills traversed by Caesar the previous day, established a two-legion camp there, and in the belief that Caesar would make the same journey more than once to get grain took up his position with a large force of cavalry and light-armed in a suitable place for an ambush.

(66) Caesar, who had in the mean time been informed by deserters of Labienus' ambush, stayed where he was for a few days until repetition of the same daily routine had made the enemy careless. Then suddenly one morning he gave orders for three* veteran legions and some of the cavalry to follow him out of the rear gate of the camp. By sending the cavalry ahead, he took the men lying in ambush in the folds of the hills by surprise and cut down about 500 of the light-armed, while the rest were ignominiously routed. Meanwhile Labienus came to the assistance of the fugitives with his entire force of cavalry. When Caesar's few cavalry were no longer able to withstand the pressure of hostile numbers, Caesar formed up his legions ready for battle and displayed them to the enemy forces. This manœuvre thoroughly dismayed and checked Labienus and Caesar was able to withdraw his cavalry before they suffered any losses. On the following day Juba crucified all the Numidians who had deserted their posts and fled back to camp.

(67) Meanwhile Caesar was suffering from a shortage of grain. He therefore concentrated all his troops in camp, leaving garrisons at Leptis, Ruspina, and Acylla, and handed the fleet over to Cispius and Aquila to mount naval blockades, the one against Hadrumetum and the other against Thapsus. He himself set fire to his camp and started out before dawn with his men drawn up ready to fight and their baggage collected together on the left. When he reached the town of Aggar, which had often previously been attacked by the Gaetulians but defended with great energy by the townspeople, he established a single* camp there on open ground and set out in person with part of the army to go round the estates and collect grain. He found a great quantity of barley, oil, wine, and figs, and a little wheat, and returned to camp with his men's morale much improved. In the mean time Scipio, having discovered that Caesar had departed, began to follow him along the ridge with all his forces, and took up a position six miles from Caesar's camp with his own troops in three well-separated camps.

(68) There was a town called Zeta, which lay ten miles from Scipio in a district and direction accessible from his camp, but was distant and difficult to reach for Caesar, who was fourteen miles from it. To this town Scipio sent two legions to collect grain. When he heard this from a deserter, Caesar moved his camp up from the level ground to a safer site on a hill, left a garrison there, and after setting out before dawn marched with his forces beyond the enemy camp and seized the town. He found out that Scipio's legions were some distance away, collecting grain in the countryside, but as he was making efforts to march towards them he noticed enemy forces coming to assist these legions. This checked his attack. So after capturing Gaius Minucius Reginus, the Roman in command of the town, who was of equestrian rank and an intimate of Scipio, and Publius Atrius, another equestrian from the association of Roman citizens at Utica,* and appropriating twenty-two camels belonging to Juba, he left a garrison there under Oppius, one of his senior officers, and began to return to camp himself.

(69) He had reached a point not far from Scipio's camp, which he had to pass, when Labienus and Afranius with all

their cavalry and light-armed sprang an ambush on him, emerging from the first hills and confronting the end of his column. On seeing this Caesar blocked the enemy thrust with his cavalry and ordered his legionaries to put their kit in a pile and attack the enemy without delay. When they started to do this, the first onslaught of the legions drove back the enemy cavalry and light-armed and dislodged them from the slope without any difficulty. Thinking them beaten and demoralized, Caesar did not expect them to go on harassing him and began to resume his march, but they soon burst on him again from the nearby hills. The attack on Caesar's legionaries was mounted exactly as I have previously described* by the Numidians and their amazingly fast-moving light-armed, who took their fighting stations between the horsemen and used to run forward and retreat in unison with them. When they did this again and again, moving in to harass Caesar's men when they were starting to move on but taking to flight in the face of an attack, never coming any closer, employing their distinctive mode of combat, and being content to inflict serious injuries on the horses with their javelins, Caesar realized their sole aim was to force him to make camp there, where there was absolutely no water, so that his animals and his hungry army, which had had nothing to eat from before dawn until late in the day, should perish of thirst.

(70) It was now just before sunset, and his progress had not amounted to 150 yards in four hours. He therefore moved his cavalry from the rear of his column, because of the death of their mounts, and substituted the legions. In this way he proceeded slowly and calmly, with the pressure of the enemy attack being more easily sustained by the legionaries. Meanwhile the Numidian cavalry would gallop on through the hills to right and left and use their numbers to form a kind of ring around Caesar's forces, while some of them harassed the rear of his column. All the while, if no more than three or four of Caesar's veteran soldiers faced about and threw their spears with all their might at the Numidians who were bothering them, more than 2,000 of them took to flight as one man; then wheeling their horses round at random they

would form up in line again, follow at a distance, and hurl their javelins at the legionaries. By alternating progress and resistance in this way, Caesar completed a rather too protracted march and brought every single man safely back to camp an hour after nightfall, with ten wounded. Labienus retired to his own camp with about 300 men dead, many more wounded, and all exhausted by the constant attacking. In the mean time Scipio, who had brought his legions out of camp and formed them up with the elephants in battle order where Caesar could see them, led them back in again.

(71) To counter enemies of this sort, Caesar trained his men not like the commander-in-chief of a triumphant veteran army with great achievements to its credit, but like a manager of gladiators training raw recruits to his troop. He told them how many feet to retreat from the enemy, in what way and in how small a space to turn and resist their opponents, how to alternate running forward with drawing back and threatening to charge, and almost where and how to throw their weapons. It was astonishing how worried and anxious the enemy light-armed had made our army. They not only prevented the cavalry from beginning an engagement, because they killed the horses with their javelins, but they wore out the legionaries, because they were so quick on their feet. For as soon as the heavy-armed soldiers had halted under their harassment and charged them, the enemy easily escaped danger by their speed in running away.

(72) Caesar was seriously concerned, because whenever battle was joined his cavalry was for these reasons incapable of matching the cavalry and light-armed of the enemy, unless it had the support of legionaries. He was also worried that the enemy legions were as yet an unknown quantity, and he did not know how he would be able to withstand his opponents' wonderful cavalry and light armed if their legions were also present. A further cause of anxiety was that the number and size of the elephants was keeping his men in constant fear. However, for the last, but only the last, problem he had found a remedy: he had ordered elephants to be brought across from Italy, so that our soldiers could become acquainted with the appearance and characteristics

of the beasts, and find out what parts of their body were easily vulnerable to weapons, and when the elephant was caparisoned and armed what part of the body was left uncovered, so that weapons could be aimed at that point. In addition, his other animals would through familiarity lose any fear of the beasts' smell, noise, and appearance. He was largely successful with these aims, for the soldiers handled the beasts and discovered their slowness, the cavalry threw spears tipped with balls at them, and the elephants' own passivity accustomed the horses to tolerate them.

(73) Caesar was worried, for the reasons I have given above. He became slower and more deliberate, and abandoned his former rapidity and style of campaigning. And no wonder: for in Gaul he possessed forces used to campaigning on open ground and against the Gauls, straightforward men not much given to trickery, whose habit in fighting was to rely on bravery, not on deceit; but now he had to strive to accustom his soldiers to recognize the tricks, traps, and schemes of the enemy and what courses of action were best to follow or avoid. Therefore, to make them learn the lesson more quickly, he was careful not to keep the legions in one place but to take them rapidly in this direction or that, ostensibly to collect grain, because he did not think the enemy forces would stop following in his tracks or go away. And two days later he brought his forces out for battle and maintained a very careful deployment as he proceeded at close quarters past the enemy camp and invited them to fight on level ground. Towards evening, realizing that they shrank from an encounter, he led the legions back to camp.

(74) Meanwhile delegates arrived from the town of Vaga, next to Zeta, which as we have explained was already in Caesar's possession. They begged and entreated him to send them a garrison, and said that they would supply him with much that was militarily useful. At the same time news came that Juba, who had been informed by deserters of their fellow citizens' intentions and their sympathy for Caesar,* had made great speed with his forces to the town before Caesar's garrison could reach it. On arrival he had surrounded it with a mass of troops, taken possession of it, and after killing

every single one of the inhabitants handed the town over to his soldiers to pillage and destroy.

(75) Caesar meanwhile performed a ceremonial purification of his army on 21 March,* and on the following day brought all his forces out, advanced five miles from his own camp, and halted with his line drawn up for battle at about two miles' distance from Scipio's camp. When it was well and truly clear to him that his opponents were refusing his invitation to battle, he led his forces back and moved camp the next day, making a rapid march towards the town of Sarsura, where Scipio had a garrison and a depot of grain. When Labienus observed this, he started to use his cavalry and light-armed to harass the rear of Caesar's column. He captured the baggage of the camp-followers and traders who were carrying their goods in carts, and taking heart from this made closer and bolder approaches to the legions, because he thought that the soldiers were tired by the weight of the kit they carried and were incapable of fighting. But this point had not escaped Caesar; he had ordered three hundred men in each legion to be in battle-readiness, and he accordingly sent them to help his own squadrons by launching an attack on Labienus' cavalry. Labienus, frightened by the sight of the standards, then turned his horses about and took to rapid and ignominious flight. The legionaries killed many of his men and wounded a good number of others, then returned to their formations and resumed their march. Labienus continued to follow at a distance along the top of a ridge of high ground to the right.

(76) When Caesar reached the town of Sarsura, he slaughtered Scipio's garrison under the eyes of his opponents, who did not have the courage to intervene, and although Publius Cornelius, a re-enlisted veteran of Scipio's who was in command there, resisted bravely, he was outnumbered and killed. Having gained possession of the town and issued grain there to his army, Caesar went on the next day to the town of Thysdra, where Considius then was with a sizeable garrison and his troop of gladiators. Caesar took stock of the town, but was put off an assault on it by the lack of water, and went on about another four miles. Here he made camp near

some water, but then set out before dawn and returned to the camp he had made at Aggar.* Scipio did the same thing, bringing his forces back to his old camp.

(77) Meanwhile the people of Thabena, who normally recognized Juba's sovereignty and whose town lay at the far end of the coastal part of his kingdom, put the king's garrison to death and sent a deputation to Caesar to tell him what they had done and to beg and entreat the Roman people* to help them, because they had done them a service. Caesar approved their intentions, and sent Marcius Crispus, a tribune, to Thabena with a cohort, some archers, and a quantity of artillery. At the same time 400 cavalry, 1,000 slingers and archers, and about 4,000 soldiers belonging to all the legions, who had been on leave or ill and had not been able to cross with the standards to Africa earlier, reached him on board a single convoy. He therefore led out all his legions including these forces and halted in battle order five miles from his own camp and two miles from Scipio's.

(78) Below Scipio's camp lay a town called Tegea, where it was his practice to keep a cavalry garrison numbering about 2,000. He deployed this cavalry to right and left from the edges of the town while he himself led his legions out of camp and halted with them drawn up in line of battle on a lower ridge no more than a mile or so in front of his own fortifications. After Scipio had waited too long in the same place and the day was passing in inactivity, Caesar ordered his squadrons of horse to make a thrust against the enemy cavalry posted by the town, and sent light-armed infantry, archers, and slingers to support them. As soon as this manœuvre was under way, and Caesar's horse had charged at the gallop, Pacideius* began to extend his line of cavalry laterally, to give them the opportunity to outflank the Caesarian squadrons without fighting any the less bravely and fiercely. On seeing this, Caesar ordered the 300 men he normally kept lightly equipped in each legion to go from the nearest legion of his battle formation to the help of the cavalry. Meanwhile Labienus sent his cavalry mounted support and supplied the exhausted and wounded men with fresher and fit reinforcements. When the 400 Caesarian cavalry proved unable to

withstand the enemy strength of about 4,000, and were suffering casualties at the hands of the Numidian light-armed and retreating step by step, Caesar sent another cavalry regiment* at speed to help his hard-pressed men. This raised their morale and they all counter-attacked the enemy and put their opponents to flight. They killed many of them and wounded more, and after pursuing them for three miles and driving them as far as the rising ground withdrew to their own lines. Caesar waited with his army still in battle formation until late in the afternoon, then retreated to his own camp without loss. In this encounter Pacideius received a severe head wound from a throwing-spear which penetrated his helmet, and several officers and all the bravest men suffered death or injury.

Caesar defeats Scipio and Juba at Thapsus

(79) When Caesar was utterly unable to induce his opponents to come down to level ground and expose their legions to danger, and perceived that inadequate water supplies prevented him from making camp any nearer the enemy, he understood that his opponents' confidence was not based on their courage, and that their disdain of him was due to his shortage of water. So on 3 April, after midnight, he left Aggar and travelled sixteen miles in the dark towards Thapsus, where Vergilius was in command with a large garrison. He made camp there and on the same day began to invest the town with earthworks and put garrisons in a number of strategic places to stop the enemy penetrating his works and seizing positions inside his lines. Meanwhile Scipio, on realizing Caesar's intentions, found himself forced to fight in order not to abandon in the most disgraceful way Vergilius and the people of Thapsus, who had shown great loyalty to his cause. He therefore hastily followed Caesar by a higher route and established himself in twin camps eight miles from Thapsus.

(80) Between a salt-water lagoon and the sea there lay a narrow gap no more than a mile and a half wide, through which Scipio was trying to pass and bring help to Thapsus.

Caesar had anticipated this development, and on the previous day had constructed a fort, where he left a garrison of three <cohorts? . . . >, while he himself with the rest of his forces worked from a crescent-shaped camp to surround Thapsus with earthworks. Scipio meanwhile, having found his initial line of march barred to him, spent the following day and night inland from the lagoon and then as the sky was growing light took up a position beside the sea, not far (a mile and a half) from the camp and fort I have mentioned, and began to fortify a camp. When the news reached Caesar, he took his men off their work, left the proconsul Asprenas* with two legions to guard his camp, and hurried to the spot himself with a force ready for battle. He left some of his fleet off Thapsus, but told the rest of his ships to come as close inshore as they could behind the enemy and keep a lookout for his signal, so that when it was given they could suddenly and unexpectedly raise a clamour and spread panic among the enemy, who would be facing the other way, and would therefore become frightened and unsettled and be forced to look over their shoulders.

(81) On reaching the spot, Caesar saw that Scipio's battle-line was drawn up in front of his camp with the elephants on the right and left wings; and also that, in spite of this, some of his soldiers were energetically at work on the camp defences. He himself adopted a triple line of battle, *with the Tenth and Fourteenth(?) legions on the right wing, the Thirteenth(?) and Ninth on the left, <two in the centre>, and to counter the elephants five cohorts of the Fifth legion* placed in a fourth line on each wing, with archers and slingers stationed on both wings and light-armed infantry between the cavalrymen. Caesar himself, on foot, quickly made the rounds of the troops and roused their fighting spirit by making persuasive appeals and recalling his veterans' qualities in previous battles. He called on the recruits, men who had never fought in a pitched battle, to emulate the courage of his veterans and to covet the fame, status, and reputation of the latter which they would themselves enjoy once victory was theirs.

(82) While going round his army in this way he noticed that there was great agitation amongst the enemy in the area

of the rampart, where they were running backwards and forwards in fright, retreating inside the gates one minute and changing their minds and coming out again in large numbers the next. When this fact began to be more widely apparent, Caesar's senior officers and re-enlisted men* suddenly implored Caesar not to hesitate to give the signal for battle, saying that it was a portent from the immortal gods that they would be victorious. As Caesar hesitated, resisting their ardour and enthusiasm, protesting that he did not agree with battle by sally, and constantly steadying the line, a trumpeter on the right wing, under pressure from the soldiers, suddenly began to sound the signal without orders from Caesar. The result was that the standards of all the cohorts began to move forward against the enemy, although the centurions turned round to face them and physically restrained their men from joining battle contrary to their commander-in-chief's orders—but to no avail.

(83) When Caesar realized that it was quite impossible to stand in his men's way, now that they had been roused to fight, he gave 'Success'* as the password, put his horse into a gallop towards the enemy, and tried to reach their leaders. Meanwhile the slingers and archers poured a constant hail of missiles from the right wing on to the elephants. At this the animals, terrified by the whistling of the slings and the impact of the stones and leadshot, turned about, trampled on the thickly packed ranks of their own men behind them, and rushed into the half-built gateways in the rampart. The Moorish cavalry, who were on the same wing as the elephants, were also deprived of their protection and were the first to take to flight. The elephants having thus been speedily disposed of, the legions gained control of the enemy fortifications, and although a few of the enemy fought bitterly and died the rest scrambled to take refuge in the camp they had left the day before.

(84) The courage of a veteran of the Fifth legion should not, I think, be passed over in silence. An elephant on the left wing was wounded, and maddened with pain had attacked an unarmed camp-follower; the animal put its foot on him, then knelt on him with all its weight, and as it was

crushing him to death, waving its trunk in the air with a mighty trumpeting, the soldier could not endure the sight and felt bound to confront the animal. When the elephant saw him coming with his sword raised to strike, it left the corpse, wound its trunk round the soldier, and lifted him right off the ground. The soldier, being the kind of man who thought that in a dangerous situation like this determination was required, kept hacking as hard as he could with his sword at the trunk in which he was wrapped, and caused the beast such pain that it threw him aside and with tremendous noise and flurry rejoined the other elephants.

(85) Meanwhile the garrison of Thapsus sallied out from the seaward gate of the town. Whether their intention was to go to the aid of their own side or whether it was to abandon the town and flee to safety, they came out and waded waist-deep through the sea towards the shore; but they were prevented from reaching it by stones and spears thrown by the slaves and boys in the camp, and retreated again to the town. Meanwhile Caesar's legions lost no time in pursuing Scipio's shattered forces, who were in flight all over the field, and gave them no space to pull themselves together. After Scipio's men had reached the camp which was the objective of their flight, hoping to refurbish it, defend themselves again, and find some leader they could obey and under whose authority and command they could go on with the struggle, they then realized that there was no one there to protect them, threw their weapons away, and continued their flight on to Juba's camp. When they reached this, they saw that it too was in the hands of Caesar's men. Despairing of their lives, they then halted on a hill, laid down their arms, and hailed the victor in military fashion.* Their action did these unfortunates little good, because the veterans were inflamed with anger and resentment and not only could not be persuaded to spare the enemy but actually wounded or killed several prominent men from Rome in their own army whom they accused of responsibility for the war. Among these was the former quaestor Tullius Rufus, who died when a soldier deliberately impaled him on his spear; and Pompeius Rufus, who suffered a sword-cut on the arm, would likewise have died if he had not swiftly run to Caesar. After this had hap-

pened, a number of senators and Romans of equestrian rank became frightened and withdrew from the battle in case they too were killed by the soldiers, who following such a crushing victory had arrogated to themselves the right to commit any sort of crime in the expectation that their great achievements would give them immunity from punishment. And so all these soldiers of Scipio's, although pleading to surrender unconditionally to Caesar, were slaughtered down to the last man under Caesar's very eyes as he begged his men to spare them.

(86) After winning control of three enemy camps, killing 5,000* of their soldiers, and putting a large number to flight, Caesar withdrew to his camp with fifty of his own men dead and a few wounded. As soon as he arrived, he took up a position in front of Thapsus, and having captured sixty-four fully equipped and armoured elephants with their turrets and accoutrements lined them up opposite the town, to see if the determination of Vergilius and those under siege with him could be broken down by evidence of the disaster which had overtaken their side. Then he himself appealed to Vergilius, inviting him to surrender and emphasizing his own leniency and clemency. But when he realized he was not going to receive an answer, he went away. On the following day he performed a religious ceremony and called an assembly in the sight of the townspeople. He praised his troops, gave a cash bonus to the whole body of veterans, and from his platform presented rewards to all who had deserved well of him by their outstanding bravery. Then after leaving the proconsul Rebilus with three legions to besiege Thapsus and Gnaeus Domitius with two to besiege Thysdra, where Considius was the commander, he sent Marcus Messalla ahead to Utica with the cavalry and marched rapidly towards the same town himself.

Events at Utica; Cato's suicide; surrender of the town

(87) Meanwhile Scipio's cavalry, who had escaped from the battle, came to the town of Parada as they were on their

way to Utica. When they were refused admittance, because the report of Caesar's victory had run ahead of them, they took the town by force, made a pile of timber in the middle of the main square, heaped the townspeople's possessions on top, and set fire to it. They then inflicted savage punishment on the inhabitants, regardless of age or status,* by tying them up and throwing them alive into the flames, and proceeded forthwith to Utica. Previous to this, Marcus Cato, who thought the population of Utica were unreliable because of the favour Caesar had done them by passing his law,* had thrown the common people unarmed out of the town and forced them to live under guard outside the Gate of Baal* in a camp which he had walled and surrounded with a ditch, admittedly small. He had also arrested the members of the town's senate. Scipio's cavalry began to attack the camp, because they knew that the people in it sympathized with Caesar, and they wanted to kill them in order to avenge the smart of their defeat by an act of destruction. The Uticans, taking heart from Caesar's victory, drove the cavalry off with sticks and clubs. And so the latter, after failing to capture the camp, poured into the town, where they killed many of the townspeople and stormed and sacked their homes. Cato was completely unable to persuade them to join him in defending the town and stop their murder and pillage, and when he understood what they wanted made them a payment of 100 sesterces each to allay their greed. Faustus Sulla did the same and bribed them out of his own pocket; he then set off with them from Utica, intending to make his way to the king's territory.

(88) Meanwhile a large number of refugees reached Utica. Cato called them all together, along with the 300 who had made payments to Scipio to finance the war, and called on them to free their slaves* and defend the town. When he realized that some of them were in favour of this, but that the others were spineless and terrified and determined to flee, he said no more but allotted them ships so that they could each go wherever they wanted. He himself carefully tidied up all his affairs and asked Lucius Caesar, who was currently his acting quaestor, to look after his children. He then went to

bed, showing no abnormality in his expression or his conversation, and without arousing any suspicion took a sword into the room with him and secretly stabbed himself. He collapsed, but before he could expire his doctor and attendants became suspicious and broke into the bedroom. They began to support him and bind up the wound, but he savagely tore it open with his own hands and killed himself in full consciousness of what he was doing.* Although the people of Utica hated him for his political views, they none the less gave him a funeral on account of his remarkable integrity, and because he had been quite different from the other leaders and had provided Utica with magnificent defences and improved the bastions. Now that Cato was dead, Lucius Caesar, in order to get some protection for himself from the event, summoned the populace and made a speech in which he urged them all to let the gates be opened, saying that he had great confidence in Caesar's mercy. So the gates were opened and he left Utica to meet Caesar and acknowledge him as his commander-in-chief. Messalla, in accordance with his orders, reached Utica and put guards on all the gates.

(89) Caesar, meanwhile, had left Thapsus and come to Usseta, where Scipio had kept a large quantity of grain, arms, missiles, and other supplies under the protection of a small force. On his arrival he took possession of these and then went on to Hadrumetum. He entered the town at once, took stock of the arms, grain, and money, and granted their lives to Quintus Ligarius* and Gaius Considius' son Gaius Considius. He then marched away from Hadrumetum the same day, leaving Livineius Regulus there with one legion, and pressed on to Utica. Lucius Caesar met him on the way and immediately threw himself to his knees, begging for his own life and nothing else. Caesar readily granted him this, following his natural inclination and custom, and made the same concession, as was his habit, to Caecina, Gaius Ateius, Publius Atrius, Lucius Cella father and son, Marcus Eppius, Marcus Aquinus, the son of Cato, and the children of Damasippus. He reached Utica about the time the lamps were being lit and stayed outside the town that night.

(90) On the next day he entered the city and called a public meeting. He urged the inhabitants to take heart and thanked them for their support of him, but delivered a sustained indictment of the Roman businessmen and those individuals who were among the 300 who had contributed money to Varus and Scipio. After dwelling at length on their crimes, he finally announced that they were to come forward without fear, because he would at least concede them their lives; he would, however, put their property up for sale— but on the understanding that if any of them bought it back themselves he would annul the sale and treat the money as a fine, so that they could remain safe.* These men had been paralysed with fear and in despair of losing their lives for what they had done, and when a means of salvation was suddenly offered they were all anxious and willing to accept the terms. So they asked Caesar to name a sum to be paid by all 300 on a single account, and when a fine of 200 million sesterces was imposed on them, to be paid to the Roman people in six instalments over three years, none of them demurred and they were delighted to thank Caesar, proclaiming that they had not known life until that day.

Collapse of resistance to Caesar. Deaths of Juba and other Pompeian supporters. Caesar distributes rewards and punishments, and returns to Rome

(91) King Juba meanwhile, when he had escaped from the battle, joined Petreius to hide in farm-buildings by day and travel on by night. Finally he reached his own kingdom and arrived at the town of Zama, where he had his residence and his wives and children. Here he had collected all the money and valuables from his whole realm, and had built very substantial fortifications on the outbreak of war. But the inhabitants, who had already heard the longed-for rumour of Caesar's victory, kept Juba out of the town because when he had gone to war against the Roman people he had stacked up wood and constructed an enormous pyre in the

middle of the town square so that if he happened to be defeated in the war he could heap all his possessions on it, kill every one of the citizens and throw them on, and then after setting light to the pyre finally commit suicide himself on top of it and be burnt to ashes along with his wives, children, subjects, and the entire royal treasure. Juba argued long and hard with the people of Zama in front of the gates, first with threats appropriate to his authority, and then, when he realized he was making no impression, with pleas that they admit him to his ancestral hearth and household gods. Realizing that they remained adamant and were moved by neither threats nor entreaties to admit him, his third course was to ask them to hand over his wives and children so that he could take them with him, but when he saw that the townspeople were making him no answer at all, he left Zama without winning any concessions from them and went off to his country estate with Marcus Petreius and a few cavalry troopers.

(92) Meanwhile the people of Zama sent a deputation to tell Caesar about this, with a request that he send them assistance before the king could collect a force and attack them. They said they were prepared to keep the town loyal to Caesar and stay loyal themselves so long as they had breath in their bodies. Caesar praised the members of the deputation and told them to go back to Zama ahead of him and announce his forthcoming arrival. The following day he left Utica and hurried with his cavalry towards the kingdom. On the way a number of commanders from the royal forces came to him, begging for his forgiveness, and after pardoning these suppliants, he arrived at Zama. Meanwhile the report of his leniency and clemency had spread, and virtually all the cavalry of the kingdom came to him at Zama and were assured by him that they need harbour no fears for their own safety.

(93) While the two opponents were thus engaged, Considius, who was in command at Thysdra and had a force consisting of his slaves, a troop of gladiators, and some Gaetulians, learnt of the slaughter of his own side. Terrified by the arrival of Domitius and the legions, he abandoned any hope

of survival, deserted the town, and slipped secretly away, accompanied by a few natives and laden with cash, in an attempt to escape to Juba's kingdom. But his Gaetulian companions, who were greedy to steal the money, murdered him on the way and disappeared wherever they could. Meanwhile Gaius Vergilius realized that his efforts were useless, blockaded as he was by land and sea; and when he learnt that the troops of his own side had been killed or routed, that Marcus Cato had committed suicide at Utica, that Juba was a wanderer deserted by his men and rejected by all, that Saburra and his forces had been destroyed by Sittius, that Caesar had been admitted without hesitation into Utica, and that there was nothing left of that huge army, he accepted a pledge of personal protection for himself and his children from the proconsul Caninius, who was besieging him, and surrendered himself, everything that was his, and the town to the proconsul.

(94) The king meanwhile, being shut out of every civic community, despaired of saving himself. After supper he and Petreius took their swords and fought a duel, so that they should appear to have died like men, and Juba, being the stronger, easily managed to finish off the weaker Petreius. He then tried to stab himself in the chest with his weapon, but could not, whereupon he successfully implored one of his slaves to kill him.

(95) Meanwhile Publius Sittius, who had defeated the army of Saburra, Juba's general, and killed Saburra himself, was marching with a few troops through Mauritania towards Caesar. By chance he came on Faustus and Afranius* who were on their way to Spain with the force of about 1,000 with which they had sacked Utica. He therefore quickly laid an ambush while it was dark, and attacked at first light. Except for a few troopers, who had escaped from the head of the column, he killed or took the rest prisoner, and captured Afranius and Faustus alive together with Faustus' wife and children. A few days later Faustus and Afranius were killed in a disturbance which broke out in the army, but Caesar granted Pompeia and Faustus' children their lives and possession of all their property.

(96) Meanwhile Scipio with his warships and accompanied by Damasippus, Torquatus, and Plaetorius Rustianus was experiencing a stormy and protracted passage in the attempt to reach Spain. When he was forced in to land at Hippo Regius, where Sittius' fleet was at that time, Scipio's smaller number of vessels was surrounded by the larger fleet and sunk, and he perished together with the others I have just mentioned.

(97) Meanwhile Caesar held an auction of the royal property at Zama and put up for sale the possessions of those Roman citizens who had taken up arms against the Roman people. He rewarded the inhabitants of the town who had made the decision not to admit the king, confiscated the income from the crown's taxes, and made the kingdom a Roman province, leaving Gaius Sallustius there as proconsul with full authority. He himself left Zama and went back to Utica, where he sold the property of those who had served as centurions under Petreius or Juba, and imposed fines as follows: on the people of Thapsus, two million sesterces, and on their association of Roman citizens, three million; on the people of Hadrumetum, three million sesterces, and on their association of Roman citizens, five million. The communities themselves and their property he protected from any injury or looting. On the people of Leptis, whose possessions had been plundered by Juba in earlier years and who had recovered their losses after they had sent a deputation of complaint to the senate which resulted in the appointment of arbitrators, he imposed an annual fine of three million pounds' weight of oil,* his reason being that at the start of the dispute between the leading men of the state* they had made an alliance with Juba and had helped him with weapons, troops, and money. On account of the insignificance of their town, he fined the people of Thysdra a fixed amount of grain.

(98) This done, he embarked at Utica on 13 June and arrived at Caralis in Sardinia with his fleet two days later. There, because they had given shelter to Nasidius and his fleet and helped him with manpower, Caesar fined the people of Sulci ten million sesterces, ordered them to pay a tithe

of $12^1/_2$ per cent instead of 10 per cent, and put the property of a few of them up for sale. He sailed on 27 June, following the coast, but because of bad weather had to stay in more than one port along the way and did not reach Rome until twenty-seven days later.

THE SPANISH WAR

Caesar attacks Sextus Pompeius in Corduba, forcing his brother Gnaeus to abandon his siege of Ulia and come to the aid of Corduba (1–5). Caesar moves to attack Ategua, Gnaeus Pompeius follows; skirmishing and diversionary tactics by Pompeius fail to prevent the fall of Ategua (6–19). Pompeius moves away, followed by Caesar; various engagements and individual exploits occur in the region around Ulia, until the armies move on to the plain of Munda (20–27). Caesar defeats Pompeius in battle at Munda (28–31). Pompeius escapes to Carteia (32). Caesar gains control of Corduba and Hispalis (33–36). Flight and death of Pompeius; death of his captor Didius (37–40). Capture of Munda, siege of Urso, and speech of Caesar at Hispalis (41–42)

(1) After the defeat of Pharnaces and the recovery of Africa, those who <*had survived*> these battles made their escape to the young Gnaeus Pompeius, when he had . . . and had gained control of Further Spain. While Caesar was detained giving shows in Italy,* . . . so that he might more easily prepare defences against an attack, Pompeius set about appealing to the loyalty of every single community. He thus assembled, partly by entreaty and partly by force, a very considerable body of men and started to plunder the province. In this situation some communities sent him help of their own accord, while others shut their gates against him. When any of the latter towns were captured, if there were any citizen of the place who had been rewarded by Pompey* his wealth would mean that some charge or other would be levelled against him, so that he could be made away with and his money used for bonuses to the brigands. In this way, as the rewards of peace . . . by the enemy . . . so Pompeius' forces increased.

Consequently the communities hostile to Pompeius sent frequent messages to Italy demanding help.

(2) Gaius Caesar was holding the dictatorship for the third time and was dictator-designate for the fourth time, and after dealing with a great deal of business set out for Spain. He made a tremendously fast journey* with the object of finishing the war, and was met by a delegation of Corduban citizens, who had withdrawn their support from Gnaeus Pompeius. They told Caesar that it was possible for him to take the town under cover of darkness, because he had reached the province without his enemies expecting it, and also because the scouts, who had been stationed everywhere by Gnaeus Pompeius to inform him of Caesar's arrival <had been intercepted, and . . . >, and they adduced much else that was plausible. Caesar was persuaded by these considerations, and informed Quintus Pedius and Quintus Fabius Maximus, whom he had previously appointed as senior officers to command the army, that he had arrived and that he needed a guard of cavalry from the province for himself. But he reached them more quickly than they expected, and did not get the cavalry guard for himself that he wanted.

(3) At this particular moment it was Gnaeus' brother Sextus Pompeius who was in command of the garrison holding Corduba, which was considered the capital of the province; Gnaeus Pompeius himself was attacking the town of Ulia and had been detained there a matter of months. Representatives from this town, when they heard about Caesar's arrival, eluded Pompeius' guards, made their way to Caesar, and started to ask him to send them help as soon as possible. <Remembering that> their community had always been extremely loyal to Rome, Caesar swiftly ordered six cohorts and an equal number of cavalry to set out before midnight. In command of them he placed a man who was well known in the province, and no fool, Lucius Vibius Paciaecus. Vibius reached Pompeius' guards at a moment when he was being lashed in the face by a storm and strong wind, and the violence of the storm so obscured the way ahead that it was hardly possible to recognize the next man. But this inconvenience proved extremely useful to them. When they came

to the place, Paciaecus ordered two men to ride on each horse, and they made directly for the town through the enemy guards. In the middle of them, they were challenged. One of our men told the guards to keep quiet, explaining that they were at that moment trying to reach the wall and take the town, and the guards were partly hampered by the storm from paying proper attention and partly put off by this answer. On approaching the gate, Paciaecus' party gave the password and the townspeople let them in. The infantry remained there, partially dispersed, while the cavalry raised a great cry and burst out to attack the enemy camp. As a result of this action a near-majority of the men in the camp, who were taken by surprise, thought they were on the point of being captured.

(4) After sending this defensive force to Ulia, with the object of making Pompeius abandon his attack, Caesar marched towards Corduba. He sent some cavalry on ahead with some tough legionary soldiers, who were taken up on to the horses when they came in view of the town. This manœuvre could not be observed by the Cordubans. As they drew nearer, and a really large number of men came out from the town to destroy the cavalry, the above-mentioned legionaries jumped down from the horses and put up a fierce fight, with the result that out of a huge number of men few got back to the town. Sextus Pompeius was frightened by this into writing to his brother to come and help him quickly, because there was a risk of Caesar taking Corduba before he himself arrived. So although Gnaeus Pompeius had almost captured Ulia, he was worried by his brother's letter and started to march with his army towards Corduba.

(5) When Caesar reached the River Baetis he was unable to cross because of the depth of the water; so he lowered baskets full of stones into the river, placed beams on top of them, and led his men in three divisions across the bridge so made to his camp. He advanced to face the town in the area of the bridge with his force divided in three, as we have said. When Pompeius arrived with his forces, he placed his camp in the same fashion opposite Caesar's. Caesar wanted to shut him off from the town and from supplies, and began

to push a bank and ditch towards the bridge;* Pompeius, whose situation was parallel, did the same. At this point there developed a race between the two generals as to which of them would seize the bridge first, and this race gave rise to minor clashes every day, of which sometimes one side and sometimes the other had the better. When the situation had reached the point of more serious struggle, both sides began a hand-to-hand fight in their increasing desire to hold their ground. Men were clustered thickly around the bridge, and those near the river bank were squeezed together and forced into the water. Here the opposing sides in turn not only piled corpse on corpse, but rivalled each other in the size of their burial mounds. After a number of days had been spent like this, Caesar was anxious, if he could manage it, to bring his adversaries down on to level ground and settle the campaign by a battle as soon as possible.

(6) He saw that his opponents had not the least wish to do this, so in order to lure them on to level ground in the same way as he had dragged them back from Ulia he took his troops across the river and ordered big fires to be lit at night. In this way he set out for Ategua, Pompeius' strongest base. When Pompeius discovered this from deserters, he <abandoned the hills and> narrow passes on the very day <he had> the chance, collected a large number of carts and loaded mules . . . and made his way to Corduba. Caesar began a siege of Ategua and started to surround it with earthworks. A message was brought that Pompeius had set out that day, and to guard against his arrival Caesar occupied several strongpoints where cavalry, in some places, and infantry, in others, could take up their positions and keep a lookout to defend his camp. But it so happened that Pompeius arrived when there was a very thick morning mist, and in the poor visibility surrounded Caesar's cavalry with some cohorts and squadrons of horse and cut them to pieces to such effect that very few escaped the slaughter.

(7) On the following night Pompeius burnt his camp, and after crossing the River Salsum made his way through narrow valleys to establish his camp on high ground between the two towns of Ategua and Ucubi. Caesar, having finished

the fortifications which were needed for his attack on Ategua, began to drive an assault mound and screens forward. The area is mountainous and unsuited to military operations, and split by the plain of the River Salsum, which is none the less very close to Ategua for about two miles. Pompeius had placed his camp on that side of the town, on the hills, in sight of both towns, but lacked the courage to come to the help of his allies. He had the eagles and standards of thirteen legions; but there were only two which he thought gave his force some solidity, the local legion* and the Second, which had both deserted from Trebonius; there was another raised from the settlers in the district, a fourth which was one of Afranius' that he had brought with him from Africa, and the remainder consisted of runaways or auxiliaries. As for light-armed and cavalry, our side were far superior both in fighting quality and in numbers.

(8) Another thing which enabled Pompeius to prolong the campaign was that the hills are steep and not unsuitable for constructing the defences to a camp. Also, throughout almost the whole of Further Spain the fertility of the soil and the equally plentiful supplies of water blunt the effect of sieges and make them difficult. In this region, too, because of the frequency of raids by the natives, every place at all distant from a town has a ring of towers and fortifications, and these are roofed with rubble, as in Africa, and not with tiles. They also have lookout posts in them, the height of which allows a view far and wide. Again, the majority of the towns of the province are given a fair degree of protection by hills and are built on naturally elevated sites, so that it is not easy to approach or climb up to them. Thus the Spanish towns have such good natural protection from siege that they are not easy for an enemy to take; and this was true in this campaign. For when Pompeius had a camp established between Ategua and Ucubi, the towns mentioned above, and in sight of both, there was, about four miles from his camp, a natural hillock called Postumius' Camp, where Caesar had located a fort to protect himself.

(9) Pompeius observed that this fort's natural protection was the same ridge that he occupied and that it was a long

way from Caesar's camp, and also that because it was cut off by the River Salsum its situation was so awkward that Caesar was unlikely to commit himself to sending help. Confident of his analysis, Pompeius set out after midnight and began to attack the fort. Having approached it, his men raised a sudden shout and began to throw masses of weapons, wounding a large number of men. This phase over, when the garrison of the fort had begun to fight back and a message had reached Caesar's main camp, Caesar set out with three legions to help our struggling side. When he reached them, many of the enemy fled in terror and were killed, and not a few captured, amongst whom were two <centurions?>. In addition, many of them threw their arms away before they fled, and eighty of their shields were recovered.

(10) The following day Arguetius arrived from Italy with some cavalry. He brought with him five units of Saguntines, taken from the inhabitants of the town. (Mention was not made in the correct place of the fact that cavalry had come to Caesar from Italy with Asprenas.)* That night Pompeius burnt his camp and started to march towards Corduba. A king by the name of Indo, who had brought his forces along together with the cavalry,* was isolated and killed by the men of the local legion as he pursued his enemies' column of march too eagerly.

(11) On the following day our cavalry went a long way in the direction of Corduba to harass those who were bringing supplies from the town to Pompeius' camp. Fifty of these men were captured and brought with their animals to our camp. On the same day Quintus Marcius, who had been one of Pompeius' military tribunes, deserted to us; and in the latter part of the night there was a determined attack from the town,* with much throwing of firebrands. After this Gaius Fundanius, a Roman equestrian, deserted to us from the enemy camp.

(12) The next day, our cavalry captured two men from the local legion. They claimed to be slaves, but when they came into camp they were recognized as deserters from Trebonius by soldiers who had previously been with Fabius and Pedius. They were given no chance of pardon and were

put to death by our men. At the same time some messengers who had been sent from Corduba to Pompeius and had come by mistake to our camp were allowed to go free after their hands had been cut off. Following their previous pattern of behaviour, in the period before midnight the defenders spent a long time throwing a lot of firebrands and great quantities of weapons from the town, and inflicted a considerable number of casualties. When the night was over they made a sally against the Sixth legion when our men were spread out constructing fortifications, and started a fierce fight; but the shock of their attack was absorbed by our men, although the townspeople had the advantage of the slope. In spite of the fact that our opponents had taken the initiative in beginning the sally, they were none the less driven back by the courage of our soldiers, even though these had to fight uphill, and they retreated into the town with many injured.

(13) The next day, Pompeius began to extend a fortification from his camp to the River Salsum, and when a few of our cavalry stationed at an outpost were discovered by a more numerous force, they were ejected from their post and three of them killed. The same day Aulus Valgius, a senator's son, whose brother had served with Pompey, left all his things behind, mounted his horse, and fled. A scout from Pompeius' Second legion was captured by soldiers and killed, and at the same time a sling-shot was hurled bearing this message:* 'On the day you approach to take the town, I shall lay down my shield.' Encouraged by this, some troops, in the hope that they could scale the wall and capture the town without danger, started work by the wall on the following day and after pulling down a good part of the outer wall . . .

Having done this they were saved by the townspeople as though they belonged to their own side . .

. . . they begged him to let go the legionaries who had been put in charge of the defence of the town by Pompeius. Caesar replied that it was his custom to lay down terms, not agree to them. When they returned to the town, and reported the answer, a cry was raised, volleys of every sort of weapon were thrown, and they began to fight all along the wall. This made the majority of the men in our camp think that they would certainly make a sally that day. So a cordon was drawn round them and a violent battle lasted for some time; at the same time an artillery missile shot by our side demolished a tower, and five of the enemy who were in the tower, along with a boy who used to keep a watch on the artillery piece, were hurled to the ground.

(14) Earlier that day Pompeius established a fort across the River Salsum, and since we did not stop him he mistakenly boasted that he held a position that was virtually in our territory. On the next day he continued the same tactics and advanced further, to a place where our cavalry had an outpost. Here an attack was made on some squadrons of ours who were supported by light-armed troops, and they were dislodged from their position and, since our cavalry were few, were trampled down along with the light-armed by the enemy squadrons. This action took place in sight of both camps and the exultant boasting of the Pompeians increased as our side began to retreat and be pursued further. However, when the Pompeians reached a place where they were received by our men with their usual outstanding courage, they made a great noise but declined a fight.

(15) In most armies, this is the rule of cavalry fighting: when a trooper abandons his horse to fight at close quarters with an infantryman, the trooper is never reckoned the equal of the latter. However, <the opposite> was true in this battle. When picked light-armed infantry arrived unexpectedly to fight our cavalry, and this was noticed in the struggle, quite a number of the cavalry dismounted. Thus the troopers soon began to fight an infantry battle, so much so that they were slaughtering the enemy very close to the ramparts of the camp.* In this engagement 123 enemy fell, a number were stripped of their arms, and many were taken back wounded to camp. Three of our men died, and twelve infantrymen and five troopers were wounded. Later the same day, fighting began after the usual pattern at the wall. After the garrison had hurled a very large quantity of missiles and firebrands at our soldiers, who took defensive action, they embarked on an unspeakable deed of the utmost cruelty: in

full view of us, they began to cut the throats of their hosts in the town and throw them down from the wall, just like savages—an action unrecorded in human history.

(16) At the very end of the same day the Pompeians sent a messenger unobserved by our forces, to tell the garrison to set fire that night to the towers and assault ramp* and break out after midnight. So after they had spent a large part of the night in throwing firebrands and a quantity of weapons, they opened the gate which was on the same side as, and in sight of, Pompeius' camp, and burst out all together. They carried with them brushwood and fascines to fill up the ditches, and throwing-hooks so that they could tear apart and burn the straw huts which our men had built for winter shelter, and also silver and clothing so that while our men were distracted by the plunder they could kill them and get away to Pompeius' protection. For the latter, in the belief that their attempt could succeed, spent the whole night patrolling the other side of the River Salsum with his army drawn up in battle order. Perhaps their plan might have succeeded if they had taken us by surprise, but our men bravely beat them back, inflicted many injuries, and penned them inside the town, seizing booty and arms from them and capturing some alive, who were put to death the next day. At the same time a deserter from the town told us that when the civilians in the town had been murdered, Junius, a sapper, had protested that he and his fellows were committing a crime of an unspeakable kind: their victims had done nothing to deserve such a punishment, in receiving them at their hearths and homes, and they themselves had criminally polluted the hospitality they had received. Junius had said much more, and the soldiers, deterred by what he had said, had called a halt to the killing.

(17) So the next day Tullius, accompanied by Cato, a Lusitanian, came to negotiate with Caesar and addressed him as follows: 'I wish the immortal gods had so acted as to make me one of your soldiers and not one of Pompeius', and that I was exhibiting this courage and resolution on the occasion of your victory, not of his affliction. But the ill-starred acclaim accorded him has sunk so low, that we Roman

citizens <stand> in need of protection, and the result of the grievous ruin of our country has been that we are numbered among her enemies; so we who have secured neither the best of fortune when he was successful in battle, nor the next best when he was unsuccessful, we who have toiled night and day under volleys of missiles and blows of swords, we who have been abandoned and deserted by Pompeius and overcome by your fighting qualities, therefore ask you to show mercy and save us, and beg you <to spare our lives.' To which Caesar replied:> 'When Roman citizens surrender, I shall behave in the same way as I have behaved towards other nations.'

(18) When the returning delegation reached the gate, Tiberius Tullius . . . and when Cato the Lusitanian did not follow him as he went in, he returned to the gate* and laid hold of the man. On seeing this Tiberius pulled out a dagger and cut his hand. So they fled to Caesar. At the same time the standard-bearer of the First legion deserted and it became known that on the day of the cavalry battle thirty-five men from his unit had died and he had not been allowed to announce it or mention in Pompeius' camp that a single man had died. A slave (whose master was in Caesar's camp, having left his wife and sons in the town) murdered his mistress, and by this means got away to Pompeius' camp unobserved by Caesar's guards and threw a sling-shot with a message informing Caesar of the preparations being made for the defence of the town. So after this note had been received, when the man who used to throw the sling-shots with the messages had returned to the town . . .

Later, two brothers, who were Lusitanians, deserted and brought news of an address to his men by Pompeius, proposing that since he could not assist the town, they should withdraw by night out of sight of the enemy, in the direction of the sea; one person had answered that it was better to go down and fight than give the signal for retreat; and the man who said this had been murdered. At the same time messengers from Pompeius were caught on their way to Ategua. Caesar passed their despatches on to the people of the town, and when they begged for their lives told them to burn down the townspeople's wooden tower: if any of them were successful, all his wishes would be granted. It was difficult for anyone to set fire to the tower without risk, and so when one of them approached it with . . . he was killed by the townspeople. The same night a deserter reported that Pompeius and Labienus had complained about the murder of the inhabitants of Ategua.

(19) Somewhat before midnight, because of the number of hits it had received, one of our wooden towers gave way at the base, so much so that the damage extended to the second and third storeys. At the same time the enemy fought fiercely along the wall and set fire to a tower of ours like the other, owing to the fact that they had the wind in the right direction. The following day, a married woman jumped down from the wall, ran across to our side, and said that she had made a compact with her household that they would all desert to Caesar but that the rest had been overpowered and killed. Also at this time a writing-tablet was thrown from the wall, on which this was found written: 'Lucius Munatius to Caesar. If you will grant me my life, since I have been deserted by Gnaeus Pompeius, I will support you with the same courage and determination as I have shown in his service.' At the same time a delegation from the townspeople which had earlier left the town had audience with Caesar and promised that if he would spare their lives they would surrender the town the next day. His answer was that he was Caesar and would keep his word. And so he took possession of the town on 19 February and was saluted 'Victorious General' by his troops.*

(20) On learning from deserters that the town had surrendered, Pompeius moved his camp towards Ucubi, established strongpoints in the area, and began to ring himself with fortifications. Caesar moved . . . and placed his camp very near Pompeius'. At the same time a legionary soldier from the local legion deserted to us one morning with the news that Pompeius had called together the people of Ucubi and given them orders to carry out careful enquiries into who was on his side and who favoured a victory by his opponents. After this, in the captured town, the slave whom we

mentioned above as having murdered his mistress was caught hiding in an underground passage and was burnt alive. At the same time eight legionary centurions from the local legion deserted to Caesar, and there was an engagement between our cavalry and that of our opponents and a few light-armed infantry were wounded and killed. That night some scouts were captured, three slaves and a soldier from the local legion. The slaves were crucified and the soldier beheaded.

(21) On the day after, some cavalry and light-armed infantry deserted to us. Concurrently about forty cavalry sallied out to attack our water-carriers, killing some and taking others away alive; of those captured, eight were cavalrymen. The following day Pompeius beheaded seventy-four of the men who were alleged to favour a Caesarian victory, and ordered the rest to be taken back to the town; of these, 120 escaped and reached Caesar.

(22) After this, a delegation from Urso, the members of which had been captured in Ategua, left with some of our side to inform the people of Urso what had happened and what they could expect from Gnaeus Pompeius, since they had themselves witnessed the murder of his hosts; furthermore, they would testify to many other crimes committed by the men whom the Ateguans had taken in to their community as protectors. When they reached Urso, none of our people who were equestrians* or senators dared to enter the town, except those who were citizens of the place. Responses were then exchanged, and when our spokesmen were rejoining the group outside the town, they were set upon by a body of armed men who <took them by surprise and> killed them. There were two survivors, who escaped and reported the episode to Caesar. <The people of Urso> sent . . . and spies to the town of Ategua, and when the latter had discovered for certain that the course of events had been as the delegation had reported, the townspeople ran together and began to throw stones and make threatening gestures at the man responsible for the killing of the delegates, saying that because of him they were lost. So having escaped by a whisker he begged them to let him go as an emissary to Caesar, promising to satisfy him. Permission was granted, and he set out.

He then procured an armed guard, and when he had put together a really large gang tricked his way into being admitted into the town at night. A bloodbath followed, and after his leading opponents had been killed he took control of the town. Later, some slaves who had deserted brought news that the property of the townspeople was being put up for sale and that it was forbidden to go outside the town's defences except in casual dress, the reason being that ever since the day that Ategua had been captured many people had been fleeing in terror to Baeturia; they had no expectation at all of victory, and if any of our side deserted they were being assigned to the light-armed and paid no more than seven denarii.*

(23) Next Caesar placed his camp near the enemy's and began to throw out a line of fortifications towards the River Salsum. While our soldiers were dispersed on the work, a considerable number of the enemy charged down from higher ground and when our men continued to work threw a large quantity of weapons and wounded quite a few of them. At this point, to quote Ennius,* our men 'withdrew for a short time'. Therefore, when it was observed that our men were giving way more than usual, two centurions from the Fifth legion crossed the river and steadied the line, and as they were displaying outstanding courage in energetically driving back superior numbers, one of them fell under a hail of weapons thrown from higher ground. So although his fellow centurion had started to fight the enemy, when he noticed that he was being completely surrounded he retreated, but tripped. When he fell . . . and a number of the enemy were rushing in to strip the decorations from this brave man, our cavalry crossed the river lower down and began to drive the enemy back to their defences. The result was that while they were too greedily intent on their killing between the enemy outposts, they were trapped by some cavalry squadrons and light-armed infantry. Had they not been extremely brave they would have been taken prisoner, because they were so cramped together by the actual fortifications of the outpost that a man on horseback scarcely had the space to defend himself. In the fighting against both sorts of troops

a number of them were wounded, including also Clodius Arquitius, and the close-quarters engagement between the sides was such that none of our men were lost apart from the two centurions who covered themselves in glory.

(24) The day after, forces of both armies clashed around Soricaria. Our men began to construct extensions to their fortifications. When Pompeius realized that he was being kept out of the stronghold of Aspavia, which is five miles from Ucubi, this inevitably demanded that he come down and offer battle; however, he did not open himself to a fight on level ground, but from a mound . . . <our men?> were about to capture a lofty hillock, so much so that he had no choice but to approach from an inferior position. As a result, when forces from both armies tried to reach this commanding hillock, the enemy were stopped by our side and pushed back on the level ground. This turned the battle in our men's favour, and they indulged in no little slaughter as their opponents gave way at every point. The latter were saved by the aid not of their courage, but of the mountainous terrain. If it had not begun to grow dark our men, whom they outnumbered, would have rendered them helpless. To prove it, their losses were 323 light-armed and 138 legionaries, in addition to those who were stripped of their arms and other equipment. This was the way the enemy made restitution for the deaths of the two centurions on the previous day.

(25) The following day, when a detachment of Pompeius' came in similar fashion to the same place, they behaved as before: apart from the cavalry, none of them dared to venture on to level ground. While our troops were at work on their fortifications, the cavalry forces began to engage. At the same time their legionaries were shouting and when they demanded a part in the action, like men accustomed to follow up—and you would have thought they were very ready to fight—our men came a good long way out of a shallow fold in the hills and took up their position on open and more level ground. But the Pompeians were definitely too timid to come down to the level ground and join battle, except for one man, Antistius Turpio. Confident in his strength,

he began to proclaim that none of his opponents was his equal. At this point, as in the tale of the duel of Achilles and Memnon,* Quintus Pompeius Niger, a man of equestrian rank from Italica, advanced from our ranks to meet him. Because Antistius' ferocity had made everyone watch instead of concentrate on their task, the battle-lines were set out: for it was unclear which of the warring principals would be victorious, so that it almost seemed that the duel would bring an end to the war. §§*Thus eager and intent, each man favoured his own side and willed it to win. Alert and courageous, they came down to flat ground to fight, and their shields and battle decorations shone in chased metal-work . . . Their fight would have been brought to an immediate end, if it had not been that the cavalry engagement, as we said above . . . He stationed the light-armed as a precaution not far from the fortifications, <near> the camp. §§* While our cavalry were coming back to camp as we withdrew, the enemy were too keen to harass them, and they all gave a shout and charged. Thus terrified, the enemy lost a considerable number of men as they fled, and returned to their camp.

(26) As a reward for courage, Caesar presented Cassius' squadron of horse with 13,000 sesterces, their unit commander with five bracelets of twisted gold, and the light-armed infantry with 12,000 sesterces. The same day Aulus Baebius, Gaius Flavius, and Aulus Trebellius, Romans of equestrian rank from Asta, deserted to Caesar with their horses practically covered with silver. They said that all the men of equestrian status in Pompeius' camp had made a secret agreement to change sides; a slave had informed on them and they had all been arrested, but they themselves had deserted when a chance offered. Again, on the same day, a letter from Gnaeus Pompeius to Urso was intercepted: 'Greetings. Although, as our good fortune would lead you to expect, we have until now repulsed the enemy as we planned, if they would give us the chance of a battle on level ground I would have put an end to the war more quickly than you think. But they are unwilling to bring their untried army down for a fight and are conducting the campaign so far <by attacking?>

our strongpoints. They have besieged individual towns, and are taking supplies from them. For this reason I shall protect the towns on our side and also finish the war as soon as possible. I intend to send you . . . cohorts. They will be deprived of supplies by our success, and will have to come down and fight.'

(27) Later, when our men were dispersed about their tasks, a number of cavalry were killed while gathering wood in an olive-grove. Some slaves deserted, bringing the information that there had been great apprehension ever since the battle at Soricaria on 5 March, and Attius Varus was now in charge of the outlying fortified sites. That day, Pompeius moved his camp and established it in an olive-grove opposite Spalis. Before Caesar set out to follow him, the moon was visible about midday. After the camps had been shifted, Pompeius gave orders to the garrison he had left in Ucubi to set fire to the town, and when the town had burnt down withdraw to the main camp. Later, <Caesar> started to attack the town of Ventipo and when it surrendered marched to Carruca and encamped opposite Pompeius. Pompeius set fire to the town, because it had refused to admit a garrison of his; and a soldier, who had murdered his brother in camp, was caught by our soldiers and clubbed to death. They marched away from here, and on arrival at the plain of Munda* Caesar established his camp opposite Pompeius.

(28) The next day, when Caesar wanted to continue his march with his forces, his scouts reported that Pompeius had been ready for battle since long before dawn. On receipt of this news, he flew his battle-flag. Pompeius' reason for leading his army out to battle was the letter he had previously sent to the community of Urso, which supported him, saying that Caesar was reluctant to come down to the valley bottom because the greater part of his army were untried men. This letter wonderfully bolstered the morale of the townspeople. So Pompeius, confident in this opinion, thought that he could finish the whole thing: he was protected both by the lie of the land and by the defences of the town itself, where he had encamped. For as we have explained above,* the high ground is sometimes fringed by hillocks, sometimes

separated by intervening flat ground; and this was true on this occasion.

(29) The plain lying between the two camps was about five miles long, so that Pompeius' supporting forces were protected by two things, the town and the height of their position. The plain extended directly from here, and was level. Before it stretched away, there came a stream which made approach to them extremely difficult, because it ran to the right in marshy and treacherous ground. Caesar was therefore quite certain, when he saw the line of battle drawn up, that his opponents would advance to the unencumbered ground and fight in the middle of the plain, which was in full view of all. In addition, it happened that the site was distinguished not only by its clear level ground, but also by the calm and sunshine of the day, so that you might think such a choice and wonderful moment had been marked out by the immortal gods for a pitched battle. Our men were glad, and some were also afraid, because the fate and fortune of all were at stake there, and it was quite unclear what chance might have in store for them after the hour of struggle. And so our men advanced to fight, which we had expected our opponents to do; but they did not dare to advance very far beyond the defences of the town, where they took up their position, there near the wall. Therefore our men advanced. From time to time the level ground tempted our opponents to press forward to victory, given such conditions; but they would not depart from their usual practice and leave either their higher position or the town. Although our men had come at a deliberate pace very close to the stream, our opponents did not cease to favour the slope.

(30) Their line of battle was composed of thirteen eagles,* which were protected on the flanks by cavalry and light-armed numbering 6,000, and in addition almost as many auxiliaries again; our forces consisted of eighty cohorts* and 8,000 cavalry. Thus when our men approached the unfavourable ground at the edge of the plain, the enemy were ready and in a better position, so that it was extremely dangerous to cross it to go on up. On seeing this Caesar began to hold his troops back from it, in case some rash and culpable

mistake were made. When the order reached their ears, they were bitter and angry at being stopped from doing battle. The delay made the enemy keener, thinking that it was fear which prevented Caesar's forces joining battle. So they poured down on to the unfavourable ground and gave us the chance to engage them, although it was very risky to approach them. On this occasion the Tenth legion occupied its usual position, the right wing, and the Third and Fifth the left, and likewise . . . the rest of the auxiliaries and cavalry. Then the battle-cry was raised and the fighting began.

(31) In this situation, although our men had the edge in courage, their opponents defended themselves vigorously from their superior position, and violent was the shouting on both sides and the meeting of the lines as the weapons flew—to such an extent that our men almost ceased to be confident of victory. For the charge and the battle-cry, the things which most terrify an enemy, were comparatively equal. After this, when they turned from these two aspects of battle, in which their courage was evenly matched, to actual fighting, a great many of the opposition were hit by javelins and fell in heaps. We have explained that the men of the Tenth were on the wing; and although they were few in number, their courage none the less enabled them to put great fear into the opposition by their efforts, because they began to exert severe pressure on the enemy's position, with the consequence that one of the opposing legions was brought across to the right wing in support, to stop our troops taking them in the flank.* As soon as this legion was moved, Caesar's cavalry began to press hard on the left wing in such a way that although the enemy could fight with splendid courage, there was no room for reinforcements to reach the line of battle. So as shouts mingled with groans, and the swish of swords fell on their ears, the inexperienced were paralysed with fear. Here, as Ennius says, 'Foot was pressed by foot, and arms were ground by arms',* and although the opposition fought fiercely our men began to drive them back. But the town helped them: broken and fleeing, they would not have survived the day of the Liberalia* unless they had taken refuge in the place they had emerged from. About 30,000 men or rather more fell in the battle, as well as

Labienus and Attius Varus (whose bodies were both given funerals), and about 3,000 Roman equestrians, some from Rome and some from Spain. On our side about 1,000 were lost, partly cavalry, partly infantry, and about 500 wounded. There were captured thirteen eagles, ... standards, ... rods of office, in addition ...

(32) ... from this rout those who had made the town of Munda their refuge, and our men were of necessity forced to blockade them by constructing a ditch and rampart. Shields and spears from the enemy arms were used instead of palings, and instead of turves, corpses were placed side by side; on top, severed heads, all facing the town, were arranged on the tips of swords <to> frighten the enemy ... <so that> the opposition might see exhibited the visible signs of our bravery and be shut inside a palisade. The Gauls then surrounded the town and began to attack it by throwing spears and darts from on top of the enemy corpses.

Young Valerius escaped from the battle with a few cavalrymen and reported what had happened to Sextus Pompeius, who was at Corduba. On receipt of this intelligence, Sextus distributed to the inhabitants of the town such cavalry and cash as he had with him, told them that he was going to discuss peace with Caesar, and left the town before midnight. Gnaeus Pompeius, accompanied by a few cavalry and some infantry, hurried in the opposite direction, to the naval force at Carteia, a town about 170 miles from Corduba. When he reached the eighth milepost from Carteia, Publius Caucilius, who had previously been the camp commander appointed by Pompeius, sent a message in Pompeius' name that the latter was not in a good state, and that the garrison were to send a litter to carry him into the town. Bearers were despatched, and Pompeius was brought into Carteia. His supporters, who supposed he had come secretly, met in the house to which he had been taken to put to him what questions they wished about the war. When the meeting had gathered, Pompeius descended from his litter and entrusted himself to their protection.

(33) Directly after the battle, Caesar, having invested <Munda>, came to Corduba. Those who had escaped there from the slaughter seized the bridge, and when we arrived

began to taunt us, asserting that not many of us had survived the battle and asking us where we were fleeing. So they began to conduct hostilities from the bridge. Caesar crossed the river and made camp. When Scapula, the moving force behind the whole revolt, reached Corduba after the battle, he summoned his household and his ex-slaves, built a pyre for himself, ordered the best possible dinner to be brought and the finest coverlets to be spread, and made presents of silver and money on the spot to his household. He himself dined unhurriedly, and repeatedly anointed himself with resin and nard-oil. Finally he gave orders to a slave and an ex-slave, who was his bedfellow, the one to slit his throat* and the other to set light to the pyre.

(34) As soon as Caesar encamped opposite the town, its inhabitants began to quarrel so fiercely that the noise reached our camp. There were in the town two legions made up <partly> of deserters and partly of slaves who had belonged to the townspeople but had been freed by Sextus Pompeius;* on Caesar's arrival these prepared to come out and do battle. The Thirteenth legion started to defend the town . . . and when they were now fighting it out, the Ninth(?)* occupied some of the towers and the wall. Again they sent representatives to Caesar, to ask him to send legions in to help them. When the deserters became aware of this, they began to set fire to the town. They were worsted by our men and 22,000 were killed, apart from those who had perished outside the wall. In this way Caesar gained possession of the town. While he was busy here, the men who had been blockaded, as we explained above, after the battle made a break-out, but were driven back into the town* with much loss of life.

(35) When Caesar marched on Hispalis, a delegation came to ask him for mercy. So on reaching the town, he sent his senior officer Caninius in with a garrison, while he himself pitched camp by the town. There was a large group of Pompeian supporters inside, and they became very resentful that the garrison had been admitted without the knowledge of a certain Philo, the man who had been the keenest partisan of the Pompeian cause, and was very well known all over Lusitania. Unobserved by the garrison, he set out for

Lusitania and at Lennium met Caecilius Niger, a native, who commanded a substantial band of Lusitanians. On returning to Hispalis, Philo was let through the wall into the town by night again, and they murdered the guards, barred the gates, and renewed their resistance.

(36) While these events were occurring, a delegation from Carteia announced that they had arrested Pompeius. Because they had previously barred their gates against Caesar, they thought that by rendering him this service they would turn their wrongdoing to advantage. At Hispalis, the Lusitanians continued to resist. Noting this, Caesar was afraid that if he pressed on with taking the town, these desperadoes would set fire to it and destroy the walls. So a plan was agreed whereby he allowed them to make a night sally, something they did not think would happen by design. So they broke out and burnt some ships which were on the River Baetis. While our men were delayed by the fire, the Lusitanians made off and were cut down by the cavalry. The town was thus recovered, and Caesar began to march towards Asta, from which community a delegation came to offer surrender. At Munda, a good number of the inhabitants who had taken refuge in the town after the battle surrendered as the siege lengthened, and when they had been conscripted into the legion formed a conspiracy among themselves that at night, when the signal was given, those who were inside the town would break out, while the others would start a massacre in the camp. The plan was discovered, and late the following night, after the order had been circulated, they were all executed outside the rampart.

(37) While Caesar attacked the rest of the towns on his route, the people of Carteia began to quarrel about Pompeius. On one side were those who had sent the delegation to Caesar, on the other those who were supporters of Pompeius. Rioting broke out . . . there was much loss of life, and Pompeius, although wounded, seized twenty warships and fled. The moment the news reached him, Didius, who was in command of the fleet at Gades, set off in rapid pursuit; infantry and cavalry also hurried to pursue Pompeius, again following rapidly. After sailing for four days, Pompeius' ships put in

to land because they had left unprepared and set out from Carteia without water. While they were watering ship, Didius came on them with his fleet, set fire to the ships, and captured several.

(38) Pompeius fled with a few men and took possession of a spot that had natural defences. The cavalry and infantry that had been sent in pursuit of him were informed of this by scouts who had gone ahead, and travelled night and day. Pompeius was badly wounded in the shoulder and left leg. In addition to this he had also twisted his ankle, which severely hampered him. So as he had been brought ashore in a litter he continued to be so carried, according the military fashion of the Lusitanians. When he was sighted by Caesar's force, he was quickly surrounded by the cavalry and cohorts. The place was difficult of access, because the reason Pompeius had occupied a place with natural defences was to ensure that however large a force was brought against him, a handful of men could keep them off from a higher position. Our troops approached from below, but were driven off by missiles. As they withdrew, the opposition pressed enthusiastically after them, and quickly slowed down their approach. When this had occurred several times it was realized that our men were being placed in great danger. The enemy set about building a defensive wall round themselves, and with equal haste our men began to construct encircling fortifications on the ridge, so that they could come to grips with their opponents on equal terms. But when the latter saw this, they took refuge in flight.

(39) As we explained above, Pompeius was wounded and had a twisted ankle. For that reason he was handicapped in making his escape, and because of the difficult terrain he was also unable to seek safety by using a horse or a vehicle. Our men indulged in widespread slaughter. Shut out of any fortification, and bereft of supporters, Pompeius made his way to an eroded gully and tried to conceal himself in a cave, so that if one of the prisoners had not pointed out the place our men would have had difficulty in finding him. This is how he was killed there. His head was brought to Hispalis on 12 April and displayed in public, when Caesar was at Gades.

(40) After young Gnaeus Pompeius had been killed, the above-mentioned Didius, highly delighted, retired into the nearest fort, hauled out some of his ships for repair, and . . .* The Lusitanians who had survived the fight gathered to their standards, and when a force of considerable size had formed went back to face Didius. Although he was careful to keep his ships safe, none the less their frequent sallies sometimes lured him out of the fort and <he was involved> in almost daily engagements <against the Lusitanians. They then> laid a trap and divided their forces into three. There was one group ready to burn the ships, and another to beat off any assistance sent to the ships once they were on fire; these were so stationed as to be <quite invisible. The rest> came out to fight in full view of all. So when Didius advanced out of the fort with his men to drive them away, the signal was hoisted by the Lusitanians and the ships were set on fire. Simultaneously, on the same signal, a great cry was raised and the men who had advanced from the fort to fight were ambushed from the rear as they pursued the fleeing ruffians. Didius died fighting bravely, along with a number of his men. After the battle some seized the small boats which were on the beach, and a fair number extricated themselves by swimming to the ships, which were anchored offshore, and after weighing anchor they began to row out to sea; this action saved their lives. The Lusitanians took possession of their booty. Caesar hurried back to Hispalis from Gades.

(41) Fabius Maximus, whom Caesar had left to besiege the defenders at Munda, had work continue night and day and encircled the town with a fortification. The blockaded inhabitants started to fight among themselves . . . after many had been killed . . . they made a . . . Our men did not let slip the chance of retaking the town and made prisoners of the remainder, 14,000 in number. Then they set out for Urso; the town was set within mighty defences, so that the very site seemed to have been fortified not only by the hand of man but by nature too. In addition, apart from a single supply inside the town itself, there was no water to be found anywhere within a radius of eight miles. This was a factor of great assistance to the townspeople. And the next point was

that it was <difficult to construct?> a siege mound ... and the timber normally used to make siege towers was impossible to find nearer than six miles away, because Pompeius had cut down the timber all around and brought it in so that the town should be safer from attack. It was therefore necessary to withdraw our troops to bring timber from Munda, which they had just captured, to Urso.

(42) While this was happening at Munda and Urso, Caesar went back from Gades to Hispalis and called a public meeting for the next day. He reminded his audience that at the start of his period of office as quaestor* he had made their province, out of all the provinces, his own particular concern and had conferred on them what favours he could at the time. In his subsequent praetorship,* an office of greater weight, he had appealed to the senate against the taxes which Metellus had imposed,* and had freed the province from payment of those sums. At the same time he had assumed the patronage of the province, introduced many deputations to the senate, and defended Spanish interests by taking up many cases, both public and private, at the cost of much personal enmity. Likewise in his consulship,* although he was not present in the province, he conferred what advantages he could on its inhabitants; but in the present war, and previously,* he had discovered that they had forgotten all these benefits and felt no gratitude towards himself or the Roman people. 'You are people who are familiar with international convention and with the institutions of Roman civil life, yet you have behaved like savages; time and again you have laid violent hands on sacrosanct magistrates of the Roman people, and you wished to commit the unspeakable crime of killing Cassius* in broad daylight in the middle of the town square. You have always been such haters of peace that there has never been a time when Roman legions were not stationed in this province. With you, favours are reckoned as injuries, and injuries as favours. Accordingly you have never been able to preserve concord in time of peace, or honour in time of war. Young Gnaeus Pompeius, a man holding no public office, found shelter with you after his escape. He seized authority and the symbols of authority, put many of

our fellow citizens to death, gathered armed support against the Roman people, and at your prompting laid waste the territory of the province. At what point were you going to emerge as victors? Did you not see that if you destroyed me the Roman people possessed legions which were able not simply to resist you but pull down even the heavens? Their glorious record and their courage . . .'*

EXPLANATORY NOTES

THE CIVIL WAR

Numbers refer to books and chapters.

1.1   *the letter should be read out in the senate*: the date is 1 January 49 BC, and the occasion the first meeting of the senate under the presidency of the new consul Lucius Cornelius Lentulus, who like his colleague Gaius Claudius Marcellus was a bitter enemy of Caesar. Some editors think that this is the first sentence of the *Civil War* as Caesar wrote it; but since the narrative neither joins up with the end of the Eighth Book of the *Gallic War* which Hirtius later wrote especially to link Caesar's two accounts, nor provides a reader with any clear facts (however slanted) about the dispute between Caesar and his enemies, it is much more likely that a chapter or more has been lost from the beginning of the work. It is uncharacteristic of Caesar not to tell us what was in such an important document as this letter. It was brought by Curio, who as a tribune had surreptitiously worked to defend Caesar's interests until his year of office terminated on 10 December, when he went to join Caesar in the Po Valley; and the tribunes who put pressure on Lentulus and Marcellus to read it out were Marcus Antonius (Mark Antony) and Quintus Cassius.

   Scipio: Q. Caecilius Metellus Pius Scipio, Pompey's father-in-law (see Glossary).

1.2   *Pompey was nearby*: Pompey could not enter the centre of Rome, that is the area within the sacred boundary called the *pomoerium*, because he was the (absentee) governor of the two provinces of Spain and held a species of authority (proconsular *imperium*) which lapsed if he entered the city. He was at this time living in his house in the suburbs.

   the two legions: to meet a threat from the Parthians, the senate had decided in the summer of 50 that Pompey and Caesar should each give up one legion, which would be sent to Syria. Pompey surrendered a legion which he had previously lent to Caesar, so that the latter effectively lost two. They were at the present time supposed to be *en route* for the East.

Marcus Rufus: M. Caelius Rufus (see Glossary).

committing an act hostile to the state: this form of words served as a warning to obstructive or revolutionary persons that force might be used against them.

1.3   *the Comitium*: this was the original civic assembly-place in the Forum, where soldiers had no place. Caesar is implying that arms had now completely invaded and taken over civil life.

one of the censors: the censorship was the crown of a civil career, since a pair of censors were elected, to hold office for eighteen months, only once every five years or so.

1.4   *Cato . . . electoral defeat*: M. Porcius Cato, one of Caesar's most determined opponents, had stood unsuccessfully for the consulship of 51 (see Glossary).

a second Sulla: L. Cornelius Sulla (see Glossary) used his power as dictator to exile or put to death hundreds of his former opponents and to profit from the confiscation of their property.

their family connection: Pompey had been married to Caesar's daughter Julia from April 59 until she died in childbirth in 54 BC. Before this alliance the two men had been in opposed political camps.

1.5   *veto . . . untouched*: Sulla saw the tribunate as a prime source of discord in the state. He therefore severely restricted the tribunes' powers to legislate, and barred them from holding higher office; but their right to veto other magistrates (and each other) was fundamental to their historic role as protectors of the commons against executive power, and he did not touch it.

the famous revolutionary tribunes of earlier times: Caesar appears to refer to P. Sulpicius and P. Antistius (88 BC), L. Appuleius Saturninus (100 BC), Gaius Gracchus (122 BC), and Tiberius Gracchus (133 BC).

last and final decree of the senate: this decree, commonly known as the *senatus consultum ultimum* or *s.c.u.*, and first used in the crisis which led to the death of Gaius Gracchus early in 121 BC, in fact conferred no powers on the magistrates that they did not already possess. It simply gave them the moral backing to act resolutely, by assuring them of the support of the senate.

1.5   *the two comitial days*: 3 and 4 Jan. were days set aside for
meetings of the electoral or legislative assemblies of the
Roman people (if required).

the tribunes: Marcus Antonius and Quintus Cassius. They
were accompanied by Curio (see first note to ch. 1) and
Caelius Rufus (see ch. 2).

1.6   *outside the city*: i.e. outside the sacred boundary, to allow
Pompey to attend (see I.2 n., *Pompey was nearby*).

Marcellus: the consul, not his brother mentioned in ch. 2.

duly recorded: decisions of the senate, unless they were
vetoed (as here), or overridden by the popular assembly,
acquired *prima facie* validity in this way.

men who were not holding office: Pompey had passed a
law in 52 BC which interposed a five-year gap between a
man's tenure of the consulship or praetorship in Rome, and
any subsequent appointment as a provincial governor. Previously, the two periods had been continuous and the executive authority (*imperium*) acquired by initial election to the
magistracy was simply *extended* by senatorial decree. Caesar
is here making a slightly theoretical and certainly contro-
versial point: since Scipio and Domitius had laid down their
imperium at the end of their consulships (52 and 54 BC respectively), they had become men 'deprived' (the root meaning of *privatus*, 'private') of that authority, and the senate
alone (unlike the assembly of the sovereign Roman people)
did not have any power to *confer* it on them again. As for
the persons mentioned, Scipio's appointment was clearly
illegal under Pompey's own five-year rule, and L. Domitius
Ahenobarbus was a fanatical opponent of Caesar, while
both the men passed over (for whatever reasons), L. Aurelius
Cotta (consul in 65) and L. Marcius Philippus (consul in
56), were not only fully legal appointees but also related
to Caesar.

<*without taking the auspices*>: before solemn acts of state,
which included departure from Rome, the consuls or other
responsible magistrates would ensure that the gods were
favourable by noting the behaviour of birds (or other animals), and particularly of the sacred chickens kept for the
purpose. This behaviour was interpreted by diviners known
as augurs.

attended by lictors: holders of *imperium* (see note above)
were escorted by lictors, attendants who carried the sym-

bols of their authority, the rods and axes. Caesar is both amplifying the point he has just made, that Scipio, Domitius, and the unnamed praetorian provincial governors were not valid holders of the *imperium* they purported to possess, and adding another—that even if this *imperium* had been valid, it was still constitutionally improper to exercise it within the city of Rome: only elected magistrates during their year of office could do so.

1.7 *an address to his soldiers*: Caesar is still at Ravenna.

Sulla . . . what they had previously possessed: on Sulla, see I.5 n. (*veto*); Pompey, as consul in 70, had restored most of the powers removed by Sulla. Caesar's argument is that this was an illusory gain, because Pompey and his supporters had now shown themselves prepared to ignore the tribunician veto, which was the bedrock, left intact even by Sulla, on which the other powers ultimately rested.

temples and commanding positions were seized: in order to gain a good position for rioting.

Saturninus and the Gracchi: L. Appuleius Saturninus, tribune in 103 and 100, Tiberius Gracchus, tribune in 133, and the latter's brother Gaius, tribune in 123 and 122, were all killed in civil violence led or instigated by senatorial 'hard-liners' during or shortly after the end of their periods of office. In the cases of Saturninus and Gaius Gracchus the *s.c.u.* was first passed (see I.5 n., *last and final decree*).

1.8 *Ariminum*: Caesar suppresses the fact that Ariminum, though not far away, lay in Italy and that *en route* he had to cross the Rubicon, the river which marked the southern boundary of Cisalpine Gaul and therefore the limit of his legal authority. By crossing it with troops, he became a mutinous lawbreaker.

ordered to follow after him: in fact, only the Eighth and Twelfth legions came on to Italy, the other six being pulled southwards from their various positions in Transalpine Gaul in order to be able to counter a possible movement of Pompey's legions overland from Spain, but still prevent much likelihood of a Gallic uprising.

1.9 *more important than his life*: it is illuminating for the values of the Roman Late Republican élite that Caesar could advance such an intensely personal reason for inflicting war on his native country. Note also Cicero's startling and almost exactly contemporary definition of the cultured man

(*Partitiones Oratoriae*, 90): 'There are two kinds of man: one uncultured and rustic [*indoctum et agreste*] who always puts his own advantage before what is right, the other cultivated and refined [*humanum atque expolitum*] who puts his standing [*dignitas*, Caesar's word] above all else.'

1.9   *candidature in absence at the next elections*: the elections are those of late summer 49, to elect magistrates for 48, when Caesar was legally entitled to be consul again after a ten-year interval (cf. III.1). At the time when Pompey passed his law allowing Caesar to stand in absence for the consulship, Caesar could have expected to have been replaced as proconsul of Gaul not before the early days of 48, since his successor would have to be one of the magistrates holding office in Rome in 49 (see Introduction, p. xviii). By bowing now to pressure to return to Rome in the summer of 49 and campaign for the consulship in person (see I.10 n.). Caesar was forfeiting six months of this expected tenure (and incidentally—an important fact he does not mention—laying himself open to prosecution, as a private individual no longer protected by tenure of office, for the illegal acts of his first consulship).

a letter to the senate: almost certainly the letter referred to at the opening of ch. 1.

1.10   *reported Caesar's demands*: probably on 23 Jan., Pompey and the consuls having left Rome on 17–18 Jan. (see ch. 14). Caesar's terms are spelt out more fully by Cicero (*Letters to his Friends*, XVI.12.3): Pompey to go to Spain, levies and forces in Italy to be dismissed, Domitius Ahenobarbus to take over Nearer and Considius Nonianus Further Gaul, himself to canvass in person and present his name as a candidate within seventeen days.

1.11   *And so from Ariminum . . .* : Caesar obscures the order of events by this apparently logical transition. We know from the contemporary correspondence of Cicero that Ariminum, Pisaurum, Arretium, and possibly Ancona had all fallen to Caesar by 16 Jan., yet he cannot have had his first interviews with Roscius and young Lucius Caesar much, if at all, before 17 or 18 Jan. His negotiations *may* have been in good faith, but their relationship with actual events has been considerably 'improved' in his account.

1.12   *praetor*: as often, for propraetor, the technically correct term for a man holding the authority but not the actual office of a praetor; Thermus was one of several former magistrates reinvested with power of command for the war against Caesar.

Attius: P. Attius Varus (see Glossary).

1.13 *imperator*: this was originally purely a title of honour, meaning 'victorious commander', bestowed by acclamation on a general by his army after a great victory (e.g. on Curio at the Bagradas, II.26). It later also came to be used as a word for 'general'. Here the former meaning is the relevant one, emphasizing the publicly and formally recognized greatness of Caesar's military achievements.

1.14 *When news . . . reached Rome, . . . Lentulus . . . fled*: the news is that of the fall of Ariminum, Pisaurum, etc. (see I.11 n.), which provoked the departure of the consuls on 18 Jan. Caesar's arrangement of the narrative makes it appear that the panic at Rome *followed* the breakdown of negotiations between himself and Pompey.

colonists . . . settled there by the Julian Law: the Romans had confiscated prime land belonging to Capua because the city had supported Hannibal, and leased it out for the public profit until Caesar's consulship in 59. Caesar's law (the Julian Law) set up a colony at Capua and settled on this land Roman poor who were the fathers of three or more children.

the Campanian Assembly: this was the name of the collectivity of Campanians (= Capuans) before 59, when they lacked local self-government. Caesar's use of the term here suggests that the municipal government restored to the city when it became a colony (see previous note) was reserved to his new colonists and that the institutions operated by the existing inhabitants continued to function in some way. It is obvious that the old inhabitants would have resented Caesar's colonists and tended to support Pompey, hence it was to them that Pompey (not Lentulus, as Caesar alleges: see Cicero, *Letters to Atticus*, VII.14.2, VIII.2.1, and Shackleton-Bailey's commentary (Cambridge, 1965–70)) distributed the gladiators. This story of Lentulus' attempt to use the gladiators as troops appears to be pure invention.

1.15 *Labienus*: for Titus Labienus, see Glossary. Cingulum was his home town, established during the process of urbanization that took place in this area of Italy during the third–first centuries BC but not given formal existence and the appropriate municipal buildings until the 60s or 50s BC.

1.15 *the Twelfth legion caught up with him*: since the Twelfth had been in Transalpine Gaul at the beginning of the winter and could never have caught up with Caesar by this time (early February) unless it had received the order to march well before Caesar crossed the Rubicon, this apparently routine statement has enormous importance for a proper assessment of Caesar's willingness to resort to force in his quarrel with the Pompeians.

dismissed him: this is a gross misrepresentation of a course of action that must have been agreed between Vibullius and Spinther, who remained in command of troops (see I.22, and Cicero, *Letters to Atticus*, VII.23.1). Since Spinther was an ex-consul, and Vibullius Rufus a mere equestrian agent of Pompey's, the suggestion that he was dismissed by Vibullius is rather like a modern report alleging, say, that a cabinet minister was dismissed by a prime minister's personal aide.

Domitius: L. Domitius Ahenobarbus. His stand at Corfinium was against Pompey's wishes; he hoped to be able to trap Caesar in the enclosed Paelignian plain between himself and Pompey's forces (see next ch.).

1.16 *Firmum was in his hands*: probably by 4 Feb.

1.17 *Pompey in Apulia*: Pompey was at Luceria.

twenty-four acres per head: the Latin measurement is 40 *iugera*; individual allotments of about this size seem to be fairly standard for settlements of the period, and the amount of land required, between 500 and 600 square miles, is not beyond the resources of a great land-holding family of the Late Republic such as the Domitii.

1.18 *Within three days the Eighth legion reached him*: i.e. by 18 Feb. See I.15 n., *Twelfth legion*, on the implications of this. With all these new forces Caesar now had the equivalent of just over five legions, which further recruiting increased to six by the time he reached Brundisium (ch. 25).

1.19 *Pompey had in fact written back*: three letters from Pompey to Domitius are preserved in Cicero's correspondence (*Letters to Atticus*, VIII.12B–12D). Pompey's points are that Caesar will not allow Domitius a battle, but would proceed by blockade, and that he himself cannot trust either the effectiveness of his new recruits or the loyalty of the two veteran legions he has acquired from Caesar.

1.22 *to assert his own freedom . . . an oligarchic clique*: this was evidently a political slogan of the time, being repeated in almost exactly the same words by Augustus in the opening sentence of his *Res Gestae* to justify his own insurrection against the state in 44–43 BC.

1.23 *Roman equestrians*: see Glossary, *s.v.* Equestrian Order.

Caecilius Rufus: as an ex-praetor (57 BC) Caecilius Rufus is given his correct ranking in the list between the two ex-consuls (of whom Domitius precedes as commander) and the serving quaestor.

Quintilius Varus: he made his way to Africa after being released by Caesar. See II.28.

on that day moved camp and completed a normal march: the day was 21 Feb. (Cicero, *Letters to Atticus*, VIII.14.1), and a normal march could apparently be as little as eight Roman miles or 12 km. (see III.76, end).

1.24 *Lucius Manlius*: L. Manlius Torquatus (see Glossary).

1.25 *he arrived at Brundisium with six legions*: on 9 March, by Caesar's own report (Cicero, *Letters to Atticus*, IX.13A).

Dyrrachium: modern Dürres (Durazzo) in Albania, the port giving access to the western end of the Via Egnatia, which led across to Macedonia.

1.26 *Magius . . . had not been sent back to him*: this was not true. A letter of Caesar's own survives (Cicero, *Letters to Atticus*, IX.13A): 'I reached Brundisium on 9 March and encamped by the walls. Pompey is in Brundisium. He sent Numerius Magius to me to discuss peace. I replied as I thought best . . .'

1.27 *. . . intended to withdraw from Italy*: from Cicero's correspondence between January and March it seems that Pompey always had it in mind to withdraw from Italy if he saw no chance of matching Caesar there, but (naturally) did not advertise his intention.

1.28 *Pompey set sail*: on 17 March.

1.29 *Gaul, Picenum, and the Straits*: 'Gaul' means the Adriatic coast of Cisalpine Gaul, including such places as Ravenna and Aquileia, and 'the Straits' the Straits of Messina, through which any ships from the western Mediterranean would have to come.

1.29 *a veteran army*: Pompey had seven legions in Spain, as detailed by Caesar in ch. 38.

1.30 *as propraetor*: Curio was to take over from Cato as governor. He did not in fact set out for Sicily until after the middle of April.

<Lucius> Tubero: L. Aelius Tubero, for whom see the following chapter.

he fled the province: 23 April.

1.31 *as described above*: ch. 13.

finding it without a governor: it is not clear why Caesar ignores the fact that the previous governor C. Considius Longus (who should have handed over to Tubero when the latter arrived) was still in the province.

1.32 *the senate was called*: on 1 April.

the legitimate interval: ten years; see I.9 n., *candidature in absence*.

in Pompey's own consulship: 52 BC. For the law, see Introduction, p. xviii.

what they demanded of a rival: Caesar means that his opponents wanted him to lay down his command, but did not make the same request of Pompey.

taking his legions: the two referred to in chs. 2 and 9.

1.33 *whatever else Caesar decided to do*: Caesar chooses not to report the famous episode in which Metellus tried to stop Caesar raiding the inner treasury (the contents of which were supposed to be reserved for use in times of national emergency). Caesar's implication in ch. 14 above that Lentulus had already opened this treasury is almost certainly false.

1.34 *When he reached the province*: on or about 19 April.

gain control of Massilia: as Domitius was fully entitled to do, being the duly (if controversially) appointed proconsul of Gaul (see ch. 6).

earlier benefits to them: see note to next chapter, *Volcae Arecomici . . .*

1.35 *the Fifteen*: Strabo describes the Massiliot constitution: 'of all aristocracies theirs is the best ordered, since they have established a council of six hundred men who hold office for life. . . . Over the council are set fifteen of its number, and to them is given the handling of day-to-day business. And three again of the fifteen preside over them, holding supreme authority' (4.179C).

a single individual: Pompey.

Volcae Arecomici . . . Helvii . . . Sallyes: these are all tribes in the neighbourhood of the (extensive) territory of Massilia; it is likely that it was Caesar who assigned the first two to the Massiliot state (in the late 50s), and Pompey the third (in the 70s), but there are difficulties both with the manuscript readings and with Caesar's meaning, and the matter is far from certain.

1.36 *three legions*: these must have been the legions under Trebonius' command (VI, X, and XIV) which had wintered in central Gaul.

1.37 *three legions*: the three legions which Fabius had brought south to Narbo (modern Narbonne) from central Gaul at the same time (December?) as Caesar withdrew the Twelfth from him for service in Italy were VII, IX, and XI.

the other legions: Caesar appears to be referring to the three veteran legions which he had been using for his Italian campaign, namely VIII, XII, and XIII, since he had no others apart from those mentioned in the two preceding notes and any newly recruited in Italy during the course of his recent campaign there. These three veteran legions had to march from southern Italy after ejecting Pompey from Brundisium, and can hardly have arrived at Massilia before the very end of May. When they did, one at least and possibly all three took over siege duties, allowing a different combination of three (which included XIV, see ch. 46) to go on to Ilerda to join Fabius' three.

the pass: almost certainly the Col de la Perche.

1.38 *as noted*: in ch. 34.

Pompey's deputies: although appointed governor of Spain in 55, Pompey never subsequently visited the two provinces. For his individual deputies, see Glossary.

1.39 *mountain peoples who border the province of Gaul*: that is, peoples living in the Massif Central and on the French side of the Alps. Caesar distinguishes the old province of Gaul established in 121 (south of the Massif Central) from the regions of the centre and north, conquered by himself.

1.40 *two bridges . . . four miles apart*: Fabius was on the same side of the river as the town, that is on the right or north-western bank, and presumably some 2–4 km. upriver of it. The bridges were temporary wooden ones, one of them by his camp and the other further upstream.

1.41 *Two days later*: about 23 June.

1.44 *their open side*: their right, unprotected by the shield which was carried on the left arm.

1.46 *a leading centurion*: in Latin *primi pili centurio*, that is the senior centurion of the whole legion, who had charge of the first century of the first cohort.

1.48 *as has been explained above*: Caesar has not in fact explained this, which may be seen as confirmation that he had not given his manuscript a final revision. The town of Ilerda, and both camps, lay on the western bank of the Segre, which flows roughly N–S; the Cinca flows into the Segre from the north-west, the confluence being about 30 km. downstream of Ilerda.

thirty miles: Caesar means thirty miles upstream from Ilerda, i.e. the point where the rivers debouch from the hills.

the cattle: on the unpopularity of meat as an item of soldiers' diet, see III.47 n.

1.52 *fifty <denarii> a bushel*: a *modius* ('bushel') contained anything between 6¼ and nearly 7 kg.; any attempt to be more precise is impossible, given the lack of standardization of ancient measures. Some idea of the normal cost of grain in the Late Republic may be gained from Cicero, who says that at one *as* (one quarter of a sesterce) per *modius* it was very cheap (*de Officiis*, 2.58), and at five *denarii* (20 sesterces) very dear. The price here seems quite extraordinarily high, and although it is not impossible one must note that it is the result of an emendation which assumes that X is an abbreviation for *denarius*, and not part of the numeral.

1.53 *Gnaeus Pompeius*: I reproduce Caesar's formal method of referring to Pompey here.

1.54 *his experience of Britain*: in the campaigns of 55 and 54 BC Caesar had met the British sea-going coracle, a more substantial affair than the better-known round or egg-shaped one-man river craft.

twenty-two miles from his camp: there is a suitable crossing-point conforming to Caesar's description, and at the right distance, just below a place called Llorenç de Montgai.

1.56 *tenants and shepherds he had brought with him*: see ch. 34.

the island which is opposite Massilia: Ratonneau, directly off Marseille, famous nowadays for the prison of Château d'If standing on a tiny islet beside it.

1.57 *front-line troops*: in Latin, *antesignani*—troops who fought 'in front of the standards'.

1.59 *fortune swiftly changed*: on the importance and mutability of fortune cf. chs. 52 and 72 and the similar idea at III.27 and 72. A calculation backwards from the known date of the end of the Ilerda campaign (ch. 83 n.) gives the end of June as the date of the sea battle.

1.61 *Celtiberia*: south and west of their present position.

the earlier war with Sertorius: for a full account of this, see Plutarch, *Sertorius*, 7-27. Quintus Sertorius had been a supporter of Marius in the civil war against Sulla, but anticipated the defeat of his side and left Italy in 83 BC to seek a base in the West. Ejected once from Spain, he made a comeback and was so successful that he kept two Roman commanders, Pompey and Metellus Pius, at bay for several years (77-74 BC). Ultimately he was forced from Celtiberia to the north side of the Ebro Valley, and was murdered (at Osca) by his subordinate Perperna (who was shortly afterwards abandoned by his allies and defeated). Afranius had served as an officer of Pompey's in this war.

1.64 *their march was six miles longer*: this means that Caesar's ford was three miles upstream of the stone bridge at Ilerda.

1.65 *mountains were close by*: Caesar refers to the wide and deep valley broken by many ridges and hills through which the Ebro finds its way on this stretch of its course. This valley's northern edge, which lies anything between 1 and 10 km. from the river, is constituted (for anyone approaching, like Caesar and his opponents, from the north) by little more than a low ridge dominated at the end nearer the Segre by the volcano-shaped cone of Montmaneu.

1.68 *very deep and difficult gullies*: these are the numerous torrent-beds which intersect the landscape. Although they are mostly wide and flat-bottomed, their sides are miniature cliffs formed of bands of crumbling rock and earth. Occasional low flat-topped hills, nearly as awkward to surmount, constitute further impediments to progress.

1.69 *to the right*: Caesar was attempting to outflank Afranius to the east, on the opposite side to the River Segre.

1.72 *their camp*: that is, the one they had left in such a hurry that morning.

1.73 *Tarraco*: this town (modern Tarragona), the capital of the Nearer province, lay about four days' march to the SE.

1.74 *the great general*: this expression attempts to convey the flavour of the fact that Afranius' troops referred to Caesar as *imperator*, a title which they should only have used for their own supreme commander Pompey.

Sulpicius: P. Sulpicius Rufus.

his earlier leniency: e.g. at Corfinium.

1.75 *his praetorian cohort*: the cohort which acted as the general's bodyguard in battle.

wrapped their left hands in their cloaks: to serve as a substitute for a shield.

1.78 *twenty-two [?] days' rations*: Roman legionaries sometimes carried provisions for more than a fortnight, but Afranius expected to reach the Ebro in two or three days, if that. Furthermore, it has been calculated that 22 days' rations would weigh 17 kg., whereas the Roman military writer Vegetius (1.19) gives the entire marching load of a legionary as 60 lb. (19.6 kg.). On both counts the figure of 22 must be corrupt; 12 or 8 are the most likely corrections, and either would make sense in the context.

1.83 *On the following day*: 2 August of the pre-Julian system, as recorded in the inscribed calendars of the Julio-Claudian period. The true (astronomical) date is early June, because of the tendency of the official calendar to run ahead of the astronomical calendar.

a ford in the River Segre: in normal times, i.e. outside the periods of snow-melt or exceptional storms, the river is shallow, running in a wide gravel bed for many miles below Ilerda.

1.84 *the ultimate punishment*: Caesar means death.

1.85   *thanks to a long period of peace needed no protection*: it was probably true that such a large army was not required in Spain so long as the object was simply to preserve the status quo; on the other hand, the later experience of Augustus, under whom the country was finally brought entirely under Roman rule, showed that a large army was definitely necessary to bring the unconquered and only half-pacified areas to the north and west under control. As to the 'long period of peace', Caesar himself had campaigned effectively enough in 61–60 to be awarded a triumph.

same man . . . absentee governor: i.e. Pompey, who was simultaneously consul (in 52) and proconsul of Spain, without ever visiting the latter.

rules for holding magistracies had been changed: see I.6 n. 'men who were not holding office'.

II.1   *washed by the sea on three sides*: namely the coast running NE to the bay of La Joliette, the nose of the promontory in the centre, and the port to the S (the modern Vieux-Port, a deep but now partly silted-up inlet to the south of the ridge on which the ancient city stood).

a siege-ramp eighty feet high: the usual siege-ramp (*agger*) was a bank made of earth with heavy timber shoring, so that it was liable to attack with fire (cf. ch. 14). Its great height here was probably made necessary by the 'very deep valley' just mentioned, plus the height of the wall it had eventually to match. The object was to advance it to the wall of the besieged town so as to allow either entry over the top, or the use of a ram or the driving of tunnels from the protection of a chamber in the front of the structure. As it was pushed forward sheds (*plutei*) and screens (*vineae*) were placed on it and around it (cf. ch. 15) to protect the workers and the other soldiers who were defending them.

II.2   *artillery*: in Latin, *tormenta*, which were like large mounted cross-bows.

a sixty-foot 'tortoise': a mobile, armoured hut under the protection of whose carapace the ground-clearing necessary for the secure foundation of the *agger* (presumably 60 feet wide at its base) could take place.

the Albici: see I.34.

II.3   *Curio*: see I.30.

II.4   *their previous battle*: see I.56–58.

Tauroeis: known to Strabo as Tauroention, one of a chain of Massiliot settlements designed to secure the coast to the east against the Sallyes of the interior.

II.6   *when the ships did lie together*: it was the aim of the out-manœuvred Caesarian ships to grapple their opponents and turn the battle into a hand-to-hand engagement on a floating platform. Conversely, the Massiliot aim was to split up and ram their opponents individually.

II.8   *height of a tower*: conventional siege-towers were made of timber and sometimes mobile.

II.9   *siege-shed and screens*: these were evidently those used to protect the tower and its builders at the beginning.

II.10   *enemy wall and tower*: the walls of Massilia included numerous stone towers; the singular is used here to denote the one which was under immediate attack from the Caesarian tower.

water . . . washing them to pieces: the bricks referred to were unbaked (Latin *later*, opposed to *testa*, baked brick).

quilts: soaked in water.

II.11   *sacred ribbons*: these were bands of coloured wool worn both by priests and by sacrificial animals. In circumstances like those described here they performed the function of the white flag in our society, but also implicitly invoked divine protection.

II.12   *highly educated men*: Massilia was famous for its schools of rhetoric.

II.13   *treachery and contempt*: translated into less partisan language, this only means the Massiliot decision to support Pompey and mount active resistance to Caesar's army.

II.14   *an act of treacherous cunning*: Dio (XLI.25.2) has a rather different version, according to which Caesar's soldiers made a night attack during a 'sort of truce', to which the inhabitants responded so vigorously that the soldiers did not dare make any further attempts. If this is true the treachery was not one-sided, and it may be the explanation of the surprising fact that even after destroying the siege-works in the manner here described the Massiliots were granted another truce on the same terms (ch. 16).

II.16   *the shortness of the range*: at short range the *tormenta* had to fire at an angle of depression. That they could not do this was presumably due to their fixed positioning relative to the wall apertures through which they fired.

II.17 *Marcus Varro*: see I.38.

II.18 *against the interests of the state*: equivalent here to 'in Caesar's interests'.

On an island: the sand-bar connecting Gades (Cadiz) to the mainland was not there in antiquity.

II.19 *Quintus Cassius, tribune of the people*: Caesar's normal motive in mentioning official positions is to stress that elected magistrates of the state were on his side, but in this case the mention of Cassius' tribunate is somewhat two-edged: tribunes of the people were not supposed to go more than a mile from the boundary of Rome during their year of office. Possibly he intended to contrast his own deputy, an elected magistrate of the Roman people, with Varro's, a mere equestrian who chanced by on a financial errand.

the association of Roman citizens: when a number of Roman citizens found themselves living in a non-Roman community, they often formed themselves into a *conventus*, a sort of club or association, which because of the power and standing of Rome had a great deal of influence, as here. Such associations of Roman citizens are found in both eastern and western halves of the empire (cf. chs. 20, 36, and III.9, 29).

cohorts of the sort called 'settler': probably recruited not from Roman citizens (who would have been eligible for the ordinary legions) but from Romanized native farmers, perhaps of Italian descent, or from Roman citizens who were too old for normal service.

II.20 *called the local one*: in Latin, *legio vernacula*; this was composed of Roman citizens born in Further Spain, and appears again in *Alexandrian War*, chs. 53 ff., and *Spanish War*, chs. 7, 10, 12, and 20.

II.21 *the four legions*: Caesar's two and Varro's two.

travelled . . . to Massilia: Caesar perhaps arrived towards the end of October.

the appointment of a dictator: the dictatorship was an emergency office, allowing a single man unlimited authority for a limited period of time (six months). The Romans made frequent use of this office for both military and political emergencies between the fifth and third centuries, but it effectively became obsolete with the rise of Rome to the status of a world power as a result of the Hannibalic war, and would have passed into oblivion had it not been needed by Sulla in 82 BC to provide him with a means whereby he could easily and without procedural opposition carry through a large number of constitutional reforms. Caesar, who at this stage was still posing as a republican constitutionalist, will not yet have wished to don Sulla's mantle (though he later did so), and the most plausible explanation for his nomination as dictator was to enable the election of consuls for the following year to take place, as those who should have carried out this task (Lentulus and Marcellus) were in Greece with Pompey. Many of the early dictators were appointed for precisely this purpose.

II.23 *Concurrently with these events*: an extremely vague indication; in fact Curio probably did not set sail for Africa until the beginning of August. Although he is represented (in ch. 32) as knowing already, when he had barely arrived at Utica, that Caesar had defeated Afranius and Petreius, which occurred on 2 August, a less rhetorical and possibly more reliable synchronism is given by the statement (in ch. 37) that news of Caesar's successes (unspecified) in Spain was starting to reach Africa some days later.

Young Lucius Caesar: the man who had acted as an intermediary in the opening stages of Caesar's invasion of Italy (I.8–10).

the war with the pirates: Pompey's Mediterranean-wide campaign of 67–66 BC.

II.24 *Scipio's Camp*: in the Latin, *Castra Cornelia*, so called because P. Cornelius Scipio Africanus (the Elder) camped there when he attacked Utica in 204/3 BC. The ridge (Kalaat el Oued) is about 60 feet high and, though now several kilometres distant from the shore, once fell steeply into the sea on three sides.

II.25 *King Juba ... Pompey ... Curio ...*: Juba was son of Hiempsal, who had been made king of Numidia by Pompey when he conquered the Marians in Africa in 81 BC; Juba had also once been involved in a physically violent altercation with Caesar when the latter was defending a Numidian noble, Masintha, against the king (Suetonius, *Divus Julius*, 71). Curio's proposal in 50 to annex Numidia as a province was not novel: according to Cicero, Hiempsal bribed the tribune Rullus to safeguard his kingdom from exactly this fate in 63 BC. Juba's loyalties in the present conflict were therefore a foregone conclusion (cf. I.6).

II.26   *hailed as 'Victorious General'*: on 'Victorious General' see note on *imperator* in I.13. A note of sarcasm is detectable in the preceding 'exploits' (*res gestae*, a term normally implying at least noteworthiness and often a very great deal more, but capable of quite literal translation as 'things done'). Curio had patently done nothing to justify such a salutation.

II.28   *as mentioned above*: I.23.

the memory of their first oath*: the Roman military oath (*sacramentum*) was binding until the general to whom it had been sworn discharged his men. Since it is very unlikely that Domitius did this, Curio's legionaries, although they would have sworn a fresh oath to Caesar, might well have felt themselves under some kind of moral pressure in their current situation.

II.29   *Civil war ... for the worse*: this passage is badly damaged in the manuscripts, and nothing is gained by trying to restore it.

II.32   *myself, whom he held very dear*: the device of having another speak allows Caesar a rare expression of personal feeling.

Sicily and Africa, without which he cannot keep Rome and Italy safe: before the annexation of Egypt in 30 BC, Africa and Sicily were the principal sources of grain for the population of Rome. If he could not feed Rome, the consequences for Caesar might be very serious.

Domitius desert you: for Domitius' behaviour at Corfinium, see I.19–20.

loss of legal rights: by surrendering, a Roman suffered *deminutio capitis*, that is forfeiture of his rights as a citizen (and *a fortiori* as a magistrate).

my conscientiousness: but note Caesar's observation (ch. 3) about Curio's carelessness.

II.36   *the populace, ... the citizens, ... the association of Romans*: Caesar distinguishes between (i) the *incolae*, who are the native population of the surrounding districts (cf. ch. 25), under the administration of the town but possessing restricted civic rights; (ii) the full citizens of the town, more privileged and less numerous than the first group; and (iii) those Roman citizens who lived or did business in Utica, for whose association (*conventus*) and its importance see note to ch. 19. What favour Caesar had conferred on group (ii) above is not known, but it was by a *lex Iulia* (*African War*, ch. 87) and presumably therefore dates to 59.

II.38   *his kingdom*: Numidia bordered the province of Africa (roughly modern Tunisia, but smaller) to the west and south.

II.39   *'You see, men . . . That the king is not present'*: Caesar uses a story-telling motif that is at least as old as Herodotus, namely the wrongly interpreted answer. Croesus thought, when the Delphic oracle said that a great empire would fall if he crossed the River Halys, that the Persian empire and not his own was meant (Herodotus, I.53). Here, Curio thinks that because the king is not at the Bagradas he is nowhere near. In both cases reflection, or further questioning, would have prevented the disaster. But Curio is driven on to his fate by his overweening confidence (cf. chs. 32, 37). The element of tragedy is further emphasized by the dramatic device of direct speech, for the third and final occasion in the book.

II.44   *with several senators in train*: Roman senators had been in the habit for at least a hundred years of giving orders to, not following in the train of, such vassal kings as Juba— who owed his throne to Pompey (see note to ch. 25). It had been Roman senators, not foreign kings, who took decisions such as the ones Juba is here represented as making. Not for the first time, Caesar emphasizes the topsy-turvy world of the Pompeians.

III.1   *as dictator*: see II.21 n.

    <Gaius> Julius and Publius Servilius . . . to become consul: (*a*) omission of third names (*cognomina*), in this case respectively Caesar and Isauricus, is a feature of formal style, and is often found in official documents or when consuls' names serve as dates. Here, this method of reference lends an air of objectivity and impersonality to Caesar's report and helps to validate, for the reader, the result of what must have been a most untypical election. (*b*) Sulla had re-enacted an older law which had come to be flagrantly disregarded in his lifetime, namely that ten years had to elapse before a

man could be re-elected to the consulship. Thus Caesar, consul in 59, could not without special dispensation hold a second consulship until 48.

since credit had become difficult: in the absence of sophisticated financial institutions, in Roman society the normal collateral for substantial loans was landed property. A great deal of this land was in the hands of the upper class, who were also required by the political system of the Late Republic to have available from time to time very large amounts of cash, which they spent on the voters of the metropolis in the expectation of being able to recoup it later by plundering the provincials or the enemies of Rome. There was thus a permanent, if shifting, indebtedness among the politically active. In addition, wealthy non-senators, who were the only people who could take the great state contracts, such as that for the collection of the taxes of the province of Asia, gave security at least partly in land. A collapse in the price of land would have been disastrous for debtors, and if there had been many forced sales of large estates by creditors attempting to recover their loans the market would have become further depressed. Another factor which contributed to the crisis of credit was the tendency of people to hoard cash in times of great political uncertainty like the present (Dio, XLI.38, reporting Caesar's edict restricting cash holdings to 60,000 sesterces in silver or gold). Hence Caesar's scheme to force creditors to accept land and other property (such as urban rented housing, brick-pits, potteries, fisheries, and ships) in settlement at pre-war values.

by praetors and tribunes: that is, not by himself. Caesar wishes to stress the constitutional propriety of his actions.

Pompey's law on electoral corruption: this law was passed in 52 BC, in Pompey's third consulship. The existing laws against electoral bribery had been insufficient to prevent flagrant misbehaviour by the consuls and consular candidates in 54 and by the candidates in 53. Pompey's law, which took into account offences from as far back as 70 BC, stiffened the penalty to exile for life, and set up a speedier judicial procedure (see next note).

trials . . . being completed each in a single day . . . give the verdict: Caesar distorts the facts: three days were allowed for the hearing of witnesses by a panel of 360 jurors, and a further day for certain formalities, before the delivery on the fifth day of the speeches for the prosecution and the defence to a lot-selected group of 81 of the jurors. These were then reduced by challenges to 51, who had to give a verdict on the same day. It is true that all 360 jurors were unlikely to have been present on the first three days, and therefore that some of the lot-selected 81 might indeed not have heard the arguments; but it is doubtful whether any such would have survived the challenges. The purpose of this machinery was to speed up court procedure and allow the settling of several old scores, though these were not all to the advantage of Pompey and his current political allies.

III.2   *eleven days*: approximately 13–24 December by the official calendar (late October by the sun).

the Gauls: Caesar's main providers of cavalry.

III.3   *tax companies of the provinces which he himself held*: these tax companies were the associations of rich non-senators who contracted (by public auction or otherwise) to collect the taxes due to Rome in the various provinces, which did not all have the same system of taxation. Since Pompey was the legally appointed governor of none but the two Spanish provinces, and the tax companies were of little importance there because the Spanish communities paid a fixed tribute, it seems that Caesar is speaking loosely and simply recognizing the fact that a number of the provinces were *de facto* in Pompey's control in 49.

III.4   *Antonius*: Gaius Antonius, younger brother of Marcus, who had been betrayed and suffered a defeat (see III.10, 67) on the island of Curicta off the Dalmatian coast at about the same time as Curio's force was annihilated by Juba in Africa.

Deiotarus ... Ariobarzanes ... Cotys ... Rhascypolis: Deiotarus, a Galatian prince, had made himself useful over the years to a series of Roman commanders, including Sulla and Pompey, and had by this time become ruler of a large part of Galatia and seen his son, like himself, recognized as a king by the Roman senate. His neighbour *Ariobarzanes* III Eusebes Philorhomaios, King of Cappadocia 52–42 BC, was the grandson of the first king of that name, who also owed his throne to Roman support. *Cotys* was king of the Astae in eastern Thrace, towards the Bosporus, and had like the other two kept on the right side of the Romans. *Rhascypolis* was another Thracian prince, ruler of the Sapaei in Western Thrace.

garrison with King Ptolemy: Gabinius, while governor of Syria, had in 55 BC used a Roman army to restore the exiled Egyptian king Ptolemy Auletes (Cleopatra's father) to his throne. Auletes had bought his restoration at a massive price in Rome, but with borrowed money. The soldiers left him by Gabinius were needed to protect him from his subjects as he strove to wring from them the vast sums he owed to his Roman creditors. 'Pompey's son' is Gnaeus, the elder of the two.

Antiochus of Commagene: Antiochus had been allowed to retain his kingdom when most of Syria became a Roman province in 63, and to annex Seleuceia and some parts of Mesopotamia. His reliability at this time was not above suspicion, but in view of the threat to his kingdom from the Parthians he needed Roman goodwill. The mounted archers he provided were a Parthian speciality, unfamiliar in Roman armies of the time.

III.5   *Gaius Marcellus*: consul of the previous year (and see Glossary for him and all the other commanders mentioned here).

III.9   *the association of Roman citizens*: see II.19 n.

to make artillery: twisted hair could be used to make the springs of catapults.

Winter was now approaching . . . Pompey at Dyrrachium: winter arrives in November in this part of the world, and this is approximately the date of Caesar's crossing from Brundisium. When Pompey makes his appearance in the narrative (ch. 11), he is in Candavia, hastening to reach Dyrrachium from Macedonia. It seems, then, that in completing his account of these early operations in the northern and central sectors of the Dalmatio-Illyrian coast, Caesar has moved on to a point in time from which, at the beginning of the following chapter, he has to backtrack to start the next chain of events. This is a characteristic of his narrative technique.

III.10   *to Pompey < . . . >*: after 'Pompey' the manuscripts have 'he [i.e. Caesar] would dismiss all his land forces everywhere(?)', but since this makes no sense in view of what Caesar has just written I prefer to indicate a lacuna.

III.11 *legitimate authority of the Roman people*: Caesar is referring to the fact that he was now a duly elected consul.

the townspeople: these seem here to be contrasted with 'the Greeks'; if so, they are the non-Greek-speaking local inhabitants, possibly not even full citizens of their community. For such distinctions elsewhere, cf. Utica (II.36).

III.13 *Labienus came forward and took an oath*: the irony is patent of having such a man, celebrated for his desertion of Caesar at the outbreak of the war, take the lead in swearing an oath of loyalty. The episode also prepares the way for his bad faith at ch. 19. (Labienus in fact remained true to his oath and finally fell fighting on the field of Munda in 45 BC.) The oath is exactly like that administered by Petreius in the Ilerda campaign (I.76), and must have been taken seriously to have been used as a means of restoring morale.

under canvas: literally, 'under skins', the material of which Roman tents were made.

III.14 *Following Caesar's instructions*: see ch. 8.

III.15 *as mentioned above*: presumably in the lacuna between chs. 8 and 9.

I have described: this is the only instance in Caesar's works of the first person singular of this verb, though the first person pural occurs 32 times.

III.16 *aedileship and praetorship*: in 65 and 62 BC respectively. Suetonius (*Life of Caesar*, 10) explains that as aedile Caesar gave games and beast-hunts both together with his colleague Bibulus, and separately, but his own lavishness was such that he derived all the credit even for their common expenditure. Bibulus thus felt that his munificence had been wasted— perhaps wrongly, because the Roman people in due course elected him consul. What the dispute was in the praetorship we do not know.

by resolution of council: this was the decision taken at the end of 49 by Pompey's 'senate' at Thessalonica. Caesar is constitutionally correct to term this body Pompey's 'council' (*consilium*).

III.18 *Vibullius . . . summoned Libo and Lucius Lucceius and Theophanes*: Libo's presence, and the information that this took place when things had settled down after Caesar's landing, indicates that we are in Pompey's camp on the Apsus (see ch. 13). On Lucceius and Theophanes, see Glossary.

after the end of the war: by 'the war' must be meant the phase of civil war terminated by the death of Pompey (ch. 104). Each of the subsequent campaigns (Alexandrian etc., African, and Spanish) is called 'a war'.

III.19 *permitted even to fugitives . . . and to pirates*: the reference is to groups of people against whom Pompey had fought in the past.

III.20 *his dais . . . official seat*: a Roman magistrate with legal authority, such as a praetor, would set his official seat (*sella curulis* on a portable platform or dais (*tribunal*) to indicate, so to speak, that his office was open for business. The urban praetor, the most senior of the college of eight praetors, dealt with civil cases between Roman citizens and therefore with all applications for recovery of debt. He had his seat in the open Forum, so that his proceedings, and Caelius' attempted challenge, were completely public.

system set up by Caesar: see ch. 1.

<on its fifth(?) anniversary>: I translate the received correction to the gibberish of the manuscripts; but an interest-free loan for five years seems excessive, and 'after six months' is perhaps more likely (correcting *sexies seni die* to *semenstri die*).

III.21 *a motion suspending Caelius from public duties*: other sources make it clear that what was also passed was the *senatus consultum ultimum* (the 'last decree of the senate', see I.5 n.). The irony of the present situation was that the developments in the senate took almost exactly the same course as they had in the first few days of 49, similarly culminating in a tribunician veto which provoked the *s.c.u.*; but now Caesar's man Servilius was in the position of Lentulus on that occasion, and the tribunes who opposed him took the parts previously played by Antony and Cassius. It is, then, hardly surprising that Caesar, who had made the earlier events a *casus belli*, glosses over these.

the Rostra: 'the Rams' was a long, elevated, speakers' platform at the north-west end of the Forum, adorned with ships' rams which had been taken as spoils of war from the people of Antium in the fourth century.

III.21 *Clodius' murder*: P. Clodius Pulcher and T. Annius Milo were political enemies, and candidates for public office for the year 52. On 18 Jan. of that year, no elections having yet been held because of the level of political violence, they met accidentally at Bovillae on the road from Rome to Lanuvium. A brawl ensued, which led to Clodius' death, followed by more disturbances in Rome and Pompey's appointment as sole consul to restore public affairs to normality. The level of public disorder was such that Pompey determined to take firm action, and a show trial ensued in which Milo, feebly defended by Cicero, was condemned for the murder. He went into exile at Massilia, whence Caelius now summoned him.

the shepherds: cf. I.24. Shepherds, whether free or (usually) slave, led an independent nomadic life, of necessity possessed weapons for self-defence, and had a reputation for toughness and willingness to take a chance to improve their lot.

III.22 *the preoccupations of the magistrates and <the problems> of the times*: Caesar means that he himself (as consul) and the other magistrates (who were now of course all his own men) were busy with the struggle against Pompey.

III.23 *from Oricum*: that is, from the neighbourhood of Oricum, perhaps the island of Sason off its gulf. Oricum itself continued to be held by Caesar.

III.25 *Many months had now elapsed and winter was far advanced*: winter draws to an end on the Dalmatian coast about the beginning of March, and Caesar had crossed from Brundisium before the middle of November by the true calendar.

Apollonian coast: in complete contrast to the Ceraunian coast where Caesar had come ashore, the Apollonian shore is low and marshy, formed by alluvial deposit brought down by the two rivers, the Apsus and the Aous, between which the town lay. It would therefore be quite safe and easy to beach transports there.

III.26 *the same south wind came up again and helped us*: the important difference between Coponius' ships and those of Calenus was that Coponius' were warships, depending chiefly on oars for propulsion and smooth water for effective fighting, while Calenus' were mostly merchantmen, dependent on sail but safer and easier to handle in bad weather than warships.

III.28 *brutally put to death*: Caesar is apt to ascribe this particular atrocity to his opponents; whether one should believe it is another matter.

withdrew . . . to join our forces: these forces must be Antonius', which as the next chapter makes clear disembarked at nearby Nymphaeum.

III.29 *the remaining infantry and cavalry*: only one legion was now left at Brundisium out of the original twelve (see chs. 2 and 6). Caesar does not state his total cavalry strength.

III.30 *the Greeks*: Dyrrachium was a Greek city. The meeting of Antonius with Caesar must have been south and inland of Dyrrachium, and most probably south of the River Genusus.

Asparagium: a place no longer certainly identifiable, lying on the north bank of the River Genusus (now Shkumbin), to the west of modern Pegin. It was probably the spot where the Apollonian and Dyrrachian arms of the Via Egnatia diverged.

III.31 '*Victorious General*': i.e. 'Imperator', see I.13 n. Note the sarcasm here.

the Parthian enemy on his borders: Scipio was proconsul of Syria.

Marcus Crassus . . . and Marcus Bibulus: Crassus had suffered a catastrophic defeat in 53 at Carrhae, and been killed. Bibulus took charge of Syria in 51–50.

III.32 *A poll tax*: neither a poll tax nor the following 'new' tax on door-posts etc. are likely to have been innovations of Scipio's.

the debt of the province was increased: in order to pay the exactions required, the provincials were driven to borrowing money, often (whether directly or indirectly) from the same people who were extorting it from them.

III.33 *shrine of Diana at Ephesus*: one of the largest and most famous temples of antiquity, numbered among the Seven Wonders of the World.

accompanied by a number of senators: to serve as official witnesses to the 'loan' of the treasures (cf. ch. 105).

III.34 *the area of this province known as 'free'*: 'the regions about Lyncus, Pelagonia, Orestias, and Elimeia, used to be called Upper Macedonia, though later on they were also called by some Free Macedonia' (Strabo VII.7.8, discussing the area of Macedonia inland from the coast of Epirus).

III.35   *Calydon and Naupactus*: these towns guarded the route from Western Greece (Epirus and Acarnania) to the Peloponnese, via the Rhion–Antirrhion crossing, and to Central Greece, via Amphissa.

III.36   *the River Haliacmon*: the middle course of the Haliacmon runs north-east along the flanks of the Olympus range, and its valley provides the easiest route, apart from the defile of Tempe, from Thessaly into Macedonia.

Cotys' cavalry: see ch. 4.

mountains which ring Thessaly: from the sequel, these appear to be the Pindus.

III.39   *as mentioned above*: ch. 34.

the inner harbour behind the town: in antiquity, Oricum stood on a spit of land projecting into the gulf, with a sheltered lagoon (now silted up) behind it to serve as a harbour.

III.41   *Pompey was near Asparagium*: the narrative resumes from the end of ch. 30.

III.42   *Petra*: the name simply means 'Rock' in Greek. It lies on the bay about 8 km. south-east of Dyrrachium.

dug out: grain was often stored in underground pits, cf. *African War*, 65.

III.44   *more men*: at Dyrrachium Pompey had nine legions, probably still well up to strength, Caesar about seven, unlikely to have been at full strength.

III.46   *about midway*: presumably, about midway along the spur leading to the hill which Caesar's men were attempting to fortify.

III.47   *in Spain the previous year*: see I.48–52.

Alesia . . . Avaricum: Caesar recounts the siege of Alesia in 52 BC in *Gallic War*, 7.68–90, but with no specific reference to shortage of food. At Avaricum earlier in the same year grain was so short that there, as here, the soldiers were driven to eat meat and their patriotism was such that they did not complain (*Gallic War*, 7.17). Meat clearly formed no part of the normal diet of Roman peasants.

III.48   *'chara'*: this episode is mentioned by Pliny (*Natural History*, XIX.144, XX.96), who calls the plant *lapsana* and describes it as being about a foot high, with hairy leaves, and resembling white mustard (*sinapis*). Modern guesses as to its identity include *arum esculentum, arum italicum*, and a sort of cabbage.

III.50 *in one place* . . . : there is a gap of some size at this point. It would appear that what is missing is not only some fighting at the fortifications but also a failed night attack by Caesar on Dyrrachium. Probably the arrival of Afranius with troops from Spain (cf. ch. 88) was also noted here.

III.53 *three at Dyrrachium and three* . . . : see preceding note.

governor of Asia: see Glossary.

double pay [etc.] . . . *military decorations*: double pay and sometimes rations were a recognized reward for outstanding service; decorations included a miniature spear (*cornuculum* or *hasta pura*), silver cup (*patera* or *patella*), twisted precious-metal necklace (*torques*), bracelet (*armilla*), and horse-boss (*phalera*).

III.56 *Achaea*: the Peloponnese.

III.57 *his original policy*: negotiating for peace.

afraid of delivering his message . . . *at an inopportune time*: this does not in fact apply to any of the intermediaries we have heard of so far, at I.10, 24, 26; III.18. Abortive negotiations not elsewhere described are, however, mentioned in ch. 18.

commanded an army in his own right: as proconsul of Syria.

III.58 *the Pompeian cavalry at Dyrrachium*: the transport of Pompey's cavalry from Petra to Dyrrachium must have been described in the lost portion of narrative between chs. 50 and 51.

III.59 *the Allobroges*: this Gallic tribe lived immediately to the west of the Alps. Their territory, south and east of the Rhône and north of the Isère, formed the northernmost part of the Roman province (later called Narbonensis) which had been established after their defeat in 121. By the the 50s the presence and influence of Rome in this region were all-pervasive.

III.62 *furthest away from Caesar's main camp*: i.e. the southern end of the fortifications, since Caesar's main camp stood between Petra and Dyrrachium.

III.64 *a military disgrace*: the loss of an eagle, regarded as the ultimate shame.

III.64 *all the centurions of the first cohort*: there were only five centurions in the first cohort, although all the other cohorts had six. The most senior was known as the *primus pilus* or *primipilus*, the second senior (as here) *princeps prior*.

III.66 *Caesar ... moved his camp ... A few days afterwards Pompey ...*: both these operations took place during the jockeying for position as Caesar attempted to complete his encirclement, before Pompey's assault and the defeat of Marcellinus' forces as just described.

III.67 *Caesar's lookouts reported*: the narrative now switches back to the present.

in double line: in a column with only two men abreast of each other. This formation, and its more usual form with three men abreast, was used when an attack was expected, so that the men had only to halt and turn through a right-angle to be ready in line facing the enemy.

'hedgehog': a great baulk of timber studded with iron spikes.

Gaius Antonius' army had been betrayed: Pullienus had evidently changed sides. He was probably either a centurion or a military tribune.

III.70 *I think*: this is the only occurrence in Caesar's works of the first person singular of this verb (*credo*), direct speech excepted.

III.71 *military standards*: these are not of course legionary standards (eagles), but the standards of individual centuries and other units.

'Victorious General': see I.13 n. Caesar's purpose in telling us in the next sentence that Pompey accepted the title is to put him in the wrong, because a triumph (for which this salutation was a necessary prerequisite) could be celebrated only over Rome's foreign enemies, not over fellow Romans.

III.73 *experienced and practised generals*: Afranius and Petreius.

nearby provinces: Sardinia and Sicily.

Gergovia: in 52 BC Caesar suffered a serious reverse at Gergovia, with the loss of 46 centurions (*Gallic War*, 7.43–51), but recovered to defeat Vercingetorix decisively at Alesia (ibid., chs. 69–88).

III.75 *ahead to Apollonia*: about 75 km. distant, i.e. 24–30 hours' hard marching.

hindered by baggage: this expresses Pompey's thinking. He did not know that Caesar had sent the baggage on ahead.

III.76   *his old camp facing Asparagium*: see chs. 30, 41.

III.77   *the way very obstructed*: as this can hardly have been true of the Via Egnatia from Asparagium to Apollonia, it seems that Caesar took a roundabout route through difficult country in the hope of shaking off pursuit. This would also account for the fact that he took three more days to cover a mere 40 km. (direct distance) when his troops were quite capable of 25 km. a day if pushed.

III.78   *anxious about Domitius*: for Domitius Calvinus' position, see chs. 34 and 36–8.

by way of Illyricum: Caesar had insufficient naval transport to follow Pompey across the Adriatic.

through Epirus and Athamania: Caesar's army, outnumbered and demoralized, had to use the high passes leading from the headwaters of the River Aous over the Pindus range to Aeginium in western Thessaly, rather than the much easier and lower route followed by the Via Egnatia from Asparagium through Heraclia to Thessalonica.

III.79   *as we explained above*: chs. 59–60.

III.80   *desperate shortage of everything*: this is the only hint Caesar gives of the privations of his army on the way from Apollonia, a journey, through mountainous terrain and over a possibly still snowbound 1,500 m. pass, which cannot have taken less than 15 days.

III.81   *the centre of his whole campaign*: there is textual damage at this point, and it may be that the name of this place (Palaepharsalus, see *Alexandrian War*, 48) has dropped out; but it would be quite characteristic of Caesar not to mention it. It is in fact on the north bank of the River Enipeus, approximately opposite the town of Pharsalus (modern Pharsala) which lies about the same distance south of the river.

III.83   *Domitius*: Ahenobarbus.

Caesar's priesthood: Caesar was Pontifex Maximus, the official head of the state religion.

III.84   *interval . . . since the battles at Dyrrachium*: Caesar reached Apollonia on the fourth, or perhaps fifth day after leaving Dyrrachium (ch. 77). Between Apollonia and Aeginium, where he met Domitius Calvinus (ch. 79), lay some 300 mountainous km. which his army can hardly have traversed in less than 15 days. There followed the march from Aeginium to Gomphi (c.30 km.), the two one-day attacks on Gomphi and Metropolis and another two days' march (c.50 km.) to reach Pharsalus—making a minimum total of 24 days. The more plausible guesses as to the date of Caesar's discomfiture at Dyrrachium range from 5 to 9 July. The battle of Pharsalus eventually took place on 9 August (all these dates pre-Julian).

III.86 *open flank*: the right-hand side, unprotected by the shield.

so strong in cavalry: Pompey had 7,000 cavalry, Caesar 1,000.

III.87 *I took part in all the battles*: a manifest exaggeration, put into Labienus' mouth by Caesar in order to point up his unreliability.

Transpadane settlers: the point of this remark is to accuse Caesar (probably correctly) of having recruited from Latin, i.e. technically non-Roman, settlers; but readers know that the further implication, that such recruits would be no match for the legally constituted army of Pompey, is nonsense.

a general of such experience: surely ironical, and referring to Labienus rather than Pompey.

III.88 *... called the First, the other the Third*: Caesar's somewhat pedantic expression arises from the fact that the Third had borne the number Fifteen when it was in his army in Gaul. See I.2 n. 'two legions' for the circumstances of the transfer.

as we said: evidently in the missing portion of narrative between chs. 50 and 51.

45,000 men: other evidence suggests that this figure is in fact roughly correct, in spite of the fact that it makes the odds against Caesar so great.

A river with difficult banks: the Enipeus.

III.89 *22,000 men in all*: this means that Caesar's units were at little more than half strength, since 80 full-strength cohorts would have numbered about 40,000 men.

III.90 *Vatinius ... Aulus Clodius ... Libo at Oricum*: see chs. 19, 57, and 16–17 respectively.

III.93 *open side*: the right side.

some very high hills: these are the (relatively) high hills which form the northern edge of the river valley where the engagement took place.

III.94   *on the left*: that is, Pompey's left.

III.95   *some very high hills*: see note to ch. 93.

III.96   *a few of his fleeing associates*: according to Plutarch (*Pompey*, ch. 73) these included Favonius and the two Lentuli (Spinther and Crus).

a group of men: his cavalry.

III.97   *A few men of senatorial rank*: that is, higher-ranking officers than the centurions and military tribunes already mentioned.

III.98   *reached Larisa on the same day*: Larisa lies about 20 km. from the place where the remnants of Pompey's army surrendered, and between 30 and 35 km. from Caesar's camp.

III.99   *two hundred*: Appian (*Civil Wars*, II.82) reports that some say Caesar's losses were 1,200, a figure which is on general grounds more believable and also has the advantage of bringing the proportion of common soldiers to centurions killed into a more probable relationship. Perhaps MCC (1,200) was at some point wrongly copied as CC (200).

the above-mentioned Crastinus: ch. 91.

III.100 *Libo*: see ch. 23.

III.101 *Cassius*: the C. Cassius mentioned in ch. 5.

quinqueremes . . . triremes: quinqueremes appear to have been the standard 'ships of the line' of the period. They were propelled by two banks of oars, of which the upper was rowed by three men per oar, the lower by two (hence the name, a 'five', from the number of men per vertical rowing unit). Triremes of the classical fifth-century type, though smaller, undeniably had three banks of oars, with one man per oar, but it is possible that by this time the word may have been used in some navies of a double-banked ship with one man on each lower oar and two on each upper.

III.102 *again*: Pompey's eastern army, with which he had fought at Pharsalus, was already a substitute for the seasoned army which he had lost the previous year in Spain.

III.103 *slaves of the tax companies*: the working personnel of the tax companies (on which see note to ch. 3).

Ptolemy . . . Cleopatra: the elder son and elder daughter of Ptolemy XII Auletes ('the oboist'), who had died in 51 after having been restored by Gabinius (see note to ch. 4). By Egyptian custom, Cleopatra was also her brother's consort.

III.103 *ties of friendship and hospitality*: Ptolemy Auletes had spent some time in Rome as Pompey's guest at his Alban villa, which he had been allowed to use as a base from which to raise the loan he needed to buy his restoration.

III.104 *his friends*: these included, apart from Achillas (mentioned below), the royal guardian and regent Pothinus and the king's tutor Theodotus of Chios.

III.105 *Minerva*: Athena.

a palm-tree: a palm-frond was a symbol of victory.

III.106 *These legions contained 3,200 men*: i.e. 1,600 men each: the average strength of Caesar's legions at Pharsalus had been only 2,750 men.

the consul's rods: these were the *fasces*, the consuls' symbol of office. It is not clear from Caesar's language whether his greeting from Gabinius' old soldiers was friendly or hostile.

III.107 *the Etesian winds*: these are northerly winds which blow, often very strongly, in the summer months in the Aegean and eastern Mediterranean.

his previous consulship: 59 BC.

III.108 *the elder of his two sons and the one of his daughters who had precedence of age*: Ptolemy Auletes' two sons were the present king, Ptolemy XIII Philopator Philadelphos, and his brother, two years younger, who was soon to succeed to the throne as Ptolemy XIV Philopator. The strangely clumsy expression to designate which of the daughters was to succeed (as consort) stems from the fact that at the time the will was drawn (59-58) there were three of them, Berenice, Cleopatra, and Arsinoe. However, Berenice, who ruled from 57 to 55, was put to death by her father when he was restored by Gabinius. Caesar's form of words is designed to avoid using the solecism 'eldest' to distinguish between the two surviving daughters, while still applying to the state of affairs which obtained when the will was made.

III.109 *While these matters were being disputed . . . on their way to Alexandria*: by completely passing over a complicated sequence of events not entirely creditable to himself, Caesar conceals his famous meeting with Cleopatra when she had herself smuggled into the palace, his favouritism of her cause, and his antagonizing of the Alexandrians by demanding that they repay Ptolemy Auletes' huge debt. These things explain Achillas' march on Alexandria.

to him: i.e. to the king.

. . . the other was killed: Dio's version of this senseless (as Caesar tells it) episode is much to be preferred. According to Dio, Serapion and Dioscorides did indeed deliver their message, that Achillas should keep the peace; but he, realizing that the command actually emanated from Caesar and interpreting it as a sign of weakness, roused the anger of his troops against Caesar and Cleopatra to such an extent that they committed the sacrilege of attacking the ambassadors (XLII.37).

III.110 *had taken wives*: soldiers in the Roman army were not allowed to marry while in service.

had killed two sons of Bibulus: Bibulus, when proconsul of Syria in 51 BC, had sent two of his sons to Alexandria, where they were mocked and killed by the army. The purpose of their visit is not known, but may have been to request help against the Parthians.

the Egyptians: that is, the native population, who were in economic and political subjection to the Greek dynasty of the Ptolemies and the privileged Greek citizen class of Alexandria.

III.111 *the part of the town which Caesar held*: it appears that this was the part to the east and south-east of the main harbour, where the royal palace extended.

in the dockyards: these were in the western part of the Great Harbour, adjoining the causeway mentioned in the next chapter.

III.112 *the Pharus*: this was the first real lighthouse in the world and ranked as one of the Seven Wonders of the World. It was at least 300 feet in height, and its three sections, respectively square, octagonal, and round, were each set in from the one below and had tapering sides to give greater stability. Part of the wonder of the structure consisted in the ramps and passageways constructed within the different levels to bring fuel up to the continuously burning fire.

a causeway nine hundred paces long: this is the structure known as the Heptastadion. Strabo's more detailed description (17.1.6) says it had two bridges in it, to allow access from one part of the Great Harbour to the other.

III.112 *seized the lighthouse*: Caesar says 'seized Pharus', which could mean either the island, or the lighthouse, or both; but the continuation (*Alexandrian War*, 17) makes it plain that he did not seize the whole island, only the lighthouse. Because it stood at the eastern tip of the island, control of it was sufficient to achieve his purpose of protecting the entry into the harbour.

the royal dockyards: these were in the eastern part of the harbour, adjacent to the palace.

King Ptolemy's younger daughter: Arsinoe, younger than Cleopatra but considerably older than Ptolemy XIII.

THE ALEXANDRIAN WAR

Numbers refer to chapters.

1 *artillery*: i.e. catapults of various sizes.

movable galleries and screens: for the first (*musculus*), see Caesar's description earlier in this volume at *Civil War*, II.10-11; the second (*testudo*) was a movable wooden screen with a sloping roof under which men could work to attack walls.

siege-huts: movable trellis-work structures to protect attackers.

the marsh: an extension of the freshwater Lake Mareotis that bounds the city to the south.

2 *along the straight avenues*: Alexandria had been laid out on a rectangular grid, with two wide avenues intersecting at right angles as principal thoroughfares and many narrower streets and alleys for access.

3 *gales*: these are the Etesian winds referred to at *Civil War*, III.107.

4 *bonuses to the soldiery*: see *Civil War*, III.112.

5 *the Nile*: the river flows some distance to the east of the city, but was connected to Lake Mareotis by canals (see the description by Caesar's near-contemporary Strabo, *Geography*, 17.1.16).

7 *their race*: the Alexandrians were Greeks, whom the Romans regarded as devious, untrustworthy, and too clever.

8 *Paraetonium . . . the island . . .*: Paraetonium is modern Mersa Matruh, some 150 miles to the west and an impossibly distant source for water. As for 'the island', this cannot be Pharos, and

unless the Delta is meant there are no other candidates. (It is likely that the author, who was not an eyewitness of the events he describes, is confused, particularly as he has failed to notice that a favourable wind for going to collect water will be an unfavourable one for returning.)

9 *surrendered Pompeian soldiers*: these will be those who had surrendered after the battle of Pharsalus, see *Civil War*, III.98; for Domitius Calvinus, see Glossary.

a fast vessel: an *actuaria navis* was light and designed for speed, under both oar and sail.

10 *taking any soldiers on board*: in naval battles of this period much fighting was done by soldiers stationed on the top decks and upperworks of the ships, either as they lay grappled together or when they were close enough to be within missile range of each other.

11 *quadrireme*: a quadrireme had two banks of oars, each oar being worked by two men; for further explanation, see *Civil War*, III.101 n.

12 *they hardly had any confidence . . . earlier occasions*: the Latin text here is corrupt, and I have translated a possible correction (by Dinter).

more than 110 warships: see *Civil War*, III.111 (end).

13 *quinqueremes*: see note above on *quadrireme* (ch. 11).

Cilician: a conjecture for 'Lycian' of the manuscripts (see ch. 1 above, opening sentence).

14 *took his fleet round Pharos*: Caesar had had to sail round the outside of Pharos because the harbour inside was divided by the causeway joining the island to the city (see *Civil War*, III.112).

half of Alexandria belongs to Africa: the allusion is to a belief or debate about where the continent of Asia ended and that of Africa began; cf. Herodotus, *Histories*, II.16: 'I shall show that the Greeks and even the Ionians cannot count when they say that the world has three parts, Europe, Asia, and Africa. They ought to add, as a fourth, the Delta of Egypt, if it belongs neither to Asia nor to Africa. For is it not the Nile which according to their argument divides Asia from Africa? But the Nile splits at the apex of this Delta, which would then be between Asia and Africa.'

15 *meeting approaching ships head-on*: the only safe direction from which to accept ramming, i.e. ram to ram. Even so, the enemy

ship could break off your oars by passing close down your side with her own oars withdrawn at the last minute, and it was important to be equally quick in withdrawing yours.

15 *except for*: I have adopted Fleischer's insertion of these words: it is hard to see how people who were actually engaged in fighting could have behaved in the way described, or conversely, why it was that those who had least real opportunity to give the battle their attention in fact did so.

17 *the island*: Pharos.

fighting from the roofs of the houses: the roofs were flat, and the fighting will have consisted of firing missiles of all sorts (arrows, slingstones, catapult javelins, fire, etc.) from them.

18 *their continuous line of high towers*: the writer means that each house, with its three or four storeys (30 ft. high, as he says below), blank walls, and cuboid form, resembled the towers which punctuated defensive walls of the epoch, so that a line of such houses was like a continuous fortification.

19 *nearer to the town*: from what follows it can be deduced that the bridge at the town (southern) end of the causeway immediately adjoined the shore.

20 *on their unprotected side*: their right, non-shield side. The Alexandrian ships were on the western side of the causeway, the Roman on the eastern.

22 *<our men were passionately . . . >*: the Latin is damaged at this point, but must have said something of this kind.

23 *release the king*: Caesar was holding the young king prisoner in his own palace; see *Civil War*, III.109 (end).

28 *sailing by the Nile*: the author appears to be using 'Nile' loosely of the canal system which connected Alexandria and Lake Mareotis (to which there was an exit from the artificial harbour known as the 'Box', which was still under the king's control) to the river proper.

said to be on the African side . . . explained above: a reference to the remark about Africa in ch. 14. Dio's account (XLII.43) makes Caesar pretend to sail east along the coast, then secretly double back and land men west of the city in order to pass south of Lake Mareotis and take Ptolemy by surprise.

a position which was naturally fortified: not now identifiable.

29 *a narrow watercourse*: this was almost certainly one of the canals connecting Lake Mareotis and the Nile. The Latin is *flumen*,

which ought to mean flowing water, but the Nile has no tributaries in the Delta.

31 *had an easier escape*: an (earthen) rampart had a matching ditch in front of it. Compare Caesar's account of the same phenomenon, *Civil War*, III.69.

33 *to the younger boy and to Cleopatra*: the younger son became Ptolemy XIV Philopator, while Cleopatra (VII) remained queen, transferring her role as sister-consort from one brother to the other. See also *Civil War*, III.108.

Caesar set off for Syria: the author loyally passes in silence over the three further months that, in spite of pressing matters elsewhere, Caesar spent in Egypt as Cleopatra's guest, during which he almost certainly fathered her child Caesarion.

34 *an external power*: that is, one that was completely outside the Roman sphere of influence.

100 cavalry: this is the reading of the manuscripts, but the conjecture D (500) for C (100) is very attractive: 200 cavalry are extremely few to support three legions.

35 *a state of affairs that was as it had been*: Domitius' point is that it was precisely Pharnaces' interference which had altered things in the first place.

37 *gaps to right and left*: the author seems to mean the gaps between the three blocks of (triple) reinforcements, which were placed behind a continuous front line, but his description is not as clear as one could wish.

40 *equestrian order*: see Glossary.

41 *his father's fortune*: that is, to become King of Pontus.

punishments more harrowing than death: see ch. 70.

42 *in the summer*: of 48 BC, the time now being the late autumn (by the sun) or two months later (by the Roman calendar).

war on its borders: Illyricum adjoined Epirus, where the greater part of the confrontation of Pompey and Caesar had taken place, at and around Dyrrachium.

Octavius: for Marcus Octavius' earlier activities in this same area, see *Civil War*, III.9.

the gulf: the northern and central Adriatic.

Gabinius: it seems that at the time of Pharsalus Gabinius had been raising extra forces for Caesar in Italy.

43 *military tribunes*: see Glossary, *s.v.* 'Tribunes'.

44 *when the army had been ferried across to Greece*: in the first half of 48 BC; see *Civil War*, III.2, 6, 25.

46 *a galley of his*: the term used in *myoparon*, a very fast light vessel, especially favoured by pirates.

47 *'five'* . . . *'twos'*: the words here used are the Greek terms *penteres* and *dicrotas*, presumably a quinquereme and biremes respectively (see note on *quadrireme*, ch. 11).

48 *Palaepharsalus*: 'Old Pharsalus', probably the correct name for the site of the battle more usually referred to as that of Pharsalus (see *Civil War*, III.81 n.).

the Further province: at this period, Spain was divided into three for military and administrative purposes (cf. *Civil War*, I.38). Nearer Spain (*Citerior*, later known as *Tarraconensis*) included the eastern coast and its hinterland, with its capital at Tarraco; Further Spain (*Ulterior*, later *Baetica*) comprised, roughly speaking, modern Andalusia, with its centre at Corduba; and the third district, a purely military command often amalgamated with one of the others, embraced as much of the land west and north of these two relatively settled and peaceful areas as the Romans could manage to control or intended to attack. For the context in which Cassius Longinus was appointed governor, see *Civil War*, II.19–21. The events which follow belong to 48 BC and the following winter.

quaestor: probably in 52 BC.

'Victorious General': on this salutation, see *Civil War*, I.13 n.

49 *not merely permitted, but required . . . himself*: that is, Cassius overstepped the conventional bounds of provincial extortion by insisting on direct cash payments to himself instead of disguising the transaction in some specious way.

50 *a new, Fifth, legion*: this legion should not be confused with the Fifth legion which Caesar had previously raised from non-Roman citizens in Gaul (*V. Alaudae*, the 'Larks', so called from the crest on the soldier's helmets). The four legions already in Further Spain were the Second and an unnumbered locally raised one which had formed Varro's force (see *Civil War*, II.20), and the Thirtieth and Twenty-first which Caesar had brought from Italy and left behind with Cassius (*Civil War*, II.19, and *Alexandrian War*, ch. 53).

52 *basilica*: a large general-purpose public hall, with a dais or tribunal from which the governor would preside over his court when he was in town.

Quintus Cassius: this man, the governor's *legatus* (a deputy in both his military and his civil capacities), is to be distinguished from the governor Quintus Cassius Longinus, who is variously described as *pro praetore*, *imperator*, and (by implication) *praetor*.

55 *ex-slaves*: that is, Cassius' own: slaves who had been freed ('freedmen', *liberti*) owed a special duty of loyalty and service to their former masters, and were often employed by them in a variety of administrative functions within their households or businesses.

L. Mercello ... Squillus: see ch. 52 above for L. Mercello; the manuscripts may be right in calling him L. Mercel(l)(i)o (or Mergelio) Squillus here, but modern editors have preferred to see this as an erroneous coalescence of two men's names.

six million ... five million sesterces: the sums are enormous, but are confirmed by Valerius Maximus' report of the same episode (9.4.2).

56 *colonies and associations of Roman citizens*: 'colonies' (*coloniae*) were towns whose full citizens all enjoyed *ipso facto* the Roman citizenship, but there is a puzzle here: Corduba, known to be the earliest colony in Baetica (the later name of Cassius' province), had certainly not yet attained this status because it still possessed an association (*conventus*) of Roman citizens (see *Alexandrian War*, ch. 57, and cf. *Civil War*, II.19). Such an association, a sort of expatriates' club, was an organization characteristic of non-Roman towns in which any number of Romans lived, and was thus quite out of place in a Roman colony. Perhaps our author is writing carelessly.

performed a ceremony of purification: a ceremony sometimes carried out before important events (e.g. a major battle or the founding of a colony) to ensure that the gods were not alienated by the presence of any pollution. In military contexts, it tended to coalesce with a review of the assembled troops, and it is possible that the expression here means little more than 'reviewed'.

57 *Naeva*: an almost certainly correct conjecture for a missing place-name; Naeva is modern *Villaverde*, which lies at plausible distances from both Ilipa and Carmo.

58 *the legions which had been Marcus Varro's*: the Second and local legions.

65 *When Caesar reached Syria*: in the spring of 47 BC.

65 *damaging riots*: for the situation in Rome, see Cassius Dio, *Roman History*, 42.26–33. The troublesome tribunes of this year (47 BC) were L. Trebellius, who championed the cause of the debtors, and P. Cornelius Dolabella (Cicero's erstwhile son-in-law). They not only quarrelled with each other, but also challenged the authority of Mark Antony, who had been named as 'Master of Horse', or deputy, by Caesar (created Dictator after his victory at Pharsalus) and sent back from Greece to take charge of Rome.

collapse of strict discipline: the troops in Campania mutinied, but Antony could not quell them. He returned to Rome to find the city in the grip of riots as a result of the activities of Trebellius and Dolabella (see previous note), but he did nothing effective until the senate called on him to intervene, when he summoned the one legion on whose loyalty he could still rely. He then took drastic action against Dolabella's supporters. Even this was not enough to restore order fully, and the city was still simmering with discontent and violence when Caesar returned later in the year.

firm friends: in this kind of context, 'friend' (*amicus*) is a diplomatic term of some precision. It meant that the 'friend' (whether ruler or state) could count upon the support and protection of Rome provided that he (or it) was prepared to behave in the Roman interest—an obligation which might go so far as having to provide troops or cash for wars which would otherwise have been of little concern to the 'friend' (for an example, see *Civil War*, III.3).

66 *sanctuary of Bellona in Cappadocia*: both Caesar's line of march (Mazaca is the later Eusebeia Caesaria Mazaca, modern Kayseri) and the evidence of Strabo (XII.3.32–4), whose mother's family were prominent in Pontus at this time, show that the text is wrong and that what is said here relates to Comana in Pontus (north of Mazaca), not to Comana in Cappadocia (south-east of Mazaca). Both places possessed an important cult of the goddess Ma, as she was known locally, and a priesthood that was almost royal. Either the author has become confused, or (more probably) 'in Cappadocia' is an erroneous note, which was made in the margin by someone who knew the more famous of the two sanctuaries, and was later incorporated into the text.

change of descent: Lycomedes was the grandson of Archelaos, priest of Ma-Bellona at Pontic Comana and general of Mithridates VI of Pontus; but Lycomedes' father, also called Archelaos and also priest of Bellona, had claimed to be a son of Mithridates and had married Berenice IV of Egypt in 56 BC (only to be defeated and put to death by Gabinius when the latter invaded Egypt in 55).

his sovereignty and power: the text here is corrupt, but the general drift must be that Caesar granted some privileges to Ariarathes to discourage him from plotting against his brother.

67 *the garb of a man summoned for prosecution*: it was the custom for defendants at Rome, before their trial came on, to put on squalid clothing, give up shaving and barbers, and present to their fellow citizens as unkempt and miserable a picture of themselves as possible in order to excite sympathy.

68 *when he was consul*: in 59 BC, during his first consulship, Caesar succeeded in ratifying the eastern settlement which had been made by Pompey at the end of his war against Mithridates, and conferred benefits on Deiotarus.

succeeded to Lentulus and Marcellus as consul: Caesar himself; see *Civil War*, III.1.

his own past favours: these are Caesar's favours to Deiotarus, as is shown by e.g. *Civil War*, I.22, where Lentulus makes the fact that Caesar has done him kindnesses in the past a reason for Caesar to be merciful to him.

72 *Mithridates' victory over Triarius*: see Glossary, *s.v.* Valerius Triarius (1).

73 *the fourth watch*: the Romans divided the night into four watches, so this is shortly before dawn.

76 *escape*: Pharnaces made his way back to the Bosporan kingdom, where he fell fighting against his son-in-law Asander, who had displaced him as ruler.

78 *earlier*: see ch. 26.

of royal stock: according to Strabo (XIII.4.3) not only did young Mithridates' father Menodotos belong to the family of the tetrarchs of Galatia, but his mother Adobogion was also the concubine of King Mithridates.

sooner than anyone expected: September 47 BC.

THE AFRICAN WAR

Numbers refer to chapters.

1 *17 December*: the year is 47 BC (when December still had only 29 days). It must be remembered that the dates used in this

work are the official Roman calendar dates, which were at this stage ten to eleven weeks in advance of the true (Julian) dates, so Caesar was in fact making his crossing early in October. It was now approximately three months since he had returned to Rome from the east, as described at the end of the preceding work.

1 *the king*: King Juba of Numidia; see *Civil War*, II.25 ff.

four legions of recruits: these were numbered XXV, XXVI, XXVIII, and XXIX; see ch. 60 below.

6 *fewer than thirty*: indeed an incredible figure. Something must be wrong with this and/or the other figures for cavalry strength.

Numidians: it is not clear why the author starts at this point to describe as 'Numidian' instead of 'Moorish' what is evidently the same body of cavalry.

7 *Leptis*: Leptis Minor, see Glossary.

9 *six cohorts*: nominally 3,000 men (6 × 500).

10 *Vatinius and Sulpicius* (Rufus): the commanders' names show that these cohorts had been marines on Caesar's Adriatic fleet.

16 *the Tenth legion*: Caesar's crack legion until 48 BC, occupying the place of honour on the right of the line at Pharsalus (*Civil War*, III.89).

19 *by what had happened to Curio*: see *Civil War*, II.40–3.

more than 12,000 men of all sorts: these would probably have been formed into three under-strength legions; 'of all sorts' means that the conscripts included persons other than Roman citizens, who alone were in theory qualified to be enrolled in the legions. (Note that the details of the anti-Caesarian forces given in this chapter are confused and repetitive, and the text unreliable: *Buthrotum* is a correction for 'Brundisium', and the numerals, as often, are suspect.)

22 *not yet a senator*: Pompey was 25 or 26 when Sulla allowed him the honour of a triumph for his recovery of Sicily and North Africa from the supporters of Marius in 82 and 81 BC. This was in spite of the fact that he did not satisfy the criteria for the award of such a coveted honour, including at the very least the holding of elected public office—the normal qualification at this date for admission to the senate. His father, Cn. Pompeius Strabo (consul in 89 BC), had died of natural causes while commanding an army in Italy in 87 BC during Marius' successful assault on Rome; it was the remains of this army, subsequently

disbanded, which Pompey re-formed and led to join Sulla, when he invaded Italy in the winter of 84–83 and proceeded to defeat the Marian government which had held power since 87 (the *criminally wicked fellow Romans* mentioned earlier in this chapter).

23 *without coming ashore again*: for the sequel to Pompeius' flight, see *Spanish War*.

24 *forces . . . described above*: see ch. 20.

28 *Marcus Messalla*: this is M. Valerius Messalla Rufus, who according to a letter of Cicero, written in Sept. 47 BC, had been 'sent packing' by some unspecified soldiery, apparently in Italy; but it is not impossible that Salienus' mutiny was merely part of the wider disaffection among the troops in Italy in August 47 (cf. *Alexandrian War*, 65 and note).

29 *'scorpion'*: a type of quick-firing artillery piece which shot heavy arrows or javelin-like darts.

31 *a rout*: that is, the dispersal of the Pompeian forces after the battle of Pharsalus.

32 *the fear and hopelessness felt by Caesar's army*: the preserved Latin text says 'his [i.e. Scipio's, or his soldiers'] fear and the hopelessness felt by Caesar's army', but this cannot be right in the light of Caesar's reported observation in the previous chapter that the enemy might think him 'submissive and fearful'. The fear here is surely Caesar's, not Scipio's.

a relation of Caesar's: Gaius Marius was Caesar's uncle by marriage to his aunt Julia. Marius was in charge of the war against the Numidian king Jugurtha from 107 to 105 BC and hence had ample opportunity to confer favours during and after the fighting. Plutarch also notes that he took some 'Moorish cavalry' back with him to Italy from Africa in 87 BC (*Marius*, ch. 41).

34 *Cercina*: see ch. 8.

36 *20 tonnes*: the Latin measure (3,000 *modii*) has been converted by taking one *modius* as equivalent to $6^2/_3$ kg.

invaded Numidia with his troops: see ch. 25.

40 *Curio's defeat*: see *Civil War*, II.42.

43 *with three cohorts*: text uncertain, both here and earlier in the sentence. For the context, see ch. 33.

through Juba's kingdom: that is, he went by a circuitous inland route to avoid the coast.

44 *Quintus Cominius*: probably a senator, because he is mentioned before the *eques* Ticida and the family had certainly produced senators in the past.

45 *<thirteen?> years?*: the manuscripts have the impossible figure XXXVI for the length of the centurion's service. Caesar's campaigns in Gaul began in 59 BC, thirteen years before the present date.

47 *the Pleiades had set*: the setting of the Pleiades, which marked the close of the sailing season for the Romans and was associated with a period of storms, occurs about 8 Nov. (Julian). This date corresponds to approximately 21 Jan. of the present narrative, the Roman calendar being between ten and eleven weeks out by the winter of 47/6 BC.

no equipment or slaves: cf. the similar situation at *Civil War*, III.6.

canvas: literally, 'hides', as Roman tents were made of leather.

48 *cavalry with reins*: see ch. 19 above.

52 *served under Curio*: see ch. 40 and note thereto.

55 *as we explained above*: in ch. 32.

56 *higher camp*: the Latin can also mean 'his previous camp', but cf. ch. 61 'Caesar's camp on the hill'.

after Sulla's victory: i.e. in 81 BC, following Pompey's defeat of the Marians in Africa (see note to ch. 22). The Numidian king Hiempsal supported Pompey, and duly reaped his reward. There were at least three occasions in Marius' military career when he *could* have been helped by Gaetulian horsemen: during his campaigns of 107 and 106 BC against Jugurtha in Africa (although Sallust's account consistently makes Gaetulians the enemies of Rome); during those of 104-101 BC against the Germanic tribes who were attempting to enter Italy from the north (perhaps the most likely context); and in 87 BC, when he returned from exile in Africa to join in the defeat of Sulla's supporters in Italy (but is perhaps unlikely to have been supported by Gaetulians unless they already owed him loyalty from an earlier connection).

59 *the legionaries*: presumably Caesar's.

60 *newly recruited ones*: these were the legions bearing numbers in the twenties. (The text of this sentence, as well as the numbers of the legions in the preceding one, is badly corrupted and I have translated following the corrections suggested by Nipperdey.)

64 *dismissed . . . by Caesar in Spain*: see *Civil War*, I.86. It may have been a condition of discharge that the men thus allowed to go free should not rejoin the fight against Caesar, but he does not actually say so. See also note to ch. 89, *Quintus Ligarius*.
Nasidius' fleet: cf. *Civil War*, II.3.

66 *three*: this is a speculative correction for the figure of VIII given by the manuscripts, since Caesar had only five veteran legions with him: V (ch. 1), IX and X (ch. 53), and XIII and XIV (ch. 34).

67 *single*: the author's reason for mentioning this may be to make a contrast with what he is about to tell us of Scipio's arrangements; but it is worth remembering that Caesar's previous camp was a double one, consisting of his first position on the ridge (chs. 51, 61) and his advanced position in front of Uzitta (chs. 56, 58, 60).

68 *association of Roman citizens at Utica*: see *Civil War*, II.19 and note.

69 *previously described*: see ch. 14.

74 *who had been informed . . . sympathy for Caesar*: the text of this clause is corrupt and the translation given here is based on an emendation by Vielhaber.

75 *ceremonial purification . . . 21 March*: see *Alexandrian War*, 56 n. However, 21 March was the middle day of the five-day festival of the Quinquatrus, in honour of Minerva, on the last day of which the Tubilustrium (purification of the ritual trumpets) took place at Rome. Gardner may therefore well be right to suggest, in her note to this passage, that here *lustrare* retains its proper meaning of 'purify', and that Caesar's action was connected with other ceremonies of purification of items associated with war which are attested in the Roman religious calendar for March—a month named after and originally sacred to Mars, the god of war.

76 *Aggar*: ch. 67.

77 *the Roman people*: the author reproduces the official language of diplomacy. Had the people of Thabena chosen to approach Scipio for some favour, they would have expressed themselves no differently. But by reproducing this official language, the author stresses Caesar's legitimacy as the representative of the Roman people.

78 *Pacideius*: evidently the commander of this part of Scipio's cavalry; see ch. 13.

78 *cavalry regiment*: the Latin is *ala*, a larger unit than the 'squadron' (*turma*).

80 *Asprenas*: L. Nonius Asprenas, who was eventually to attain the consulate in 36 BC as a supporter of Octavian.

81 **with the Tenth . . . Fifth legion**: the text between the asterisks is corrupt. The basis of the reconstruction here offered is that Caesar, who had nine legions in all (see ch. 60 and note thereto), had left two (doubtless two of his four recruit legions) in camp, and therefore must have had seven to deploy in battle; also, given that he had two legions on each wing and that the Latin, though damaged, seems to be telling us that he had split the Fifth to stiffen the two wings against Scipio's elephants, his centre must have consisted of the remaining two—probably the other two recruit legions, because the wings were where the battle was likely to be won or lost.

82 *re-enlisted men*: these were by definition experienced soldiers, like P. Cornelius (ch. 76) and probably included a high proportion of former NCOs like the ex-centurion Crastinus (*Civil War*, III.91).

83 *'Success'*: in Latin, *Felicitas*.

85 *hailed the victor in military fashion*: that is, they used the normal military formula to salute Caesar as their new commanding officer. (The date of Caesar's victory was 6 April by the official calendar.)

86 *killing 5,000*: the numeral in the Latin is 50,000 (*L milibus*), but this seems quite impossible even allowing for the habitual tendency of ancient sources to exaggerate numbers of dead and wounded. I have therefore followed Gardner in emending *L* to *V* (a common corruption in numerals).

87 *status*: that is, they did not distinguish between slaves and free men, or between citizens of Parada and those of other places who might happen to be there.

by passing his law: in the Latin, *lex Iulia*. See *Civil War*, II.36 and note.

Gate of Baal: cf. *Civil War*, II.25. There, as here, the manuscripts have converted *Belica* ('of Baal', the chief Semitic god) to the ordinary Latin adjective *bellica* ('of war').

88 *free their slaves*: slaves did not serve as soldiers, but in emergencies might be freed so that they could be conscripted for military service.

killed himself . . . what he was doing: for a fully worked-up account of this, the most famous suicide of antiquity, see Plutarch, *Life of the Younger Cato*, chs. 66–70, or (somewhat briefer) Appian, *Civil Wars*, II.98–9.

89 *Quintus Ligarius*: this man had been one of the elder Considius' deputies (*legati*) in the province before the Civil War broke out, and had stayed on when Considius abdicated and allowed Attius Varus to take over (*Civil War*, I.31). Later in 46 BC he was defended before Caesar by Cicero in an extant speech (*Pro Q. Ligario*) against the charge of abetting the Pompeian effort against Caesar in Africa. He had two brothers, but since they were both alive at the time of the speech the P. Ligarius of ch. 64 above cannot be one of them, unless he somehow escaped execution.

90 *remain safe*: it appears that forced sale of property, whether as a punishment (as here) or in response to legal action for recovery of debt, besmirched a man's record and in some way disadvantaged him or laid him open to further action.

95 *Faustus and Afranius*: see ch. 87.

97 *three million pounds' weight of oil*: this has been calculated at one million litres and is some indication of the fertility of the African coast at this time (see D. Mattingly, *Libyan Studies* vol. 19 (1988), 21–41). Caesar accepted opposition, but disliked ingratitude: cf. the fate of P. Ligarius (ch. 64).

the dispute between the leading men of the state: diplomatic language for 'the Civil War'.

THE SPANISH WAR

Numbers refer to chapters.

1 *giving shows in Italy*: this refers to the dinners, entertainments, and spectacles provided for the populace of Rome by Caesar after he had celebrated a quadruple triumph in September 46 BC for his victories over the Gauls, Egypt, Pharnaces, and Juba.

rewarded by Pompey: Pompey had commanded armies in Nearer Spain between 76 and 71 BC, and been governor, albeit absentee, of both provinces from 55 to 49 BC. As a result he had enjoyed ample opportunities to establish a wide patronage of both individuals and communities. (I take 'Cn. Pompeius' in the text to refer to the father, whom I call 'Pompey' to distinguish him from his son, also named Cn. Pompeius.)

2 *a tremendously fast journey*: Caesar covered the *c.*1,950 km. between Rome and Saguntum (just north of modern Valencia) in 17 days (Orosius VI.16.6), composing a poem about his journey on the way, and the further 450 km. to Obulco, 55 km. from Corduba, in another 10 days (Strabo III.4.9).

5 *the bridge*: this appears to mean the permanent stone bridge which connected the town (on the north bank) with the other side of the river (cf. the situation at Ilerda, *Civil War*, I.40). It is not clear which end of the bridge was being contested, nor on which side of the River Gnaeus Pompeius was encamped.

7 *the local legion*: see *Civil War*, II.20 and *Alexandrian War*, 53.

10 (*Mention was not made . . . Asprenas*): this aside seems to be evidence for the compilation of the *Spanish War*, at least in part, from existing military documents or reports.

together with the cavalry: the cavalry are presumably those raised by Arguetius at Saguntum; it is likely, therefore, that Indo was ruler of a tribe living in Nearer Spain.

11 *from the town*: I read *ex oppido* for *in oppido* (accepted by all other editors), because the next chapter makes it clear that this was an attack by the defenders of Ategua on Caesar's troops. Had the struggle taken place *in* the town, the siege would already have been over, and plainly it was not.

13 *bearing this message*: lead sling-shot was occasionally inscribed (examples carrying brief slogans uncomplimentary to the enemy, or comforting to the sender, survive from the siege of Perugia in 41–40 BC), but a message as long as this must have been written on material which was wrapped round the shot (cf. ch. 18).

15 *the camp*: apparently, Caesar's camp. Cavalry did not normally become involved in the sort of fighting which took place at the point of assault on fortifications.

16 *towers and assault ramp*: the standard structures used by a besieging force, and either entirely made of, or containing, timber. Cf. *Civil War*, II.2, 8–9 (the tower here being exceptional in that it was built of brick and therefore fireproof).

18 *he returned to the gate*: 'he' cannot be Tullius, at least as the Latin now stands in our editions. It appears that something has gone seriously wrong with the text between 'Tiberius Tullius' and this point. Most probably some kind of fracas took place between Cato and one of the guards at the gate, but it is impossible to restore sense without wholesale and speculative emendation.

19 *was saluted 'Victorious General' by his troops*: see *Civil War*, I.13 n.

22 *equestrians*: i.e. *equites Romani*; see Glossary, *s.v.* Equestrian Order.

seven denarii: if this is the correct decipherment of the numeral XVII found in the manuscripts, i.e. X (= denarius, originally 10 *asses*) VII, it *may* be a monthly rate of pay, in which case it is little more than a third of what a legionary received.

23 *Ennius*: Q. Ennius (239–169 BC), who came from SE Italy and became a Roman citizen quite late in life, composed amongst much else the first Latin epic poem to be written in hexameters, the metre used by Homer and all Greek epic poetry. This poem, a patriotic version of Roman history entitled *Annales*, became a classic and formed part of the school curriculum at least down to the reign of the emperor Tiberius.

25 *Achilles and Memnon*: the duel between Achilles and Priam's nephew the Ethiopian king Memnon, son of Eos (Aurora, the Dawn) and Tithonus, formed part of the subject-matter of the *Aethiopis*, one of the lost epic poems which continued the story of Homer's *Iliad*.

§§*Thus eager and intent . . . <near> the camp* §§: the text of this whole passage is too defective to permit even speculative restoration.

27 *Munda*: normally identified with modern Montilla, 35 km. S of Corduba; but R. Corzo Sánchez has argued in *Habis*, 4 (1973), 241–52, that the battle should be placed some 30 km. to the SW of this, near Osuna (ancient Urso).

28 *above*: perhaps the reference is to ch. 24, where the text is badly defective.

30 *eagles*: i.e. legions.

eighty cohorts: eight legions.

31 *taking them in the flank*: see *Civil War*, III.93 (end)–94 for the dramatic consequences if this were allowed to happen.

'*Foot was pressed . . . arms*': on Ennius, see note to ch. 23; although unmetrical as they presently stand in the Latin, the words *armis teruntur arma* are proved by a similar conjunction in Silius Italicus' *Punica* (IV.352) to be part of the quotation.

Liberalia: a Roman festival which took place on 17 March.

33 *slit his throat*: it is quite unclear from the Latin whether the ex-slave was the bedfellow of Scapula or of the other slave,

or whose throat was slit (though one would suppose it was Scapula's).

34 *freed by Sextus Pompeius*: only in the direst emergencies were slaves enrolled as soldiers, and they were always given their freedom first.

the Ninth(?): the identification is uncertain.

the town: Munda.

40 *and . . .* : I have not attempted to translate or restore to sense the corrupt and deficient six words which follow (*quodvis essent bracchium ex utrisque partibus*), but the general sense is likely to be that Didius extended his fortifications to guard against whatever danger might threaten from the Lusitanians.

42 *quaestor*: Caesar served as quaestor in Further Spain in 69–68 BC.

praetorship: in Rome, 62 BC, followed by a term as governor of Further Spain.

the taxes which Metellus had imposed: Q. Metellus Pius was proconsul of Further Spain from 79 to 71 BC, fighting against the Marian and native forces under the leadership of Q. Sertorius and M. Perperna, who represented the last remaining opposition to the government set up in Rome by Sulla. The taxes were presumably a penalty laid on those communities which had supported Sertorius.

consulship: 59 BC.

previously: in 49 BC; see *Civil War*, I.

Cassius: see *Alexandrian War*, 52–3.

and their courage . . . : Caesar's speech, and the work as a whole, breaks off here. It is possible that the author was modelling the end of his narrative on the end of *Civil War* I (chs. 85–7), where Caesar gives himself a longish self-justificatory speech, followed by a brief factual conclusion to the narrative. The speech itself, in both its parts (the indirect and the direct), shows a much more elaborately balanced and rhythmical oratorical style, resembling that of the speech placed in the mouth of Tullius in ch. 17, than the plain but often clumsy writing of the rest of the narrative. It is tempting to suppose that the author either lifted it, with suitable modification, from some handbook of rhetorical examples (such as those contained in Book IV of the pseudo-Ciceronian *Rhetorica ad Herennium*), or else that he had access to a version of the speech which Caesar actually delivered.

GLOSSARY

All dates are BC *unless otherwise specified.*

ACARNANIA *(Civ.* III.56, 58): a district of NW Greece lying SE of the Gulf of Arta.

ACHAEA *(Civ.* III.3, 4, 5, 56, 57, 106; *Alex.* 44): the Peloponnese.

ACHILLAS *(Civ.* III.104, 108–12; *Alex.* 4): commander of the army of Ptolemy XIII.

ACHILLES *(Span.* 25): the Homeric hero of the *Iliad*.

Marcus ACILIUS Canin(i)(an)us *(Civ.* III.15, 16, 39, 40): Caesarian officer, placed in command of Oricum in 48.

ACUTIUS Rufus *(Civ.* III.83): a senator in Pompey's following in 48.

ACYLLA *(Afr.* 33, 43, 67): a town in Africa.

ADBUCILLUS *(Civ.* III.59): a Gallic chieftain, father of Egus and Roucillus.

ADRIATIC *(Civ.* I.25): the sea of this name.

AEGIMURUS *(Afr.* 44): a small island off the entrance to the Bay of Tunis.

AEGINIUM *(Civ.* III.79): an Illyrian town on the fringes of western Thessaly, at the mouth of the upper Peneios Valley.

Lucius AELIUS Tubero *(Civ.* I.30, 31): the legitimate governor of Africa in 49, excluded from the province by Attius Varus.

Marcus AEMILIUS Lepidus *(Civ.* II.21; *Alex.* 59, 63–4): praetor in 49, became consul in 46, and then a member, with Octavian and Mark Antony, of the Triumvirate which ruled the Roman world from 43 to 33.

AETOLIA(N) *(Civ.* III.34, 35, 56, 61): a district of Greece N of the Gulf of Corinth.

AFRANIUS *(Civ.* I.74, 84): son of the following.

Lucius AFRANIUS *(Civ.* I.37–43, 46–54, 60–76, 78, 83–4, 87; II.17, 18; III.83, 88; *Afr.* 69, 95; *Span.* 7): consul in 60, a deputy *(legatus)* for Pompey in Spain 55–49; defeated there by Caesar, fought again at Pharsalus and in Africa, and put to death after being captured as he attempted to leave Africa for Spain.

AFRICA(N) *(Civ.* I.30, 31; II.23, 28, 32, 37; III.10; *Alex.* 9, 14, 28, 47, 51, 56; *Afr.* 2, 3, 8, 10, 19–26, 34, 47, 54, 64–5, 77; *Span.* 1, 7, 8): normally, the Roman province, corresponding approximately to modern Tunisia; but used in the wider sense of the whole continent at *Alex.* 9, 14, 28.

AGGAR (*Afr.* 67, 76, 79): an African town.

AHENOBARBUS: *see* DOMITIUS.

ALBA (FUCENS) (*Civ.* I.15, 24): a town in Central Italy E of Rome.

ALBICI (*Civ.* I.34, 56–8; II.2, 6): a Gallic tribe living near Massilia.

ALESIA (*Civ.* III.47): a town in Gaul, scene of a famous siege conducted by Caesar against Vercingetorix in 52.

ALEXANDRIA (*Civ.* III.4, 103–12; *Alex.* 1–33 *passim*, 38, 48, 69): the capital of Egypt.

Aulus ALLIENUS (*Afr.* 2, 26, 34, 44): the governor (*pro praetore*) of Sicily in 47–46.

ALLOBROGES (*Civ.* III.59, 63, 79, 84): a Gallic tribe which furnished Caesar with cavalry.

AMANTIA (*Civ.* III.12, 40): a town in Epirus, near Apollonia.

AMANUS (*Civ.* III.31): a part of the Taurus mountain range in SE Asia Minor.

AMBRACIA (*Civ.* III.36): the region to the N of the Gulf of Arta in NW Greece.

AMPHILOCHIA (*Civ.* III.56): the region to the E of the Gulf of Arta in NW Greece.

AMPHIPOLIS (*Civ.* III.102): the chief town of eastern Macedonia, lying on the Via Egnatia, near the mouth of the River Strymon.

Titus AMPIUS Balbus (*Civ.* III.105): praetor in 59 and governor of Asia in the following year. Senior assistant (*legatus pro praetore*) to Fannius, the governor of Asia in 49–48.

ANAS (*Civ.* I.38): a river in Spain forming the northern boundary of Further Spain; now called the Gaudiana.

ANCONA (*Civ.* I.11): a town on the NE coast of Italy, still bearing the same name.

ANDROSTHENES (*Civ.* III.80): the chief magistrate of Thessaly in 48; attempted to hold Gomphi against Caesar.

Titus ANNIUS Milo (*Civ.* III.21, 22): tribune of the plebs in 57, exiled in 52 for the murder of his political rival Publius Clodius Pulcher, and not recalled by Caesar when he permitted other exiles to return; came back to Italy illegally to support the insurrection of Caelius Rufus in 48, and was killed attacking Compsa in southern Central Italy.

ANNIUS Scapula (*Alex.* 55): a Corduban involved in the plot against Q. Cassius Longinus.

ANQUILLARIA (*Civ.* II.23): a small port near Cape Bon in Tunisia, site unknown.

ANTIOCH (*Civ.* III.102, 105): Antiochia in northern Syria, the most famous of the many towns bearing the name.

ANTIOCHUS (*Civ.* III.4): king of Commagene.

ANTISTIUS Turpio (*Span.* 25): a Pompeian soldier.

Gaius ANTONIUS (*Civ.* III.10, 67): younger brother of Marcus Antonius; commander of a Caesarian force defeated in the Dalmatian archipelago in 49; later praetor (44).

Marcus ANTONIUS (*Civ.* I.2, 11, 18; III.4, 24–30, 34, 40, 46, 65, 89): tribune of the plebs in 49, and one of Caesar's most trusted and energetic commanders; was in office as consul when Caesar was murdered in 44; in 42 joined Octavian and Lepidus to form the Triumvirate which ruled the Roman world until 33, but lost the subsequent struggle with Octavian for sole mastery of the state and committed suicide in Alexandria in 30, dying in Cleopatra's arms.

APOLLONIA (*Civ.* III.5, 11–13, 25, 26, 30, 75, 78, 79): an important port on the Illyrian coast.

APONIANA (*Afr.* 2): the largest of the Aegates group, lying off the western end of Sicily; today Favignana.

Lucius APPULEIUS Saturninus (*Civ.* I.7): populist tribune of the plebs in 103 and 100.

APSUS (*Civ.* III.13, 19, 30): a river in Epirus, N of Apollonia; today the Semeni.

APULIA (*Civ.* I.14, 17, 23; III.2): the region of Italy bordering the Adriatic between Larinum and the territory of Tarentum.

Quintus AQUILA (*Afr.* 62–3, 67): a squadron commander with Caesar's fleet in Africa.

Marcus AQUINUS (*Afr.* 57, 89): a Pompeian senator.

AQUITANIA (*Civ.* I.39): the SW district of France, bordering on the Atlantic.

ARECOMICI (*Civ.* I.35): see VOLCAE.

ARELATE (*Civ.* I.36; II.5): a town on the coast of southern Gaul; today Arles.

ARGUETIUS (*Span.* 10): commander of a troop of cavalry.

ARIARATHES (*Alex.* 66): brother of Ariobarzanes.

ARIMINUM (*Civ.* I.8, 10–12): the most northerly town within Italy on the Adriatic coast; today Rimini.

ARIOBARZANES III Eusebes Philorhomaios (*Civ.* III.4; *Alex.* 34, 66): king of Cappadocia from 52 to 42 and grandson of the first king of that name, who like Deiotarus owed his throne to Roman opposition to Mithridates VI of Pontus in the 90s and 80s. He supported Pompey in 48.

ARMENIA MINOR (*Alex.* 34–6, 67): a kingdom to the E of Cappadocia.

ARRETIUM (*Civ.* I.11): a town on the borders of Tuscany and Umbria; today Arezzo.

ARSINOE (*Civ.* III.112; *Alex.* 4, 33): younger sister of Cleopatra VII.

ASCULUM (*Civ.* I.15): a town in Picenum in N Italy; today Ascoli Piceno.

ASCURUM (*Afr.* 23): a Mauretanian town.

ASIA(N) (*Civ.* I.4; III.3–5, 7, 40, 42, 53, 105–7; *Alex.* 13, 34, 40, 65, 78): a province bordering the eastern Aegean Sea; the first and richest of the several Roman provinces which came to embrace nearly all of modern Asia Minor.

ASPARAGIUM (*Civ.* III.30, 41, 76): a place no longer identifiable, lying on the River Genusus.

ASPAVIA (*Span.* 24): a fortified settlement near Ucubi.

ASPRENAS: *see* NONIUS.

ASTA (*Span.* 26, 36): a town in Further Spain not far from Gades.

ATEGUA (*Span.* 6–8, 22): a town SE of Corduba.

Gaius ATEIUS Capito (*Afr.* 89): a Pompeian senator.

ATHAMANIA (*Civ.* III.78): a district of N Greece, lying in the mountains between Epirus and Thessaly.

ATHENS (*Civ.* III.3): the same.

ATLANTIC (*Oceanus*) (*Civ.* I.38): the same.

Publius ATRIUS (*Afr.* 68, 89): a Roman equestrian living at Utica.

Gaius AT(T)IUS (*Civ.* I.18): a Paelignian supporter of Pompeius Magnus.

Publius ATTIUS Varus (*Civ.* I.12, 13, 31; II.23, 25, 27–8, 30, 33–6, 43–4; *Afr.* 44, 62–4, 90; *Span.* 27, 31): attained the praetorship by 53 and governed Africa in 52; held a command (perhaps as a *legatus* to Pompey) in N Italy in 49; Pompeian governor in Africa 49–46, escaped to Spain and died at Munda in 45.

Quintus AT(T)IUS Varus (*Civ.* III.37): a cavalry commander serving with Caesar's army in Greece.

Lucius AURELIUS Cotta (*Civ.* I.6): consul in 65, and a distant relation of Caesar through the latter's mother Aurelia.

Marcus AURELIUS Cotta (*Civ.* I.30): praetor in the 50s; Pompeian supporter and legitimate governor of Sardinia in 49, ejected by the inhabitants.

AUSETANI (*Civ.* I.60): a tribe of Nearer Spain.

AUXIMUM (*Civ.* I.12, 13, 15, 31): a town in northern Picenum, today Osimo.

AVARICUM (*Civ.* III.47): site of a notable siege conducted by Caesar in Gaul in 52.

Gaius AVIENUS (*Afr.* 54): a military tribune of Caesar's Tenth legion.

Aulus BAEBIUS (*Span.* 26): a Roman equestrian from Asta.

BAETIS (*Alex.* 59, 60; *Span.* 5, 36): today the Guadalquivir, the chief river of Further Spain.

BAETURIA (*Span.* 22): the region extending N and W of Corduba as far as the River Anas.

BAGRADAS (*Civ.* II.24, 26, 38, 39): a river E of Utica; today the Medjerdah.

BALBUS: *see* AMPIUS, CORNELIUS.

BALEARIC ISLANDS (*Afr.* 23): the same.

BELLONA (*Alex.* 66): the Roman goddess of war, identified with the Pontic and Cappadocian goddess Ma.

BERONES (*Alex.* 53): a Celtic or possibly Iberian tribe who lived around the upper Ebro.

BESSI (*Civ.* III.4): a tribe living to the N of Macedonia.

BIBULUS: *see* CALPURNIUS.

BITHYNIA(N) (*Civ.* III.3; *Alex.* 65–6, 78): a kingdom on the S shore of the Black Sea, W of Pontus; annexed by Rome in 74.

BOCCHUS (*Afr.* 25): joint king of Mauretania, with Bogud.

BOEOTIA (*Civ.* III.4): the district of central Greece N of Attica.

BOGUD (*Alex.* 59, 62; *Afr.* 23): joint king of Mauretania, with Bocchus.

BOSPHORUS (*Alex.* 78): a kingdom lying to the NW of the straits of the same name.

BRITAIN (*Civ.* I.54): the same.

BRUNDISIUM (*Civ.* I.24–8, 30; III.2, 6, 8, 14, 23–5, 87, 100; *Alex.* 44, 47): a port on the 'heel' of Italy; today Brindisi.

BRUTTIUM (*Civ.* I.30): the 'toe' of Italy, modern Calabria.

BRUTUS: *see* JUNIUS.

BUTHROTUM (*Civ.* III.16; *Afr.* 19): a town on the coast of Epirus; today Butrint.

BYLLIS (*Civ.* III.12, 40): a town in Epirus, near Apollonia.

C. (*passim*): the abbreviation for the Roman first name Gaius, used because Latin did not originally possess a separate letter G.

Titus CAECILIUS (*Civ.* I.46): one of Afranius' centurions.

Lucius CAECILIUS Metellus (*Civ.* I.33): tribune of the plebs in 49.

Quintus CAECILIUS Metellus Pius (*Span.* 42): Sulla's colleague as consul in 80, subdued resistance in Spain to the government in Rome, 79–71.

Quintus CAECILIUS Metellus Pius Scipio (*Civ.* I.1, 2, 4, 6; III.4, 31, 33, 36–8, 57, 78–83, 88, 90; *Afr.* 1, 4, 8, 20, 24–32, 35–52, 57–61, 67–70, 75–81, 85–90, 96): adoptive son of the foregoing, became father-in-law and consular colleague of Cn. Pompeius Magnus in 52; proconsul of Syria 49–48, fought at Pharsalus; escaped to command the Pompeian forces in Africa in 47–46, including the men brought overland from Cyrenaica by Cato, but died attempting to reach Spain after his defeat at Thapsus.

CAECILIUS Niger (*Span*. 35): a native Lusitanian leader.

Lucius CAECILIUS Rufus (*Civ*. I.23): an ex-praetor (57) captured and released at Corfinium in 49 by Caesar.

CAECINA (*Afr*. 89): perhaps the Aulus Caecina who was later exiled for writing a pamphlet attacking Caesar.

Marcus CAELIUS Rufus (*Civ*. I.2; III.20–2): a talented and unstable young reprobate, brilliantly defended by Cicero in 56; a newcomer to the senate, he held the tribunate in 52 and was a prominent supporter of Caesar, but came to regret that political choice and after attempting, as praetor, to whip up opposition to Caesar in Rome early in 48 led an armed insurrection in which he met his death.

Marcus CAELIUS Vinicianus (*Alex*. 77): as tribune of the plebs in 53, a strong supporter of Pompey; probably governor of the joint province of Bithynia & Pontus in 47, but when he came over to Caesar is not known.

CAESAR: *see* JULIUS.

CALAGURRIS (*Civ*. I.60): a town in the upper Ebro Valley; today Calahorra.

CALENUS: *see* FUFIUS.

Marcus CALIDIUS (*Civ*. I.2): a leading orator of the day, who had held the praetorship in 57.

Marcus CALPURNIUS Bibulus (*Civ*. III.5, 7, 8, 14–18, 31, 110): although Caesar's colleague as aedile (65), praetor (62), and consul (59), ranks with Domitius Ahenobarbus as one of his bitterest and most determined enemies; proconsul of Syria 51–50, died serving as Pompeian naval commander-in-chief in the Adriatic early in 48.

Gnaeus CALPURNIUS Piso (Frugi) (*Afr*. 3, 18): probably proquaestor for Pompeius Magnus in Spain in 49; commanded cavalry under Metellus Scipio in Africa in 47–46; survived the civil wars and became consul in 23, in his late fifties.

Lucius CALPURNIUS Piso (Caesoninus) (*Civ*. I.3): consul in 58, censor in 49, and Caesar's father-in-law from 59.

CALPURNIUS Salvianus (*Alex*. 53, 55): a would-be assailant of Q. Cassius Longinus.

CALVINUS: *see* DOMITIUS.

Gaius CALVISIUS Sabinus (*Civ*. III.34, 35, 56): served as an officer with Caesar in Greece in 48; later praetor (46?) and consul (39) and a pillar of Octavian's regime during the Triumviral period.

CALYDON (*Civ*. III.35): a town in Aetolia.

CAMERINUM (*Civ*. I.15): a town in Picenum.

CAMPANIA (*Civ.* I.14): the coastal district of Italy adjoining Latium to the S.

CANDAVIA (*Civ.* III.11, 79): a region of inland Illyria around Lake Ohrid, on the Via Egnatia.

CANIN(I)US: *see* ACILIUS.

Gaius CANINIUS Rebilus (*Civ.* I.26; II.24, 34; *Afr.* 86, 93; *Span.* 35): a senior officer of Caesar's, who served in Gaul, Italy, and Africa and became praetor in 48(?); chiefly famous for his one-day consulship at the end of 45.

CANOPUS (*Alex.* 25): a town at the mouth of the W arm of the Nile.

CANTABRI (*Civ.* I.38): a N Spanish tribe.

Lucius CANULEIUS (*Civ.* III.42): a senior officer (*legatus*) serving under Caesar in Greece in 48.

CANUSIUM (*Civ.* I.24): an inland town in central Apulia.

CAPITOLIUM (*Civ.* I.6): the precinct of Jupiter Optimus Maximus on the Capitol hill in Rome.

CAPPADOCIA (*Civ.* III.4; *Alex.* 34–5, 40, 66): a kingdom lying between Cilicia and Pontus.

CAPUA (*Civ.* I.10, 14; III.21, 71): the chief town of Campania, deprived of municipal self-government as a punishment for supporting Hannibal in the second Punic War, until it became a colony by Caesar's legislation of 59.

CARALIS (*Civ.* I.30: *Afr.* 98): the chief town of Sardinia; today Cagliari.

Decimus CARFULENUS (*Alex.* 31): an officer serving under Caesar at Alexandria, later to die as a legionary commander at Mutina in 43.

CARMO (*Civ.* II.19; *Alex.* 57, 64): a town in Further Spain between Corduba and Hispalis; today Carmona.

CARRUCA (*Span.* 27): a town in Further Spain.

CARTEIA (*Span.* 32, 36–7): a coastal town in Further Spain, a little NE of Gibraltar.

CASILINUM (*Civ.* III.21): a town in Campania.

CASSIUS (*Span.* 26): a Caesarian prefect of cavalry.

Quintus CASSIUS (*Alex.* 52, 57): deputy (*legatus*) to Q. Cassius Longinus in Spain.

Gaius CASSIUS Longinus (*Civ.* III.5, 101): the later tyrannicide, cousin(?) of Quintus Cassius Longinus; quaestor to Crassus in Syria in 53, escaped from the disaster at Carrhae and organized a highly successful defence of the province against the Parthians in 52–51; tribune in 49; commanded a Pompeian fleet in the Adriatic in 49–48.

Lucius CASSIUS Longinus (*Civ.* III.34–6, 56): younger(?) brother of the above, served under Caesar in Greece in 48, and became tribune of the plebs in 44.

Quintus CASSIUS Longinus (*Civ.* I.2, 5; II.19, 21; *Alex.* 48–64; *Span.* 42): tribune of the plebs in 49, fleeing Rome to join Caesar and his army as war broke out; left by Caesar to govern Spain at the end of 49, he provoked a rising in 48 and met his end the following winter.

CASTOR: *see* TARCONDARIUS.

CASTRA CORNELIA (*Civ.* II.24, 25, 30, 37): the site of Scipio's camp near Utica when he crossed to Africa to fight Hannibal.

CASTULO (*Civ.* I.38): a town in Further Spain, near modern Linares, in the upper reaches of the valley of the River Baetis.

CATO (*Span.* 17): a Lusitanian. *See also* PORCIUS.

Publius CAUCILIUS (*Span.* 32): a Pompeian officer.

Lucius CELLA (*Afr.* 89): father and son, Pompeian supporters in Africa.

CELTIBERIA (*Civ.* I.38, 61): the mountainous and upland region lying to the S and SW of the Ebro Valley and dividing it from the headwaters of the great westward-flowing rivers of Spain.

CENTURION (*passim*): the senior 'warrant officer' rank in the Roman army; each of the 59 centuries that composed a full-strength legion was commanded by a centurion. Centurions might be either experienced soldiers who had risen from the ranks, or men of good birth at or near the beginning of a public or military career (note P. Valerius Flaccus, son of a senator and therefore by definition of equestrian status, serving as a centurion with Caesar in 48).

CERAUNIA (*Civ.* III.6): the steep cliff-bound range running along the coast of Epirus N of Corcyra.

CERCINA (*Afr.* 8, 34): an island in the Gulf of Sfax; today Chergui/Shergi/Kerkenna.

CHERSONENSUS (*Alex.* 10): a small anchorage to the W of Alexandria.

CILICIA(N) (*Civ.* III.3, 4, 88, 101–2, 110; *Alex.* 1, 13, 25–6, 34, 65–6); the SW coastal region of Asia Minor; became a Roman province about 100.

CINGA (*Civ.* I.48): a tributary of the River Sicoris; today the Cinca.

CINGULUM (*Civ.* I.15): a town in northern Picenum (*see also* LABIENUS).

CIRTA (*Afr.* 25): the leading town of Numidia; today Constantine.

Lucius CISPIUS (*Afr.* 62, 67): a squadron commander with Caesar's fleet in Africa.

Gaius CLAUDIUS Marcellus (*Civ.* I.6, 14; III.5; *Alex.* 68): consul in 49, a less passionate opponent of Caesar than his colleague Lentulus.

Marcus CLAUDIUS Marcellus (*Civ.* I.2): consul in 51, elder brother of the consul of 49.

Marcus CLAUDIUS Marcellus Aeserninus (*Alex.* 57–64): quaestor to Q. Cassius Longinus in Spain in 48; survived the civil wars to become consul in 22.

Tiberius CLAUDIUS Nero (*Alex.* 25): an officer serving under Caesar at Alexandria, father of the future Emperor Tiberius.

CLEOPATRA [VII] (*Civ.* III.103, 107–8; *Alex.* 33): born *c.*70, middle daughter of Ptolemy XII Auletes, queen-consort successively of her two younger brothers Ptolemy XIII and XIV.

CLODIUS Arquitius (*Span.* 23): a cavalry commander serving under Caesar in Spain in 46.

Aulus CLODIUS (*Civ.* III.57, 90): a friend of Caesar and Scipio.

Publius CLODIUS Pulcher (*Civ.* III.21): a fiercely ambitious aristocrat, famous as the enemy of Cicero and Milo, and brother of Catullus' lover 'Lesbia' (Clodia), he renounced patrician status (and even adopted the plebeian spelling of his family name Claudius), to become tribune in 58; aedile in 56, he was standing for the praetorship in 52 when killed in a brawl with Milo's retinue.

CLUPEA (*Civ.* II.23; *Afr.* 2, 3): a small port on the outer (E) coast of the E arm of the Bay of Tunis.

Gaius CLUSINAS (*Afr.* 54): a centurion of Caesar's Tenth legion.

CN. (*passim*): the abbreviation for the Roman first name Gnaeus, used because Latin did not originally possess a separate letter G.

COHORT (*passim*): the basic tactical unit of the Roman army, comprising six 'centuries' of a nominal strength of 80 men each, although some cohorts, notably the first in each legion, were double-strength. Ten cohorts made up a legion.

COMANA (*Alex.* 34–5): a town in Pontus.

COMANA (*Alex.* 66): a town in Cappadocia (probably here an error for the preceding; see note on the passage).

Quintus COMINIUS (*Afr.* 44, 46): a senator (?) serving under Caesar in the African campaign.

COMMAGENE (*Civ.* III.4): a small kingdom tucked in to the NW of the great bend of the Euphrates north of Zeugma, between the river and the ranges of Amanus and the eastern Taurus.

COMPSA (*Civ.* III.22): a town on the inland borders of Campania.

Gaius CONSIDIUS (*Afr.* 89): son of the following.

Gaius CONSIDIUS Longus (*Civ.* II.23; *Afr.* 3–5, 33, 43, 76, 86, 93): praetor in the 50s, governor of Africa 51(?)–50, refused to hand over the province to his legitimate successor, L. Aelius Tubero, in 49, and placed himself and his legion first under the authority of P. Attius Varus when the latter arrived from Italy later that year, and then under Scipio in 47–46.

CONSUL: one of the two annually elected magistrates (minimum qualifying age: 42) to whom the Romans entrusted overall charge of the state and command of its armies; expected, but not compelled, to act in accordance with the advice of the senate.

Gaius COPONIUS (*Civ.* III.5, 26): praetor in 49, Pompeian fleet commander in 48.

CORCYRA (*Civ.* III.3, 7, 8, 11, 15, 16, 58, 100): the island now called Corfu or Kerkyra.

CORDUBA (*Civ.* II.19–21; *Alex.* 49, 52, 54, 57–61, 64; *Span.* 2–4, 6, 10–12, 32–4): the leading town of Further Spain (*Ulterior*), lying on the River Baetis; today Cordoba.

CORFINIUM (*Civ.* I.15–21, 23–5, 34; II.28, 32; III.10): the capital of the Paeligni, situated in an inland plain in the mountains E of Rome.

Publius CORNELIUS (*Afr.* 76): a re-enlisted veteran serving as a garrison commander under Scipio in Africa in 47–46.

Lucius CORNELIUS Balbus (*Civ.* III.19): a native of Gades, granted Roman citizenship at the end of the Sertorian war; like his identically named uncle (who earned a consulship in 40), a supporter and agent of Caesar's; became quaestor in 44.

Lucius CORNELIUS Lentulus Crus (*Civ.* I.1, 2, 4, 5, 14; III.4, 96, 102, 104; *Alex.* 68): consul in 49, one of the most diehard of Caesar's enemies; survived Pharsalus, but was killed afterwards in Egypt.

Publius CORNELIUS Lentulus Marcellinus (*Civ.* III.62, 64, 65): son or nephew of Gnaeus Cornelius Lentulus Marcellinus, the consul of 56, a staunch Pompeian but dead by 49; served as an officer under Caesar at Dyrrachium in 48.

Publius CORNELIUS Lentulus Spinther (*Civ.* I.15, 16, 21–3; III.83, 102): elected a Pontifex after 63; urban praetor in 60 and governor of Nearer Spain in 59; consul in 57 and governor of Cilicia 56–54, winning a triumph which he eventually celebrated in 51; the most senior of the Pompeian commanders in the N of Italy in 49, occupying the strongest town with the largest force that we hear of; pardoned by Caesar on being captured at Corfinium, he rejoined Pompey's forces in Greece, and escaped after Pharsalus to Rhodes, dying not long afterwards.

Faustus CORNELIUS Sulla (*Civ.* I.6; *Afr.* 87, 95): son of the following, and son-in-law to Pompeius Magnus; quaestor in 54, held commands (as *proquaestor pro praetore*) in Greece and Africa 49–46.

Lucius CORNELIUS Sulla (Felix) (*Civ.* I.4, 5, 7; *Afr.* 56): consul in 88 and 80; believer in strong senatorial government; victor of the civil war between himself and Marius and followers which lasted from 87 to 82, and dictator 82–81.

Publius CORNELIUS Sulla (*Civ.* III.51, 89, 99): nephew of the preceding; elected consul in 65, but barred from taking up office after being convicted of electoral bribery, he joined the conspiracy of Catiline in 63 and was successfully defended by Cicero, in a still extant speech, against a charge of public violence.

Quintus CORNIFICIUS (*Alex.* 42–4, 47): quaestor to Caesar as consul in 48, placed in charge of Illyricum after Pharsalus.

COSA (*Civ.* I.34): a town on the Tyrrhenian coast of Italy *c.*100 km. NW of Rome; today Ansedonia.

COTTA: *see* AURELIUS.

COTYS (*Civ.* III.4, 36): a Thracian king allied to Pompey.

CRASSUS: *see* LICINIUS, OTACILIUS.

CRASTINUS (*Civ.* III.91, 99): an ex-centurion serving with Caesar.

CREMONA (*Civ.* I.24): a town in the Po Valley, still called the same.

CRETE (*Civ.* III.4–5; *Alex.* 1): annexed from Egypt by Rome in 58.

CRISPUS: *see* MARCIUS, SALLUSTIUS.

CURICTA (*Civ.* III.10): an island of the Dalmatian archipelago; today Krk.

CURIO: *see* SCRIBONIUS.

CURIUS: *see* VIBIUS.

CYCLADES (*Civ.* III.3): the group of islands in the Aegean still known by this name.

CYPRUS (*Civ.* III.102, 106): the same.

CYRENE (*Civ.* III.5): the coastal area of North Africa immediately W of Egypt.

DALMATIANS (*Civ.* III.9): inhabitants of the central part of the E Adriatic coast.

DAMASIPPUS: *see* LICINIUS.

DARDANI (*Civ.* III.4): a tribe living to the NW of Thrace.

DECIDIUS Saxa, Lucius (*Civ.* I.66): an officer, probably of émigré Italian stock, serving with Caesar in Spain in 49; went on to become tribune of the plebs in 43, leaving Rome to join Antony; chiefly notorious for his defeat by the Parthians in 40 when commanding an army in Syria for Antony.

Gaius DECIMIUS (*Afr.* 34): an ex-quaestor commanding the Pompeian garrison at Cercina in 47.

DEIOTARUS (*Civ.* III.4; *Alex.* 34, 39, 40, 67–70, 77–8): began his career in the 80s as tetrarch of one of the Galatian tribes and came to rule almost the whole people; recognized as King of Galatia by the Roman senate, he duly paid his debt by supporting Pompey in Greece in 48.

DELPHI (*Civ.* III.56): a town on the N side of the Corinthian Gulf, still called the same.

DIANA (*Civ.* III.33, 105): the Roman name for the goddess Artemis.

Gaius DIDIUS (*Span.* 37, 40): commander of Caesar's fleet at Gades in 45.

DIOSCORIDES (*Civ.* III.109): an Alexandrian notable.

Gnaeus DOMITIUS (*Civ.* II.42): a cavalry commander serving under Curio in Africa.

Lucius DOMITIUS Ahenobarbus (*Civ.* I.6, 15–17, 19–21, 23, 34, 36, 56, 57; II.3, 18, 22, 28, 32; III.83, 99): one of Caesar's bitterest foes; consul in 54, appointed to take over from Caesar in Gaul at the beginning of 49, he briefly commanded a considerable force at Corfinium in February 49, and was captured and let go free by Caesar. He took command at Massilia but was unable to prevent Caesar's forces taking the city and fled to join Pompey in Greece in winter 49–48; he was killed immediately after the battle of Pharsalus.

Gnaeus DOMITIUS Calvinus (*Civ.* III.34, 36–8, 78–9, 89; *Alex.* 9, 34–40, 65, 69, 74; *Afr.* 86, 93): consul in 53; one of the most senior of Caesar's supporters, played an important part in the fighting in Greece in 48 and after Pharsalus was left in charge of Asia and the adjoining provinces. Campaigned unsuccessfully against Pharnaces in early 47.

DOMNILAUS (*Civ.* III.4): a Galatian prince.

DYRRACHIUM (*Civ.* I.25, 27; III.5, 9, 11, 13, 26, 30, 41–2, 44, 53, 57–8, 62, 78–80, 84, 87, 89, 100; *Alex.* 48): earlier known by its Greek name of Epidamnus, the best port on the coast of Epirus; today Dürres (Durazzo) in Albania.

EBRO: *see* HIBERUS.

EGUS (*Civ.* III.59, 61, 79, [84]): a Gallic prince, serving with Caesar's cavalry in Greece, who deserted to Pompey.

EGYPT(IAN) (*Civ.* III.3, 5, 40, 104, 106, 110, 112; *Alex.* 2, 3, 8, 13, 26, 33–4, 65, 78): Latin *Aegypt(i)us*.

ELIS (*Civ.* III.105): a city in the W Peloponnese.

ENNIUS, Quintus (*Span.* 23, 31): epic and tragic poet, pioneer of Latin hexameter verse.

EPHESUS (-IA) (*Civ.* III.33, 105): the leading city of the province of Asia; today Efes.

EPIDAURUS (*Alex*. 44): a town in Illyria; today Cavtat, just S of modern Dubrovnik.

EPIRUS (*Civ*. III.4, 12, 13, 42, 47, 61, 78, 80): a region on the NW border of Greece, extending from the Pindus ranges to the sea and from N of the Gulf of Arta to beyond Dyrrachium.

Marcus EPPIUS (*Afr*. 89): quaestor by 52, commanded troops under Scipio in Africa in 46.

EQUESTRIAN ORDER (*Civ*. I.23; *Alex*. 40; and *passim*): the Roman upper class, comprising men qualified, by cavalry service, free birth, and possession (or their fathers' possession) of 400,000 sesterces' worth of property, to be enrolled in the 18 voting centuries of *equites* (cavalry)—although by the Late Republic the military connection was largely theoretical (though not quite so unreal as in the case of the modern British knighthood) and the ordinary cavalry of the Roman army was no longer drawn from this source. Senators were simply members of this élite who decided to enter public life by standing for the office of quaestor. If elected, they ceased to be *equites*, but their sons, brothers, and fathers remained so unless and until they too embarked on the same course. None the less, it appears that sons of senators and holders of posts which normally preceded election to the quaestorship, such as military tribunates, in practice enjoyed higher status than that accorded to men who (or whose ancestors) held no public office. It appears from the *Spanish War* that a substantial number of Roman settlers in Further Spain had attained equestrian status.

EUPHRANOR (*Alex*. 15, 25): a Rhodian admiral.

Gaius FABIUS (*Civ*. I.37, 40, 48): a senior officer commanding some of Caesar's legions in Spain in 49; possibly the same man as the praetor of 58.

Quintus FABIUS Maximus (*Span*. 2, 12, 41): praetor in 49, one of Caesar's senior commanders in Spain 46–45, rewarded with a suffect consulship in 45.

FANUM (FORTUNAE) (*Civ*. I.11): a town at the mouth of the Metaurus on the Adriatic coast of Italy, between Ariminum and Ancona; today Fano.

Marcus FAVONIUS (*Civ*. III.36, 57): praetor in 49, a committed supporter and adviser of Pompey.

Gaius FELGINAS (*Civ*. III.71): a Roman equestrian from Placentia, killed while serving with Caesar at Dyrrachium.

FIRMUM (*Civ*. I.16): a town in Picenum, near the Adriatic coast; today Fermo.

FLACCUS: *see* VALERIUS.

Gaius FLAVIUS (*Span.* 26): a Roman of equestrian status from Asta.

FLEGINAS: *see* FELGINAS.

Aulus FONTEIUS (*Afr.* 54): a military tribune of Caesar's Tenth legion.

FRENTANI (*Civ.* I.23): a people occupying the central Adriatic seaboard of Italy, between Picenum and the Marrucini.

Quintus FUFIUS Calenus (*Civ.* I.87; III.8, 14, 26, 56, 106; *Alex.* 44): one of Caesar's most senior officers; in 49, fought in Spain; in 48, sent by Caesar to southern Greece during the blockade at Dyrrachium, and remained in charge there after Pharsalus. Became consul in 47.

Quintus FULGINIUS (*Civ.* I.46): a re-enlisted centurion.

FULVIUS Postumus (*Civ.* III.62): one of Caesar's officers at Dyrrachium.

Gaius FUNDANIUS (*Span.* 11): a Roman of equestrian status.

Aulus GABINIUS (*Civ.* III.4, 103, 110; *Alex.* 3, 42–3): consul in 58; becoming proconsul of Syria, he invaded Egypt in 55 to restore Cleopatra's father, Ptolemy XII Auletes, to his throne for an alleged sum of 10,000 talents. He was exiled around the end of 54 for misconduct as governor of Syria, and restored by Caesar in 49.

GADES (*Civ.* II.18, 20, 21; *Span.* 37, 39, 40, 42): an important seaport at the mouth of the River Baetis; today Cadiz.

GAETULI(AN) (*Afr.* 25, 32, 35, 43, 55–6, 61–2, 67, 93): a Berber people living predominantly S of the Atlas range, along the southern borders of Mauretania and Numidia.

GALATIA (*Civ.* III.4; *Alex.* 67, 78): an area in central Asia Minor occupied and settled by several tribes of invading Gauls in the 3rd century BC; also called (in Latin) Gallograecia.

GALLI(A): *see* GAUL(S).

Gaius GALLONIUS (*Civ.* II.18, 20): a Roman equestrian.

GALLUS: *see* TUTICANUS.

GANYMEDES (*Alex.* 4, 5, 12, 23, 33): guardian to Arsinoe and successor to Achillas as commander of the Egyptian army.

GAUL(S) (*Civ.* I.6, 7, 10, 18, 29, 33, 39, 48, 51; II.1, 40; III.2, 4, 22, 42, 59, 79, 87; *Alex.* 17; *Afr.* 6, 19, 20, 29, 34, 40, 73): Transalpine Gaul (usually called simply Gaul by Caesar) corresponds roughly to modern France; the country was a prime source of auxiliary cavalry at this period; Cisalpine Gaul means the Po Valley, an area which was heavily Romanized by 49 BC.

GENUSUS (*Civ.* III.75, 76): a river flowing into the sea between Dyrrachium and Apollonia; today the Shkumbin.

GERGOVIA (*Civ.* III.73): a fortress in Gaul, scene of a famous but unsuccessful siege by Caesar in 52.

GERMANS, GERMANY (*Civ.* I.7, 83; III.4, 52, 87; *Alex.* 29; *Afr.* 19, 29, 40): a catch-all term used to describe the inhabitants and the country northward and eastward from the Alps and the Rhine Valley. Some 'German' tribes lived W of the Rhine.

GOMPHI (*Civ.* III.80, 81): a town in W Thessaly.

GRACCHI: *see* SEMPRONIUS.

Aulus GRANIUS (*Civ.* III.71): a Roman equestrian from Puteoli, killed while serving with Caesar at Dyrrachium.

GREECE, GREEKS (*Civ.* I.25; III.11, 30, 102, 105; *Alex.* 15, 44, 47): the same.

HADRUMETUM (*Civ.* II.23; *Afr.* 3, 21, 24, 33, 43, 62–3, 67, 89, 97): a port on the E coast of Tunisia; today Sousse.

HALIACMON (*Civ.* III.36, 37): a river on the border of Thessaly and Macedonia, still called the same.

HEGESARETOS (*Civ.* III.35): an influential Thessalian.

HELVII (*Civ.* I.35): a tribe of southern Gaul.

HERACLIA (*Civ.* III.79): here, Heraclia Lyncestis, a place on the borders of Macedonia and Epirus.

HERCULES (*Civ.* II.18, 21): the Greek hero-god.

HERMINIAN MTS (*Alex.* 48): mountains in Lusitania.

HIBERUS (*Civ.* I.60–3, 65, 68, 69, 72, 73; *Alex.* 64): the principal river of Nearer Spain, debouching into the sea S of Tarraco; today the Ebro.

HIEMPSAL (*Afr.* 56): father of Juba; installed as king of Numidia by Pompeius Magnus in 81.

HIPPO REGIUS (*Afr.* 96): an important port on the coast of Numidia, and alternative seat of its kings (*see* ZAMA).

HIRPINI (*Civ.* III.22): an Italian people occupying territory inland from Campania.

HIRRUS: *see* LUCILIUS.

HISPALIS (*Civ.* II.18, 20; *Alex.* 56–7; *Span.* 35–6, 39, 40, 42): an important town on the site of modern Seville.

IACETANI (*Civ.* I.60): a tribe of Nearer Spain.

IADER (*Alex.* 42): an Illyrian town.

IGILIUM (*Civ.* I.34): an island about 30 km. off the Italian coast N of Rome; today Giglio.

IGUVIUM (*Civ.* I.12): a town in Umbria, today Gubbio.

ILERDA (*Civ.* I.38, 41–9, 56, 59, 63, 69, 73, 78; II.17): a town occupying a steep hill beside the River Sicoris; today Lérida, some 150 km. W of Barcelona.

ILIPA (*Alex.* 57): today Alcalá del Rio, a little N of Hispalis.

ILLURGAVONENSES (*Civ.* I.60): a Spanish tribe living along the Ebro.

ILLYRICUM (*Civ.* III.9, 78; *Alex.* 42–4): the name given by the Romans to the Adriatic coast and its hinterland between approximately modern Trieste/Trst and Albania.

INDO (*Span.* 10): a native Spanish ruler.

ISSA (*Civ.* III.9; *Alex.* 47): an island of the Dalmatian archipelago, today Vis.

ISTHMUS (*Civ.* III.56): the isthmus of Corinth.

ITALICA (*Civ.* II.20; *Alex.* 52, 57; *Span.* 25): a town near modern Seville, founded by Scipio Africanus in 205 after his defeat of the Carthaginians; so called because it was the first settlement of Italian veterans in Spain.

ITALY, ITALIAN (*Civ.* I.2, 6, 9, 25, 27, 29, 30, 35, 48, 53; II.17, 18, 22, 32; III. 1, 4, 6, 10, 12, 13, 18, 21, 22, 29, 39, 42, 57, 73, 78, 82, 87; *Afr.* 22, 36, 54, 72; *Alex.* 53, 68, 77–8; *Span.* 1, 10): modern peninsular Italy, S of the Po Valley.

ITURAEA (*Afr.* 20): the region between, and including, the Lebanon and Antilebanon ranges.

JUBA (I) (*Civ.* I.6; II.25–6, 36–44; *Afr.* 6, 25, 36, 43, 48, 52, 55, 57–9, 66, 74, 77, 91–7; *Alex.* 51): king of Numidia from before 50 (when Curio had attempted to pass a law annexing his kingdom as a Roman province) until the defeat at Thapsus in 46; he enjoyed inherited ties with Pompey and was a personal enemy of Caesar, who had once physically assaulted him in Rome.

JULIAN LAW (*Civ.* I.14; *Afr.* 87): a law passed on the proposal of a Julius, in both the present cases Gaius Julius Caesar (see notes *ad loc.*).

Gaius JULIUS Caesar (*passim*): b. 100(?), praetor 62, consul 59, proconsul of Cisalpine and Transalpine Gaul 58–49 and conqueror of the latter 58–51, consul 48 and 46–44, dictator 49, 48–47, 46–45, 45–44, and for life. Political ally of Pompeius 60–52, then his rival and opponent, defeating him at Pharsalus in Greece in 48, his followers at Thapsus in Africa in 46, and his sons at Munda in Spain in 45. Murdered in the senate, 15 March 44.

Lucius JULIUS Caesar (*Civ.* I.8, 10; II.23; *Afr.* 88–9): son of the identically named consul of 64, who was a distant relative of the dictator; unlike his father, a Pompeian sympathizer, and later supporter; proquaestor to Cato at Utica in 46.

Sextus JULIUS Caesar (*Civ.* II.20; *Alex.* 66): grandson of Sex. Julius Caesar, consul in 91, who was probably the dictator's uncle.

JUNIUS (*Span.* 16): a Pompeian soldier at Ategua.

Decimus JUNIUS Brutus Albinus (*Civ.* I.36, 56, 57; II.3, 5, 6, 22); one of Caesar's senior officers in Gaul 50–49, and placed in charge of Transalpine Gaul 48–46; later, praetor in 45(?) and one of the conspirators against Caesar in 44.

Lucius JUVENTIUS Laterensis (*Alex.* 53–5): a Roman officer involved in the plot against Q. Cassius Longinus.

Titus LABIENUS (*Civ.* I.15; III.13, 19, 71, 87; *Afr.* 13, 15–16, 19–21, 24, 29, 33, 38–40, 49–52, 61, 65–6, 69, 70, 75, 78; *Span.* 18, 31): of the local aristocracy of Cingulum in Picenum, and a commissioner for its formal constitution as a municipality; became tribune of the plebs in 63, perhaps praetor by 59; served as a senior officer (*legatus*) with Caesar in Gaul 58–49, deserted to Pompey at the start of the civil war, fought for him in Greece, Africa, and Spain, and died at Munda.

LACEDAEMON (*Civ.* III.4): the SE Peloponnese, chief town Sparta.

Decimus LAELIUS (*Civ.* III.5, 7, 40, 100): tribune in 54; served as a special emissary from Pompey to the consuls at Capua in February 49, and commanded a Pompeian fleet in the Adriatic in 48.

LARINUM (*Civ.* I.23): a town on the borders of Apulia and the territory of the Frentani; today Larino.

LARISA (*Civ.* III.80, 81, 96–8): the chief town of Thessaly, still known by the same name.

LATERENSIS: *see* JUVENTIUS.

LEGION:

I	*Civ.* III.88; *Span.* 18
II	*Alex.* 53–4, 57; *Span.* 13
III	*Civ.* III.88; *Span.* 30
IV	*Afr.* 35, 52
V (*Alauda?*)	*Afr.* 1, 28, 47, 60, 81, 84
V (Spanish)	*Alex.* 50, 52–5, 57; *Span.* 23, 30
VI	*Alex.* 33, 69, 76–7; *Afr.* 35, 52; *Span.* 12
VIII	*Civ.* I.18; III.89
IX	*Civ.* I.45; III.45, 46, 62, 66, 67, 89; *Afr.* 53, 60, 62, 81; *Span.* 34(?)
X	*Civ.* III.89, 91; *Afr.* 16, 53–4, 60, 81; *Span.* 30, 31
XI	*Civ.* III.34
XII	*Civ.* I.15; III.34
XIII	*Civ.* I.7, 12, 18; *Afr.* 34, 60, 62, 81; *Span.* 34
XIV	*Civ.* I.46; *Afr.* 34, 45, 60, 62, 81
XXI	*Alex.* 53–4, 57
XXV	*Afr.* 60
XXVI	*Afr.* 60
XXVII	*Civ.* III.34
XXVIII	*Afr.* 60
XXIX	*Afr.* 60
XXX	*Alex.* 53–4, 57

XXXVI	*Alex.* 34, 39, 40
XXXVII	*Alex.* 9
Cilician ('*Gemella*')	*Civ.* III.4, 88
Deiotarus'	*Alex.* 34, 39, 40, 68–9
Local (*Vernaculae*)	*Civ.* II.20; *Alex.* 53–4, 57; *Span.* 7, 10, 12, 20
Pontic	*Alex.* 34, 39, 40
Recruit	*Civ.* III.28, 29, 34; *Alex.* 42

LENNIUM (*Span.* 35): a place in Lusitania.

LENTULUS: *see* CORNELIUS.

LEPIDUS: *see* AEMILIUS.

LEPTIS (MINOR) (*Civ.* II.38; *Afr.* 7, 9, 10, 29, 61–3, 67, 97); a port on the E coast of the province of Africa between Hadrumetum and Thapsus; also known as Leptiminus.

LIBERALIA (*Span.* 31): a Roman festival which took place on 17 March.

LIBO: *see* SCRIBONIUS.

Marcus LICINIUS Crassus (*Civ.* III.31): consul in 70 and 55, a partner with Caesar and Pompey in the so-called 'First Triumvirate', whose end was precipitated by his death fighting the Parthians at Carrhae in the Syrian desert in 53.

Publius LICINIUS Crassus Damasippus (*Civ.* II.44; *Afr.* 96): a Pompeian senator who fought under Juba and Scipio in Africa, 48–46.

Lucius LICINIUS Squillus (*Alex.* 52, 55): an assailant of Q. Cassius Longinus.

Publius LIGARIUS (*Afr.* 64): see note to *Afr.* 89 on Q. Ligarius.

Quintus LIGARIUS (*Afr.* 89): a deputy (*legatus*) to C. Considius as governor of Africa in 50; later defended by Cicero before Caesar on the charge of abetting the Pompeian war effort.

LILYBAEUM (*Afr.* 1, 2, 34, 37): a port at the W end of Sicily.

LISSUS (*Civ.* III.26, 28, 29, 40, 42, 78): a strategically important town some 30 miles N of Dyrrachium.

Lucius LIVINEIUS Regulus (*Afr.* 89): a senator serving under Caesar in Africa in 46.

LONGINUS: *see* CASSIUS.

LONGUS: *see* CONSIDIUS.

LUCANIA (*Civ.* I.30): the area of Italy which lies between Campania to the N and Bruttium to the S.

Lucius LUCCEIUS (*Civ.* III.18): praetor in 67, turned down the governorship of Sardinia in the following year, prosecuted Catiline in 64, and was an unsuccessful candidate for the consulship in

59; wrote history (of which none survives), and is famous as recipient of his friend Cicero's request (*Letters to his Friends*, V.12) to write a laudatory monograph on part of his (Cicero's) career.

LUCERIA (*Civ.* I.24): an important town in the N of Apulia; today Lucera.

Gaius LUCILIUS Hirrus (*Civ.* I.15; III.82): tribune in 53, cousin to Pompey and one of his commanders in N Italy early in 49; negotiated with the Parthians on Pompey's behalf in 48, and survived long enough to have to flee the proscriptions in 43.

Quintus LUCRETIUS Vespillo (*Civ.* I.18; III.7): a Roman senator, commanding Pompeian troops at Sulmo in 49 and ships in the Adriatic in 48.

LUPUS: *see* RUTILIUS.

LUSITANIA (*Civ.* I.38; *Alex.* 48, 51; *Span.* 35): the region of Spain lying NW of the valley of the Baetis.

LUSITANIANS (*Civ.* I.44, 48; *Span.* 18, 35–6, 38, 40): inhabitants of Lusitania, some of whom lived by raiding and made effective light-armed troops.

LYCOMEDES (*Alex.* 66): a Bithynian of high birth, installed by Caesar in 47 as priest of Ma-Bellona at Comana.

MACEDONIA (*Civ.* III.4, 11, 33, 34, 36, 57, 79, 102; *Alex.* 42): the extensive region lying N and E of the Olympus range.

Numerius MAGIUS (*Civ.* I.24, 26): a Roman equestrian officer of Pompey's.

MALACA (*Alex.* 64): a port on the S coast of Spain, today Malaga.

MALCHUS (*Alex.* 1): king of Nabataea, a small kingdom lying on the E side of the head of the Red Sea.

MANILIUS Tusculus (*Alex.* 53): a would-be assailant of Q. Cassius Longinus.

Lucius MANLIUS Torquatus (*Civ.* I.24; III.11; *Afr.* 96): one of the Pompeian commanders in Italy in 49, probably praetor shortly before that date; garrison commander at Oricum in 48, fought in Africa in 46, died attempting to reach Spain.

MARCELLINUS: *see* CORNELIUS Lentulus.

MARCELLUS: *see* CLAUDIUS.

Quintus MARCIUS (*Span.* 11): a military tribune.

MARCIUS Crispus (*Afr.* 77): a military tribune serving under Caesar in Africa.

Lucius MARCIUS Philippus (*Civ.* I.6): consul in 56, stepfather of the future Augustus.

Lucius MARCIUS Philippus (*Civ.* I.6): son of the foregoing, tribune of the plebs in 49.

MARCIUS Rufus (*Civ*. II.23, 24, 43): quaestor in 49, served under Curio in Africa.

Gaius MARIUS (*Afr*. 32, 35, 56): uncle by marriage of Julius Caesar, he was the first man of his family and of his town (Arpinum) to attain the consulship, which he did in 107 as a result of a popular reaction against the inefficient conduct by the traditional aristocracy of a war against the Numidian king, Jugurtha. His success in Numidia, and a simultaneous threat to Italy by migrating German tribes, swept him to five further consulships (104–100) and the status of national saviour, somewhat sullied by his ultimately and dramatically repudiated alliance with the party of the demagogic tribune Appuleius Saturninus (*q.v.*). In 88, in the political quarrelling and resulting civil war which followed the Social War (the great struggle of the non-Roman peoples of the peninsula to reshape their relationship with the Roman state), he emerged as a deadly rival to the consul L. Cornelius Sulla. Sulla led his army on Rome, but Marius and several others with a price on their heads saved themselves by flight to Africa. On Sulla's subsequent departure to the East to campaign against Mithridates VI of Pontus, Marius returned, raised troops, and allied himself with other anti-Sullan leaders. Together with them he took Rome at the end of 87, intent on vengeance, but died, at the age of 71 or 72, a few days after entering on his seventh consulship in 86.

MARRUCINI (*Civ*. I.23; II.34): a people occupying the central Adriatic seaboard of Italy, between the Vestini to the N and the Frentani to the S.

MARSI (*Civ*. I.15, 20; II.27, 29): a people of central Italy, E of Rome.

MASSILIA (-IOTS) (*Civ*. I.34–6, 56–8; II.1, 3–7, 14, 15, 17, 18, 21, 22): a Greek city near the mouth of the Rhône, independent of Rome until 49; today Marseilles.

MAURETANIA (*Civ*. I.6, 39, 60; *Alex*. 51–2, 59; *Afr*. 22–3, 95): the region of N Africa lying W of the Roman province and Numidia.

MAXIMUS: *see* FABIUS.

MAZACA (*Alex*. 66): a town in Cappadocia, modern Kayseri.

MEDOBREGA (*Alex*. 48): a town in Lusitania.

MEMNON (*Span*. 25): legendary king of Ethiopia, killed by Achilles at Troy.

MENEDEMUS (*Civ*. III.34): a Macedonian notable.

Lucius MERCELLO (*Alex*. 52, 55): an assailant of Q. Cassius Longinus.

MESSALLA: *see* VALERIUS.

MESSANA (*Civ*. II.3; III.101; *Afr*. 28): modern Messina, a Sicilian town at the N end of the straits bearing its name.

Gaius MESSIUS (*Afr.* 33, 43): an ex-aedile serving under Caesar in Africa.

METELLUS: *see* CAECILIUS.

METROPOLIS (-ITAE) (*Civ.* III.80, 81): a town in W. Thessaly.

MILO: *see* ANNIUS.

Gaius MINUCIUS Reginus (*Afr.* 68): a Pompeian garrison commander, of equestrian rank.

MINUCIUS Rufus (*Civ.* III.7): a Pompeian squadron commander in the Adriatic in 48.

MINUCIUS Silo (*Alex.* 52-3, 55): an assailant of Q. Cassius Longinus.

Quintus MINUCIUS Thermus (*Civ.* I.12): supporter and fellow tribune of Cato in 62, praetor in 53, governor of the province of Asia 52-50, propraetor in Umbria in 49.

MITHRIDATES the Pergamene (*Alex.* 26-8, 78): son of a Galatian petty ruler but reputed to be the bastard of Mithridates VI.

MITHRIDATES VI Eupator (*Alex*: 72-3, 78): king of Pontus 120-63, a lifelong opponent of Rome.

MOORS (*Afr.* 3, 6, 7, 83): inhabitants of Mauretania.

MUNATIUS Flaccus (*Alex.* 52): an assailant of Q. Cassius Longinus.

Lucius MUNATIUS Flaccus (*Span.* 19): the Pompeian commander in Ategua (see Dio XLIII.33-4); perhaps the same man as the foregoing.

Lucius MUNATIUS Plancus (*Civ.* I.40; *Afr.* 4): commanded legions in Gaul in 54 and 53; served under Caesar in Spain in 49 and in Africa in 46 as a legionary commander (*legatus*); eventually played an important part in the events that followed the death of Caesar, became consul in 42, founded the colony of Lugdunum (Lyons), and by adroitly timed changes of loyalty survived the conflict of Antony and Octavian to become a pillar of the Augustan state.

MUNDA (*Span.* 27, 32-4, 36, 41-2): a town in Further Spain, normally identified with modern Montilla, but perhaps lying further W, near Osuna, where lead sling-shot bearing Pompeius' name have been found; site of the decisive battle between Gnaeus Pompeius the younger and Caesar on 17 March 45.

MURCUS: *see* STAIUS.

MYTILENE (*Civ.* III.102): the chief town and port of the island of Lesbos.

NABATAEA (*Alex.* 1): the region around the modern Gulf of Aqaba at the head of the Red Sea.

NARBO (*Civ.* I.37; II.21): a Roman colonial foundation in SW Gaul; today Narbonne.

Lucius NASIDIUS (*Civ.* II.3, 4, 7; *Afr.* 64, 98): a Pompeian fleet commander.

NAUPACTUS (*Civ.* III.35): an Aetolian town on the N shore of the narrows of the Gulf of Corinth.

NEAPOLIS (1) (*Civ.* III.21): Naples.

NEAPOLIS (2) (*Afr.* 2): a small port S of Clupea (*q.v.*).

NERO: *see* CLAUDIUS.

NICOPOLIS (*Alex.* 36–7): a town in Lesser Armenia.

NILE (*Alex.* 5, 13, 27–30): the chief river of Egypt.

NONIUS Asprenas (*Afr.* 80; *Span.* 10): a senator serving under Caesar in Africa and in Spain in 47–45.

NORICUM (*Civ.* I.18): an Alpine kingdom.

NUMIDIA(N) (*Civ.* II.25, 38, 39, 41; *Afr.* 6, 13–15, 18–19, 22, 32, 35–6, 38–40, 43, 48, 52, 59, 61, 66, 69, 70, 75, 78; *Alex.* 51): a North African kingdom whose territory lay to the W and S of the Roman province of Africa.

NYMPHAEUM (*Civ.* III.26): an anchorage near Lissus in Epirus.

OBUCULA (*Alex.* 57): a place in Further Spain.

OCEANUS: *see* ATLANTIC.

Marcus OCTAVIUS (*Civ.* III.5, 9; *Afr.* 44; *Alex.* 42–7); son of the consul of 76 and one of Pompey's fleet commanders in the Adriatic 49–47.

Marcus OPIMIUS (*Civ.* III.38): a Caesarian cavalry commander in Greece in 48.

Spurius(?) OPPIUS (*Afr.* 68): a senior officer (*legatus*) serving under Caesar in Africa.

ORCHOMENUS (*Civ.* III.56): a town in Boeotia.

ORICUM (*Civ.* III.7, 8, 11–16, 23, 24, 39, 40, 78, 90): a port in northern Epirus, at the head of the Gulf of Valona (modern Vlone).

OSCA (*Civ.* I.60): a town in the northern part of the middle Ebro basin.

OTACILIUS Crassus (*Civ.* III.28, 29): the Pompeian commander in Lissus.

OTOGESA (*Civ.* I.61, 68, 70): a place on the River Ebro a little downstream from its confluence with the Segre.

PACIAECUS: *see* VIBIUS.

PACIDEIUS (*Afr.* 13, 78): two brothers(?) commanding forces under Scipio in Africa.

PAELIGNI(AN) (*Civ.* I.15, 18; II.29, 35): a mountain people inhabiting a small territory between the Marsi and the peoples of the Adriatic coast.

PALAEPHARSALUS (*Alex.* 48): the site of the battle of Pharsalus.

PALAESTE (*Civ.* III.6): a cove (modern Palasë) N of Panormus (modern Palermo) on the Ceraunian coast.

PARADA (*Afr.* 87): a town between Thapsus and Utica.

PARAETONIUM (*Alex.* 8): a port on the Libyan coast W of Alexandria.

PARTHINI (*Civ.* III.11, 41, 42): an Illyrian people living in the area around Dyrrachium.

PARTHIA(NS) (*Civ.* I.9; III.31, 82): a powerful people occupying Mesopotamia and in direct contact with the Roman empire along the Syrian border.

Quintus PATISIUS (*Alex.* 34): an officer serving under Domitius Calvinus in Asia Minor.

Quintus PEDIUS (*Civ.* III.22; *Span.* 2, 12): nephew of Caesar, held a praetorship in 48 and commanded under Caesar in Spain in 46–45. Died as suffect consul in 43.

PELUSIUM (*Civ.* III.103, 108; *Alex.* 26): a town at the mouth of the E arm of the Nile delta.

PERGAMUM (*Civ.* III.31, 105; *Alex.* 78): an important city in the N of the province of Asia, formerly seat of the Attalid kings.

PETRA (*Civ.* III.42): a small promontory in the bay S of Dyrrachium.

PETRAEUS (*Civ.* III.35): a Thessalian noble.

Marcus PETREIUS (*Civ.* I.38–43, 53, 61–7, 72–6, 87; II.17, 18; *Afr.* 18–20, 24, 91, 94, 97): praetor 64(?), *legatus* governing Lusitania for Pompeius 55–49, joined the latter in Greece in 48 having been spared by Caesar after being defeated (together with Afranius) by him in Spain in 49, survived Pharsalus to command troops under Scipio in Africa; one of the earliest identifiable examples of a 'professional' military man.

PHARNACES (*Alex.* 34–41, 65, 69–76, 78; *Span.* 1): recognized by Rome as ruler of the Bosporan kingdom since 63, when having forced his father Mithridates VI of Pontus to commit suicide at the end of his long struggle against Rome, he brought his corpse to Pompey. Took advantage of the war between Pompey and Caesar to invade Pontus and attempt to re-establish his father's power. Defeated by Caesar at Zela in 47.

PHAROS: *see* PHARUS.

PHARSALUS (*Alex.* 42): a town in S Thessaly, near the site of the decisive battle between Caesar and Pompey in 48. *See also* PALAEPHARSALUS.

PHARUS (*Civ.* III.111–12; *Alex.* 14–19, 26): the island, famous for its lighthouse bearing the same name, forming the outer side of the harbour at Alexandria; also the name of an island in the Adriatic archipelago.

PHILIPPUS: *see* MARCIUS.

PHILO (*Span.* 35): a leader of the Pompeian party in Hispalis.

PHOENICIA (*Civ.* III.3, 101): the region approximately corresponding to the coastal regions of modern Lebanon and Israel.

PICENUM (*Civ.* I.12, 15, 29): a district of Italy lying between Umbria and the Adriatic, from Ancona in the N to Hadria (today Atri) in the S.

PISAURUM (*Civ.* I.11, 12): a town on the Adriatic seaboard N of Picenum, modern Pesaro.

PISO: *see* CALPURNIUS.

PLACENTIA (*Civ.* III.71): a town in the Po Valley; today Piacenza.

Gaius PLAETORIUS (*Alex.* 34): quaestor in Bithynia & Pontus in 48.

PLAETORIUS Rustianus (*Afr.* 96): a senator serving with Scipio in Africa in 47–46.

PLANCUS: *see* MUNATIUS.

Marcus PLOTIUS (*Civ.* III.19): an officer serving in Greece in 48.

POMPEIA (*Afr.* 95): daughter of Pompeius and wife of Faustus Sulla.

Gnaeus POMPEIUS (*Civ.* III.4, 5, 40; *Afr.* 22–3; *Span. passim*): elder son of Pompeius Magnus, probably born in the early 70s. Leader of the Pompeian resistance to Caesar in Spain, 46–45. Killed after his defeat at Munda.

Sextus POMPEIUS (*Span.* 3, 4, 32, 34): younger son of Pompeius Magnus, born c.66; too young to fight at Pharsalus, he led continuing resistance to Caesar in Spain after his brother Gnaeus' death in the aftermath of the battle of Munda in 45. Recalled from exile in the period following Caesar's murder, he established himself with a strong fleet in Sicily by 43, but never reached a satisfactory accommodation with the Triumvirs and was ultimately defeated by Octavian in 36. Fled to Asia, where he was captured and put to death on Antony's orders in 35.

Gnaeus POMPEIUS Magnus ('Pompey') (*Civ.* I.1–10, 13–15, 17, 19, 24–30, 32–5, 38, 39, 53, 60, 61, 76, 84; II.3, 17, 18, 25, 32; III *passim*; *Alex.* 3, 42, 48, 51, 56, 58–9, 67, 69, 70; *Afr.* 64; *Span.* 1): b. 106, son of Cn. Pompeius Strabo (consul in 89). Supported Sulla in the civil war of 84–82, defeated the Marian opposition in Africa and (after Sulla's death) in Spain, and became consul for the first time in 70 although he had held no previous elected office and was not yet a senator. Brought Asia Minor and the Levant positively under Roman control in the 60s, with campaigns against the pirates and Mithridates. In 59, joined with Caesar and M. Licinius Crassus to form a political alliance (traditionally but inaccurately called the 'First Triumvirate') which largely succeeded in dominating the state until the late 50s, when after Crassus' death (53) he fell out with Caesar and precipitated the second civil war. Held further consulships in 55 and 52, and command of Spain and the strong army there from 55. Defeated by Caesar in Greece in 48, he fled to Egypt and was murdered there on 28 Sept. on the recommendation of the king's advisers.

Quintus POMPEIUS Niger (*Span.* 25): a Roman equestrian from Italica.

POMPEIUS Rufus (*Afr.* 85): an officer serving under Caesar at Thapsus.

POMPEY: *see* Gnaeus POMPEIUS Magnus.

Marcus POMPONIUS (*Civ.* III.101): one of Caesar's admirals in 48.

PONTUS (*Civ.* III.3, 4; *Alex.* 13–15, 34–5, 39, 41, 65, 67, 69, 70, 72, 77): a kingdom extending southwards from the SE shore of the Black Sea, partly annexed as a province by Rome after the defeat of its last king Mithridates VI and administered together with Bithynia to its W.

Marcus PORCIUS Cato (*Civ.* I.4, 30, 32; *Afr.* 22, 36, 87–8, 93): praetor in 54; famous for his obstinate moral rectitude, patterned on that of his 2nd-century ancestor Cato the Censor, and his constant attempts to uphold qualities allegedly associated with an earlier and better epoch of the Republic; one of Caesar's bitterest opponents, who fought for Pompeius in Greece (and subsequently for Scipio in Africa) without entirely approving of him.

POSTUMIUS' CAMP (*Span.* 8): Latin *Castra Postumiana*, a site near Ucubi. Named after L. Postumius Albinus, the Roman commander in Further Spain in 180–179.

POSTUMUS: *see* FULVIUS, RABIRIUS.

POTHINUS (*Civ.* III.108, 112): an Alexandrian eunuch, tutor to Ptolemy XIII.

PRAETOR: one of eight annual magistrates (minimum age: 39), ranking immediately below consuls and possessing in their absence the same authority (*imperium*) to command troops, dispense justice, and summon senate or people for deliberation or legislation. In the Late Republic they acted as presidents of various standing courts in Rome during their year of office and proceeded to govern provinces subsequently, with the title of proconsul or, in the older provinces like Sicily, Spain, or Asia, praetor.

PROCONSUL: the title used to describe an ex-consul or ex-praetor who at the conclusion of his year of office had had his period of authority extended to enable him to govern a province and/or command an army, just as though he were a consul.

PTOLEMAIS (*Civ.* III.105): the name of a number of towns in the E Mediterranean, in this case probably either Ptolemais-Ake on the Phoenician coast, Ptolemais of Cyrene, or Ptolemais on the Pamphylian coast.

PTOLEMY XIII AULETES (*Civ.* III.4, 103, 107–10, 112; *Alex.* 4, 33): king of Egypt 80–51.

PTOLEMY XIII (*Civ.* III.103–4, 106–9, 112; *Alex.* 23–5, 27–31): born 61; with his elder sister Cleopatra as consort, succeeded his father Ptolemy XII Auletes on the throne of Egypt in 51.

Titus PULLIENUS (*Civ.* III.67): perhaps a centurion or military tribune, serving with Pompey in 48 after betraying C. Antonius at Curicta the previous year.

Lucius PUPIUS (*Civ.* I.13): a leading centurion (*primus pilus*) in Pompey's army in 49, and previously.

PUTEOLI (*Civ.* III.71): a port in Campania, near Naples; today Pozzuoli.

PYRENEES (*Civ.* I.37; III.19): the same.

QUAESTOR: the most junior (minimum qualifying age: 30) of the magistracies which marked a public career; twenty were elected annually to undertake financial and administrative duties in Italy and the provinces, in the latter case as assistants and deputies to the governor; at the end of their year of office they became senators.

QUINCTIUS Scapula (*Span.* 33): leader of the Pompeian party in Corduba.

Sextus QUINTILIUS Varus (*Civ.* I.23; II.28): quaestor in 49, of Pompeian sympathies; captured and released at Corfinium, he joined Attius Varus in Africa.

Gaius RABIRIUS Postumus (*Afr.* 8, 26): an eminent member of the equestrian class promoted by Caesar to the senate and rewarded with a praetorship, probably in 48, and placed in charge of Caesar's commissariat for the African campaign of 46; earlier in the 50s, he had been the funder of Ptolemy XII Auletes' debts (and briefly his financial minister) in the interest of Pompey and Caesar, and was defended by Cicero in an extant speech, *pro Rabirio Postumo.*

Lucius RACILIUS (*Alex.* 52–3, 55): an assailant of Q. Cassius Longinus.

RAVENNA (*Civ.* I.5): a town on the Adriatic coast of Italy, just within the province of Cisalpine Gaul.

REBILUS: *see* CANINIUS.

REGINUS: *see* MINUCIUS.

REGULUS: *see* LIVINEIUS.

RHASCYPOLIS (*Civ.* III.4): a Macedonian prince.

RHODES (-IAN) (*Civ.* III.5, 26, 27, 102, 106; *Alex.* 1, 11, 13–15, 25; *Afr.* 20): the island, still an independent power before 42.

RHÔNE (*Civ.* II.1): the river.

The ROMAN PEOPLE (*Populus Romanus*) (*Civ.* I.7, 9, 22, 35; III.11, 12, 107, 108, 110; *Alex.* 3, 24, 33–4, 36, 65, 67–8, 78; *Afr.* 4, 54, 57, 77, 90–1, 97; *Span.* 3, 42): the Romans, viewed as a constitutional body.

ROME (*or* 'the city') (*Civ.* I.2, 3, 5, 6, 9, 14, 32–4, 53; II.22, 32; III.1, 2, 10, 83, 108, 109; *Alex.* 65, 68, 71; *Afr.* 19, 22, 64, 98; *Span.* 31): the same.

Lucius ROSCIUS Fabatus (*Civ.* I.3, 8, 10): served with Caesar in Gaul; praetor in 49, and informal ambassador to Caesar from the senate just before war broke out.

ROUCILLUS (*Civ.* III.59, 61, 79, [84]): a Gallic prince, serving with Caesar's cavalry in Greece, who deserted to Pompey.

Lucius RUBRIUS (*Civ.* I.23): a Pompeian senator captured at Corfinium.

RUFUS: *see* ACUTIUS, CAECILIUS, CAELIUS, MARCIUS, MINUCIUS, POMPEIUS, SULPICIUS, TULLIUS, VIBULLIUS.

RUSPINA (*Afr.* 6, 9–11, 20, 28, 33–7, 53, 67): a coastal town between Hadrumetum and Leptis Minor.

RUSTIANUS: *see* PLAETORIUS.

RUTENI (*Civ.* I.51): a Gallic people who lived in the W Massif Central, N of the River Tarn.

Publius RUTILIUS Lupus (*Civ.* I.24; III.56): praetor and commander of a Pompeian force in Italy in 49, placed in charge of S Greece (Achaea) by Pompey in 48.

SABINUS: *see* CALVISIUS.

SABURRA (*Civ.* II.38–42; *Afr.* 48, 93, 95): Juba's general.

Marcus SACRATIVIR(?) (*Civ.* III.71): a military tribune serving with Caesar in Greece.

SADALAS (*Civ.* III.4): son of the Thracian king Cotys.

SAGUNTUM (*Span.* 10): a town on the coast of Nearer Spain; today Sagunto, a little N of Valencia.

Titus SALIENUS (*Afr.* 28, 54): a centurion of Caesar's Fifth legion.

Gaius SALLUSTIUS Crispus (*Afr.* 8, 34, 97): the historian Sallust; praetor in 46, he served under Caesar in Africa and remained to govern the province after Caesar left.

SALLYES (*Civ.* I.35): a tribe of S Gaul.

SALONA or SALONAE (*Civ.* III.9; *Alex.* 43): the chief port for Illyria; today Solin, on the outskirts of Split (Spalato).

SALSUM (*Span.* 7, 9, 13, 14, 16, 23): the modern River Guadajoz, a tributary of the Baetis.

SALVIANUS: *see* CALPURNIUS.

SARDINIA (*Civ.* I.30, 31; III.10; *Afr.* 8, 24, 97): the island.

SARSURA (*Afr.* 75–6): a town in the province of Africa.

Gaius SASERNA (*Afr.* 9, 29, 57): an officer serving under Caesar in Africa.

Publius SASERNA (*Afr.* 10): brother of the preceding.

SASON (*Civ.* III.8): an island lying off the entrance to the Gulf of Valona (Vlone) on the coast of Epirus.

SATURNINUS: *see* APPULEIUS.

SAXA: *see* DECIDIUS.

SCAEVA (*Civ.* III.53): a centurion of Caesar's Sixth legion, famous for his bravery at Dyrrachium (family name given by other sources as either Caesius or Minucius).

SCAPULA: *see* ANNIUS, QUINCTIUS.

SCIPIO: *see* CAECILIUS Metellus.

SCIPIO'S CAMP: *see* CASTRA CORNELIA.

Gaius SCRIBONIUS Curio (*Civ.* I.12, 18, 30, 31; II.3, 23–43; III.10; *Afr.* 19, 40, 52): spendthrift son of a pillar of the traditional aristocracy, and apparently an opponent of Caesar, he secured a tribunate in 50, but when his debts were paid by Caesar he surreptitiously switched political allegiance; served as one of Caesar's lieutenants during the invasion of Italy, but lost his life later in 49 while commanding the forces attempting to recover the province of Africa from the Pompeians.

Lucius SCRIBONIUS Libo (*Civ.* I.26; III.5, 15–18, 23, 24, 90, 100): a close associate of Pompey's, perhaps praetor before 49; his daughter later married Pompey's younger son, Sextus, and his sister the future emperor Augustus.

SEGOVIA (*Alex.* 57): a small town a few miles SW of Corduba (not to be confused with the more famous place of the same name in central Spain).

SEGRE: *see* SICORIS.

Gaius and Tiberius SEMPRONIUS Gracchus (*Civ.* I.7): brothers who became tribunes of the people in (respectively) 123–122 and 133, in both cases on a popular reforming platform; both died by violence at the hands of their political opponents at or soon after the end of their period in office.

SENATE (see esp. *Civ.* I.1–6, 32–3): the *c.*600-strong advisory council of the consuls, comprising (at this period) all magistrates and ex-magistrates of the rank of quaestor or above. Opinions were given in order of seniority, which meant that it was rare for anyone other than ex-consuls or serving magistrates of the year to be able to express a view. Its resolutions (*senatus consulta*) were in practice binding unless vetoed (cf. *Civil War*, I.2), or amended by legislation carried in the sovereign popular assembly (*comitia*), but had strictly speaking no independent legal authority.

Lucius SEPTIMIUS (*Civ.* III.104): a military tribune who killed Pompey.

SERAPION (*Civ.* III.109): an Alexandrian notable.

Quintus SERTORIUS (*Civ.* I.61): praetor in 83; went as governor to Spain in 82, refused to acknowledge the authority of Sulla after he had overthrown the government in Rome, and conducted a largely successful war of resistance against the Sullan generals Pompey and Metellus until he was murdered by his subordinate M. Perperna in 72.

Publius SERVILIUS Isauricus (*Civ.* III.1, 21): son of the man of the same name who had earned his last name (*cognomen*) by suppressing the Isaurian pirates of western Cilicia in the 70s, but on the opposite side in politics (cf. Curio). Consular colleague of Caesar in 48, he went on to hold a second consulship in 41.

SESTERCE (*Sestertius*): the Roman unit of account, worth (in so far as such comparisons can be made at all) something between £2 and £5 sterling at 1990s prices. 4 *asses* made 1 *sestertius*, and 4 *sestertii* made 1 *denarius*, the common silver coin of the Republic and early empire.

Publius SESTIUS (*Alex.* 34): an officer serving under Domitius Calvinus in Asia.

Quintus SESTIUS (*Alex.* 55): a conspirator against Q. Cassius Longinus.

SICILY (*Civ.* I.25, 30, 31; II.3, 23, 30, 32, 34, 37, 43, 44; III.10, 42, 101; *Afr.* 2, 8, 20, 22, 24, 26, 44, 47, 53–4, 62): the island, which constituted a province and was not regarded as part of Italy.

SICORIS (*Civ.* I.40, 48, 61–3, 83): the modern River Segre, a tributary of the Ebro.

SILO: *see* MINUCIUS.

Publius SITTIUS (*Afr.* 25, 36, 48, 93, 95–6): a non-senator from the town of Nuceria in Campania, who was exiled for his part in the Catilinarian conspiracy (63) and became a mercenary captain under King Bocchus in North Africa, ultimately throwing in his lot with Caesar and destroying Juba's army under Saburra.

SINGILIS (*Alex.* 57): a tributary of the River Guadalquivir in Further Spain; now the River Genil.

SORICARIA (*Span.* 24, 27): the site of a battle between the armies of Gnaeus Pompeius and Caesar, near Ucubi.

SPAIN (*as a general term*) (*Civ.* I.10, 30, 34, 37–9, 74, 85–7; II.1, 32, 37; III.2, 10, 47, 73, 83; *Alex.* 48, 52, 62; *Afr.* 64, 95–6; *Span.* 2, 8): the same.

SPAIN (*Further province*, Ulterior) (*Civ.* I.22, 29, 38, 39, 48, 49; II.7, 17, 18, 21; III.10, 73; *Afr.* 95–6; *Alex.* 59, 63): as a settled Roman province, approximately modern Andalusia, but the governor might operate militarily further N and W.

SPAIN (*Nearer province*, Citerior) (*Civ.* I.29, 38, 39; II.17–21; *Alex.* 48–50, 53, 56–8, 64; *Afr.* 64; *Span.* 1–3, 8, 31, 42): the coast from the Sierra Nevada to the Pyrenees together with substantial areas of the hinterland, especially in the Ebro Valley. As with the Further province, the governor might operate far inland, where the Roman writ did not at this epoch run.

SPALIS (*Span.* 27, *name corrupt?*): a town in Further Spain.

SPANIARD (*Civ.* II.21, 40; III.22, 88; *Alex.* 62; *Afr.* 28, 39): the native inhabitants of Spain.

SPINTHER: *see* CORNELIUS Lentulus.

Lucius STABERIUS (*Civ.* III.12): the Pompeian garrison commander in Apollonia in 48.

Lucius STAIUS Murcus (*Civ.* III.15, 16): a senior officer serving under Caesar in Greece in 48; later prominent as a fleet commander in the civil wars of 42–39.

SUFFECT: the technical adjective describing a magistrate appointed to replace another who had died or resigned during his year of office; see, e.g., Q. FABIUS Maximus above.

SULCI (*Afr.* 98): a Sardinian town.

SULLA: *see* CORNELIUS.

SULMO (*Civ.* I.18): a town in central Italy in the territory of the Paeligni, today Sulmona.

Servius SULPICIUS (*Civ.* II.44): a Roman senator of Pompeian sympathies, probably the son of the consul of 51.

Publius SULPICIUS Rufus (*Civ.* I.74; III. 101; *Afr.* 10): one of Caesar's legionary commanders in Gaul in 55 and 52; served in Spain in 49 and became praetor in 48.

SYRIA(N) (*Civ.* I.4, 6; III.3–5, 31, 88, 103, 105, 110: *Alex.* 1, 25–6, 33–4, 38, 65–6; *Afr.* 20): the Roman province embracing roughly modern Israel, Lebanon, and Syria.

TARCONDARIUS CASTOR (*Civ.* III.4): a Galatian prince.

TARRACINA (*Civ.* I.24): a coastal town in S Latium; today Terracina.

TARRACO (*Civ.* I.60, 73, 78; II.21): the capital of Nearer Spain (*Citerior*); today Tarragona.

TARSUS (*Alex.* 66): the capital of Cilicia.

TAURIS (*Alex.* 45): a small island towards the S end of the Dalmatian archipelago, lying between Corcyra Nigra (today Korcula) and Pharos (today Hvar).

TAUROEIS (*Civ.* II.4): an outlying coastal settlement of Massilia.

TEGEA (*Afr.* 78): a small town near Leptis Minor.

Aulus TERENTIUS Varro (*Civ.* III.19): a Pompeian supporter and friend of Cicero's who survived to become curule aedile in 44.

Marcus TERENTIUS Varro (*Civ.* I.38; II.17, 19–21; *Alex.* 58): praetor in the 60s (date uncertain), deputy (*legatus*) for the absentee governor Pompey in S Spain in (55?)–49, having served in Spain under Pompey in the 70s; more famous as a polymath, antiquary, and writer of a still extant work on agriculture (*de Re Rustica*).

THABENA (*Afr.* 77): a Numidian coastal town just S of the Roman province.

THAPSUS (*Afr.* 28, 44, 46, 53, 62, 67, 79, 80, 85–6, 89, 97): an established harbour town on the E coast of the Roman province of Africa, S of Hadrumetum; site of the decisive battle of the campaign of 46.

THEBES (*Civ.* III.56): the chief town of Boeotia.

THEOPHANES (*Civ.* III.18): Cn. Pompeius Theophanes (to give him his full name at this time) was a cultured and influential Greek from Mytilene who probably first met Pompey in 67 at the time of the campaign against the pirates, and became a member of his retinue during the subsequent war against Mithridates; published a eulogistic and doubtless tendentious account of his patron's deeds, was rewarded for this and other services with the Roman citizenship, and continued to advise Pompey until the latter's death.

THERMUS: *see* MINUCIUS.

THESSALY (-IAN) (*Civ.* III.4, 5, 34–6, 79–82, 100, 101, 106, 111): the large area of NE Greece formed by the basin of the rivers Peneios and Enipeus.

Titus THORIUS (*Alex.* 57–8): a citizen of Italica.

THRACE (-IAN) (*Civ.* III.4, 95): the region lying between the Hellespont and Macedonia.

THURII (*Civ.* III.21, 22): a town of S Italy.

THYSDRA (*Afr.* 36, 76, 86, 93, 97): a strongly fortified town in the SE part of the Roman province of Africa; today El Djem.

Lucius TIBURTIUS (*Civ.* III.19): an officer serving in Greece in 48.

Lucius TICIDA (*Afr.* 44, 46): a Roman of equestrian status serving in Caesar's forces in 46.

Quintus TILLIUS (*Civ.* III.42): a senior officer (*legatus*) serving under Caesar in Greece in 48.

Marcus TIRO (*Afr.* 54): a centurion serving with either the Ninth or Tenth legion.

Lucius and (—) TITIUS (*Alex.* 57; *Afr.* 28): military tribunes of the Fifth legion.

TORQUATUS: *see* MANLIUS.

TRALLES (*Civ.* III.105): a town in the province of Asia.

Aulus TREBELLIUS (*Span.* 26): a Roman equestrian from Asta.

Gaius TREBONIUS (*Civ.* I.36; II.1, 5, 13, 15; III.20–1; *Alex.* 64; *Span.* 7, 12): one of Caesar's most experienced and able commanders; served with him in Gaul before the Civil War and conducted the siege of Massilia in 49; succeeded Q. Cassius Longinus as governor of Further Spain 47–46, became consul in 45, and joined the conspiracy against Caesar in 44.

TRIARIUS: *see* VALERIUS.

TRIBUNES (a) MILITARY: officers of equestrian or senatorial standing, six to each legion, who ranked between the legionary commander and the centurions; (b) OF THE PEOPLE (OR PLEBS): a college of ten annually elected magistrates possessing important and potentially revolutionary powers of legislation and veto; supposedly defenders of the basic rights of the common people, they were now always senators (albeit relatively junior ones).

TUBERO: *see* AELIUS.

Tiberius TULLIUS(?) (*Span.* 17, 18): a Roman serving with Gnaeus Pompeius at Ategua.

TULLIUS Rufus (*Afr.* 85): an ex-quaestor in Caesar's army at Thapsus, killed by a mutinous soldier after the battle.

TULLUS: *see* VOLCACIUS.

TURPIO: *see* ANTISTIUS.

TUSCULUS: *see* MANILIUS.

Titus(?) TUTICANUS Gallus (*Civ.* III.71): a senator's son serving as a military tribune with Caesar in Greece in 48.

UCUBI (*Span.* 7, 8, 20, 24, 27): a town SE of Corduba; today Espejo.

ULIA (*Alex.* 61, 63; *Span.* 3, 4, 6): a town some 30 km. S of Corduba; today Montemayor.

URSO (*Span.* 22, 26, 28, 41, 42): an important town *c.*75 km. SW of Corduba and a similar distance E of Hispalis; today Osuna.

USSETA (*Afr.* 89): a small town between Thapsus and Hadrumetum.

UTICA (*Civ.* I.31; II.23–6, 36–8, 44; *Afr.* 7, 22–4, 36, 62, 68, 86–90, 92–3, 95, 97–8): the chief port of the province of Africa, lying on the Bay of Tunis not far W of Carthage.

UZITTA (*Afr.* 41, 51–9): a small town near Ruspina.

VAGA (*Afr.* 74): a town near Zeta (not to be confused with the more celebrated town of the same name some 100 km. W of Carthage).

VALERIUS (*Span.* 32): a Pompeian officer at Munda.

Lucius and Publius VALERIUS Flaccus (*Civ.* III.53): Lucius, the father, praetor in 63, was governor of Asia in 62 and subsequently defended by Cicero on a charge of extortion. Publius, the son, served as a centurion in Caesar's army in Greece in 48.

Marcus VALERIUS Messalla Rufus (*Afr.* 28, 86, 88): consul in 53, exiled for his part in a spectacularly corrupt bargain to rig the consular elections for 52; sought Caesar's protection and acted as a senior officer (*legatus*) to him in Italy and Sicily in 47 and in Africa in 46.

Quintus VALERIUS Orca (*Civ.* I.30, 31): a senior officer (*legatus*) of Caesar's in 49.

Gaius VALERIUS Triarius (1) (*Alex.* 72–3): a Roman army commander (*legatus*) who operated under the overall authority of L. Lucullus against Mithridates from 73 to 67, in which year he suffered a disastrous defeat near Zela.

Gaius VALERIUS Triarius (2) (*Civ.* III.5, 92): probably son of the above, a senator who commanded a Pompeian fleet in the Adriatic in 49–48 and fought at Pharsalus.

Aulus VALGIUS (*Span.* 13): a senator's son serving with Caesar in Spain.

VARRO: *see* TERENTIUS.

VAR (*Civ.* I.86, 87): a river entering the sea at modern Nice and marking the eastern boundary of Transalpine Gaul.

VARUS: *see* ATTIUS, QUINTILIUS.

Titus VASIUS (*Alex.* 52): an assailant of Q. Cassius Longinus.

Publius VATINIUS (*Civ.* III.19, 90, 100; *Alex.* 44–7; *Afr.* 10): famous as the tribune of the plebs who legislated in Caesar's interest when the latter was consul in 59; he went on to serve under Caesar in Gaul before becoming praetor in 55; from 51 one of Caesar's senior officers.

VENTIPO (*Span.* 27): a town in Further Spain.

Gaius VERGILIUS (*Afr.* 28, 44, 79, 86, 93): an ex-praetor (62) commanding the Pompeian garrison of Thapsus in 46.

VESPILLO: *see* LUCRETIUS.

Publius VESTRIUS (*Afr.* 64): a Roman equestrian of Pompeian sympathies.

VETTONES (*Civ.* I.38): a Spanish people.

VIBIUS Curius (*Civ.* I.24): a Caesarian cavalry commander in 49.

Lucius VIBIUS Paciaecus (*Span.* 3): an officer of Caesar's in Spain.

VIBO (*Civ.* III.101): in Greek, Hipponium, a town on the E seaboard of Bruttium; today Vibo Valentia.

Lucius VIBULLIUS Rufus (*Civ.* I.15, 34, 38; III.10, 11, 15, 18, 22): a Roman of equestrian status, acted as confidential messenger and agent of Pompey's in 56 and 54. Taken prisoner, and released, by Caesar at Corfinium and again in Spain in 49, he continued to act as a go-between and messenger on both Pompey's and Caesar's behalf in 48.

VINICIANUS: *see* CAELIUS.

Gaius (or Lucius?) VOLCACIUS Tullus (*Civ*. III.52): a Gaius Volcacius Tullus is mentioned by Caesar as serving under him as a junior officer in Gaul in 53. The man mentioned here may be this man or his brother(?) Lucius, who eventually became consul in 33 and was the uncle of that Tullus to whom some of Propertius' poems are addressed.

VOLCAE ARECOMICI (*Civ*. I.35): a tribe of S Gaul.

Gaius VOLUSENUS (*Civ*. III.60): served with Caesar in Gaul as a military tribune in 56 and 55 and as a cavalry commander in 53 and 51; also in the latter function in Greece in 48.

ZAMA (*Afr*. 91–2, 97): the main residence of the Numidian royal family, famous as the site of Hannibal's defeat by Scipio Africanus in 202.

ZELA (*Alex*. 72): a town in Pontus.

ZETA (*Afr*. 68, 74): a small town in the E part of the Roman province of Africa.

A SELECTION OF   OXFORD WORLD'S CLASSICS

An Anthology of Elizabethan Prose Fiction

An Anthology of Seventeenth-Century Fiction

APHRA BEHN   Oroonoko and Other Writings

JOHN BUNYAN   Grace Abounding
                      The Pilgrim's Progress

SIR PHILIP SIDNEY   The Old Arcadia

IZAAK WALTON   The Compleat Angler

ECTION OF   OXFORD WORLD'S CLASSICS

RONIUS	The Satyricon
LATO	Defence of Socrates, Euthyphro, and Crito
	Gorgias
	Phaedo
	Republic
	Symposium
PLAUTUS	Four Comedies
PLUTARCH	Selected Essays and Dialogues
PROPERTIUS	The Poems
SOPHOCLES	Antigone, Oedipus the King, and Electra
STATIUS	Thebaid
TACITUS	The Histories
VIRGIL	The Aeneid
	The Eclogues and Georgics

MORE ABOUT OXFORD WORLD'S CLASSICS

American Literature

British and Irish Literature

Children's Literature

Classics and Ancient Literature

Colonial Literature

Eastern Literature

European Literature

History

Medieval Literature

Oxford English Drama

Poetry

Philosophy

Politics

Religion

The Oxford Shakespeare

A complete list of Oxford Paperbacks, including Oxford World's Classics, OPUS, Past Masters, Oxford Authors, Oxford Shakespeare, Oxford Drama, and Oxford Paperback Reference, is available in the UK from the Academic Division Publicity Department, Oxford University Press, Great Clarendon Street, Oxford OX2 6DP.

In the USA, complete lists are available from the Paperbacks Marketing Manager, Oxford University Press, 198 Madison Avenue, New York, NY 10016.

Oxford Paperbacks are available from all good bookshops. In case of difficulty, customers in the UK can order direct from Oxford University Press Bookshop, Freepost, 116 High Street, Oxford OX1 4BR, enclosing full payment. Please add 10 per cent of published price for postage and packing.